The
Princeton
Review®

PrincetonReview.com

THE BEST VALUE
COLLEGES

75 Schools That Give You the Most for Your Money

13th Edition

**By Robert Franek, David Soto,
Stephen Koch, and
The Staff of The Princeton Review**

Penguin
Random
House

The Princeton Review
110 East 42nd Street, 7th Floor
New York, NY 10017
E-mail: editorialsupport@review.com

Terms of Service: The Princeton Review Online Companion
Tools ("Student Tools") for retail books are available for only
the two most recent editions of that book. Student Tools may
be activated only once per eligible book purchased for a total
of 24 months of access. Activation of Student Tools more than
once per book is in direct violation of these Terms of Service
and may result in discontinuation of access to Student Tools
Services.

ISBN: 978-0-525-56926-8
ISSN: 2163-6095

The Princeton Review is not affiliated with Princeton
University.

Editors: Aaron Riccio and Brian Saladino
Production Editors: Liz Dacey and Emma Parker
Production Artist: Deborah Weber
Content Contributors: Jen Adams and Andrea Kornstein

Printed in the United States of America.

10   9   8   7   6   5   4   3   2   1

13th Edition

Editorial
Rob Franek, Editor-in-Chief
David Soto, Director of Content Development
Stephen Koch, Survey Manager
Deborah Weber, Director of Production
Gabriel Berlin, Production Design Manager
Selena Coppock, Managing Editor
Aaron Riccio, Senior Editor
Meave Shelton, Senior Editor
Christopher Chimera, Editor
Eleanor Green, Editor
Orion McBean, Editor
Brian Saladino, Editor
Patricia Murphy, Editorial Assistant

Penguin Random House Publishing Team
Tom Russell, VP, Publisher
Alison Stoltzfus, Publishing Director
Amanda Yee, Associate Managing Editor
Ellen Reed, Production Manager
Suzanne Lee, Designer

Contents

Get More (Free) Content

at PrincetonReview.com/guidebooks

As easy as 1·2·3

1 Go to PrincetonReview.com/guidebooks and enter the following ISBN for your book:
9780525569268

2 Answer a few simple questions to set up an exclusive Princeton Review account.
(If you already have one, you can just log in.)

3 Enjoy access to your **FREE** content!

Once you've registered, you can...

- Read full profiles for 125 additional best value colleges

- Take a full-length practice SAT and ACT

- Get valuable advice about applying to college

- Access a list of great schools for the highest paying majors, as well as an alphabetical and location-based index for ease of use

- Check for any post-print updates or errata

Need to report a potential **content** issue?

Contact **EditorialSupport@review.com** and include:

- full title of the book
- ISBN
- page number

Need to report a **technical** issue?

Contact **TPRStudentTech@review.com** and provide:

- your full name
- email address used to register the book
- full book title and ISBN
- operating system (Mac/PC) and browser (Firefox, Safari, etc.)

How Does College Pay You Back?

Introduction

The Princeton Review has long encouraged college applicants to seek out the schools that fit them best academically, culturally, and financially. As the cost of attending college continues to rise dramatically, applicants and their families are increasingly concerned about post-graduation job prospects. Tuition is an investment in the future, and like investors, students want to see a return on that investment. To continue our mission of helping students find the right college for them, we have combined alumni career outcome data with the institutional data and student surveys we collect to create a Return on Investment (ROI) rating for each of 200 schools, 75 of which are published in these pages, and 125 of which can be accessed online once you register this book. (See page iv for details.) We know that students invest more than money in their educations, however—they invest their time, energy, and passion. The ROI on your education is much more than a high salary.

History

In 2008, we began publishing America's Best Value Colleges online (in partnership with USA Today), and in 2011, we turned that list into a book. The schools that we covered in *Best Value Colleges* were chosen based on more than thirty factors covering three areas: academics, cost of attendance, and financial aid, including student ratings of their financial aid packages. The aim of our Best Value Colleges franchise was to highlight schools that offer excellent academics as well as excellent need and non-need-based aid.

Career Outcomes

Career outcomes have become as important to students and parents as academic quality and campus life when choosing a school. Increasingly, colleges and universities are moving their offices of career services closer to their admissions offices, providing visiting prospective students with a glimpse of what they can offer. Career services advisors are engaging with students earlier in their time on campus, often in the first few weeks of their first year. These trends in career services aren't a result of colleges pressuring students to plan out their futures before they are ready—rather, colleges and universities are beginning to help students identify their interests, strengths, and passions, and use those to build the foundation of an effective long-term career strategy.

In order to provide meaningful career metrics for each school profiled in this book, we partnered with PayScale.com, which surveys alumni about salary and career. On each of the 200 school profiles in *The Best Value Colleges*, you'll find PayScale.com's median starting salary and mid-career salary for graduates of that school. To cover professions that have high social value but may offer lower salary numbers, such as teaching or non-profit management, we have also included the percentage of alumni who feel that their job makes the world a better place. All of these statistics are printed on each school's profile, and were incorporated into the overall ROI rating for each school. When available, salary data is broken out for alumni who pursued further study, and the percentage of alumni with science/technology/engineering/ math (STEM) majors appears in some school profiles.

The Real Cost of College

When we set out to develop our ROI rating and determine which schools to include in this book, we started with the same cost analysis we used to create our Best Value Colleges criteria: We calculate the sticker price of each college (often referred to as "cost of attendance," this figure includes tuition, required fees, and room and board) and subtract the average gift aid (scholarships and grants) awarded to students. We don't subtract work-study or student loans, since those are costs that students ultimately have to bear. Out of the 656 schools we considered for this project, the 200 we chose offer great academics combined with affordable costs and stellar career outcomes.

Going Beyond Cold Hard Cash

We defined "value" as inclusive of excellent academics, facilities, and on-campus resources in addition to generous financial aid packages, because we believe colleges pay you back in more than a high salary. The colleges and universities that appear in this book were chosen based on more than forty factors. These factors include PayScale.com's alumni career information, the cost of attendance, financial aid (based on both demonstrated need and merit), selectivity, academics, and student opinion surveys. This methodology goes beyond the bottom line to provide a complete picture of a school's value, and as a result these 200 schools are diverse in academic programs, size, region, and type.

About Our Student Survey

Surveying tens of thousands of students on hundreds of campuses is a mammoth undertaking. In 1992, our survey was a paper survey. We worked with school administrators to set up tables in centrally-trafficked locations on their campuses at which students filled out the surveys. To reach a range of students, freshmen to seniors, this process sometimes took place over several days and at various on-campus locations. That process yielded about 125 surveys per college.

However, the launch of our online survey several years ago made our survey process more efficient, secure, and representative. Our student survey is also now a continuous process. Students submit surveys online from all schools in the book and they can submit their surveys at any time at https://www.princetonreview.com/survey. (However, our site will accept only one survey from a student per academic year per school (it's not possible to "stuff" the ballot box, as it were).) In addition to those surveys we receive from students on an ongoing basis, we also conduct "formal" surveys of students at each school in the book at least once every three years. (We conduct these more often once every three years if the colleges request that we do so (and we can accommodate that request) or we deem it necessary.)

How do we do conduct those "formal" surveys? First, we notify our administrative contacts at the schools we plan to survey. We depend upon these contacts for assistance in informing the student body of our survey (although we also get the word out to students about our survey via other channels independent of the schools). An increasing number of schools have chosen to send an e-mail to the entire student body about the availability of our online survey; in such cases this has yielded robust response rates. Our average number of student surveys (per college) is now 359 students per campus (and at some schools we hear from more than 3,000 students).

And of course, surveys we receive from students outside of their schools' normal survey cycles are always factored into the subsequent year's ranking calculations, so our pool of student survey data is continuously refreshed.

The survey has more than eighty questions divided into four sections: "About Yourself," "Your School's Academics/Administration," "Students," and "Life at Your School." We ask about all sorts of things, from "How many out-of-class hours do you spend studying each day?" to "How do you rate your campus food?" Most questions offer students a five-point grid on which to indicate their answer choices (headers may range from "Excellent" to "Awful"). Eight questions offer students the opportunity to expand on their answers with narrative comment. These essay-type responses are the sources of the student quotations that appear in the school profiles. Once the surveys have been completed and responses stored in our database, every college is given a score (similar to a grade point average) for its students' answers to each question. This score enables us to compare students' responses to a particular question from one college to the next. We use these scores as an underlying data point in our calculation of the ratings in the profile sidebars and the ranking lists in the section of the book titled "School Rankings and Lists."

Once we have the student survey information in hand, we write the college profiles. Student quotations in each profile are chosen because they represent the sentiments expressed by the majority of survey respondents from the college; or, they illustrate one side or another of a mixed bag of student opinion, in which case there will also appear a counterpoint within the text. In order to guard against producing a write-up that's off the mark for any particular college, we send our administrative contact at each school a copy of the profile we intend to publish prior to its publication date, with ample opportunity to respond with corrections, comments, and/or outright objections. In every case in which we receive requests for changes, we take careful measures to review the school's suggestions against the student survey data we collected and make appropriate changes when warranted.

How to Use This Book

It's pretty self-explanatory. We have done our best to include lots of helpful information about choosing colleges and gaining admission. The profiles we have written contain the same basic information for each school and follow the same basic format. The Princeton Review collects all of the data you see in the sidebars of each school. As is customary with college guides, our numbers usually reflect the figures for the academic year prior to publication. Since college offerings and demographics significantly vary from one institution to another and some colleges report data more thoroughly than others, some entries will not include all of the individual data described. Please know that we take our data-collection process seriously. We reach out to schools numerous times through the process to ensure we can present you with the most accurate and up-to-date facts, figures, and deadlines. Even so, a book is dated from the moment it hits the printing press. Be sure to double-check with any schools to which you plan to apply to make sure you are able to get them everything they need in order to meet their deadlines.

How This Book Is Organized

Each of the colleges and universities in this book (and online) has its own four-page profile. To make it easier to find and compare information about the schools, we've used the same profile format for every school. First, at the very top of the profile you will see the school's address, telephone, and fax numbers for the admissions office, the telephone number for the financial aid office, and the school's website and/or e-mail address. You'll also find a grey sidebar box on each page, split into the following four categories: Campus Life, Academics, Selectivity, and Financial Facts. Third, at the bottom of the last page you will find a PayScale.com Career Information box with the each school's ROI rating and salary figures. Finally, there are seven headings in the narrative text: About the School, Bang for Your Buck, Student Life, Career, General Info, Financial Aid, and Bottom Line.

Sidebars

The sidebars contain various statistics culled from our surveys of students attending the school and from questionnaires that school administrators complete at our request in the fall of each year. Keep in mind that not every category will appear for every school—in some cases the information is not reported or not applicable. We compile the eight ratings— Quality of Life, Fire Safety, Green Rating, Academic, Profs Interesting, Profs Accessible, Admissions Selectivity, and Financial Aid—listed in the sidebars based on the results from our student surveys and/or institutional data we collect from school administrators.

These ratings are on a scale of 60–99. If a 60* (60 with an asterisk) appears as any rating for any school, it means that the school reported so few of the rating's underlying data points by our deadline that we were unable to calculate an accurate rating for it. (These measures are outlined in the ratings explanation below.) Be advised that, because the Admissions Selectivity Rating is a factor in the computation that produces the Academic Rating, a school that has 60* (60 with an asterisk) as its Admissions Selectivity Rating will have an Academic Rating that is lower than it should be. Also bear in mind that each rating places each college on a continuum for purposes of comparing colleges within this edition only. Since our ratings computations may change from year to year, it is invalid to compare the ratings in this edition to those that appear in any prior or future edition.

PayScale.com Career Information Box

This box includes up to seven data points: our unique ROI rating; median starting salary reported by alumni and median mid-career salary reported by alumni, both those holding just a bachelor's degree and those with a higher degree; the percentage of alumni that report having high job meaning (i.e., feeling that their job makes the world a better place); and the percentage of degrees the school awarded in STEM (science, technology, engineering, and math). Alumni survey information comes from PayScale.com's 2019–2020 College Salary Report. Some school profiles do not include all of these data points, as PayScale.com only reports survey results based on a statistically significant sample of responses. The data used for PayScale.com's annual College Salary Report is collected through their ongoing, online compensation survey. You can read more about their survey and methodology online at www.PayScale.com/college-salary-report/methodology.

ROI Rating

Our ROI rating is based on data we collected from fall 2018 through fall 2019 via our institutional and student surveys. It is calculated using more than forty data points covering academics, costs, financial aid, career outcomes, and student and alumni survey data.

We asked students to rate their schools career services office, the opportunities for internships and experiential learning, and the strength of their alumni network on campus. Starting and mid-career salary data was taken from PayScale.com's 2019–20 College Salary Report. In addition to salary data, PayScale.com provided data on alumni who reported high job meaning.

Also considered are the percentage of graduating seniors who borrowed from any loan program and the average debt those students had at graduation. The percentage of students graduating within four and six years was also taken into account.

Additional criteria included the following breakdown of Princeton Review's ratings:

Academic Rating

To tally this rating, we analyze a large amount of data the schools report to us about their academic selectivity and admissions, plus opinion data we collect from students reporting on the education they are receiving at their schools. The admissions statistics shed light on how difficult it is to gain acceptance: they include SAT/ACT scores and high school GPA of enrolled freshmen as well as other data factors. The student data reveals how students at the school rate their professors' teaching ability as well as how accessible the professors are outside of class.

Financial Aid Rating

This rating measures how much financial aid a school awards and how satisfied students are with that aid. This rating is based on school-reported data on the percentage of students who were determined to have need and received aid, the percentage of need met for those students, and the percentage of students whose need was fully met. Student survey data that measures students' satisfaction with the financial aid they receive is also considered.

Nota Bene: *The following ratings appear in each school profile, but were not included in the ROI methodology.*

Quality of Life Rating

On a scale of 60–99, this rating is a measure of how happy students are with their campus experiences outside the classroom. To compile this rating, we weighed several factors, all based on students' answers to questions on our survey. They included the students' assessments of: their overall happiness; the beauty, safety, and location of the campus; comfort of dorms; quality of food; ease of getting around campus and dealing with administrators; friendliness of fellow students; and the interaction of different student types on campus and within the greater community.

Fire Safety Rating

On a scale of 60–99, this rating measures how well prepared a school is to prevent or respond to campus fires, specifically in residence halls. We asked schools several questions about their efforts to ensure fire safety for campus residents. We developed the questions in consultation with the Center for Campus Fire Safety (www.campusfiresafety.org). Each school's responses to seven questions were considered when calculating its Fire Safety Rating. They cover:

1. The percentage of student housing sleeping rooms protected by an automatic fire sprinkler system with a fire sprinkler head located in the individual sleeping rooms.
2. The percentage of student housing sleeping rooms equipped with a smoke detector connected to a supervised fire alarm system.

3. The number of malicious fire alarms that occur in student housing per year.
4. The number of unwanted fire alarms that occur in student housing per year.
5. The banning of certain hazardous items and activities in residence halls, like candles, smoking, halogen lamps, etc.
6. The percentage of student housing fire alarm systems that, if activated, result in a signal being transmitted to a monitored location, where security investigates before notifying the fire department.
7. The percentage of student housing fire alarm systems that, if activated, result in a signal being transmitted immediately to a continuously monitored location.

Schools that did not report answers to a sufficient number of questions receive a Fire Safety Rating of 60* (60 with an asterisk).

Green Rating

We asked all the schools we collect data from annually to answer a number of questions that evaluate the comprehensive measure of their performance as an environmentally aware and responsible institution. The questions were first developed in consultation with ecoAmerica (www.ecoAmerica.org), a research and partnership-based environmental nonprofit that convened an expert committee to design this comprehensive rating system, and cover: 1) whether students have a campus quality of life that is both healthy and sustainable; 2) how well a school is preparing students not only for employment in the clean energy economy of the twenty-first century, but also for citizenship in a world now defined by environmental challenges; and 3) how environmentally responsible a school's policies are.

Additionally, The Princeton Review and the Association for the Advancement of Sustainability in Higher Education (AASHE) continue to collaborate on an effort to streamline the reporting process for institutions that choose to participate in various higher education sustainability assessments. The intent of this initiative is to reduce and streamline the amount of time campus staff spend tracking sustainability data and completing related surveys.

Please find more information here:

http://www.princetonreview.com/green-data-partnership

Each school's responses to ten questions were considered when calculating The Princeton Review's Green Rating.

They include:

1. The percentage of food expenditures that go toward local, organic, or otherwise environmentally preferable food.
2. Whether the school offers programs including mass transit programs, bike sharing, facilities for bicyclists, bicycle and pedestrian plan, car sharing, carpool discount, carpool/vanpool matching, cash-out of parking, prohibiting idling, local housing, telecommuting, and condensed work week.
3. Whether the school has a formal committee that is devoted to advancing sustainability on campus.
4. Whether school buildings that were constructed or underwent major renovations in the past three years are LEED certified.
5. The schools overall waste-diversion rate.
6. Whether the school offers at least one sustainability-focused undergraduate major, degree program, or equivalent.
7. Whether the school's students graduate from programs that include sustainability as a required learning outcome or include multiple sustainability learning outcomes.
8. Whether the school has a formal plan to mitigate its greenhouse gas emissions.
9. What percentage of the school's energy consumption is derived from renewable resources.
10. Whether the school employs a dedicated full-time (or full-time equivalent) sustainability officer.

Colleges that did not supply answers to a sufficient number of the green campus questions for us to fairly compare them to other colleges receive a Green Rating of 60*.

Check out our free resource area, The Princeton Review's Guide to 399 Green Colleges at www.princetonreview.com/green-guide.

In addition to these ratings, we have compiled the following information about each school. Keep in mind that not all schools responded to our requests for information, so not all of this information will appear in every profile.

Type of school: Whether the school is public or private.

Affiliation: Any religious order with which the school is affiliated.

Environment: The type and size of the setting.

- Metropolis (In a major city, pop. 300,000 or more, or within its metropolitan area)

- City (In a small/medium city, pop. 75,000–299,999, or within its metropolitan area)
- Town (In a large town, pop. 25,000–74,999, or near a large town)
- Village (In a small town, pop. 5,000–24,999, or near a small town)
- Rural (In or near a rural community, pop. Under 5,000)

Total undergrad enrollment: The total number of degree-seeking undergraduates who attend the school.

"% male/female" through "# countries represented": Demographic information about the full-time undergraduate student body, including male to female ratio, ethnicity, and the number of countries represented by the student body. Also included are the percentages of the student body who are from out of state, attended a public high school, freshmen living on campus, and belong to Greek organizations.

Academic Rating: On a scale of 60–99, this rating is a measure of how hard students work at the school and how much they get back for their efforts. The rating is based on results from our surveys of students and data we collect from administrators. Factors weighed included how many hours students reported that they study each day outside of class, students' assessments of their professors' teaching abilities and of their accessibility outside the classroom and the quality of students the school attracts as measured by admissions statistics.

4-year graduation rate: The percentage of degree-seeking undergraduate students graduating in four years or less.

6-year graduation rate: The percentage of degree-seeking undergraduate students graduating within six years.

Calendar: The school's schedule of academic terms. A "semester" schedule has two long terms, usually starting in September and January. A "trimester" schedule has three terms, one usually beginning before Christmas and two after. A "quarterly" schedule has four terms, which go by very quickly: the entire term, including exams, usually lasts only nine or ten weeks. A "4-1-4" schedule is like a semester schedule, but with a month-long term in between the fall and spring semesters. (Similarly, a "4-4-1" has a short term following two longer semesters.) It is always best to call the admissions office for details.

Student/faculty ratio: The ratio of full-time undergraduate instructional faculty members to all undergraduates.

Profs interesting rating: On a scale of 60–99, this rating is based on levels of surveyed students' agreement or disagreement with the statement: "Your instructors are good teachers."

Profs accessible rating: On a scale of 60–99, this rating is based on levels of surveyed students' agreement or disagreement with the statement: "Your instructors are accessible outside the classroom."

Most common regular class size; Most common lab size: The most commonly occurring class size for regular courses and for labs/discussion sections.

Most popular majors: The majors with the highest enrollments at the school.

Admissions Selectivity Rating: On a scale of 60–99, this rating is a measure of how competitive admission is at the school. This rating is determined by several factors, including the class rank of entering freshmen, test scores, and percentage of applicants accepted.

# of applicants: The total number of applicants to a school.

% of applicants accepted: The percentage of applicants to whom the school offered admission.

% of acceptees attending: The percentage of accepted students who eventually enrolled at the school.

 # accepting a place on wait list: The number of students who decided to take a place on the wait list when offered this option.

% admitted from wait list: The percentage of applicants who opted to take a place on the wait list and were subsequently offered admission. These figures will vary tremendously from college to college, and should be a consideration when deciding whether to accept a place on a college's wait list.

# of early decision applicants: The number of students who applied under the college's early decision or early action plan.

% accepted early decision: The percentage of early decision or early action applicants who were admitted under this plan. By the nature of these plans, the vast majority who are admitted ultimately enroll.

Range SAT EBRW, Range SAT Math, Range ACT Composite: The middle 50 percent range of test scores for entering first-year students. Don't be discouraged from applying to the school of your choice even if your scores are below the average, because you may still have a chance of getting in. Remember that many schools value other aspects of your application (e.g., your grades, how good a match you make with the school) more heavily than test scores.

Average HS GPA: The average grade point average of entering freshman. We report this on a scale of 1.0–4.0 (occasionally colleges report averages on a 100 scale, in which case we report those figures). This is one of the key factors in college admissions.

% graduated top 10%, top 25%, top 50% of class: Of those students for whom class rank was reported, the percentage of entering freshmen who ranked in the top tenth, quarter, and half of their high school classes.

Early decision/action deadlines: The deadline for submission of application materials under the early decision or early action plan.

Early decision, early action, priority, and regular admission deadlines: The dates by which all materials must be postmarked (we suggest "received in the office") in order to be considered for admission under each particular admissions option/cycle for matriculation in the fall term.

Early decision, early action, priority, and regular admission notification: The dates by which you can expect a decision on your application under each admissions option/cycle.

Nonfall registration: Some schools will allow incoming students to register and begin attending classes at times other than the fall term, which is the traditional beginning of the academic calendar year. Other schools will allow you to register for classes only if you can begin in the fall term. A simple "yes" or "no" in this category indicates the school's policy on nonfall registration.

Financial Aid Rating: On a scale of 60–99, this rating is a measure of the financial aid the school awards and how satisfied students are with the aid they receive. It is based on school-reported data on financial aid and students' responses to the survey question, "If you receive financial aid, how satisfied are you with your financial aid package?"

Annual in-state tuition: The tuition at the school, or for public colleges, the cost of tuition for a resident of the school's state. Usually much lower than out-of-state tuition for state-supported public schools.

Annual out-of-state tuition: For public colleges, the tuition for a non-resident of the school's state. This entry appears only for public colleges, since tuition at private colleges is generally the same regardless of state of residence.

Room and board: Estimated annual room and board costs.

Required fees: Any additional costs students must pay beyond tuition in order to attend the school. These often include fitness center fees and the like. A few state schools may not officially charge in-state students tuition, but those students are still responsible for hefty fees.

Tuition and fees: In cases when schools do not report separate figures for tuition and required fees, we offer this total of the two.

Comprehensive fee: A few schools report one overall fee that reflects the total cost of tuition, room and board, and required fees. If you'd like to see how this figure breaks down, we recommend contacting the school.

Books and supplies: Estimated annual cost of necessary textbooks and/or supplies.

Average need-based scholarship: The average need-based scholarship and grant aid awarded to students with need.

% needy frosh receiving need-based scholarship or grant aid: The percentage of all degree-seeking freshmen who were determined to have need and received any need-based scholarship or grant.

% needy UG receiving need-based scholarship or grant aid: The percentage of all degree-seeking undergraduates who were determined to have need and received any need-based scholarship or grant.

% needy frosh receiving non-need-based scholarship or grant aid: The percentage of all degree-seeking freshmen, determined to have need, receiving any non-need based scholarship or grant aid.

% needy UG receiving non-need-based scholarship or grant aid: The percentage of all degree-seeking undergraduates, determined to have need, receiving any non-need based scholarship or grant aid.

% needy frosh receiving need-based self-help aid: The percentage of all degree-seeking freshmen, determined to have need, who received any need-based self-help aid.

% needy UG receiving need-based self-help aid: The percentage of all degree-seeking undergraduates, determined to have need, who received any need-based self-help aid.

% frosh receiving any financial aid: The percentage of all degree-seeking freshmen receiving any financial aid (need-based, merit-based, gift aid).

% UG receiving any financial aid: The percentage of all degree-seeking undergraduates receiving any financial aid (need-based, merit-based, gift aid).

% UG borrow to pay for school: The percentage who borrowed at any time through any loan programs (institutional, state, Federal Stafford Subsidized and Unsubsidized, private loans that were certified by your institution, etc., exclude parent loans). Includes both Federal Direct Student Loans and Federal Family Education Loans (prior to the FFEL program ending in June 2010).

Average Indebtedness: The average per-borrower cumulative undergraduate indebtedness of those who borrowed at any time through any loan programs (institutional, state, Federal Stafford Subsidized and Unsubsidized, private loans that were certified by your institution, etc.; excluding parent loans).

% frosh and ugrad need fully met: The percentage of needy degree-seeking students whose needs were fully met (excludes PLUS loans, unsubsidized loans and private alternative loans).

Average % of frosh and ugrad need met: On average, the percentage of need that was met of students who were awarded any need-based aid. Excludes any aid that was awarded in excess of need as well as any resources that were awarded to replace EFC (PLUS loans, unsubsidized loans and private alternative loans).

Nota Bene: *The statistical data reported in this book, unless otherwise noted, was collected from the profiled colleges from fall 2018 through the fall of 2019. In some cases, we were unable to publish the most recent data because schools did not report the necessary statistics to us in time, despite our repeated outreach efforts. Because the enrollment and financial statistics, as well as application and financial aid deadlines, fluctuate from one year to another, we recommend that you check with the schools to make sure you have the most current information before applying.*

We made the above information available to contacts at each school for review and approval. You may also cross-reference our print profiles with our online school profiles at PrincetonReview.com, which list the most up-to date data as reported by schools.

Don't be discouraged from applying to the school of your choice even if your combined SAT scores are 80 or even 120 points below the average, because you may still have a chance of getting in. Remember that many schools value other aspects of your application (e.g., your grades, how good a match you make with the school) more heavily than test scores.

The Narrative

These sections share the straight-from-the-campus feedback we get from the school's most important customers: The students attending them. They summarize the opinions of freshmen through seniors we've surveyed and they include direct quotes from scores of them. When appropriate, they also incorporate statistics provided by the schools. The sections based on student survey responses are divided into four subsections:

About the School

This section provides a general overview of the school including student descriptions of the school environment and often tells you which programs or academic departments students rated most favorably and how professors interact with students. Student opinion regarding administrative departments also works its way into this section.

Bang For Your Buck

Here you will find information about scholarship and fellowship programs, the school's commitment to meeting demonstrated need, and student opinion regarding financial aid. Details on particular offerings related to funding are also included.

Student Life

The student life section describes life outside the classroom and addresses questions ranging from "How comfortable are the dorms?" to "How popular are fraternities and sororities?" In this section, students describe what they do for entertainment both on-campus and off, providing a clear picture of the social environment at their particular school. This section will also give you the lowdown on the types of students the school attracts and how the students view the level of interaction among various groups, including those of different ethnic, socioeconomic, and religious backgrounds.

Career

In this section, you will find information about the career resources at each school including career services departments, job fairs, and internship programs. We spotlight specific experiential learning opportunities that could have real-world advantages in terms of your career and include student opinions about the career services offered to them.

The other three sections included in the profile are:

General Info

This section lists student activities, organizations, athletics, and other campus highlights that each school's admissions office would you to know about their institution.

Financial Aid

Here you'll find out what you need to know about the financial aid process at the school, namely what forms you need and what types of merit-based aid and loans are available. Information about need-based aid is contained in the financial aid sidebar. This section includes specific deadline dates for submission of materials as reported by the colleges. We strongly encourage students seeking financial aid to file all forms—federal, state, and institutional—carefully, fully, and on time.

Bottom Line

Here we breakdown the cost of attendance for each school by tuition, fees, and housing, and give you the final totals for in-state and out-of-state students.

Ranking Lists

The Best Value Colleges contains seven ranking lists, all of which focus on different aspects of financial aid and career preparation. For lists that cover sixty-two topics on academics, facilities, and campus culture, check out our book *The Best 385 Colleges*, or visit PrincetonReview.com.

Top 75 Best Value Colleges

The seventy-five schools that received the highest ROI rating (described on page 7), ranked in order. Each of these school's profiles also includes a banner with its rank.

1. Princeton University
2. Massachusetts Institute of Technology
3. Harvey Mudd College
4. Stanford University
5. California Institute of Technology
6. Yale University
7. Williams College
8. Harvard College
9. The Cooper Union for the Advancement of Science and Art
10. University of California—Berkeley
11. Georgia Institute of Technology
12. University of Virginia
13. Vanderbilt University
14. Rice University
15. Columbia University
16. Dartmouth College
17. Pomona College
18. Amherst College
19. Duke University
20. Rose-Hulman Institute of Technology
21. University of North Carolina at Chapel Hill
22. Claremont McKenna College
23. University of California—Santa Barbara
24. Brown University
25. Bowdoin College
26. Wabash College
27. Cornell University
28. University of Pennsylvania
29. University of Chicago
30. Swarthmore College
31. Lehigh University
32. Worcester Polytechnic Institute
33. Carleton College
34. Haverford College
35. Brigham Young University (UT)
36. University of California—Los Angeles
37. Johns Hopkins University
38. Carnegie Mellon University
39. University of California—San Diego
40. Grinnell College
41. Colgate University
42. University of Florida
43. College of William and Mary
44. Wellesley College
45. Hamilton College
46. Emory University
47. Middlebury College
48. Washington University in St. Louis
49. Purdue University—West Lafayette
50. Vassar College
51. North Carolina State University
52. Rhodes College
53. Lafayette College
54. Wesleyan University
55. Case Western Reserve University
56. City University of New York—Baruch College
57. University of Wisconsin-Madison
58. Babson College
59. University of Michigan—Ann Arbor

60. Trinity University
61. Union College (NY)
62. University of Richmond
63. Bates College
64. Denison University
65. Smith College
66. Rensselaer Polytechnic Institute
67. Florida State University
68. Tufts University
69. Bucknell University
70. St. Olaf College
71. University of Notre Dame
72. University of Texas at Austin
73. University of California—Davis
74. University of California—Riverside
75. Thomas Aquinas College

Top 25 Best Value Colleges for Students With No Demonstrated Need

To create this list, we used the same methodology for our ROI rating, but removed need-based aid information. If you don't qualify for financial aid, these are your twenty-five best value schools.

1. Harvey Mudd College
2. Georgia Institute of Technology
3. Massachusetts Institute of Technology
4. University of California—Berkeley
5. Stanford University
6. University of Virginia
7. California Institute of Technology
8. Princeton University
9. Brigham Young University (UT)
10. University of North Carolina at Chapel Hill
11. University of California—Santa Barbara
12. College of William and Mary
13. University of Florida
14. University of California—Los Angeles
15. Williams College
16. Worcester Polytechnic Institute
17. Yale University
18. Rose-Hulman Institute of Technology
19. Rice University
20. Dartmouth College
21. Purdue University—West Lafayette
22. Claremont McKenna College
23. North Carolina State University
24. Carnegie Mellon University
25. University of Michigan—Ann Arbor

Top 25 Best Alumni Networks

These twenty-five schools have the strongest and most active alumni networks, based on current students' ratings of alumni activity and visibility on campus.

1. Wabash College
2. Hampden-Sydney College
3. Pennsylvania State University—University Park
4. St. Lawrence University
5. Hollins University
6. University of Virginia
7. Texas Christian University
8. Georgia Institute of Technology
9. Agnes Scott College
10. Wellesley College
11. Clemson University
12. Worcester Polytechnic Institute
13. Mount Holyoke College
14. Bryn Mawr College
15. Williams College
16. Wheaton College (IL)
17. Emory University
18. Washington State University
19. Wofford College
20. The University of the South
21. The University of Alabama—Tuscaloosa
22. Tulane University
23. Florida State University
24. Clarkson University
25. College of William and Mary

Top 25 Best Schools for Internships

This top twenty-five list is based on students' ratings of accessibility of internships at their school.

1. Wabash College
2. The University of Alabama—Tuscaloosa
3. Rose-Hulman Institute of Technology
4. Bentley University
5. Franklin W. Olin College of Engineering
6. University of Richmond
7. Northeastern University
8. Grove City College
9. Clemson University
10. Texas Christian University
11. University of Dayton
12. Stevens Institute of Technology
13. Southwestern University
14. Hampden-Sydney College
15. The University of the South
16. Coe College
17. College of William and Mary
18. College of Wooster
19. Marquette University
20. Worcester Polytechnic Institute
21. Hollins University
22. Vanderbilt University
23. Lake Forest College
24. Bradley University
25. Stonehill College

Top 25 Best Career Placement

This top twenty-five list is based on students' ratings of career services at their school, and on PayScale.com's median starting and mid-career salary information.

1. Harvey Mudd College
2. Massachusetts Institute of Technology
3. Stanford University
4. California Institute of Technology
5. Princeton University
6. Worcester Polytechnic Institute
7. Rose-Hulman Institute of Technology
8. Harvard College
9. University of Pennsylvania
10. Carnegie Mellon University
11. Stevens Institute of Technology
12. Duke University
13. Dartmouth College
14. Babson College
15. Rensselaer Polytechnic Institute
16. Lehigh University
17. Yale University
18. Claremont McKenna College
19. Georgia Institute of Technology
20. Columbia University
21. Cornell University
22. University of California—Berkeley
23. Clarkson University
24. Colgate University
25. Franklin W. Olin College of Engineering

Top 25 Best Schools for Financial Aid

The twenty-five schools in this book that receive the highest financial aid rating (described on page 8).

1. Vassar College
2. Princeton University
3. Vanderbilt University
4. Pomona College
5. Williams College
6. Grinnell College
7. Washington University in St. Louis
8. Bowdoin College
9. Yale University
10. Rice University
11. Thomas Aquinas College
12. Reed College
13. Gettysburg College
14. California Institute of Technology
15. Stanford University
16. Colgate University
17. Kenyon College
18. Franklin W. Olin College of Engineering
19. Carleton College
20. Amherst College
21. Lehigh University
22. Wabash College
23. Brown University
24. Wellesley College
25. Hamilton College

Top 25 Best Schools for Making an Impact

These twenty-five schools were selected based on student ratings and responses to our survey questions covering community service opportunities at their school, student government, sustainability efforts, and on-campus student engagement. We also took into account PayScale.com's percentage of alumni from each school that reported that they had high job meaning.

1. Wesleyan University
2. Southwestern University
3. Lawrence University
4. Saint Louis University
5. Williams College
6. Brown University
7. Brandeis University
8. Dickinson College
9. Furman University
10. Whitman College
11. Mount Holyoke College
12. Wheaton College (IL)
13. Reed College
14. Union College (NY)
15. Hobart and William Smith Colleges
16. College of William and Mary
17. Emory University
18. Tulane University
19. Grinnell College
20. St. Olaf College
21. Clark University
22. Hampden-Sydney College
23. Allegheny College
24. Creighton University
25. Macalester College

School Profiles

Amherst College

Campus Box 2231, Amherst, MA 01002 • Admissions: 413-542-2328 • Fax: 413-542-2040

#18 BEST VALUE COLLEGE

CAMPUS LIFE	
Quality of Life Rating	85
Fire Safety Rating	60*
Green Rating	82
Type of school	Private
Environment	Town

STUDENTS	
Total undergrad enrollment	1,855
% male/female	50/50
% from out of state	87
% frosh from public high school	62
% frosh live on campus	100
% ugrads live on campus	98
# of fraternities	0
# of sororities	0
% African American	11
% Asian	15
% Caucasian	44
% Hispanic	13
% Native American	<1
% Pacific Islander	0
% Two or more races	7
% Race and/or ethnicity unknown	2
% international	8
# of countries represented	61

ABOUT THE SCHOOL

Situated on a lush 1,015-acre campus in Amherst, Massachusetts, Amherst College offers students an intellectual atmosphere fostered by friendly and supportive faculty members. Amherst College has an exploratory vibe with a virtually requirement-free curriculum that gives students unprecedented academic freedom. There are no core or general requirements. Beyond the first-year seminar and major coursework, students can choose what they want to study. One student told us, "I love the open curriculum and that you can do whatever you want here." That doesn't mean you can slack off, though: students say you must be "willing to read a text forward and backward and firmly grasp it" and "skimming will do you no good." The most popular majors are economics, political science, and English, and alumni have a solid track record in gaining admission to postgraduate programs. In fact, some students view Amherst as "prep school for grad school." Students can also receive credit for courses at neighboring colleges Smith, Mount Holyoke, Hampshire, and the University of Massachusetts Amherst for a total selection of more than 6,000 courses. Students say that they love the "abundant academic and social opportunities" provided by the consortium. Almost half of Amherst students also pack their bags during junior year to study abroad. Students say that professors "are always available, and they want to spend time with us outside of the classroom."

BANG FOR YOUR BUCK

Amherst College is a no-loan institution, which means the college does not include loans in its financial aid packages but focuses on providing

Amherst College

Financial Aid: 413-542-2296 • E-mail: admission@amherst.edu • Website: www.amherst.edu

grant and scholarship aid instead. It is possible to graduate from Amherst with no debt. In addition to a need-blind admissions policy, Amherst meets 100 percent of students' demonstrated need, be they international or domestic. Every year, Amherst awards grants and scholarships to more than half the student body. All students who apply for financial aid are automatically considered for grant and scholarship funds. In 2018–2019, the school provided over $59 million in scholarship and grant aid to students, and the average award was over $54,000.

STUDENT LIFE

While students at Amherst are "focused first and foremost on academics, nearly every student is active and enjoys life outside of the library." In their spare time, "students love to get involved in extracurriculars. It seems like everyone plays a sport, is a member of an a cappella group, and has joined an affinity group." "There's a club or organization for every interest" here, and students assure us that if there isn't one that you're interested in, "the school will find the money for it." Amherst's small size "means that no group is isolated, and everyone interacts and more or less gets along." And truly, "diversity—racial, ethnic, geographic, socioeconomic—is more than a buzzword here." The campus is also "a politically and environmentally conscious" place, and the town of Amherst and the surrounding areas are "incredibly intellectual." Still, the "awesome" dorms tend to serve as the school's social hubs, as Amherst did away with its Greek system in 1984.

CAREER

The Loeb Center for Career Exploration and Planning at Amherst is focused on empowering students to think about their futures reflectively and strategically. The Amherst Select Internship Program allows students to get a

ACADEMICS

Academic Rating	94
% students returning for sophomore year	96
% students graduating within 4 years	85
% students graduating within 6 years	93
Calendar	Semester
Student/faculty ratio	7:1
Profs interesting rating	89
Profs accessible rating	86

Most classes have 10–19 students. Most lab/discussion sessions have 10–19 students.

MOST POPULAR MAJORS

English Language and Literature, General; Psychology, General; Economics, General

SELECTIVITY

Admissions Rating	98
# of applicants	9,724
% of applicants accepted	13
% of acceptees attending	39
# offered a place on the wait list	1,482
% accepting a place on wait list	56
% admitted from wait list	0
# of early decision applicants	472
% accepted early decision	38

taste of different fields over the summer and truly test out their options. Other resources like Quest, Career Beam, and the Liberal Arts Career Network list job and internship opportunities for gaining professional experience. Students can easily connect with alumni through the Alumni-in-Residence program that brings alumni back to campus for a series of candid conversations designed to help students explore career options, build relationships, and get real-world advice. Those grads who visited PayScale.com report starting salaries of about $63,800, and 52 percent believe their work makes the world a better place.

GENERAL INFO

Activities: Campus Ministries; Choral groups; Concert band; Dance; Drama/theater; International Student Organization; Jazz band; Literary magazine; Model UN; Music ensembles; Musical theater; Opera; Pep band; Radio station; Student government; Student newspaper; Student-run film society; Symphony orchestra; Yearbook. 150 registered organizations, 6 religious organizations, 0 fraternities, 0 sororities, on campus. **Athletics (Intercollegiate):** *Men:* baseball, basketball, cross-country, diving, football, golf, ice hockey, lacrosse, soccer, squash, swimming, tennis, track/field (outdoor), track/field (indoor). *Women:* basketball, cross-country, diving, field hockey, golf, ice hockey, lacrosse, soccer, softball, squash, swimming, tennis, track/field (outdoor), track/field (indoor), volleyball. **On-Campus Highlights:** Mead Art Museum, Beneski Museum of Natural History, Russian Cultural Center, Japanese Peace Garden, Wilder Observatory.

FINANCIAL AID

Students should submit: CSS/Financial Aid PROFILE; FAFSA; Noncustodial PROFILE. Priority filing deadline is 1/1. The Princeton Review suggests that all financial aid forms be submitted as soon as possible after October 1. *Need-based scholarships/grants offered*: College/university scholarship or grant aid from institutional funds; Federal Pell; Private scholarships; SEOG; State scholarships/grants. *Loan aid offered*: Direct PLUS loans; Direct Subsidized Stafford Loans; Direct Unsubsidized Stafford Loans. Applicants will be notified of awards on or about 4/1. Federal Work-Study Program available. Institutional employment available.

BOTTOM LINE

Annual tuition, fees, and room and board cost roughly $73,950 at Amherst. Once you consider books, supplies, personal expenses, and transportation, you can expect to spend anywhere from $76,000 to $81,000 per year. In the end, you'll get much more than what you pay for. The school meets 100 percent of its student body's demonstrated need without loans, and those who choose to take them out graduate with little debt (relative to the indebtedness of graduates of many similar schools). Students feel it is "hard to find somewhere better" and believe Amherst is "the best of the small, elite New England colleges."

CAREER INFORMATION FROM PAYSCALE.COM

ROI Rating	94
Bachelors and No Higher	
Median starting salary	$63,800
Median mid-career salary	$116,500
At Least Bachelors	
Median starting salary	$66,500
Median mid-career salary	$136,300
Alumni with high job meaning	52%
Degrees awarded in STEM subjects	32%

FINANCIAL FACTS

Financial Aid Rating	98
Annual tuition	$57,640
Room and board	$15,310
Required fees	$1,000
Books and supplies	$1,000
Average frosh need-based scholarship	$58,880
Average UG need-based scholarship	$54,715
% needy frosh rec. need-based scholarship or grant aid	100
% needy UG rec. need-based scholarship or grant aid	100
% needy frosh rec. non-need-based scholarship or grant aid	0
% needy UG rec. non-need-based scholarship or grant aid	0
% needy frosh rec. need-based self-help aid	83
% needy UG rec. need-based self-help aid	88
% frosh rec. any financial aid	62
% UG rec. any financial aid	56
% UG borrow to pay for school	30
Average cumulative indebtedness	$13,710
% frosh need fully met	100
% ugrads need fully met	100
Average % of frosh need met	100
Average % of ugrad need met	100

Amherst College

Babson College

231 Forest Street, Babson Park, MA 02457 • Admission: 781-239-5522 • Fax: 781-239-4006

CAMPUS LIFE

Quality of Life Rating	86
Fire Safety Rating	95
Green Rating	91
Type of school	Private
Environment	Village

STUDENTS

Total undergrad enrollment	2,361
% male/female	52/48
% from out of state	71
% frosh live on campus	100
% ugrads live on campus	78
# of fraternities	
(% ugrad men join)	4 (13)
# of sororities	
(% ugrad women join)	3 (26)
% African American	4
% Asian	12
% Caucasian	36
% Hispanic	11
% Native American	<1
% Pacific Islander	<1
% Two or more races	2
% Race and/or ethnicity unknown	5
% international	28
# of countries represented	81

#58 BEST VALUE COLLEGE

ABOUT THE SCHOOL

Massachusetts' Babson College cultivates an entrepreneurial mindset through a rigorous business curriculum with liberal arts woven throughout. More than 2,100 undergraduates are educated under the school's Entrepreneurial Thought & Action methodology, which teaches students to use entrepreneurship as a way to look at the world. Students find the "achievement-driven culture of Babson" offers access to unique programs, institutes, and fundamental experiences like the Foundations of Management and Entrepreneurship (FME) program, in which teams of first-years create, launch, and run a business using a loan from the college. More generally, "small class sizes inherently keep classes more discussion-based than lecture-based," and faculty are often current or former professionals who "are always available for … advice and sharing of connections and resources." It is "truly incredible to see the real world experiences of our professors and how they shape class discussions."

BANG FOR YOUR BUCK

Those who enter Babson gain access to "an amazingly responsive network" and "incredible resources." One such resource is The Lewis Institute, which focuses on seeking social innovation solutions. Another is the Babson College Fund (BCF), which is an accredited course that allows select students to manage a portion of the school's endowment. In addition to these options (and several others), Babson also has an off-campus collaborative agreement with both the nearby F. W. Olin College of Engineering and Wellesley College, which allows students to participate in even more joint research, curricular projects, conferences, and classes. Across the board, the goal of

Babson College

Financial Aid: 781-239-4015 • E-mail: ugradadmission@babson.edu • Website: www.babson.edu

the school's services and resources is to ensure "the experience you have seems to replicate the real world as much as it can." One noteworthy exception comes from Babson's generous financial assistance, which is designed to ensure that students have access to the school: about half receive some form of aid, and the school meets 100 percent of students' need in the first year. In fact, assuming there is no change in the students' circumstances, Babson commits to that level of aid for all four years. Merit scholarships are available to select students, including scholarships for returning students based on their academic and leadership achievements on campus the previous year, such as the Dean's Scholarship (of up to $5,000 a year).

SCHOOL LIFE

The always active enrollees at Babson often fill their time "working on professional development, their own ventures, or internships," which means they are also often "heavily involved in student organizations." Everyone "is encouraged to take on some type of leadership position or at least be engaged in one or multiple clubs." "Google Calendar is an absolute must," shares one undergrad, citing the "need to be self-disciplined to survive here." If that seems like a lot of pressure, rest assured that "people also love to just eat and talk [and] watch TV together," though "fun is something that is saved for weekends or late nights" for most. And since there are no Friday classes at Babson, "students will take weekend trips to New York City, Maine, New Hampshire, and Vermont." In addition, "Wellesley is a beautiful place to explore, grab a bite to eat, and shop."

CAREER

Given the entrepreneurial focus of Babson, students here "tend to be heavily invested in their life after Babson and in setting themselves up for a comfortable career." It's also helpful that "the alumni network is

ACADEMICS

Academic Rating	85
% students returning for sophomore year	95
% students graduating within 4 years	89
% students graduating within 6 years	91
Calendar	Semester
Student/faculty ratio	14:1
Profs interesting rating	86
Profs accessible rating	88
Most classes have 20–29 students.	

MOST POPULAR MAJORS
Business Administration and Management, General

SELECTIVITY

Admissions Rating	95
# of applicants	6,383
% of applicants accepted	24
% of acceptees attending	35
# offered a place on the wait list	1,852
% accepting a place on wait list	40
% admitted from wait list	1
# of early decision applicants	431
% accepted early decision	39

very responsive given how small and community-like Babson is." That adds together and proves to be successful too, as the school has "wonderful job and graduate placement numbers": 99 percent of students were employed or attending graduate school within six months of graduation. The Center for Career Development "is one of the most active voices on campus and constantly has extremely useful events" that connect students with advising and experiential learning opportunities such as Management Consulting Field Experience. Additionally, the "extensive time taken to teach students here how to view the world through an entrepreneurial lens" is well-known to employers, "making Babson standout candidates for jobs."

GENERAL INFO

Activities: Campus Ministries; Choral groups; Dance; Drama/theater; International Student Organization; Literary magazine; Model UN; Music ensembles; Musical theater; Radio station; Student government; Campus Activities Board (CAB); Student-run film society. 120 registered organizations, 2 honor societies, 8 religious organizations, 4 fraternities, 3 sororities, on campus. **Athletics (Intercollegiate):** *Men:* baseball, basketball, cross-country, diving, golf, ice hockey, lacrosse, skiing (downhill/alpine), soccer, swimming, tennis, track/field (outdoor). *Women:* basketball, cross-country, diving, field hockey, lacrosse, skiing (downhill/alpine), soccer, softball, swimming, tennis, track/field (outdoor), volleyball. **On-Campus Highlights:** Reynolds Campus Center, The Commons at Horn Library, Trim Dining Hall, Weissman Foundry, Sorenson Center for the Arts, Recreation and Athletics Complex (BRAC). **Environmental Initiatives:** Investment of $4 million into energy efficiency and capital improvements to save energy.

Babson College

FINANCIAL AID

Students should submit: CSS/Financial Aid PROFILE; FAFSA; Noncustodial PROFILE. Priority filing deadline is 2/1. The Princeton Review suggests that all financial aid forms be submitted as soon as possible after October 1. *Need-based scholarships/ grants offered*: College/university scholarship or grant aid from institutional funds; Federal Pell; Private scholarships; SEOG; State scholarships/grants. *Loan aid offered*: Direct PLUS loans; Direct Subsidized Stafford Loans; Direct Unsubsidized Stafford Loans. Applicants will be notified of awards on or about 4/1. Federal Work-Study Program available. Institutional employment available.

BOTTOM LINE

Babson College currently charges $52,608 for its annual tuition. Undergrads (and their families) should also expect to pay $10,828 for room (the price of the average double) and an additional $5,948 for a meal plan. Books and classroom supplies will likely cost another $1,144. The college also estimates that personal expenses come to roughly $1,850. And there's a $50 federal direct loan fee. That makes the total (estimated) cost of attendance about $72,428.

FINANCIAL FACTS	
Financial Aid Rating	94
Annual tuition	$52,608
Room and board	$16,776
Books and supplies	$1,144
Average frosh need-based scholarship	$39,582
Average UG need-based scholarship	$41,446
% needy frosh rec. need-based scholarship or grant aid	93
% needy UG rec. need-based scholarship or grant aid	96
% needy frosh rec. non-need-based scholarship or grant aid	14
% needy UG rec. non-need-based scholarship or grant aid	15
% needy frosh rec. need-based self-help aid	90
% needy UG rec. need-based self-help aid	80
% frosh rec. any financial aid	46
% UG rec. any financial aid	47
% UG borrow to pay for school	40
Average cumulative indebtedness	$37,866
% frosh need fully met	100
% ugrads need fully met	63
Average % of frosh need met	100
Average % of ugrad need met	99

CAREER INFORMATION FROM PAYSCALE.COM	
ROI Rating	91
Bachelors and No Higher	
Median starting salary	$72,000
Median mid-career salary	$133,800
At Least Bachelors	
Median starting salary	$71,400
Median mid-career salary	$149,400
Alumni with high job meaning	37%
Degrees awarded in STEM subjects	0%

Babson College

Bates College

23 Campus Avenue, Lindholm House, Lewiston, ME 04240 • Admissions: 207-786-6000 • Fax: 207-786-6025

CAMPUS LIFE

Quality of Life Rating	91
Fire Safety Rating	98
Green Rating	97
Type of school	Private
Environment	Town

STUDENTS

Total undergrad enrollment	1,832
% male/female	50/50
% frosh from public high school	53
% frosh live on campus	100
# of fraternities	0
# of sororities	0
% African American	5
% Asian	4
% Caucasian	71
% Hispanic	8
% Native American	<1
% Pacific Islander	<1
% Two or more races	4
% Race and/or ethnicity unknown	<1
% international	8
# of countries represented	71

ABOUT THE SCHOOL

Bates was founded in 1855, more than 150 years ago, by people who believed strongly in freedom, civil rights, and the importance of a higher education for all who could benefit from it. Bates is devoted to undergraduates in the arts and science, and commitment to teaching excellence is central to the college's mission. The college is recognized for its inclusive social character; there are no fraternities or sororities, and student organizations are open to all. Bates College has stood firmly for the ideals of academic rigor, intellectual curiosity, egalitarianism, social justice, and freedom since its founding just before the Civil War. "The willingness of everyone to hear differing viewpoints and opinions even if they disagree" is very attractive to one student. Another is impressed that "Bates is an institution that challenges me to critically think in a way I never have before." Students who can demonstrate the intellectual soundness and potential value of an initiative—whether it's for a senior thesis project, a performance, or an independent study—will receive every possible backing from the college. And one enrollee is very pleased to find that "you will not find it hard to gain access to resources." Bates has long understood that the privilege of education carries with it responsibility to others. Commitment to social action and the environment is something students here take seriously. Learning at Bates is connected to action and to others beyond the self. Bates faculty routinely incorporate service-learning into their courses, and about half of students take part in community-based projects in the Lewiston-Auburn region.

Bates College

Financial Aid: 207-786-6096 • Website: www.bates.edu

BANG FOR YOUR BUCK

With 200 instructors at the school, those students fortunate enough to actually enroll can expect to find an outstanding student-to-faculty ratio of 10:1. More than 90 percent of freshmen return as sophomores and just a few percent less graduate within four years. Diversity is paramount at Bates; 89 percent of students are from out-of-state, and fifty-five different countries are represented on campus—extremely impressive for such a small institution. Internships and experiential learning opportunities are heavily encouraged; through the Purposeful Work Internship program, for example, students explore the world of work throughout their four years. Ninety-eight percent of students complete a senior thesis and the other 2 percent complete a capstone project. More than two-thirds of alumni enroll in graduate study within ten years. Bates highly values its study-abroad programs, unique calendar (4-4-1), and the many opportunities available for one-on-one collaboration with faculty. "The size of the student body allows for a relationship beyond that of typical professor-student and creates a sense of academic equality that produces incredible levels of scholarship at the undergraduate level."

ACADEMICS

Academic Rating	94
% students returning for sophomore year	94
% students graduating within 4 years	86
% students graduating within 6 years	89
Calendar	4-4-1
Student/faculty ratio	10:1
Profs interesting rating	93
Profs accessible rating	94
Most classes have fewer than 10 students.	

MOST POPULAR MAJORS

Psychology, General; Political Science and Government, General; History, General

SELECTIVITY

Admissions Rating	96
# of applicants	7,685
% of applicants accepted	18
% of acceptees attending	38
# offered a place on the wait list	1,903
% accepting a place on wait list	52
% admitted from wait list	0
# of early decision applicants	741
% accepted early decision	45

STUDENT LIFE

Bates undergrads promise you'll never have a dull moment on this campus. A lot of the fun can be attributed to the industrious "Student Activities Office, [which] puts on a tremendous [number] of exciting events/shows/trips for students to participate in." For example, they sponsored "the Snoop Dog concert last year, D.E.A.P. ('drop everything and play') concert in May, [the] weekly 'Village Club Series' concerts where up-and-coming artists perform café-style shows [and] the annual Winter Carnival in January." There are also nearly 100 student-run clubs to join, ranging "from Chess Club to Environmental Club to the DJ Society and, of course, the champion debating society." Additionally, you'll find "wild dances with all different themes, as well as crazy traditions like the puddle jump." And, of course, the minute that first snow fall hits, plenty of Batesies will head to the slopes to ski and/or snowboard.

CAREER

Bates' tremendous Career Development Center really helps undergrads plot their post-collegiate life. To begin with, the office provides the standard workshops in resume building, cover letter writing and interviewing techniques. Students can also participate in a new, short-term job shadowing program that offers both career insight and networking opportunities. Additionally, undergrads have access to JobCat, an exclusive Bates-only site that gives them the opportunity to browse a number of job postings/openings. Batesies looking to continue their education can attend the office's annual graduate and professional school fair. This event usually brings around 100 admissions representatives to campus. And, of course, the Career Development Center invites numerous employers (from various industries) to campus each year to conduct interviews and information sessions. Finally, recent graduates have managed to nab jobs with companies such as Sony Music Entertainment, Boston Consulting Group, GoldmanSachs, The Metropolitan Museum of Art, High Mountain Institute, and Trapeze School New York.

GENERAL INFO

Activities: Campus Ministries; Choral groups; Concert band; Dance; Drama/theater; International Student Organization; Jazz band; Literary magazine; Model UN; Music ensembles; Musical theater; Radio station; Student government; Student newspaper; Student-run film society; Symphony orchestra; Yearbook. 111 registered organizations, 3 honor societies, 11 religious organization, 0 fraternities, 0 sororities, on campus. **Athletics (Intercollegiate):** *Men:* baseball, basketball, crew/rowing, cross-country, diving, football, golf, lacrosse, skiing (downhill/alpine), skiingnordiccross-country, soccer, squash, swimming, tennis, track/field (outdoor), track/field (indoor). *Women:* basketball, crew/rowing, cross-country, diving, field hockey, golf, lacrosse, skiing (downhill/alpine), skiingnordiccross-country, soccer, softball, squash, swimming, tennis, track/field (outdoor), track/field (indoor), volleyball. **On-Campus Highlights:** Pettengill Hall, Bates College Museum of Art, Dining Commons, The George and Helen

Bates College

Ladd Library, Merrill Gymnasium/Underhill Arena. **Environmental Initiatives:** Developing sustainable building guidelines and campus energy goals.

FINANCIAL AID

Students should submit: CSS/Financial Aid PROFILE; FAFSA; Noncustodial PROFILE. Priority filing deadline is 1/1. The Princeton Review suggests that all financial aid forms be submitted as soon as possible after October 1. *Need-based scholarships/ grants offered*: College/university scholarship or grant aid from institutional funds; Federal Pell; Private scholarships; SEOG; State scholarships/grants. *Loan aid offered*: Direct PLUS loans; Direct Subsidized Stafford Loans; Direct Unsubsidized Stafford Loans. Applicants will be notified of awards on or about 4/1. Federal Work-Study Program available. Institutional employment available.

BOTTOM LINE

The education that one receives at an institution like Bates College does not come without a price. The total cost of tuition, room, board, and fees comes to $72,188. But, have no fear, students and parents: on average Bates College also meets 100 percent of need. The average total need-based scholarship is a whopping $44,590. Forty-two percent of all undergrads receive financial aid. The average graduate can expect to leave school with about $21,525 of loan debt. Additionally, scholarships and grants are plentiful, for international as well as domestic students. One student was excited that Bates "provided me the greatest amount of financial aid. It was very generous."

FINANCIAL FACTS	
Financial Aid Rating	97
Annual tuition	$55,683
Room and board	$15,705
Books and supplies	$800
Average frosh need-based scholarship	$44,644
Average UG need-based scholarship	$44,590
% needy frosh rec. need-based scholarship or grant aid	100
% needy UG rec. need-based scholarship or grant aid	100
% needy frosh rec. non-need-based scholarship or grant aid	0
% needy UG rec. non-need-based scholarship or grant aid	0
% needy frosh rec. need-based self-help aid	98
% needy UG rec. need-based self-help aid	99
% frosh rec. any financial aid	42
% UG rec. any financial aid	42
% UG borrow to pay for school	35
Average cumulative indebtedness	$21,525
% frosh need fully met	100
% ugrads need fully met	100
Average % of frosh need met	100
Average % of ugrad need met	100

CAREER INFORMATION FROM PAYSCALE.COM	
ROI Rating	91
Bachelors and No Higher	
Median starting salary	$59,500
Median mid-career salary	$111,900
At Least Bachelors	
Median starting salary	$60,200
Median mid-career salary	$127,000
Alumni with high job meaning	51%
Degrees awarded in STEM subjects	23%

Bates College

Bowdoin College

5000 College Station, Bowdoin College, Brunswick, ME 04011-8441 • Admissions: 207-725-3100

Quality of Life Rating	**97**
Fire Safety Rating	**95**
Green Rating	**98**
Type of school	Private
Environment	Village
STUDENTS	
Total undergrad enrollment	1,825
% male/female	49/51
% from out of state	89
% frosh from public high school	53
% frosh live on campus	100
% ugrads live on campus	90
# of fraternities	0
# of sororities	0
% African American	8
% Asian	8
% Caucasian	61
% Hispanic	10
% Native American	<1
% Pacific Islander	<1
% Two or more races	6
% Race and/or ethnicity unknown	1
% international	6
# of countries represented	42

#25 BEST VALUE COLLEGE

ABOUT THE SCHOOL

Founded in 1794, Maine's Bowdoin College is a historic liberal arts school that cultivates its curriculum around a commitment to the common good. The school promotes social responsibility and critical thinking alongside its academics, and more than 200 students take part in faculty-mentored research. Around a quarter of the most recent graduating class were double majors, choosing from more than forty options. The school is structured with nine College Houses that are an integral part of Bowdoin life, creating smaller communities that share special meals, events, and field trips. Bowdoin "does a good job of making sure that students have more of an interdisciplinary education," and it's "really common to have multiple learning styles" throughout classes. It helps that students feel those classes are taught by some of the best: "The professors at Bowdoin are truly incredible" and they "value their teaching more than anything, [which] shows through their thoughtfully developed curriculums, discussion facilitations, accessibility outside of class, and the thorough feedback they give students."

BANG FOR YOUR BUCK

First, the main event: the school stopped using loans in their financial aid packages in 2008, replacing them with grants instead. Nearly half of the student body receives aid, and the school even waives the application fee for any student applying for financial aid. And the financial assistance doesn't end there: Once you're in at this small school, there "are tons of opportunities for grants, independent studies, and funded internships." On top of that, a Bowdoin education is a well-rounded one that travels beyond campus

Bowdoin College

Fax: 207-725-3101 • Financial Aid: 207-725-3273 • E-mail: admissions@bowdoin.edu • Website: www.bowdoin.edu

borders: The Center for Co-curricular Opportunities features a group of advisors who help students apply their classroom learnings to the real-world through fellowships, research, and study abroad (more than half of students take their studies to another country at some point).

STUDENT LIFE

The school "works hard to foster a community within the campus setting" by organizing "tons of events throughout the year from lectures to museum nights to the notorious Bowdoin-Colby hockey game." Other common forms of entertainment include improv comedy and live music. They also want their students to eat well: "Food is an immensely important part of campus life," and the fare on offer at the dining halls "means students eat healthily and can concentrate on schoolwork, social life, and sleeping well without worrying about what they're going to eat." As one candidly shares, "The food is honestly good to a point where I feel bad for my other college friends." Those wanting time off campus are also pleased as "Brunswick is a fantastic college town." The school's Outing Club helps make "weekend trips into other parts of Maine ... popular." Overall, students "keep themselves incredibly busy at Bowdoin."

ACADEMICS

Academic Rating	95
% students returning for sophomore year	98
% students graduating within 4 years	88
% students graduating within 6 years	95
Calendar	Semester
Student/faculty ratio	9:1
Profs interesting rating	95
Profs accessible rating	97

Most classes have 10–19 students. Most lab/discussion sessions have 10–19 students.

MOST POPULAR MAJORS

Political Science and Government, General; Economics, General; Mathematics, General

SELECTIVITY

Admissions Rating	98
# of applicants	9,081
% of applicants accepted	10
% of acceptees attending	55
# of early decision applicants	1,093
% accepted early decision	23

CAREER

Bowdoin implements a Career Exploration and Development office, the goal of which is to support students as they "Explore, Experience, and Pursue" career opportunities around the world. The office is "helpful for students looking for internships, jobs, or advice," and students are encouraged to engage with their career planning early on during the Explore portion of the model so they can recognize the motivations behind their academic path. Additionally, the Bowdoin Career Advisory Network (BCAN) of alumni and parents provides connections to internships and guidance, and the

On-Campus Recruiting Program hosts more than seventy employers each year. The school itself offers "generous fellowships, especially for summer jobs," and "if you want an internship or a paid summer research job, all the steps are there for you." As one student sums up their quest to maximize career development opportunities, "Rarely have I ever heard anyone say, 'No, that's not possible.'"

GENERAL INFO

Activities: Choral groups; Concert band; Dance; Drama/theater; International Student Organization; Jazz band; Literary magazine; Model UN; Music ensembles; Musical theater; Radio station; Student government; Student newspaper; Student-run film society; Symphony orchestra. 130 registered organizations, 1 honor society, 6 religious organizations, 0 fraternities, 0 sororities, on campus. **Athletics (Intercollegiate):** *Men:* baseball, basketball, cross-country, diving, football, golf, ice hockey, lacrosse, sailing, skiing (nordic, cross-country), soccer, squash, swimming, tennis, track/field (outdoor), track/field (indoor). *Women:* basketball, cross-country, diving, field hockey, golf, ice hockey, lacrosse, rugby, sailing, skiing (nordic, cross-country), soccer, softball, squash, swimming, tennis, track/field (outdoor), track/field (indoor), volleyball. **On-Campus Highlights:** Bowdoin College Museum of Art, Peary-MacMillan Arctic Museum, Peter Buck Center for Health and Fitness, David Saul Smith Union, Schwartz Outdoor Leadership Center, The Edwards Center for Art and Dance. **Environmental Initiatives:** Bowdoin achieved carbon neutrality in 2018, two years ahead of schedule. The College is now developing an even more ambitious climate action plan to guide its sustainability efforts through 2030, and is joining with four Massachusetts liberal arts colleges to help fund a 75-megawatt solar project in Farmington, Maine. In 2018, Bowdoin opened the new Roux Center for the Environment, which serves as home for its interdisciplinary environmental studies program. The school's Schiller Center for Coastal Studies is undergoing a major expansion that will open in the late summer of 2020. A new Center for Arctic Studies will open in 2022.

Bowdoin College

FINANCIAL AID

Students should submit: Business/Farm Supplement; CSS/Financial Aid PROFILE; FAFSA; Noncustodial PROFILE. Priority filing deadline is 2/1. The Princeton Review suggests that all financial aid forms be submitted as soon as possible after October 1. *Need-based scholarships/grants offered*: College/university scholarship or grant aid from institutional funds; Federal Pell; Private scholarships; SEOG; State scholarships/grants. *Loan aid offered*: Direct Subsidized Stafford Loans; Direct Unsubsidized Stafford Loans. Federal Work-Study Program available. Institutional employment available.

BOTTOM LINE

Tuition for new students at Bowdoin is $53,418 per year, with an additional $504 student activities fee. The on-campus housing and meal plans add another $14,698 to the total, but these amenities are recognized as being some of the best in the nation. After factoring in tuition, fees, and books the annual cost of attendance is roughly 69,460.

FINANCIAL FACTS	
Financial Aid Rating	99
Annual tuition	$53,418
Room and board	$14,698
Required fees	$504
Books and supplies	$840
Average frosh need-based scholarship	$48,856
Average UG need-based scholarship	$47,522
% needy frosh rec. need-based scholarship or grant aid	100
% needy UG rec. need-based scholarship or grant aid	100
% needy frosh rec. non-need-based scholarship or grant aid	0
% needy UG rec. non-need-based scholarship or grant aid	0
% needy frosh rec. need-based self-help aid	98
% needy UG rec. need-based self-help aid	99
% frosh rec. any financial aid	52
% UG rec. any financial aid	50
% UG borrow to pay for school	27
Average cumulative indebtedness	$25,482
% frosh need fully met	100
% ugrads need fully met	100
Average % of frosh need met	100
Average % of ugrad need met	100

CAREER INFORMATION FROM PAYSCALE.COM	
ROI Rating	93
Bachelors and No Higher	
Median starting salary	$61,300
Median mid-career salary	$112,000
At Least Bachelors	
Median starting salary	$63,500
Median mid-career salary	$130,600
Alumni with high job meaning	54%
Degrees awarded in STEM subjects	37%

Bowdoin College

Brigham Young University

A-153 ASB, Provo, UT 84602-1110 • Admissions: 801-422-2507 • Fax: 801-422-0005

#35 BEST VALUE COLLEGE

ABOUT THE SCHOOL

Owned by the Church of Jesus Christ of Latter-Day Saints, BYU is all about "high moral standards" and "educating the best LDS students efficiently." Students love the "religious atmosphere" that helps in "isolating its students from what they believe will wrongly influence their choices." Also, "the tuition cost is relatedly cheap." The "academically accomplished" professors are "smart and interesting people" and "very well trained in their field." The school offers a "large variety of majors" with almost 200 in total. Popular majors include exercise science, elementary education, psychology, management, and English. The roughly 30,000 students on campus—25,733 of whom are undergraduates—make it the largest religious university in the United States. "It offers everything I wanted," one student says, "good education, my major, people who would support me in my beliefs and morals, large campus, and it was all at a great price!"

BANG FOR YOUR BUCK

Tuition is affordable, especially if you are an LDS member. BYU cuts tuition in half for LDS members, claiming it is the equivalent of in-state tuition for state universities. In addition, BYU offers about one quarter of their incoming freshmen academic scholarships of varying amounts. These scholarships are mostly paid for by tithes on LDS church members. The scholarships do not renew, but instead are awarded on a yearly basis. Students must apply every year, which also means that you may receive a scholarship in later years even if you do not get one initially. Students may also apply for federal grants and loans.

Brigham Young University

Financial Aid: 801-422-4104 • E-mail: admissions@byu.edu • Website: www.byu.edu

STUDENT LIFE

BYU's student population "is pretty homogeneous due to the fact that 98 percent of us are LDS." "The average student is kind, conservative, dedicated to school, and very religious," one student explains. "Everyone pretty much fits in," "as long as a person doesn't wear clothes or have a hairstyle that stands out obnoxiously." Student life is shaped in large part by the school's religious rules, which enforce standards of appearance and ban alcohol, drugs, and premarital sex. Consequentially, many "people think about getting married…[and] for fun, people go on dates." "Good clean fun" is the rule, and students enjoy outdoor activities "like skiing, mountain biking, hiking, climbing, etc." "There are many social activities either through the church you attend or through the school," and students "like to watch movies, dance, cook, play games, sing, or make up their own ways to have fun."

CAREER

"Professors are very attuned to career opportunities" at BYU and help students get connected with jobs. "The alumni network is amazing," although "there needs to be more help for incoming freshman to figure out what they want to do." PayScale.com reports a median starting salary of $59,200 for BYU graduates. "BYU does emphasize book smarts but that is not the main emphasis," one student explains. "Hands-on experience, internships, and study abroad are highly encouraged," which helps students get jump-starts on their post-college careers.

ACADEMICS

Academic Rating	82
% students returning for sophomore year	90
% students graduating within 4 years	23
% students graduating within 6 years	83
Calendar	Semester
Student/faculty ratio	20:1
Profs interesting rating	77
Profs accessible rating	73

Most classes have 10–19 students.

MOST POPULAR MAJORS

Elementary Education and Teaching; Exercise Physiology; Business/Commerce, General

SELECTIVITY

Admissions Rating	93
# of applicants	12,858
% of applicants accepted	52
% of acceptees attending	81

FRESHMAN PROFILE

Range SAT EBRW	610–710
Range SAT Math	600–700
Range ACT Composite	27–32
# submitting SAT scores	1,538
% submitting SAT scores	28
# submitting ACT scores	5,108
% submitting ACT scores	94
Average HS GPA	3.8
% graduated top 10% of class	54
% graduated top 25% of class	85
% graduated top 50% of class	98

DEADLINES

Regular	
Deadline	12/15
Nonfall registration?	Yes

GENERAL INFO

Activities: Choral groups; Concert band; Dance; Drama/theater; Jazz band; Literary magazine; Marching band; Music ensembles; Musical theater; Opera; Pep band; Radio station; Student government; Student newspaper; Student-run film society; Symphony orchestra; Television station. 390 registered organizations, 22 honor societies, 25 religious organizations, 0 fraternities, 0 sororities, on campus. **Athletics (Intercollegiate):** *Men:* baseball, basketball, cheerleading, cross-country, diving, football, golf, swimming, tennis, track/field (outdoor), track/field (indoor), volleyball. *Women:* basketball, cheerleading, cross-country, diving, golf, gymnastics, soccer, softball, swimming, tennis, track/field (outdoor), track/field (indoor), volleyball. **On-Campus Highlights:** Monte L. Bean Life Science Museum, The Museum of Art, Gordon B. Hinckley Alumni & Visitors Center, Harold B. Lee Library, Wilkinson Student Center.

FINANCIAL AID

Students should submit: FAFSA. Priority filing deadline is 4/15. The Princeton Review suggests that all financial aid forms be submitted as soon as possible after October 1. *Need-based scholarships/grants offered*: College/university scholarship or grant aid from institutional funds; Federal Pell; Private scholarships. *Loan aid offered*: Direct PLUS loans; Direct Subsidized Stafford Loans; Direct Unsubsidized Stafford Loans.

Brigham Young University

BOTTOM LINE

The cost of BYU depends on your religious affiliation. LDS members pay $5,790 a year while non-LDS members pay roughly double that amount. Room and board will bring those totals to just about $14,000 for LDS members and about $18,450 for non-LDS students.

CAREER INFORMATION FROM PAYSCALE.COM

ROI Rating	93
Bachelors and No Higher	
Median starting salary	$59,200
Median mid-career salary	$108,000
At Least Bachelors	
Median starting salary	$61,700
Median mid-career salary	$120,600
Alumni with high job meaning	61%
Degrees awarded in STEM subjects	25%

FINANCIAL FACTS

Financial Aid Rating	74
Annual tuition	$5,790
Room and board	$7,766
Average frosh need-based scholarship	$4,721
Average UG need-based scholarship	$5,017
% needy frosh rec. need-based scholarship or grant aid	49
% needy UG rec. need-based scholarship or grant aid	79
% needy frosh rec. non-need-based scholarship or grant aid	65
% needy UG rec. non-need-based scholarship or grant aid	50
% needy frosh rec. need-based self-help aid	26
% needy UG rec. need-based self-help aid	25
% frosh rec. any financial aid	53
% UG rec. any financial aid	64
% UG borrow to pay for school	26
Average cumulative indebtedness	$14,998
% frosh need fully met	2
% ugrads need fully met	2
Average % of frosh need met	28
Average % of ugrad need met	33

Brigham Young University

Brown University

Box 1876, 1 Prospect Street, Providence, RI 02912 • Admissions: 401-863-2378 • Fax: 401-863-9300

CAMPUS LIFE

Quality of Life Rating	96
Fire Safety Rating	92
Green Rating	91
Type of school	Private
Environment	City

STUDENTS

Total undergrad enrollment	6,752
% male/female	46/54
% from out of state	95
% frosh from public high school	53
% frosh live on campus	100
% ugrads live on campus	72
# of fraternities	
(% ugrad men join)	9 (14)
# of sororities	
(% ugrad women join)	5 (10)
% African American	6
% Asian	15
% Caucasian	43
% Hispanic	11
% Native American	<1
% Pacific Islander	<1
% Two or more races	6
% Race and/or ethnicity unknown	6
% international	11
# of countries represented	100

ABOUT THE SCHOOL

Ivy League Brown University's fervent dedication to free inquiry and undergraduate freedom means that rather than fulfilling distribution requirements, students are educated through the school's famous Open Curriculum and may dictate the course of their own liberal arts study. Under this plan, students can pick whether a course is taken for a letter grade, and have the option to pursue more than eighty majors, with a strong advising network and numerous centers and institutes (such as the public service-oriented Swearer Center) to aid in their research and action. Brown is "about constantly questioning what could make the world and our school a better place," and study abroad programs and international collaboration are stressed, as is social action. No matter what area of study a student may choose to focus on, Brown provides "an atmosphere of both strong support and intense debate."

BANG FOR YOUR BUCK

Brown allows students to "gain both practical knowledge and a traditional liberal arts education," and the Open Curriculum ensures that students can mesh very different studies into a unique blend and "gets the opportunity to map their own journey." With a "Shopping Period" to test out classes during the first two weeks of the semester and "the ability to design your own courses easily," students can easily get exactly what they pay for no matter what they're paying. Indeed, a lot of students are paying a reduced price; around 99 percent of needy students receive need-based scholarship or grant aid, with the average award totaling $50,240.

Brown University

Financial Aid: 401-863-2721 • E-mail: admission_undergraduate@brown.edu • Website: www.brown.edu

STUDENT LIFE

Everyone at Brown is "absolutely brilliant in one way or another" and "spends as much time developing skills outside of the classroom as within," yet still strives to have a thriving social life. There is a "strong activist culture" with demonstrations happening frequently, and there are "lectures, movie screenings, improv shows, dance performances, [and] a cappella showcases constantly" happening around campus. Generally, people "fill their weekdays with schoolwork and extracurricular activities and their weekends with friends and leisure." For fun, there are clubs in downtown Providence, parties or low-key room hangs, and people "dance, work out, paint, tutor, cook…and have fun in any way possible." "Really anyone can have fun in their own way at Brown, and that's lovely," says a student.

CAREER

These free-thinkers are more likely to carve their own paths than "just go to the normative career options," and Brown welcomes this approach with open arms. All post-graduate coordination (aside from supporting graduate education in the health professions, law and business) is done through the CareerLAB, the Center for Careers and Life after Brown, which arranges for on-campus recruiting, job fairs, skills workshops, boot camps, and more. "Career and internship placement has become a top priority of the new university administration," and students enjoy the fruits of Brown's reputation when applying for jobs. Brown grads who visited PayScale.com report a median starting salary of $68,200 and 51 percent believe their work makes the world a better place.

ACADEMICS

Academic Rating	95
% students returning for sophomore year	98
% students graduating within 4 years	85
% students graduating within 6 years	95
Calendar	Semester
Student/faculty ratio	6:1
Profs interesting rating	95
Profs accessible rating	91

Most classes have 10–19 students.

MOST POPULAR MAJORS

Computer and Information Sciences, General; Biology/Biological Sciences, General; Econometrics and Quantitative Economics

SELECTIVITY

Admissions Rating	99
# of applicants	35,437
% of applicants accepted	8
% of acceptees attending	61
# of early decision applicants	3,501
% accepted early decision	21

GENERAL INFO

Activities: Campus Ministries; Choral groups; Concert band; Dance; Drama/theater; International Student Organization; Jazz band; Literary magazine; Marching band; Model UN; Music ensembles; Musical theater; Opera; Pep band; Radio station; Student government; Student newspaper; Student-run film society; Symphony orchestra; Television station; Yearbook. 495 registered organizations, 3 honor societies, 25 religious organizations, 9 fraternities, 5 sororities, on campus. **Athletics (Intercollegiate):** *Men:* baseball, basketball, crew/rowing, cross-country, diving, fencing, football, golf, ice hockey, lacrosse, soccer, squash, swimming, tennis, track/field (outdoor), track/field (indoor), water polo, wrestling. *Women:* basketball, crew/rowing, cross-country, diving, equestrian sports, fencing, field hockey, golf, gymnastics, ice hockey, lacrosse, skiing (downhill/alpine), soccer, softball, squash, swimming, tennis, track/field (outdoor), track/field (indoor), volleyball, water polo. **On-Campus Highlights:** The College Green (Main Green), Nelson Fitness Center, Libraries-including the John Hay Library, Orwig Music Library, Rockefeller Library, Sciences Library., Stephen Robert '62 Campus Center, Granoff Center for the Creative Arts. **Environmental Initiatives:** Reduce GHG emissions by 75 percent by 2025, and achieve net-zero emissions no later than 2040.

FINANCIAL AID

Students should submit: CSS/Financial Aid PROFILE; FAFSA; Noncustodial PROFILE. Priority filing deadline is 2/1. The Princeton Review suggests that all financial aid forms be submitted as soon as possible after October 1. *Need-based scholarships/grants offered*: College/university scholarship or grant aid from institutional funds; Federal Pell; Private scholarships; SEOG; State scholarships/grants. *Loan aid offered*: No loans packaged in financial aid awards, but aid is packaged with University grants. *Optional loan aid offered:* Direct PLUS loans; Direct Subsidized Stafford Loans; Direct Unsubsidized Stafford Loans; college/university loans from institutional funds. Applicants will be notified of awards on or about 4/1. Federal Work-Study Program available. Institutional employment available.

Brown University

BOTTOM LINE

Brown tuition is a steep $57,112 per year with another $15,532 for room and board and $1,292 in fees. But aid is everywhere; 100 percent of every student's demonstrated need is met with a financial aid award that includes scholarship and work only—no loans.

CAREER INFORMATION FROM PAYSCALE.COM

ROI Rating	93
Bachelors and No Higher	
Median starting salary	$68,200
Median mid-career salary	$127,600
At Least Bachelors	
Median starting salary	$69,300
Median mid-career salary	$142,600
Alumni with high job meaning	51%
Degrees awarded in STEM subjects	43%

FINANCIAL FACTS

Financial Aid Rating	97
Annual tuition	$57,112
Room and board	$15,332
Required fees	$1,292
Books and supplies	$1,632
Average frosh need-based scholarship	$49,256
Average UG need-based scholarship	$50,240
% needy frosh rec. need-based scholarship or grant aid	99
% needy UG rec. need-based scholarship or grant aid	99
% needy frosh rec. non-need-based scholarship or grant aid	0
% needy UG rec. non-need-based scholarship or grant aid	0
% needy frosh rec. need-based self-help aid	83
% needy UG rec. need-based self-help aid	88
% frosh rec. any financial aid	55
% UG rec. any financial aid	51
% UG borrow to pay for school	35
Average cumulative indebtedness	$29,620
% frosh need fully met	100
% ugrads need fully met	100
Average % of frosh need met	100
Average % of ugrad need met	100

Brown University

Bucknell University

Freas Hall, Bucknell University, Lewisburg, PA 17837 • Admissions: 570-577-1101 • Financial Aid: 570-577-1331

CAMPUS LIFE

Quality of Life Rating	87
Fire Safety Rating	94
Green Rating	97
Type of school	Private
Environment	Village

STUDENTS

Total undergrad enrollment	3,583
% male/female	49/51
% from out of state	79
% frosh from public high school	62
% frosh live on campus	100
% ugrads live on campus	92
# of fraternities	
(% ugrad men join)	8 (35)
# of sororities	
(% ugrad women join)	10 (40)
% African American	4
% Asian	6
% Caucasian	72
% Hispanic	7
% Native American	<1
% Pacific Islander	0
% Two or more races	4
% Race and/or ethnicity unknown	<1
% international	7
# of countries represented	50

#69 BEST VALUE COLLEGE

ABOUT THE SCHOOL

Bucknell University delivers the quintessential East Coast college experience, and one student says it offers a balanced combination of "great academics, a liberal arts education, sterling reputation, and a great social scene." Lewisburg is located in central Pennsylvania, and the campus is described as both beautiful and safe. Another student shares his experience, saying, "Bucknell was the perfect next step from my high school; it is small enough that your teachers know your name but big enough that you don't know every person on campus. I felt the most comfortable at Bucknell, and I felt that the school actually cared about me as a person, compared to some of the larger state schools to which I applied." Overall, Bucknell balances reputation with accessibility in a neat package. "It's extremely prestigious, beautiful, and the perfect size," shares one junior. A recent graduate sums up by saying, "Bucknell University is small enough to affect change, but big enough to attract national attention. It is a school where academics are amazing, school spirit is everywhere, and the people genuinely care." Another new student is excited that "campus pride is obvious, and as a large liberal arts college there are a myriad of opportunities, but I don't have to compete with a ton of people to take advantage of them."

BANG FOR YOUR BUCK

Bucknell pride extends into the community, and students become involved socially in many area projects and activities. One student relates, "Bucknell just felt like home. It is big enough where alumni and community connections are a huge benefit, but the campus is small enough that I'm not just a

Bucknell University

E-mail: admissions@bucknell.edu • Fax: 570-577-3538 • Website: www.bucknell.edu

number. Professors take time to know me, and being included in class discussions is not a challenge." Another resident "wanted a small school where I could form close relationships with faculty and have the opportunity to do undergraduate research. So far it has exceeded my expectations, and the faculty and administration have made sure opportunities are within my reach." As another student notes appreciatively, "I also received a scholarship that allowed me to have an internship on campus, giving me work experience on top of my education."

STUDENT LIFE

At Bucknell "more than half of eligible students are members of a Greek Organization." "The typical student at Bucknell is upper/middle class, friendly, driven, well educated and preppy." Still, "people tend to be very accepting of alternate cultures and lifestyles." "Generally, academics are the number one priority" and "Bucknellians work extremely hard all week." In addition to Greek life, Bucknell hosts "engaging guest speakers" and concerts at the Weis Center for the Performing Arts. "Lewisburg, a quaint town, feels like a true metropolis" with "an adorable old fashioned movie theater" and late night carnivals. In general, student sentiment echoes that at Bucknell, "there is a place for everyone." "Most people find one, two, or 100 extracurricular activities to join."

CAREER

"Bucknell University allows students, no matter what their academic or social preferences are, to find opportunities to really explore their interests. Students are encouraged to develop projects or clubs to enhance the campus community." Most are "impressed" with the career services and "networking opportunities" available, especially the alumni "dedication."

ACADEMICS

Academic Rating	94
% students returning for sophomore year	92
% students graduating within 4 years	85
% students graduating within 6 years	88
Calendar	Semester
Student/faculty ratio	9:1
Profs interesting rating	93
Profs accessible rating	95

Most classes have 10–19 students. Most lab/discussion sessions have 10–19 students.

MOST POPULAR MAJORS

Psychology, General; Economics, General; Accounting and Finance

SELECTIVITY

Admissions Rating	94
# of applicants	10,144
% of applicants accepted	33
% of acceptees attending	29
# offered a place on the wait list	2,726
% accepting a place on wait list	44
% admitted from wait list	7
# of early decision applicants	719
% accepted early decision	56

Alumni are "valuable" assets to future Bucknellians and remain involved with the school and students long after graduation. Also, the career development center is "amazing" as are the study abroad programs, internships, and undergrad research opportunities. Bucknell "has a huge focus on service learning and community service which is phenomenal." Students receive guidance and opportunities through their professors and pre-professional advisors. According to the website PayScale.com, the median starting salary for graduates is $66,700 with a mid-career average at $122,900.

GENERAL INFO

Activities: Campus Ministries; Choral groups; Concert band; Dance; Drama/theater; International Student Organization; Jazz band; Literary magazine; Model UN; Music ensembles; Musical theater; Opera; Pep band; Radio station; Student government; Student newspaper; Student-run film society; Symphony orchestra; Yearbook. 150 registered organizations, 12 honor societies, 12 religious organizations, 8 fraternities, 10 sororities, on campus. **Athletics (Intercollegiate):** *Men:* baseball, basketball, cross-country, diving, football, golf, lacrosse, soccer, swimming, tennis, track/field (outdoor), track/field (indoor), water polo, wrestling. *Women:* basketball, crew/rowing, cross-country, diving, field hockey, golf, lacrosse, soccer, softball, swimming, tennis, track/field (outdoor), track/field (indoor), volleyball, water polo. **On-Campus Highlights:** Weis Center for the Performing Arts, Outdoor Primate Facilities, Uptown Night Club, Stadler Poetry Center, Library with Technology and Media Commons. **Environmental Initiatives:** In May 2009, the Bucknell University Environmental Center (BUEC) completed a campus-wide environmental assessment of the university's operations, involving over 70 faculty, students, staff, and community members in a highly educational and collaborative project. Teams conducted research on ten indicators of sustainability, including administration/policy, education, energy, water, solid waste, hazardous materials, purchasing, dining, built environment, and landscape.

Bucknell University

FINANCIAL AID

Students should submit: CSS/Financial Aid PROFILE; FAFSA. Priority filing deadline is 1/15. The Princeton Review suggests that all financial aid forms be submitted as soon as possible after October 1. *Need-based scholarships/grants offered*: College/university scholarship or grant aid from institutional funds; Federal Pell; Private scholarships; SEOG; State scholarships/grants. *Loan aid offered*: Direct PLUS loans; Direct Subsidized Stafford Loans; Direct Unsubsidized Stafford Loans. Applicants will be notified of awards on or about 4/1. Federal Work-Study Program available. Institutional employment available.

BOTTOM LINE

Bucknell University provides students with a fine educational experience. The yearly tuition does reflect that monetarily, at $57,882 a year. With room and board adding another $14,174, students are making a large but wise investment in their future. The school does provide a variety of options to offset the cost of attending here, with 87 percent of needy freshmen receiving need-based scholarships or grants. Forty-six percent of students borrow to pay for school, and around 60 percent of students receive some form of financial aid. Upon graduating, for those who take out loans, the average total loan debt is $31,087. "The school has been generous and fair in financial assistance, and easy to work with," relates a satisfied undergraduate.

FINANCIAL FACTS	
Financial Aid Rating	94
Annual tuition	$57,882
Room and board	$14,174
Required fees	$314
Books and supplies	$900
Average frosh need-based scholarship	$32,000
Average UG need-based scholarship	$31,600
% needy frosh rec. need-based scholarship or grant aid	87
% needy UG rec. need-based scholarship or grant aid	95
% needy frosh rec. non-need-based scholarship or grant aid	28
% needy UG rec. non-need-based scholarship or grant aid	27
% needy frosh rec. need-based self-help aid	100
% needy UG rec. need-based self-help aid	100
% frosh rec. any financial aid	50
% UG rec. any financial aid	60
% UG borrow to pay for school	46
Average cumulative indebtedness	$31,087
Average % of frosh need met	92
Average % of ugrad need met	92

CAREER INFORMATION FROM PAYSCALE.COM	
ROI Rating	91
Bachelors and No Higher	
Median starting salary	$66,700
Median mid-career salary	$122,900
At Least Bachelors	
Median starting salary	$68,000
Median mid-career salary	$139,000
Alumni with high job meaning	46%
Degrees awarded in STEM subjects	40%

Bucknell University

California Institute of Technology

1200 East California Boulevard, Pasadena, CA 91125 • Admissions: 626-395-6341

CAMPUS LIFE

Quality of Life Rating	89
Fire Safety Rating	89
Green Rating	60*
Type of school	Private
Environment	City

STUDENTS

Total undergrad enrollment	948
% male/female	55/45
% from out of state	63
% frosh from public high school	72
% frosh live on campus	100
% ugrads live on campus	86
# of fraternities	0
# of sororities	0
% African American	1
% Asian	40
% Caucasian	27
% Hispanic	14
% Native American	0
% Pacific Islander	0
% Two or more races	8
% Race and/or ethnicity unknown	0
% international	9
# of countries represented	23

#5 BEST VALUE COLLEGE

ABOUT THE SCHOOL

Caltech's swagger is completely out of proportion with its small size of about 1,000 students. Thirty-seven Caltech alumni and faculty have won the Nobel Prize; fifty-eight have won the National Medal of Science; thirteen have won the National Medal of Technology and Innovation; and 125 have been elected to the National Academies combined. To say that this science and engineering powerhouse is world-class is an understatement. Located in the suburbs of Los Angeles ("Where else do you have beaches, mountains, and desert all within a two-hour drive?"), Caltech boasts a long history of excellence, with a list of major research achievements that reads like a textbook in the history of science. It goes without saying that academics are highly rigorous and competitive; if you are used to getting straight As, Caltech may be a shock to the system. "If you were the top student all your life, prepare to experience a big dose of humility, because you'll have to work hard just to stay in the middle of the pack," says a student. Techers say the learning experience here is "like trying to drink from a firehose," which is "as accurate a statement as can be made, given the breadth, intensity, and amount of coursework required."

BANG FOR YOUR BUCK

Caltech is extremely affordable, while the school's immense reputation and plethora of opportunities ensure a bright future in research or academia for Caltech graduates. Caltech operates need-blind admissions for all U.S. citizens and permanent residents. Every year, financial aid awards meet 100 percent of demonstrated student need. Of particular note, the school makes every effort to limit a student's debt, awarding aid packages with

California Institute of Technology

Financial Aid: 626-395-6280 • E-mail: ugadmissions@caltech.edu • Website: admissions.caltech.edu

little work-study or loans. Across the board, the maximum loan expectation for Caltech students is just around $5,500 annually, and the average loan debt for Caltech students is just over $16,337 for all four years. The school also offers substantial need-based packages for international students, a rarity among private institutions. Caltech scholarships are awarded based on demonstrated financial need.

STUDENT LIFE

We're told that at Caltech, most "of the social interaction is centered around the eight student houses, which are somewhere between dorms and frats/sororities, but closest to the houses in Harry Potter." Indeed, undergrads here can participate in a myriad of activities through their respective houses. Events might include "scavenger hunts, inter-house dodgeball [and] frisbee, paint balling...pumpkin carving competition, Project Euler new problem solving session and New Yorker caption contest." Outside of the houses, "there are many music and theatre groups on campus, and countless clubs" in which students can participate. It's common for "most people [to be] involved with at least one non-academic thing." And while there is a small party scene, it's "much less traditional...than at other schools." A senior clarifies, "We're more likely to throw themed parties, with things to do other than dance, because we're kind of awkward."

CAREER

We'll get right to the point—Caltech students do very well for themselves. In fact, according to PayScale.com, the median starting salary for recent graduates is $84,100. Certainly, the school's Career Development Center should take some of the credit for this success. After all, the office provides some stellar career counseling. It also hosts a number of workshops

ACADEMICS

Academic Rating	92
% students returning for sophomore year	98
% students graduating within 4 years	81
% students graduating within 6 years	92
Calendar	Quarter
Student/faculty ratio	3:1
Profs interesting rating	78
Profs accessible rating	77

Most classes have 10–19 students. Most lab/discussion sessions have 10–19 students.

MOST POPULAR MAJORS

Computer and Information Sciences, General; Mechanical Engineering; Physics, General

SELECTIVITY

Admissions Rating	99
# of applicants	8,208
% of applicants accepted	7
% of acceptees attending	43
# offered a place on the wait list	634
% accepting a place on wait list	81
% admitted from wait list	1

covering an array of topics such as connecting with recruiters, projecting confidence in interviews and social media networking. Undergrads also have access to the TecherLink which connects them with job, internship and work study opportunities as well as the career center's activities. Perhaps most importantly, the office hosts two big career fairs each year (one in the fall, one in the winter). Finally, companies that frequently hire Caltech grads include Google, Inc., National Institutes of Health (NIH) and Oracle Corp.

GENERAL INFO

Activities: Choral groups; Concert band; Dance; Drama/theater; International Student Organization; Jazz band; Literary magazine; Music ensembles; Musical theater; Pep band; Student government; Student newspaper; Student-run film society; Symphony orchestra; Yearbook. 113 registered organizations, 2 honor societies, 7 religious organizations, 0 fraternities, 0 sororities, on campus. **Athletics (Intercollegiate):** *Men:* baseball, basketball, cross-country, diving, fencing, soccer, swimming, tennis, track/field (outdoor), water polo. *Women:* basketball, cross-country, diving, fencing, swimming, tennis, track/field (outdoor), volleyball, water polo. **On-Campus Highlights:** Caltech Bookstore, Moore Laboratory, Mead Chemistry Laboratory, Broad Center for the Biological Sciences, Red Door Cafe. **Environmental Initiatives:** Energy efficiency and retro-commissioning programs financed through the use of a green revolving loan fund (sustainability.caltech.edu/energy/CECIP).

California Institute of Technology

FINANCIAL AID

Students should submit: Business/Farm Supplement; CSS/Financial Aid PROFILE; FAFSA; Institution's own financial aid form; Noncustodial PROFILE; State aid form. Priority filing deadline is 3/2. The Princeton Review suggests that all financial aid forms be submitted as soon as possible after October 1. *Need-based scholarships/grants offered*: College/university scholarship or grant aid from institutional funds; Federal Pell; Private scholarships; SEOG; State scholarships/grants. *Loan aid offered*: Direct PLUS loans; Direct Subsidized Stafford Loans; Direct Unsubsidized Stafford Loans. Applicants will be notified of awards on or about 4/15. Federal Work-Study Program available. Institutional employment available.

BOTTOM LINE

In 2015 Caltech's endowment was just under $2.1 billion. It's no wonder generous financial aid and scholarship packages are commonplace here. Tuition at Caltech is $52,506 annually, plus another $2,000-plus in student fees. Once you factor in $16,644 for room and board and $1,428 more for books and supplies, the estimated annual cost is $72,672 per year. Few students pay the full cost, while everyone benefits from the world-class education, making this school a best buy. Financial aid packages for undergraduates include a $47,564 need-based grant on average.

FINANCIAL FACTS	
Financial Aid Rating	98
Annual tuition	$52,506
Room and board	$16,644
Required fees	$2,094
Books and supplies	$1,428
Average frosh need-based scholarship	$46,749
Average UG need-based scholarship	$47,564
% needy frosh rec. need-based scholarship or grant aid	100
% needy UG rec. need-based scholarship or grant aid	100
% needy frosh rec. non-need-based scholarship or grant aid	0
% needy UG rec. non-need-based scholarship or grant aid	0
% needy frosh rec. need-based self-help aid	53
% needy UG rec. need-based self-help aid	61
% frosh rec. any financial aid	61
% UG rec. any financial aid	58
% UG borrow to pay for school	31
Average cumulative indebtedness	$16,337
% frosh need fully met	100
% ugrads need fully met	100
Average % of frosh need met	100
Average % of ugrad need met	100

CAREER INFORMATION FROM PAYSCALE.COM	
ROI Rating	98
Bachelors and No Higher	
Median starting salary	$84,100
Median mid-career salary	$151,600
At Least Bachelors	
Median starting salary	$89,900
Median mid-career salary	$156,900
Alumni with high job meaning	53%
Degrees awarded in STEM subjects	97%

California Institute of Technology

Carleton College

100 South College Street, Northfield, MN 55057 • Admissions: 507-222-4190 • Fax: 507-222-4526

#33 BEST VALUE COLLEGE

ABOUT THE SCHOOL

Carleton College emphasizes rigor and intellectual growth without competition or hubris. Students attracted to Carleton's campus seek meaningful collaboration without the distraction of divisive academic one-upping. The opportunities to work with bright and engaged students and professors are plentiful. One student explains that "Carleton is not a research college, so while professors do some research, they are much more focused on students." Carleton operates on a trimester calendar, which many students enjoy, saying that "it's nice to be only taking three classes, though more intensely, rather than spreading yourself over four or five." An endless array of social and cocurricular activities is on offer at Carleton, as well as numerous programs for off-campus studies. These opportunities combine rural and urban experiences in a friendly Midwestern environment; students can master Chinese, Japanese, Arabic, and modern Hebrew; they can study in the shadow of a wind turbine generating electricity for the campus; they can choose to live in an environmentally conscious way from their dorm arrangements to the food they eat. Students love the "great study abroad office," which provides students here with "opportunities to travel to China, Thailand, Spain, and Africa." Experiential learning opportunities are immense here. Carleton Scholars is Carleton's highest-visibility experiential learning program and consists of taste-of-industry tours that introduce a variety of organizations in a particular field of interest, through site visits, panel discussions, receptions, and social activities. The 30 Minutes initiative provides students with access to one-on-one time, group discussion, and candid interviews with Carleton alumni luminaries in many fields. Carleton's Externships program

Carleton College

Financial Aid: 507-222-4138 • E-mail: admissions@carleton.edu • Website: www.carleton.edu

connects students with alumni for one- to four-week job shadowing and short-term project experiences, and generally includes home-stays with their alumni hosts.

BANG FOR YOUR BUCK

Carleton's financial aid program is primarily need-based, and the college commits to meeting the need of admitted students fully. This means that a student's aid award will include grants and scholarships from Carleton, applicable government grants, on-campus work, and a reasonable amount of loan. Students graduate with about $21,000 in loan debt on average. Carleton's financial aid program helps support the unique culture and character of this college through its goal of enrolling diverse students regardless of their ability to pay for college. With nearly three-fifths of the student body receiving need-based grant aid, there is a broad socioeconomic representation across the student body, and students laud Carleton for its "generous financial aid."

STUDENT LIFE

The "creative, warm, compassionate, and helpful" undergrads of Carleton are "quirky," but "everyone is accepting of these little eccentricities." One physics major praises the inclusive nature of the school, noting that "the moment that I first stepped foot on campus I felt as if I belong here." The "average Carl is . . . very physically active and loves to spend time outdoors." Even the cold Minnesota weather can be a good thing: "Minnesota winters teach you how to appreciate sunny, forty degree Spring days!" Carleton is "everything I wanted in a school: small, Midwest, great campus community, professors who really care," notes an English major. Despite the academically rigorous atmosphere, on the weekends there are "movie screenings, plays, dance performances,

ACADEMICS

Academic Rating	98
% students returning for sophomore year	97
% students graduating within 4 years	88
% students graduating within 6 years	93
Calendar	Trimester
Student/faculty ratio	9:1
Profs interesting rating	98
Profs accessible rating	98

Most classes have 10–19 students.
Most lab/discussion sessions have 10–19 students.

MOST POPULAR MAJORS

Computer and Information Sciences, General; Biology/Biological Sciences, General; Political Science/International Relations

SELECTIVITY

Admissions Rating	97
# of applicants	7,092
% of applicants accepted	20
% of acceptees attending	38
# offered a place on the wait list	1,486
% accepting a place on wait list	37
% admitted from wait list	6
# of early decision applicants	850
% accepted early decision	26

lectures, [and] musicians [on] campus." "Carleton boasts a tight-knit community, strong academics and fun campus life." One undergrad details weekend plans—"on Fridays I go to the Sci-Fi interest house . . . then go to an improv/sketch comedy group"—and highlights the general camaraderie of the school: "Conversations are often simultaneously totally goofy and deeply intellectual. I just love it here, and I'm convinced there's no better place for me."

CAREER

PayScale.com reports that 50 percent of Carleton graduates feel their careers help make the world a better place. The median starting salary for a Carleton grad is $58,800. Biology, economics, and computer science are three of the most popular majors at the school. A biology major notes that "there are great resources for academic and career help, and all kinds of interests are encouraged." Carleton's Career Center offers assistance to students at all levels of the job (and internship) hunting process. According to the school's website, two online resources, The Tunnel and Going Global, give students the opportunity to search for internships, participate in on-campus recruiting, and learn about international job and internship opportunities, respectively. Students note that Carleton professors "are very helpful in finding students summer...job opportunities."

GENERAL INFO

Activities: Campus Ministries; Choral groups; Concert band; Dance; Drama/theater; International Student Organization; Jazz band; Literary magazine; Model UN; Music ensembles; Musical theater; Radio station; Student government; Student newspaper; Student-run film society; Symphony orchestra; Yearbook. 328 registered organizations, 3 honor societies, 15 religious organizations, 0 fraternities, 0 sororities, on campus. **Athletics (Intercollegiate):** *Men:* baseball, basketball, cross-country, diving, football, golf, soccer, swimming, tennis, track/field (outdoor), track/field (indoor). *Women:* basketball, cross-country, diving, golf, soccer, softball, swimming, synchronized swimming, tennis, track/field (outdoor), track/field (indoor), volleyball. **On-Campus Highlights:** Cowling Arboretum, Weitz Center for Creativity, Historic Goodsell Observatory, Japanese Garden, Recreation Center, Evelyn M. Anderson Hall. **Environmental Initiatives:** 2nd Wind Turbine provided power directly to the campus grid; completed phase one

Carleton College

of a two-phase plan to utilize four forms of renewable energy—wind, solar photovoltaic, solar thermal, and geothermal.

FINANCIAL AID

Students should submit: CSS/Financial Aid PROFILE; FAFSA; Noncustodial PROFILE. Priority filing deadline is 1/15. The Princeton Review suggests that all financial aid forms be submitted as soon as possible after October 1. *Need-based scholarships/grants offered*: College/university scholarship or grant aid from institutional funds; Federal Pell; Private scholarships; SEOG; State scholarships/grants. *Loan aid offered*: Direct PLUS loans; Direct Subsidized Stafford Loans; Direct Unsubsidized Stafford Loans. Applicants will be notified of awards on or about 3/31. Federal Work-Study Program available. Institutional employment available.

BOTTOM LINE

At Carleton College, the total cost for tuition and fees and room and board comes to about $71,769 annually. Fortunately, the folks writing the checks at Carleton believe that cost should not be an obstacle to achieving a Carleton education. The average financial aid package for frosh includes scholarships and grants totaling $43,187—that gets you halfway there. When you factor in Carleton's other financial aid offerings in the form of work-study and loans, the dollar amount will seem much more manageable.

FINANCIAL FACTS	
Financial Aid Rating	98
Annual tuition	$56,778
Room and board	$14,658
Required fees	$333
Books and supplies	$866
Average frosh need-based scholarship	$43,187
Average UG need-based scholarship	$42,350
% needy frosh rec. need-based scholarship or grant aid	100
% needy UG rec. need-based scholarship or grant aid	100
% needy frosh rec. non-need-based scholarship or grant aid	10
% needy UG rec. non-need-based scholarship or grant aid	13
% needy frosh rec. need-based self-help aid	99
% needy UG rec. need-based self-help aid	98
% frosh rec. any financial aid	55
% UG rec. any financial aid	55
% UG borrow to pay for school	12
Average cumulative indebtedness	$21,020
% frosh need fully met	100
% ugrads need fully met	100
Average % of frosh need met	100
Average % of ugrad need met	100

CAREER INFORMATION FROM PAYSCALE.COM	
ROI Rating	93
Bachelors and No Higher	
Median starting salary	$58,800
Median mid-career salary	$109,900
At Least Bachelors	
Median starting salary	$59,900
Median mid-career salary	$125,300
Alumni with high job meaning	50%
Degrees awarded in STEM subjects	45%

Carleton College

Carnegie Mellon University

5000 Forbes Avenue, Pittsburgh, PA 15213 • Admissions: 412-268-2082 • Fax: 412-268-7838

#38 BEST VALUE COLLEGE

CAMPUS LIFE

Quality of Life Rating	88
Fire Safety Rating	90
Green Rating	96
Type of school	Private
Environment	Metropolis

STUDENTS

Total undergrad enrollment	6,843
% male/female	50/50
% from out of state	86
% frosh live on campus	100
% ugrads live on campus	58
# of fraternities	
(% ugrad men join)	13 (16)
# of sororities	
(% ugrad women join)	10 (11)
% African American	4
% Asian	30
% Caucasian	26
% Hispanic	9
% Native American	<1
% Pacific Islander	<1
% Two or more races	4
% Race and/or ethnicity unknown	6
% international	22
# of countries represented	54

ABOUT THE SCHOOL

Primarily known for its incredibly strong STEM and drama programs, Carnegie Mellon University enjoys a worldwide reputation as a research university. Professors are experts in their respective fields, and the difficulty of the classes and high expectations from faculty push students to do their best work. In return, they are given "a lot of trust from the administration" in regards to self-governance and their courses of study. "I am not limited to take classes in any one particular college," says a student. "It is nice to know I will get a good degree, but that it is also unique to me." The school offers "more opportunities to excel than you could possibly use in one four-year period" and most here treat the university as an intellectual and creative playground. "Carnegie Mellon is the only place where you will see engineers working while an art installation goes in above their heads," says a student.

BANG FOR YOUR BUCK

Students who fill out and submit the requisite forms and materials for federal and state grants and the CSS Profile will be considered for a Carnegie Mellon Undergraduate Grant. Thirty-nine percent of students receive some form of need-based financial aid, and 96.5 percent of all such need is met. Additionally, there are many student employment opportunities on campus.

Carnegie Mellon University

Financial Aid: 412-268-8186 • E-mail: admission@andrew.cmu.edu • Website: www.cmu.edu

STUDENT LIFE

Students report that "there are a million ways to find your niche on campus" beginning with orientation, and "eventually the labels 'artist' or 'scientist' fade and you become friends with people from all over campus." The challenging academics put everyone in the same time constrained boat, and so "the work-heavy culture becomes a social thing." The student body "isn't so small that you'll know everyone...[but] it's not so big that you'll disappear either." Everyone here fits in somewhere, and even people who were outcasts in high school "easily find large groups of people just like them on campus." Students at CMU are very dedicated to a variety of clubs and interests, and adhere to the logic "study or be trampled, but make sure you still have some fun."

CAREER

At CMU, the interdisciplinary approach to education means that students are taught to be versatile problem solvers with a key sense of community. The school is "great for engineering, math, science, or physics students (or drama or design)," who find that the world "practically throws opportunities (internships, guidance) at these majors." You would be hard-pressed to find a junior or senior who did not have an internship or research position in the summer; "it almost seems expected of you because of the caliber of student you are." CMU's academic diversity and rigor "put its students in an excellent position to start their careers." "People will hire you because they know you can work since you have been doing nothing but working the past four years of your life," says a student. For those students who visited PayScale.com, 48 percent reported feeling that their job was making a meaningful impact on the world.

ACADEMICS

Academic Rating	91
% students returning for sophomore year	97
% students graduating within 4 years	75
% students graduating within 6 years	89
Calendar	Semester
Student/faculty ratio	13:1
Profs interesting rating	83
Profs accessible rating	85

Most classes have 10–19 students. Most lab/discussion sessions have 20–29 students.

MOST POPULAR MAJORS

Business Administration; Computer Science; Electrical and Computer Engineering

SELECTIVITY

Admissions Rating	98
# of applicants	24,351
% of applicants accepted	17
% of acceptees attending	38
# offered a place on the wait list	3,677
% accepting a place on wait list	63
% admitted from wait list	5
# of early decision applicants	1,641
% accepted early decision	21

GENERAL INFO

Activities: Campus Ministries; Choral groups; Concert band; Dance; Drama/theater; International Student Organization; Jazz band; Literary magazine; Marching band; Model UN; Music ensembles; Musical theater; Pep band; Radio station; Student government; Student newspaper; Student-run film society; Symphony orchestra; Yearbook. 325 registered organizations, 34 religious organizations, 13 fraternities, 10 sororities, on campus. **Athletics (Intercollegiate):** *Men:* basketball, cross-country, football, golf, soccer, swimming and diving, tennis, track/field (indoor and outdoor). *Women:* basketball, cross-country, golf, soccer, swimming and diving, tennis, track/field (indoor and outdoor), volleyball. **On-Campus Highlights:** Hunt Library, The Cut, Cohon University Center (Student Center), Tepper Quad. **Environmental Initiatives:** CMU purchases renewable electricity certificates for 100% of our campus electricity use and, at minimum, USGBC LEED Silver guidelines are required for all building projects and most renovations. The majority of our projects are LEED Gold Certified. The Scotty Goes Green Office Certification program promotes sustainable office practices in several administrative and academic departments (www.cmu.edu/environment/).

FINANCIAL AID

Students should submit: CSS Profile; FAFSA; Noncustodial Profile. Priority filing deadline is 2/15. The Princeton Review suggests that all financial aid forms be submitted as soon as possible after October 1. *Need-based scholarships/grants offered:* College/university scholarship or grant aid from institutional funds; Federal Pell; SEOG; State scholarships/grants. *Loan aid offered:* Direct PLUS loans; Direct Subsidized Loans; Direct Unsubsidized Loans. Outside scholarships accepted. Applicants will be notified of awards on or about 4/1. Federal Work-Study Program available. Institutional employment available.

Carnegie Mellon University

BOTTOM LINE

As a private institution, the cost of tuition is set at $55,816 for all students regardless of state residence; add on another $14,662 for room and board (all incoming freshmen are required to live on campus). Once all fees and additional expenses (such as books and supplies) are factored in, incoming freshmen can expect to pay about $73,806. International students are not eligible to receive financial aid.

CAREER INFORMATION FROM PAYSCALE.COM

ROI Rating	93
Bachelors and No Higher	
Median starting salary	$75,900
Median mid-career salary	$136,100
At Least Bachelors	
Median starting salary	$78,300
Median mid-career salary	$141,000
Alumni with high job meaning	48%
Degrees awarded in STEM subjects	66%

FINANCIAL FACTS

Financial Aid Rating	**94**
Annual tuition	$55,816
Room and board	$14,662
Required fees	$928
Books and supplies	$2,400
Average frosh need-based scholarship	$43,090
Average UG need-based scholarship	$41,432
% needy frosh rec. need-based scholarship or grant aid	100
% needy UG rec. need-based scholarship or grant aid	96
% needy frosh rec. non-need-based scholarship or grant aid	25
% needy UG rec. non-need-based scholarship or grant aid	31
% needy frosh rec. need-based self-help aid	96
% needy UG rec. need-based self-help aid	93
% frosh rec. any financial aid	44
% UG rec. any financial aid	39
% UG borrow to pay for school	59
Average cumulative indebtedness	$27,818
% frosh need fully met	59
% ugrads need fully met	69
Average % of frosh need met	97
Average % of ugrad need met	97

Carnegie Mellon University

Case Western Reserve University

Wolstein Hall, Cleveland, OH 44106-7055 • Admissions: 216-368-4450 • Fax: 216-368-5111

#55 BEST VALUE COLLEGE

ABOUT THE SCHOOL

Nearly 100 programs of study, small class sizes, and a 11:1 student-to-faculty ratio guarantee that students at Case Western Reserve University have access to a unique combination of all the opportunities of a big school with all of the individual attention of a small school. The research behemoth stresses a lot of interdisciplinary learning from a research, clinical, experiential, classroom, and social perspective, and the strong SAGES program (Seminar Approach to General Education and Scholarship) offers undergrads a series of small, interdisciplinary seminars throughout the entirety of their time at CWRU. Professors are "sociable and eminently approachable" and "truly believe that their job is to educate students, be it in the laboratory or in the classroom." CWRU relies heavily on student initiative, creating "a close knit community centered around the cultivation of the intellect."

BANG FOR YOUR BUCK

CWRU doesn't want sticker prices to deter any student from receiving an education, and is "very generous with aid, whether it is financial or merit-based," working with each student to develop a tailored assistance package. Case Western Reserve meets 100% of demonstrated need (beginning with the class that started in fall of 2017). In addition to need-based scholarships, students may receive general academic scholarships, including a variety of awards based on specific academic interests, such as the Bolton Scholarship, Michelson-Morley STEM Scholarship, and University Scholarship. Students are automatically considered for most available scholarships when they apply to CWRU.

Case Western Reserve University

Financial Aid: 216-368-4530 • E-mail: admission@case.edu • Website: www.case.edu

STUDENT LIFE

Case Western Reserve's location in Cleveland offers a campus that still feels "collegiate" with the cultural benefits of a city; the school has a free access program to most museums, and the programming board "does a great job of planning events to restaurants, events, and concerts." In the summer, the beach is nearby, and skiing and snowboarding are equally a cinch in the winter. Students tend to be "Renaissance men and women," "jack[s]-of-all-trades" who get along "because there is something we end up working on together at some point." Most balance a full schedule, multiple campus organizations, and "still find time to go out and have fun on weekends." Leaders on campus often talk about how CWRU is "over-programmed"; there are "so many active organizations putting together events all the time that it`s impossible to go to everything."

CAREER

The academic atmosphere at CWRU is "full of opportunities for research or internship experience." Opportunities for co-ops, lab experience, shadowing, and volunteering with some of the world's top organizations help to overlay classroom theory with hands-on applications, and Case Western Reserve's science and tech programs act as a natural feeder to the booming healthcare and biotechnology industries in Cleveland and across the country. "A student need only simply look, or ask career services," says one. In addition to being academics, professors include "professionals in the work force who bring those experiences to the classroom for a much more enhanced education," and can become the foundation of a contact network for jobs after graduation. Many engineering students at Case Western Reserve also take part in a co-op, which is a full-time, two-semester-long, paid work experience that gives students a head start with potential employers. Students in

ACADEMICS

Academic Rating	91
% students returning for sophomore year	94
% students graduating within 4 years	65
% students graduating within 6 years	83
Calendar	Semester
Student/faculty ratio	11:1
Profs interesting rating	82
Profs accessible rating	84

Most classes have 10–19 students.
Most lab/discussion sessions have 10–19 students.

MOST POPULAR MAJORS

Bioengineering and Biomedical Engineering; Mechanical Engineering; Biology/Biological Sciences, General

SELECTIVITY

Admissions Rating	95
# of applicants	26,642
% of applicants accepted	29
% of acceptees attending	18
# of early decision applicants	566
% accepted early decision	42

the College of Arts & Sciences can take part in a similar (but shorter) experience called a practicum. The median starting salary for graduates who visited PayScale.com was $66,600, and 48 percent of these same graduates reported feeling that their job had a meaningful impact on the world.

GENERAL INFO

Activities: Campus Ministries; Choral groups; Concert band; Dance; Drama/theater; International Student Organization; Jazz band; Literary magazine; Marching band; Model UN; Music ensembles; Musical theater; Pep band; Radio station; Student government; Student newspaper; Student-run film society; Symphony orchestra; Yearbook. 249 registered organizations, 7 honor societies, 14 religious organizations, 17 fraternities, 10 sororities, on campus. **Athletics (Intercollegiate):** *Men:* baseball, basketball, cross-country, football, soccer, swimming, tennis, track/field (outdoor), track/field (indoor), wrestling. *Women:* basketball, cross-country, soccer, softball, swimming, tennis, track/field (outdoor), track/field (indoor), volleyball. **On-Campus Highlights:** Kelvin Smith Library, Thwing Center, Health Education Campus, Jolly Scholar, Starbucks, Biomedical Research Building Dining Commons. **Environmental Initiatives:** In 2008 President Barbara Snyder signed the American and College and University Presidents' Climate Commitment, now called the Carbon Commitment which is a public declaration that CWRU will aim to be a carbon neutral campus by 2050. The commitment requires public reporting of CWRU's greenhouse gas inventory and other sustainability metrics. CWRU is proud to be a community steward and leader on this vital topic and works with the City of Cleveland and other entries to share strategies and best practices. The University is making progress towards the goal through energy efficiency investments, green buildings, and behavior change campaigns.

Case Western Reserve University

FINANCIAL AID

Students should submit: CSS Profile; FAFSA; Noncustodial Profile. Priority filing deadline is 2/15. The Princeton Review suggests that all financial aid forms be submitted as soon as possible after October 1. *Need-based scholarships/grants offered*: College/university scholarship or grant aid from institutional funds; Federal Pell; Private scholarships; SEOG; State scholarships/grants. *Loan aid offered*: Direct PLUS loans; Direct Subsidized Student Loans; Direct Unsubsidized Student Loans. Applicants will be notified of awards upon admission. Federal Work-Study Program available. Institutional employment available.

BOTTOM LINE

Tuition runs at $50,450, with $16,874 being added on for room and board. With $474 in fees incorporated, the total cost for freshman year is $67,798. CWRU suggests that students all live on campus, but those returning students who choose to commute typically receive less need-based grant assistance (around $12,300 less) than those who live on campus.

FINANCIAL FACTS	
Financial Aid Rating	96
Annual tuition	$50,450
Room and board	$16,874
Required fees	$474
Books and supplies	$1,200
Average frosh need-based scholarship	$34,419
Average UG need-based scholarship	$31,693
% needy frosh rec. need-based scholarship or grant aid	96
% needy UG rec. need-based scholarship or grant aid	97
% needy frosh rec. non-need-based scholarship or grant aid	40
% needy UG rec. non-need-based scholarship or grant aid	19
% needy frosh rec. need-based self-help aid	92
% needy UG rec. need-based self-help aid	95
% frosh rec. any financial aid	87
% UG rec. any financial aid	85
% UG borrow to pay for school	49
Average cumulative indebtedness	$32,377
% frosh need fully met	96
% ugrads need fully met	71
Average % of frosh need met	100
Average % of ugrad need met	90

CAREER INFORMATION FROM PAYSCALE.COM	
ROI Rating	91
Bachelors and No Higher	
Median starting salary	$66,600
Median mid-career salary	$117,800
At Least Bachelors	
Median starting salary	$68,100
Median mid-career salary	$124,100
Alumni with high job meaning	48%
Degrees awarded in STEM subjects	37%

Case Western Reserve University

City University of New York—Baruch College

Undergraduate Admissions, 151 East 25th Street, New York, NY 10010 • Admissions: 646-312-1400 • Fax: 646-312-1363

CAMPUS LIFE

Quality of Life Rating	89
Fire Safety Rating	60*
Green Rating	61
Type of school	Public
Environment	Metropolis

STUDENTS

Total undergrad enrollment	14,629
% male/female	52/48
% from out of state	3
% frosh from public high school	90
% frosh live on campus	8
% ugrads live on campus	2
# of fraternities	0
# of sororities	0
% African American	9
% Asian	32
% Caucasian	20
% Hispanic	26
% Native American	<1
% Pacific Islander	<1
% Two or more races	1
% Race and/or ethnicity unknown	0
% international	11
# of countries represented	168

#56 BEST VALUE COLLEGE

ABOUT THE SCHOOL

Situated in the heart of New York City, Baruch College and its three schools—Weissman School of Arts and Sciences, Marxe School of Public and International Affairs, and the Zicklin School of Business, which is the largest—maintains a strong "academic reputation" as one of the ten senior colleges within the City University of New York system. Here students can gain a "quality" education that won't break the proverbial bank. Many students rush to highlight the "great business school" and note that it's "one [of] the nation's finest." Others call out the Marxe School of Public and International Affairs as "extremely good" and say it does a great job of maintaining a "family-like feel" on a larger campus of about 15,000 undergrads. Should students struggle, Baruch provides several "amazing resources such as peer counseling, the writing center and tutoring." Of course, students can also turn to their "excellent" professors who clearly have "a passion for what they teach." Many instructors have "first-hand experience," which they readily bring into the classroom. As one undergrad explains, "Some of my business professors came from leading huge corporations, and their anecdotes…help students internalize the material." Most importantly, Baruch professors "want the students to thrive and succeed."

BANG FOR YOUR BUCK

Many undergrads are drawn to Baruch in large part because of its "affordability." After all, "tuition is not expensive" and "the financial aid is generous." As one grateful student shares, "I am on a full tuition scholarship with free laptops and priority scheduling and even a study abroad stipend.…"

City University of New York—Baruch College

Financial Aid: 646-312-1360 • E-mail: admissions@baruch.cuny.edu • Website: www.baruch.cuny.edu

[Baruch] really hook[s] you up." More specifically, the Baruch College Fund (BCF) distributes over $2 million in scholarship funds annually. Designed to encourage both academic excellence and leadership, many of these scholarships are awarded to students who maintain a high level of academic performance. For example, the Arthur Milton Memorial Scholarship is given to incoming freshmen who earned a strong SAT score and maintained a high GPA throughout high school. The Barbara and Arthur Gallagher Scholarship is awarded to students who demonstrate both financial need and a commitment to service.

SCHOOL LIFE

When asked about life at Baruch, many undergrads caution that Baruch is "a commuter school" and "most students go to classes and go home." Thankfully, they acknowledge that "there are great clubs and events always happening [on campus]." When they find a break in their day, students often head over to "the game room where there are foosball tables and a billiards table as well." Additionally, "Baruch's student affairs [office frequently sponsors] fun weekend trips" to places like "Boston," "Niagara Falls," or even "apple picking" at an orchard just outside the city. These students certainly capitalize on their prime Manhattan location. As one student points out, whether "you like art, music, galleries, museums, theater, [or] partying," there is "always something to do in New York City."

CAREER

Students at Baruch have access to some "impressive" career resources. To begin with, undergrads can easily tap into "a strong alumni network." Baruch's Starr Career Services Center routinely invites "top companies [to campus] to network with students and talk about their jobs." The Center "provides services to help students prepare for these events," which can cover everything from LinkedIn 101—for students to learn how to leverage the

ACADEMICS

Academic Rating	81
% students returning for sophomore year	89
% students graduating within 4 years	40
% students graduating within 6 years	69
Calendar	Semester
Student/faculty ratio	18:1
Profs interesting rating	84
Profs accessible rating	79

Most classes have 20–29 students. Most lab/discussion sessions have 10–19 students.

MOST POPULAR MAJORS
Accounting; Finance, General

SELECTIVITY

Admissions Rating	91
# of applicants	21,469
% of applicants accepted	39
% of acceptees attending	20

site and make their profile stand out—to mastering a job interview. Additionally, the Starr Career Services Center offers some unique programs like the dining etiquette workshop, which allows students to prep for networking events that involve food. Of course, most importantly, Baruch hosts some amazing career fairs that put students in direct contact with top firms like Bank of America, Citi, Target, and Goldman Sachs.

GENERAL INFO

Activities: Campus Ministries; Choral groups; Dance; Drama/theater; Literary magazine; Model UN; Musical theater; Radio station; Student government; Student newspaper; Yearbook. 120 registered organizations, 9 honor societies, 7 religious organizations, 0 fraternities, 0 sororities, on campus. **Athletics (Intercollegiate):** *Men:* baseball, basketball, cross-country, soccer, swimming, tennis, volleyball. *Women:* basketball, cheerleading, cross-country, softball, swimming, tennis, volleyball. **On-Campus Highlights:** Student Club Area-Vertical Campus Building, Newman Library, Outdoor Plaza- 25th Street, Food Court- Vertical Campus Building, College Fitness Center-Vertical Campus.

FINANCIAL AID

Students should submit: FAFSA; State aid form. Priority filing deadline is 4/15. The Princeton Review suggests that all financial aid forms be submitted as soon as possible after October 1. *Need-based scholarships/grants offered*: College/university scholarship or grant aid from institutional funds; Federal Pell; Private scholarships; SEOG; State scholarships/grants. *Loan aid offered*: Direct PLUS loans; Direct Subsidized Stafford Loans; Direct Unsubsidized Stafford Loans. Applicants will be notified of awards on a rolling basis beginning 4/15. Federal Work-Study Program available. Institutional employment available.

City University of New York—
Baruch College

BOTTOM LINE

New York residents who attend Baruch full-time face a relatively modest tuition bill of $6,930 per year. Undergraduates who hail from out-of-state should expect to pay $18,600. Students should budget about $1,364 for books and supplies and $1,088 for transportation. Undergrads living away from home will need a minimum of $12,880 for room and board. Additionally, the college estimates that personal expenses might amount to $4,416 for the academic year. Lastly, all full-time students must pay a $125 technology fee, $124.15 activity fee and a $15 consolidated service fee.

CAREER INFORMATION FROM PAYSCALE.COM

ROI Rating	91
Bachelors and No Higher	
Median starting salary	$58,800
Median mid-career salary	$107,100
At Least Bachelors	
Median starting salary	$58,900
Median mid-career salary	$112,500
Alumni with high job meaning	38%
Degrees awarded in STEM subjects	8%

FINANCIAL FACTS

Financial Aid Rating	80
Annual in-state tuition	$6,930
Annual out-of-state tuition	$18,600
Room and board	$12,880
Required fees	$531
Books and supplies	$1,364
Average frosh need-based scholarship	$7,504
Average UG need-based scholarship	$6,574
% needy frosh rec. need-based scholarship or grant aid	92
% needy UG rec. need-based scholarship or grant aid	91
% needy frosh rec. non-need-based scholarship or grant aid	8
% needy UG rec. non-need-based scholarship or grant aid	6
% needy frosh rec. need-based self-help aid	11
% needy UG rec. need-based self-help aid	25
% frosh rec. any financial aid	64
% UG rec. any financial aid	62
% UG borrow to pay for school	14
Average cumulative indebtedness	$12,117
% frosh need fully met	4
% ugrads need fully met	3
Average % of frosh need met	36
Average % of ugrad need met	37

Claremont McKenna College

888 Columbia Avenue, Claremont, CA 91711 • Admissions: 909-621-8088 • Fax: 909-621-8516

CAMPUS LIFE

Quality of Life Rating	94
Fire Safety Rating	88
Green Rating	60*
Type of school	Private
Environment	Town

STUDENTS

Total undergrad enrollment	1,318
% male/female	52/48
% from out of state	54
% frosh live on campus	100
% ugrads live on campus	96
# of fraternities	0
# of sororities	0
% African American	4
% Asian	11
% Caucasian	42
% Hispanic	15
% Native American	0
% Pacific Islander	<1
% Two or more races	6
% Race and/or ethnicity unknown	6
% international	16
# of countries represented	43

#22 BEST VALUE COLLEGE

ABOUT THE SCHOOL

Part of a new generation of liberal arts colleges, Claremont McKenna was founded in 1946—more than a century later than many of its East Coast counterparts—but it has steadily built a reputation as one of the nation's best small schools. With a total enrollment of just 1,300 students, the average class size is under twenty, making it easy for students to work directly with the school's talented faculty. One literature and government major gushes that her "academic experience has been so rich—full of dinners with professors outside of class and conversations that make me a better scholar and person. I have been doing research on Robert Frost's letters that would usually be reserved for graduate students." Despite the comfortable environment, academics are surprisingly rigorous and varied.

Offering a pragmatic approach to the liberal arts, the college is divided into ten academic departments offering major programs in fields like biochemistry and history, as well as interdisciplinary minor programs or "sequences" in areas such as data science and leadership. The most popular majors are government, international relations, psychology, and philosophy-politics-economics. A psychology major relates that "the campus environment is extremely friendly, open, and career-focused. Students at CMC are motivated to make something of themselves in the world." As a part of the seven Claremont colleges, Claremont McKenna offers students the intimacy of a small college with the variety of a larger system. Jointly, the colleges offer more than 2,500 courses, and cross-registration is encouraged (as is eating in neighboring colleges' dining halls).

Claremont McKenna College

Financial Aid: 909-621-8356 • E-mail: admission@cmc.edu • Website: www.cmc.edu

BANG FOR YOUR BUCK

Not only is CMC need-blind for U.S. applicants in its admission policies, but the college is committed to fully meeting every student's financial need through a combination of merit-based scholarships and need-based awards. In addition to state and federal grants, the school offers a number of merit-based scholarship awards derived from gifts and endowments given to the college. Army ROTC Scholarships are also available. The school's website offers detailed information about the amount of aid granted to incoming students in recent years based on their family's income level. Furthermore, for students interested in an unpaid internship with a public or nonprofit organization, the Sponsored Internship & Experiences Program will provide funding for students to pursue internships anywhere in the world.

STUDENT LIFE

The incredibly content undergrads here happily declare that "life at CMC is unbeatable." For starters, students love to take advantage of the beautiful SoCal weather. And many an individual "can often be found throwing around a Frisbee, playing bocce ball, or setting up a slip-n-slide." Of course, these smart students also enjoy intellectual pursuits. Indeed, "there are numerous 'academic' things that people do for fun, such as Mock Trial or attending lectures." Students also rave about the welcoming and fun social scene. Unlike a lot of other schools, the "student government sends out emails weekly informing the students of the events taking place that weekend." This helps to "unify the whole school and creates a really fun community." Lastly, when undergrads are itching to get away, they can head to "amazing places...such as Los Angeles, the beaches, the San Gabriel Mountains, and even as far as Las Vegas and Lake Tahoe."

ACADEMICS

Academic Rating	**94**
% students returning for sophomore year	96
% students graduating within 4 years	81
% students graduating within 6 years	93
Calendar	Semester
Student/faculty ratio	8:1
Profs interesting rating	**93**
Profs accessible rating	**92**
Most classes have 10–19 students.	

MOST POPULAR MAJORS

Economics, General; Political Science Government, General; Psychology, General; International Relations; and Philosophy-Politics-Economics

SELECTIVITY

Admissions Rating	**98**
# of applicants	6,272
% of applicants accepted	9
% of acceptees attending	56
# offered a place on the wait list	1,037
% accepting a place on wait list	63
% admitted from wait list	4
# of early decision applicants	771
% accepted early decision	25

CAREER

Undergrads at Claremont McKenna love to shower the "AMAZING career services center" with praise. And it's no secret why! The office is with students every step of the way, from initial career exploration to landing that first job offer. Through their alumni career contacts database, the office makes it fairly simple for current students to connect with alums working in industries of interest. Even better, their Experts-in-Residence program allows students to find an accomplished alum or parent and engage with him/her to provide valuable insights into his/her working world, offer professional (and educational) guidance and networking opportunities. Beyond great support, CMC students benefit from many hands-on opportunities, such as one-week networking treks to New York, San Francisco, and Washington, D.C., as well as one-day job shadowing experiences around the globe. With all of these outlets, it's no wonder CMC grads are so successful.

GENERAL INFO

Activities: Acapella groups; Drama/theater; International Student Organization; Mock Trial; Model UN; Student government; Student newspaper; 60 registered organizations. **Athletics (Intercollegiate):** *Men:* baseball, basketball, cross-country, diving, football, golf, soccer, swimming, tennis, track/field (outdoor), water polo. *Women:* basketball, cross-country, diving, golf, lacrosse, soccer, softball, swimming, tennis, track/field (outdoor), volleyball, water polo. **On-Campus Highlights:** Marian Miner Cook Athenaeum, Roberts Pavillion, Emett Student Center (The Hub), Kravis Center, Keck Science Center.

Claremont McKenna College

FINANCIAL AID

Students should submit: Business/Farm Supplement; CSS/Financial Aid PROFILE; FAFSA; Noncustodial PROFILE; State aid form. Priority filing deadline is 1/5. The Princeton Review suggests that all financial aid forms be submitted as soon as possible after October 1. *Need-based scholarships/grants offered*: College/university scholarship or grant aid from institutional funds; Federal Pell; Private scholarships; SEOG; State scholarships/grants. *Loan aid offered*: Direct PLUS loans; Direct Subsidized Stafford Loans; Direct Unsubsidized Stafford Loans. Applicants will be notified of awards on or about 4/1. Federal Work-Study Program available. Institutional employment available.

BOTTOM LINE

Full-time tuition at Claremont McKenna College is $54,160 annually. Meal plans and housing range in price, but together room and board generally run about $16,705 per year. As at any private school, the annual cost to attend CMC can be a bit pricey; however, the school offers aid to students in a wide range of financial situations.

FINANCIAL FACTS

Financial Aid Rating	92
Annual tuition	$54,160
Room and board	$16,705
Required fees	$245
Average frosh need-based scholarship	$55,880
Average UG need-based scholarship	$48,754
% needy frosh rec. need-based scholarship or grant aid	99
% needy UG rec. need-based scholarship or grant aid	98
% needy frosh rec. non-need-based scholarship or grant aid	43
% needy UG rec. non-need-based scholarship or grant aid	49
% needy frosh rec. need-based self-help aid	92
% needy UG rec. need-based self-help aid	90
% frosh rec. any financial aid	43
% UG rec. any financial aid	47
% UG borrow to pay for school	34
Average cumulative indebtedness	$19,355
% frosh need fully met	100
% ugrads need fully met	99
Average % of frosh need met	100
Average % of ugrad need met	100

CAREER INFORMATION FROM PAYSCALE.COM

ROI Rating	94
Bachelors and No Higher	
Median starting salary	$68,500
Median mid-career salary	$125,400
At Least Bachelors	
Median starting salary	$71,100
Median mid-career salary	$144,800
Alumni with high job meaning	48%
Degrees awarded in STEM subjects	16%

Claremont McKenna College

Colgate University

13 Oak Drive, Hamilton, NY 13346 • Admissions: 315-228-7401 • Fax: 315-228-7544

CAMPUS LIFE

Quality of Life Rating	82
Fire Safety Rating	97
Green Rating	98
Type of school	Private
Environment	Rural

STUDENTS

Total undergrad enrollment	2,934
% male/female	45/55
% from out of state	74
% frosh from public high school	56
% frosh live on campus	100
% ugrads live on campus	92
# of fraternities	5
# of sororities	3
% African American	5
% Asian	5
% Caucasian	65
% Hispanic	9
% Native American	<1
% Pacific Islander	<1
% Two or more races	4
% Race and/or ethnicity unknown	3
% international	9
# of countries represented	49

#41 BEST VALUE COLLEGE

ABOUT THE SCHOOL

Since 1819, Hamilton, New York, has hosted Colgate University, a small liberal arts college that has a "very rigorous academic curriculum" and that will prove challenging to students—gratifyingly so, since those who choose Colgate tend to be looking for a focus on "high-intensity" academics. The science, medicine and health, music, and other programs at this "prestigious institution" win praise from those who attend. Students will be taught by professors who "love being at Colgate as much as the students do." Incoming students should expect small classrooms and hands-on teaching by professors, with class sizes that "allow for personal attention and a higher level of learning." Yet it's not all academics at Colgate. Those attending will also enjoy "strong Division I athletics, a wide variety of extracurricular activities, and a very special community." Football, softball, tennis, and other sports give students challenges to overcome outside the classroom. Students say Colgate offers "the perfect balance between academics and extracurricular activities." A strong sense of community helps. Success both in school and beyond is attributed to the "Colgate connection," a bond among the school's 2,900 students that lasts beyond their years here. The school's philosophical core, and by extension its student body, is career-minded. This is reflected in an extensive set of career-development programs and services. Among others, these include shadowing programs, internship recruiting and off-campus recruiting, and the innovative Summer on the Cuyahoga program, which gives those accepted an unprecedented opportunity to network with executives, politicians, and business owners. According to the school administration,

Colgate University

Financial Aid: : 315-228-7431 • E-mail: admission@colgate.edu • Website: www.colgate.edu

"These programs offer many dynamic opportunities for students to connect with alumni, staff, faculty, and others to learn about and discuss interests and goals."

BANG FOR YOUR BUCK

Financial aid packages can be sizable at Colgate, averaging just more than $52,075 for the class of 2021. The list of available grants and scholarships is extensive; graduating students call it "strong" and "generous." Over the next several years, school administration aims to lower the average debt for exiting students—and even that may be washed away easily for many students. One year after graduation, 78.6 percent of the class of 2018 is employed and 18 percent are attending graduate school.

STUDENT LIFE

Colgate boasts a "happy and enthusiastic student body" that "follows the motto 'work hard, play hard.'" A sophomore says, "Imagine J. Crew models. Now give them brains, and that is who is walking around Colgate's campus." Fraternities and sororities are popular: "Greek life does have a huge presence in the social life at Colgate," but "it is not exclusive to just those who are members," a sentiment backed up by an art history major who states that "many students do not take part in the preppy, Greek, party-every-night lifestyle that dominates Colgate's reputation," and that "there IS diversity at Colgate, but you have to work quite hard to find it. It is nice to know that it DOES exist if you want to seek it out," while an English major adds that "with the addition of the Ho Science Building, the science department is getting more popular, but be warned because the chemistry major is one of the toughest in the country. No one tells you this before you apply but it falls just behind MIT and CalTech in difficulty."

ACADEMICS

Academic Rating	91
% students returning for sophomore year	94
% students graduating within 4 years	84
% students graduating within 6 years	89
Calendar	Semester
Student/faculty ratio	9:1
Profs interesting rating	94
Profs accessible rating	96

MOST POPULAR MAJORS

Psychology, General; Economics, General; Political Science and Government, General

SELECTIVITY

Admissions Rating	97
# of applicants	9,716
% of applicants accepted	25
% of acceptees attending	34
# offered a place on the wait list	1,788
% accepting a place on wait list	56
% admitted from wait list	0
# of early decision applicants	962
% accepted early decision	41

FRESHMAN PROFILE

Range SAT EBRW	650–730
Range SAT Math	670–780
Range ACT Composite	31–34
# submitting SAT scores	363
% submitting SAT scores	45
# submitting ACT scores	452
% submitting ACT scores	55
Average HS GPA	3.7
% graduated top 10% of class	77
% graduated top 25% of class	94
% graduated top 50% of class	100

DEADLINES

Early decision	
Deadline	11/15
Notification	12/15
Other ED Deadline	1/15
Other ED Notification	Rolling
Regular	
Deadline	1/15
Notification	3/25
Nonfall registration?	No

CAREER

The typical Colgate University graduate has a starting salary of around $68,400, and 47 percent of graduates feel their jobs have a lot of meaning in their lives. Students feel that Colgate University has "good financial aid and good career prep." One student feels that "the alumni system is amazing," and that said alumni would "jump over any hurdle for you." Students feel that "the Career Services is phenomenal," because it offers "an incredible selection of opportunities for students to prepare for life after graduation, starting with a major event for sophomores called Sopho*MORE* Connections which gives students an opportunity to connect with the alumni network and learn more about career paths, job opportunities, and networking in general." Colgate also offers many grants to support summer career exploration, internships, and research. As of September 2018, Benton Hall is the new home of Career Services.

GENERAL INFO

Activities: Campus Ministries; Choral groups; Concert band; Dance; Drama/theater; International Student Organization; Jazz band; Literary magazine; Model UN; Music ensembles; Musical theater; Opera; Pep band; Radio station; Student government; Student newspaper; Symphony orchestra; Yearbook. 167 registered organizations, 12 honor societies, 10 religious organizations, 5 fraternities, 3 sororities, on campus. **Athletics (Intercollegiate):** *Men:* basketball, crew/rowing, cross-country, diving, football, golf, ice hockey, lacrosse, soccer, swimming, tennis, track/field (outdoor). *Women:* basketball, crew/rowing, cross-country, diving, field hockey, ice hockey, lacrosse, soccer, softball, swimming, tennis, track/field (outdoor), volleyball. **On-Campus Highlights:** O'Connor Campus Center, Chobani at Hieber Cafe in Case-Geyer Library, ALANA Cultural Center, Ho Tung Visualization Lab, Trudy Fitness Center. **Environmental Initiatives:** All electricity used on campus is hydroelectric, with some supplemental nuclear power. Colgate's wood-chip-burning heating plant utilizes a renewable energy source to provide about 70% of our total requirement.

Colgate University

FINANCIAL AID

Students should submit: CSS/Financial Aid PROFILE; FAFSA; Noncustodial PROFILE. Priority filing deadline is 1/15. The Princeton Review suggests that all financial aid forms be submitted as soon as possible after October 1. *Need-based scholarships/grants offered*: College/university scholarship or grant aid from institutional funds; Federal Pell; SEOG. *Loan aid offered*: Direct PLUS loans; Direct Subsidized Stafford Loans; Direct Unsubsidized Stafford Loans. Applicants will be notified of awards on or about 3/25. Federal Work-Study Program available. Institutional employment available.

BOTTOM LINE

If the $57,695 in annual tuition seems daunting, your fears should be offset by the fact that the school's generous need-based financial aid programs help carry a large share of that burden. Colgate meets 100 percent of student need through need-based scholarships, grants, and self-help aid.

FINANCIAL FACTS

Financial Aid Rating	98
Annual tuition	$57,695
Room and board	$14,540
Required fees	$350
Books and supplies	$1,040
Average frosh need-based scholarship	$55,163
Average UG need-based scholarship	$50,922
% needy frosh rec. need-based scholarship or grant aid	100
% needy UG rec. need-based scholarship or grant aid	100
% needy frosh rec. non-need-based scholarship or grant aid	0
% needy UG rec. non-need-based scholarship or grant aid	0
% needy frosh rec. need-based self-help aid	93
% needy UG rec. need-based self-help aid	82
% frosh rec. any financial aid	52
% UG rec. any financial aid	52
% UG borrow to pay for school	32
Average cumulative indebtedness	$24,243
% frosh need fully met	100
% ugrads need fully met	100
Average % of frosh need met	100
Average % of ugrad need met	100

CAREER INFORMATION FROM PAYSCALE.COM

ROI Rating	92
Bachelors and No Higher	
Median starting salary	$68,400
Median mid-career salary	$130,600
At Least Bachelors	
Median starting salary	$67,300
Median mid-career salary	$143,700
Alumni with high job meaning	47%
Degrees awarded in STEM subjects	26%

Colgate University

College of William and Mary

Office of Admissions, PO Box 8795, Williamsburg, VA 23187-8795 • Admissions: 757-221-4223 • Fax: 757-221-1242

CAMPUS LIFE

Quality of Life Rating	96
Fire Safety Rating	92
Green Rating	77
Type of school	Public
Environment	Town

STUDENTS

Total undergrad enrollment	6,377
% male/female	43/57
% from out of state	31
% frosh from public high school	77
% frosh live on campus	100
% ugrads live on campus	71
# of fraternities	
(% ugrad men join)	19 (28)
# of sororities	
(% ugrad women join)	14 (29)
% African American	7
% Asian	8
% Caucasian	59
% Hispanic	9
% Native American	<1
% Pacific Islander	<1
% Two or more races	5
% Race and/or ethnicity unknown	6
% international	6
# of countries represented	50

#43 BEST VALUE COLLEGE

ABOUT THE SCHOOL

The minute incoming students set foot on the campus of William & Mary in Williamsburg, Virginia, they join an "extremely close-knit and supportive" community. What's more, students here say the school's "incredible academic reputation" is well deserved noting the "rigor" of their coursework. William & Mary attracts students who love learning and maintain a desire to "satisfy…[their] curiosity." To that end, many individuals here relish the fact that "opportunit[ies] for undergraduate research" abound. They also value receiving a "liberal arts education" which helps to foster "well-rounded" individuals. "Small class sizes" allow for an intimate learning environment. Just as important, undergrads are greeted by professors who "challenge [students] to think for [themselves]" and encourage them "to come up with answers" on their own. They're also "extremely knowledgeable." As a satisfied student notes, "Professors seem like they really are here for us rather than their personal research which is nice."

BANG FOR YOUR BUCK

Affordability is synonymous with a William & Mary education. For starters, the college meets 100 percent of the demonstrated need for Virginia residents. Out-of-state students fear not; you won't be left in the dust. Indeed, qualified undergrads receive grant aid that covers 25 percent of the total cost of attendance. The college also provides numerous scholarships. For example, the James Monroe Scholars Program is offered to the top 10 to 15 percent of the applicant pool. Recipients receive a $3,000 research stipend, special housing and priority course registration. And the William &

College of William and Mary

Financial Aid: 757-221-2420 • E-mail: admission@wm.edu • Website: www.wm.edu

Mary Scholars Program is given to incoming students who come from underrepresented communities and/or have overcome adversity. The program awards the equivalent amount of in-state tuition. It's also renewable assuming the student remains in good academic standing.

SCHOOL LIFE

It's virtually impossible to be bored at William & Mary. After all, the college "is home to over 450 clubs and organizations." These groups "range from the Quidditch team to the Exotic Cheese club." Additionally, the school invites "many [prominent] speakers" to campus. Past lecturers have included "the Dali Lama [and] Condoleezza Rice." Many students also highlight "Alma Mater Productions (AMP) [which] plans and hosts free (or very low cost) events almost every day of the weekend." For example, there's "Screen on the Green, an inflatable movie screen that plays a double feature on the Sunken Gardens… [along with] more interactive activities like Zombie Apocalypse…[where] students have to fight zombies with nerf guns." Of course, when students want to get off campus, they often head to neighboring Colonial Williamsburg which always provides a nice respite from studying.

ACADEMICS

Academic Rating	94
% students returning for sophomore year	95
% students graduating within 4 years	85
% students graduating within 6 years	92
Calendar	Semester
Student/faculty ratio	11:1
Profs interesting rating	93
Profs accessible rating	96

Most classes have 10–19 students. Most lab/discussion sessions have 10–19 students.

MOST POPULAR MAJORS

Biology/Biological Sciences, General; Political Science and Government, General; Business Administration and Management, General

SELECTIVITY

Admissions Rating	96
# of applicants	14,644
% of applicants accepted	37
% of acceptees attending	29
# offered a place on the wait list	4,133
% accepting a place on wait list	53
% admitted from wait list	4
# of early decision applicants	922
% accepted early decision	58

CAREER

William & Mary students have little trouble on the job market. Undergrads readily assert that this is because the "school has a powerful reputation that allows employers and graduate schools to feel comfortable with William & Mary student's ability to perform in a real job situation." "William & Mary does a great job networking their students with alumni," plus, undergrads can turn to the fantastic Cohen Career Center for insight and support. Students have access to top notch services including resume review and mock interviews. Undergrads can also participate in unique programs like "Ask an Executive," wherein executives from a range of industries meet with students to answer their career questions.

GENERAL INFO

Activities: Campus Ministries; Choral groups; Concert band; Dance; Drama/theater; International Student Organization; Jazz band; Literary magazine; Model UN; Music ensembles; Musical theater; Opera; Pep band; Radio station; Student government; Student newspaper; Student-run film society; Symphony orchestra; Television station; Yearbook. 475 registered organizations, 19 honor societies, 30 religious organizations, 19 fraternities, 14 sororities, on campus. **Athletics (Intercollegiate):** *Men:* baseball, basketball, cheerleading, cross-country, diving, football, golf, gymnastics, soccer, swimming, tennis, track/field (outdoor), track/field (indoor). *Women:* basketball, cheerleading, cross-country, diving, field hockey, golf, gymnastics, lacrosse, soccer, swimming, tennis, track/field (outdoor), track/field (indoor), volleyball. **On-Campus Highlights:** Wren Building (oldest academic building), Sunken Garden, Sadler Center, Swem Library, Kaplan Arena.

FINANCIAL AID

Students should submit: CSS/Financial Aid PROFILE; FAFSA; Institution's own financial aid form. Priority filing deadline is 3/1. The Princeton Review suggests that all financial aid forms be submitted as soon as possible after October 1. *Need-based scholarships/grants offered:* College/university scholarship or grant aid from institutional funds; Federal Pell; Private scholarships; SEOG; State scholarships/grants. *Loan aid offered:* Direct PLUS loans; Direct Subsidized Stafford Loans; Direct Unsubsidized Stafford Loans. Applicants will be notified of awards on or about 3/15. Federal Work-Study Program available. Institutional employment available.

College of William and Mary

BOTTOM LINE

As with all state schools, William & Mary's price tag varies depending on each student's residency. Undergrads who are from Virginia face a tuition bill of $16,728 and miscellaneous fees of $6,194. Students from out-of-state are charged $40,089 for tuition along with $6,245 for fees. Room and board for all students comes to $12,926. Books, travel and incidental expenses can range from $3,544 to $3,622 (depending on residency).

CAREER INFORMATION FROM PAYSCALE.COM

ROI Rating	92
Bachelors and No Higher	
Median starting salary	$59,000
Median mid-career salary	$108,900
At Least Bachelors	
Median starting salary	$60,300
Median mid-career salary	$122,700
Alumni with high job meaning	47%
Degrees awarded in STEM subjects	21%

FINANCIAL FACTS

Financial Aid Rating	84
Annual in-state tuition	$16,728
Annual out-of-state tuition	$40,089
Room and board	$12,926
Required fees	$6,194
Books and supplies	$1,425
Average frosh need-based scholarship	$19,108
Average UG need-based scholarship	$17,561
% needy frosh rec. need-based scholarship or grant aid	90
% needy UG rec. need-based scholarship or grant aid	89
% needy frosh rec. non-need-based scholarship or grant aid	42
% needy UG rec. non-need-based scholarship or grant aid	37
% needy frosh rec. need-based self-help aid	49
% needy UG rec. need-based self-help aid	58
% frosh rec. any financial aid	40
% UG rec. any financial aid	36
% UG borrow to pay for school	35
Average cumulative indebtedness	$25,409
% frosh need fully met	27
% ugrads need fully met	24
Average % of frosh need met	82
Average % of ugrad need met	81

College of William and Mary

Columbia University

212 Hamilton Hall MC 2807, 1130 Amsterdam Ave., New York, NY 10027 • Phone: 212-854-2522

#15 BEST VALUE COLLEGE

ABOUT THE SCHOOL

Columbia University provides prestigious academics and top-of-the-line resources for an Ivy League education with a liberal arts college feel. Located on the Upper West Side of New York City, Columbia attracts prospective students with its "high academic rigor, amazing diversity, unlimited resources, the city of New York, [and the] beautiful campus." The Core Curriculum is a large draw, providing students with a solid liberal arts education on which to base their future studies. Pair this with a location that provides unparalleled access to internships, community service, and research opportunities, and you have a recipe for a melting pot of possibility. Columbia undergraduates represent every socioeconomic, racial, and ethnic background and hail from all fifty states and all over the world. Students' distinct interests and talents are reflected by their diverse academic pursuits: undergraduates study in more than ninety different academic fields. Engagement within the global community is central at Columbia, where "the students are very aware of the world around them" and "activism is essential to the Columbia experience, in fact, it is encouraged by the school itself." Being in the heart of the city is like holding a passport to opportunity with a side of arts, culture, and entertainment.

BANG FOR YOUR BUCK

With nearly all undergraduate students living on campus, students are active participants in campus life through the "multitude of opportunities that extend from clubs to study abroad programs and its proximity to one of the greatest cities in the world," which offers "so much to do outside of class [to] learn about culture and meet other people." Students boast about

Columbia University

Fax: 212-894-1209 • Website: undergrad.admissions.columbia.edu

the "range and quality of classes, academic resources, [and] many opportunities to satiate intellectual curiosity," including "Nobel Professors" and events like the "World Leaders Forum with speakers [who] historically have included presidents and prime ministers from countries far and wide." Columbia's Core Curriculum, a broad range of humanities and science classes required for all students, "teaches you to think critically and develop your opinion," which students say allows them to step outside their field: "Finally, I could escape the STEM bubble I was already part of and get myself to read books from Greek Literature, take a writing class, study philosophy, arts and music," one student explains.

STUDENT LIFE

It is no surprise that at an academically rigorous school, "the Monday to Thursday grind is usually pretty tough," "but since Columbia students generally don't have classes on Fridays, we still have enough time to enjoy the perks of living in New York City." Students enjoy going "into a city and watch plays or go to galleries," or stay on campus and "[party] at the most popular senior dorm or at one of the fraternities." While some students point out that taking advantage of the cultural experiences in NYC can be expensive, "Columbia also has a great Arts Initiative which is perfect for getting things cheaper." Student clubs and organizations are popular "and almost every student is part of at least one." "Even though studying at Columbia is pretty intense," students have plenty of opportunities to "get out of the Columbia bubble" and "devote...time to extracurriculars that [they] enjoy."

CAREER

The Columbia University brand goes far in this country, even though many students only need it to work downtown. Students are thankful for the wealth of resources (referring primarily to internships) available to a student at Columbia University, as well as the accessible professors and the "enormous

ACADEMICS

Academic Rating	92
% students returning for sophomore year	99
% students graduating within 4 years	88
% students graduating within 6 years	96
Calendar	Semester
Student/faculty ratio	6:1
Profs interesting rating	81
Profs accessible rating	79

Most classes have 10–19 students.

MOST POPULAR MAJORS

Political Science and Government; English Language and Literature; Engineering

SELECTIVITY

Admissions Rating	99
# of applicants	40,203
% of applicants accepted	6
% of acceptees attending	63
# of early decision applicants	4,085

FRESHMAN PROFILE

Range SAT EBRW	710–760
Range SAT Math	740–800
Range ACT Composite	33–35
# submitting SAT scores	867
% submitting SAT scores	61
# submitting ACT scores	745
% submitting ACT scores	52
% graduated top 10% of class	96
% graduated top 25% of class	99
% graduated top 50% of class	100

DEADLINES

Early decision	
Deadline	11/1
Notification	12/15
Regular	
Deadline	1/1
Notification	4/1
Nonfall registration?	No

investment in undergraduate research." Internships in New York are an excellent entry point for students trying to make themselves known to employers, and it doesn't hurt that the city is rife with Columbia alumni. The Center for Career Education offers a multitude of resources to get students on their way, including counseling sessions, practice interviews, dossier assessments, and old reliable career fairs. Graduates who visited PayScale.com reported median starting salary of $71,400; 48 percent of these students said they felt their job had a meaningful impact on the world.

GENERAL INFO

Activities: Campus Ministries; Choral groups; Concert band; Dance; Drama/theater; International Student Organization; Jazz band; Literary magazine; Marching band; Model UN; Music ensembles; Musical theater; Opera; Pep band; Radio station; Student government; Student newspaper; Student-run film society; Symphony orchestra; Television station; Yearbook. 500 registered organizations, 30 religious organizations, 17 fraternities, 11 sorority, on campus. **Athletics (Intercollegiate):** *Men:* baseball, basketball, crew/rowing, cross-country, diving, fencing, football, golf, soccer, swimming, tennis, track/field (outdoor), track/field (indoor), wrestling. *Women:* archery, basketball, crew/rowing, cross-country, diving, fencing, field hockey, golf, lacrosse, soccer, softball, swimming, tennis, track/field (outdoor), track/field (indoor), volleyball. **On-Campus Highlights:** Low Library and Plaza, Butler Library, Postcrypt Coffee House, Ferris Booth Commons, Levien Gym. **Environmental Initiatives:** Greenhouse gas reduction program and clean heat initiative to improve air quality and asthma rates by phasing out the use of heavy heating oils to cleaner fuels like natural gas and low-sulfur #2 oil. Columbia has also converted its entire 14 car public safety fleet to hybrid vehicles. As part of our energy efficiency initiatives, 45% of all food purchased is local and/or organic. All honey and apples are purchased through vendors at the on-campus green market from NY farmers. Annually, Dining Services contracts with a local NY farmer and canner to make all the salsa and strawberry jam for the year. In addition, all milk is local and hormone free. Liquid eggs are certified humane. All coffee is roasted locally and is fair-trade, organic, shade grown and bird friendly. Tomatoes are also fair trade. All bakery items and grab-and-go sandwiches are purchased from local vendors. 50% of daily meals served in the dining halls are vegetarian and Meatless Mondays are run every Monday.

Columbia University

FINANCIAL AID

Students should submit: CSS/Financial Aid PROFILE; FAFSA; Noncustodial PROFILE. Priority filing deadline is 2/15. The Princeton Review suggests that all financial aid forms be submitted as soon as possible after October 1. *Need-based scholarships/ grants offered*: College/university scholarship or grant aid from institutional funds; Federal Pell; Private scholarships; SEOG; State scholarships/grants. *Loan aid offered*: Direct PLUS loans; Direct Subsidized Stafford Loans; Direct Unsubsidized Stafford Loans. Applicants will be notified of awards on or about 4/1. Federal Work-Study Program available. Institutional employment available.

BOTTOM LINE

Earning an acceptance letter from Columbia is no easy feat. Admissions officers are looking to build a diverse class that will greatly contribute to the university. It's the Ivy League, folks, and it's New York City, and there is a price tag that goes with both. A year's tuition is $58,920. Additionally, count on $14,490 in room and board. Columbia's New York City campus means that every manner of distraction is literally at your fingertips, so you'll want to factor in another nice chunk of change for things like transportation, personal expenses, outings, etc. These figures are nothing to sneeze at. Take heart: If you get over the first hurdle and manage to gain admittance to this prestigious university, you can be confident that the university will help you pay for it.

FINANCIAL FACTS	
Financial Aid Rating	96
Annual tuition	$58,920
Room and board	$14,490
Required fees	$2,930
Books and supplies	$1,294
Average frosh need-based scholarship	$56,829
Average UG need-based scholarship	$55,691
% needy frosh rec. need-based scholarship or grant aid	99
% needy UG rec. need-based scholarship or grant aid	99
% needy frosh rec. non-need-based scholarship or grant aid	10
% needy UG rec. non-need-based scholarship or grant aid	4
% needy frosh rec. need-based self-help aid	69
% needy UG rec. need-based self-help aid	78
% frosh rec. any financial aid	53
% UG rec. any financial aid	50
% UG borrow to pay for school	23
Average cumulative indebtedness	$27,908
% frosh need fully met	100
% ugrads need fully met	100
Average % of frosh need met	100
Average % of ugrad need met	100

CAREER INFORMATION FROM PAYSCALE.COM	
ROI Rating	94
Bachelors and No Higher	
Median starting salary	$71,400
Median mid-career salary	$126,800
At Least Bachelors	
Median starting salary	$73,100
Median mid-career salary	$138,600
Alumni with high job meaning	48%
Degrees awarded in STEM subjects	30%

Columbia University

The Cooper Union for the Advancement of Science and Art

30 Cooper Square, New York, NY 10003 • Admissions: 212-353-4120 • Fax: 212-353-4342

#9 BEST VALUE COLLEGE

CAMPUS LIFE

Quality of Life Rating	85
Fire Safety Rating	97
Green Rating	60*
Type of school	Private
Environment	Metropolis

STUDENTS

Total undergrad enrollment	858
% male/female	61/39
% from out of state	35
% frosh from public high school	65
% frosh live on campus	56
% ugrads live on campus	13
# of fraternities	
(% ugrad men join)	2 (4)
% African American	3
% Asian	21
% Caucasian	31
% Hispanic	10
% Native American	0
% Pacific Islander	0
% Two or more races	6
% Race and/or ethnicity unknown	8
% international	21

ABOUT THE SCHOOL

Believe it or not, the generous scholarship policy isn't the only reason gifted students clamor for a spot at The Cooper Union for the Advancement of Science and Art. The school's reputable, rigorous academics and location in the heart of New York's East Village are equally big draws. Classes are small (total enrollment is fewer than 900), and students must handle a highly demanding workload. The size of the school allows for very close relationships between the faculty and the students, and that partnership is the intellectual pulse of the institution. Practicing architects, artists, and engineers come to The Cooper Union while continuing their own personal research and work at various points in their careers, giving students frontline access to real-world experience and insight from professionals who want to teach. Group projects are a major part of the curriculum, regardless of academic discipline, furthering the school's problem-solving philosophy of education. A degree from The Cooper Union is enormously valuable in the job market, and many graduates become world-class leaders in the disciplines of architecture, fine arts, design, and engineering. As an all-honors private college, The Cooper Union offers talented students rigorous, humanistic learning enhanced by the process of design and augmented by the urban setting. In addition to outstanding academic programs in architecture, art, and engineering, it offers a Faculty of Humanities and Social Sciences. "An institution of the highest caliber," the school has a narrow academic focus, conferring degrees only in fine arts, architecture, and engineering, with "plenty of opportunities for independent study in your field." Those who go on to the School of Art have easy "access to established and interesting artists."

The Cooper Union for the Advancement of Science and Art

Financial Aid: 212-353-4130 • E-mail: admissions@cooper.edu • Website: www.cooper.edu

BANG FOR YOUR BUCK

The school's founder, Peter Cooper, believed that an "education of the first rank" should be "as free as air and water," and while the current economic climate has recently changed the school's scholarship practices, The Cooper Union remains committed to providing financial support to its accomplished, ambitious student body. An example of this is every enrolled student receives a minimum half-tuition scholarship. The engineering program is considered one of the best in the nation, and a degree from The Cooper Union is a ticket into an excellent professional career. Forty percent of graduates go on to top-tier graduate programs, and the small school has produced thirty-nine Fulbright scholars since 2001. The Cooper Union's location in the East Village adds value to students' experience as well. In the limited time they spend outside of the lab or the studio, students here have access to the nearly infinite range of cultural events, restaurants, museums, and other adventures available in New York City.

STUDENT LIFE

Artists, engineers, and architects abound on this East Village campus filled with "very unique, interesting people" eager to learn and cross-pollinate between departments. This goal is supported by the architecture of The Cooper Union's distinctive academic building which was designed by Thom Mayne to enhance interaction between enrollees of all three schools. Across the board, students in every major are serious about their studies, and most of The Cooper Union's selective admits are "super intelligent, super creative, and/or just super hardworking." Still, The Cooper Union's prime location allows the City That Never Sleeps to act as The Cooper Union's extended campus with plenty of "comedy clubs, movies, bowling, lounges, and bars" to entice students to take a break from their studies. Students say their school will "push you to

ACADEMICS

Academic Rating	89
% students returning for sophomore year	91
% students graduating within 4 years	71
% students graduating within 6 years	88
Calendar	Semester
Student/faculty ratio	7:1
Profs interesting rating	85
Profs accessible rating	82

Most classes have 10–19 students.

MOST POPULAR MAJORS

Electrical and Electronics Engineering; Mechanical Engineering; Fine and Studio Arts

SELECTIVITY

Admissions Rating	98
# of applicants	2,447
% of applicants accepted	16
% of acceptees attending	55
# offered a place on the wait list	182
% accepting a place on wait list	100
% admitted from wait list	6
# of early decision applicants	260
% accepted early decision	29

your limits, push you to succeed, and this common goal unites all the students as well," which makes for a "close-knit community," not to mention an exciting, motivating experience.

CAREER

The Center for Career Development encourages "self-accountability," "initiative," and "autonomy" in all Cooper students as they transition to a professional practice. With that in mind, the Center offers ample resources to help students find their way, like online timelines and career counseling tailored to each school as well as the Cooper Career Connection that informs students about all career-related events, programs, and forums. The Career Resource Library is another excellent way to keep abreast of trends and ideas in your relevant field. Alumni lead by example, and the CU @ Lunch program allows recent grads to "speak about the vital issues they face following graduation." Those graduates who visited PayScale.com report a median starting salary of $68,500, and 55 percent believe their work makes the world a better place.

GENERAL INFO

Activities: Choral groups; Dance; Drama/theater; International Student Organization; Jazz band; Music ensembles; Musical theater; Student government; Student newspaper; Student-run film society; Symphony orchestra; Yearbook. 50 registered organizations, 15 honor societies, 5 religious organizations, 1 fraternity, on campus. **Athletics (Intercollegiate):** *Men:* basketball, soccer, volleyball. *Women:* basketball, soccer, volleyball. **On-Campus Highlights:** Great Hall, 41 Cooper Square, Foundation Building, Houghton and 41 Cooper Square Gallery, Frankie's Kitchen.

The Cooper Union for the
Advancement of Science and Art

FINANCIAL AID

Students should submit: FAFSA. Priority filing deadline is 5/1. The Princeton Review suggests that all financial aid forms be submitted as soon as possible after October 1. *Need-based scholarships/grants offered*: College/university scholarship or grant aid from institutional funds; Federal Pell; Private scholarships; SEOG; State scholarships/grants. *Loan aid offered*: Direct PLUS loans; Direct Subsidized Stafford Loans; Direct Unsubsidized Stafford Loans. Applicants will be notified of awards on a rolling basis beginning 12/20. Federal Work-Study Program available. Institutional employment available.

BOTTOM LINE

Students are accepted on the basis of student's academic achievement as well as their potential, creativity, talent and critical thinking skills. As of Fall 2015 every admitted student receives a half-tuition scholarship valued at $21,000 annually. For remaining expenses, including room and board, The Cooper Union provides additional aid based upon financial need. Health insurance adds an additional $1,200 for those that require it. Financial aid is available to assist with payment of all fees.

FINANCIAL FACTS	
Financial Aid Rating	91
Annual tuition	$44,550
Room and board	$16,638
Required fees	$2,150
Books and supplies	$1,800
Average frosh need-based scholarship	$24,749
Average UG need-based scholarship	$25,221
% needy frosh rec. need-based scholarship or grant aid	100
% needy UG rec. need-based scholarship or grant aid	100
% needy frosh rec. non-need-based scholarship or grant aid	100
% needy UG rec. non-need-based scholarship or grant aid	100
% needy frosh rec. need-based self-help aid	12
% needy UG rec. need-based self-help aid	28
% frosh rec. any financial aid	100
% UG rec. any financial aid	100
% UG borrow to pay for school	18
Average cumulative indebtedness	$17,037
% frosh need fully met	52
% ugrads need fully met	41
Average % of frosh need met	74
Average % of ugrad need met	76

CAREER INFORMATION FROM PAYSCALE.COM	
ROI Rating	96
Bachelors and No Higher	
Median starting salary	$68,500
Median mid-career salary	$126,200
At Least Bachelors	
Median starting salary	$71,600
Median mid-career salary	$138,600
Alumni with high job meaning	55%
Degrees awarded in STEM subjects	56%

Cornell University

Undergraduate Admissions, 410 Thurston Ave, Ithaca, NY 14850 • Admissions: 607-255-5241 • Fax: 607-255-0659

CAMPUS LIFE

Quality of Life Rating	90
Fire Safety Rating	96
Green Rating	98
Type of school	Private
Environment	Town

STUDENTS

Total undergrad enrollment	15,105
% male/female	47/53
# of fraternities	
(% ugrad men join)	38 (26)
# of sororities	
(% ugrad women join)	20 (24)
% African American	7
% Asian	19
% Caucasian	37
% Hispanic	14
% Native American	<1
% Pacific Islander	<1
% Two or more races	5
% Race and/or ethnicity unknown	8
% international	11
# of countries represented	85

#27 BEST VALUE COLLEGE

ABOUT THE SCHOOL

"Any person, any study." Perhaps no motto does a better job of summing up the spirit of a school than Ithaca, New York's Cornell University, an Ivy League school in upstate New York consisting of seven undergraduate colleges and schools. Cornell University is not just Ivy League, it's the largest of the Ivy League schools—and it has a curriculum to match. The "unbelievably broad curriculum" at Cornell offers a "large variety of academic programs" and "a plethora of classes to chose from," giving credence to the school's famous motto. There are nearly forty different majors at the College of Arts and Sciences alone. Factor in six other colleges and schools, and it's clear that students have a wealth of options before them. Specializations in science, agriculture, and environmental studies are especially popular here, though engineering, premed, and other studies receive just as much attention by attendees. "The research opportunities have been incredible," one student says. Another notes that, thanks to the hard work it demands of students and the school's great reputation, Cornell is a "difficult school with great job placement after." With all the educational opportunities Cornell has to offer, it should come as no surprise that the campus features an "intellectually mature student body" who are intent on focusing on the school's "rigorous" academics. "The intellectual caliber of the student body here is really unmatched." When study time ends, students exploring the "bustling student life" will see that "diversity here is definitely apparent...I love the fact that you can be surrounded by dairy farmers and Wall Street wannabes all in the same quad." About the only thing tying Cornell's student population together is the fact that everyone is "very focused on performing well in the classroom." Outside the classroom, recreation is just as diverse as the classes. Being in Ithaca, New York, opportunities for outdoor adventure abound, and Greek life thrives. Sports are as popular here as

Cornell University

Financial Aid: 607-255-5147 • E-mail: admissions@cornell.edu • Website: www.cornell.edu

partying—wrestling, track, and hockey are the school's top sports—and students note that "if I want to go study in a library at 3 A.M. on Saturday night, I will find a busy library full of other eager students, but if I want to go to a hockey game on a Saturday afternoon, I will find just as many screaming fans to share the fun."

BANG FOR YOUR BUCK

Need-based Federal Pell, SEOG, state scholarships/grants, private scholarships, school scholarship, or grant aid from institutional funds are all available to prospective students. Loan aid is also available in the form of Direct Subsidized Stafford loans, Direct Unsubsidized Stafford, Direct PLUS, and university loans from institutional funds.

STUDENT LIFE

Since Cornell is such a rigorous school, it's not surprising that "most of the time people are thinking about studying and getting their work done." "People are always thinking about the next prelim or paper they have to suffer through, but it's not always immediately at the forefront of their mind," says a student, so "people work hard here, and people certainly know how to play hard as well. "People here do anything and everything they can for fun: sports, parties, hanging out with friends or even getting involved with the clubs here on campus." With 30 to 40 percent of kids participating, "Greek life is big here. Not overwhelming, but definitely big." "Frat parties are really popular freshman and sophomore years, but then the crowd tends to migrate to the bars in Collegetown during junior and senior years." But while "it is not hard to find alcohol on campus, there really is no pressure to drink, [and] there are also a lot of campus run events on the weekends and also throughout the week to encourage students to do other things." "The campus is so diverse and the range of activities is endless. You will find a club or organization here that interests you, and there's always

ACADEMICS

Academic Rating	93
% students returning for sophomore year	97
% students graduating within 4 years	88
% students graduating within 6 years	95
Calendar	Semester
Student/faculty ratio	9:1
Profs interesting rating	84
Profs accessible rating	84

Most classes have 10–19 students.
Most lab/discussion sessions have 10–19 students.

MOST POPULAR MAJORS

Biology/Biological Sciences, General;
Hotel/Motel Administration/Management;
Labor and Industrial Relations

SELECTIVITY

Admissions Rating	98
# of applicants	51,324
% of applicants accepted	11
% of acceptees attending	60
# offered a place on the wait list	6,683
% accepting a place on wait list	68
% admitted from wait list	4
# of early decision applicants	6,325
% accepted early decision	24

FRESHMAN PROFILE	
Range SAT EBRW	680–750
Range SAT Math	710–790
Range ACT Composite	32–34
# submitting SAT scores	2,329
% submitting SAT scores	71
# submitting ACT scores	1,461
% submitting ACT scores	44
% graduated top 10% of class	83
% graduated top 25% of class	97
% graduated top 50% of class	100

DEADLINES	
Early decision	
Deadline	11/1
Notification	mid-Dec
Regular	
Deadline	1/2
Notification	4/1
Nonfall registration?	Yes

the possibility of establishing something new if that's what you're interested in here." So even if "the size of the student body may be overwhelming at first," students will find that "it's easy to find a close group of people."

CAREER

Cornell students are definitely a career-focused bunch: "People are kind of paranoid of failure," says a student. "They go crazy looking for internships and career opportunities as early as second semester freshman year." Fortunately for those students, consensus seems to be that "Cornell offers great career assistance to help students write resumes, cover letters, and find jobs/internships." The center offers counseling for students looking to explore their interests and determine a career path, resources for finding jobs and internships, career fairs and on campus recruiting, and even resources for those seeking international work experience. In addition to a central office in Barnes Hall that serves all students, each of Cornell's seven undergraduate colleges has its own office with resources tailored to the students in that college.

GENERAL INFO

Activities: Campus Ministries; Choral groups; Concert band; Dance; Drama/theater; International Student Organization; Jazz band; Literary magazine; Marching band; Model UN; Music ensembles; Musical theater; Pep band; Radio station; Student government; Student newspaper; Student-run film society; Symphony orchestra; Television station; Yearbook. 1,041 registered organizations, 15 honor societies, 24 religious organizations, 38 fraternities, 20 sororities, on campus. **Athletics (Intercollegiate):** *Men:* baseball, basketball, crew/rowing, cross-country, diving, football, golf, ice hockey, lacrosse, polo, soccer, squash, swimming, tennis, track/field (outdoor), track/field (indoor), wrestling. *Women:* basketball, crew/rowing, cross-country, diving, equestrian sports, fencing, field hockey, gymnastics, ice hockey, lacrosse, polo, soccer, softball, squash, swimming, tennis, track/field (outdoor), track/field (indoor), volleyball. **On-Campus Highlights:** Lynah Rink, The Trillium, The Lindseth Climbing Wall, Ho Plaza, Willard Straight Hall. **Environmental Initiatives:** "Where is the Human in Climate Change" is a podcast and essay series focused on the latest thinking from across the disciplines about the relationship between humans and the environment. The series explores a range of topics cultivated by students, faculty, and staff including Human Ecosystem Engineers, Future Fashion,

Cornell University

City Planning, and Planetary Health from lectures and professors from departments including Fiber Science and Apparel, Comparative Literature, City and Regional Planning, and Earth and Atmospheric Sciences. The podcast is geared towards a global audience with the goal of exploring complex issues from a humanist perspective. This series launched on Cornell's Humanities Webpage and iTunes and SoundCloud streaming platforms on April 17 and were released weekly in the spring.

FINANCIAL AID

Students should submit: CSS/Financial Aid PROFILE; FAFSA; Noncustodial PROFILE. Priority filing deadline is 2/15. The Princeton Review suggests that all financial aid forms be submitted as soon as possible after October 1. *Need-based scholarships/grants offered*: College/university scholarship or grant aid from institutional funds; Federal Pell; Private scholarships; SEOG; State scholarships/grants. *Loan aid offered*: Direct PLUS loans; Direct Subsidized Stafford Loans; Direct Unsubsidized Stafford Loans. Applicants will be notified of awards on or about 4/1. Federal Work-Study Program available. Institutional employment available.

FINANCIAL FACTS	
Financial Aid Rating	97
Annual tuition	$54,584
Room and board	$14,816
Required fees	$604
Books and supplies	$950
Average frosh need-based scholarship	$42,946
Average UG need-based scholarship	$42,228
% needy frosh rec. need-based scholarship or grant aid	97
% needy UG rec. need-based scholarship or grant aid	96
% needy frosh rec. non-need-based scholarship or grant aid	0
% needy UG rec. non-need-based scholarship or grant aid	0
% needy frosh rec. need-based self-help aid	89
% needy UG rec. need-based self-help aid	92
% frosh rec. any financial aid	45
% UG rec. any financial aid	64
% UG borrow to pay for school	41
Average cumulative indebtedness	$29,762
% frosh need fully met	100
% ugrads need fully met	100
Average % of frosh need met	100
Average % of ugrad need met	100

BOTTOM LINE

An Ivy League education at Cornell University will cost attendees just more than $55,188 per year in tuition and fees. Add to that $14,816 for room and board, and another $950 for books and supplies, and costs come to about $71,000 annually. Students are graduating from Cornell with an average accumulated debt of $29,762.

CAREER INFORMATION FROM PAYSCALE.COM	
ROI Rating	93
Bachelors and No Higher	
Median starting salary	$70,100
Median mid-career salary	$128,200
At Least Bachelors	
Median starting salary	$72,500
Median mid-career salary	$135,900
Alumni with high job meaning	48%
Degrees awarded in STEM subjects	43%

Cornell University

Dartmouth College

6016 McNutt Hall, Hanover, NH 03755 • Admissions: 603-646-2875 • Fax: 603-646-1216

CAMPUS LIFE

Quality of Life Rating	92
Fire Safety Rating	89
Green Rating	87
Type of school	Private
Environment	Village

STUDENTS

Total undergrad enrollment	4,417
% male/female	50/50
% from out of state	97
% frosh from public high school	55
% frosh live on campus	100
% ugrads live on campus	85
# of fraternities	
(% ugrad men join)	17 (44)
# of sororities	
(% ugrad women join)	11 (46)
% African American	7
% Asian	15
% Caucasian	50
% Hispanic	10
% Native American	2
% Pacific Islander	<1
% Two or more races	5
% Race and/or ethnicity unknown	2
% international	10
# of countries represented	73

ABOUT THE SCHOOL

A member of the Ivy League, Dartmouth is a small, student-centered undergraduate and graduate college, with three leading professional schools— Geisel School of Medicine, Thayer School of Engineering, and the Tuck School of Business. It is known for its commitment to excellence in undergraduate education and has a reputation as a place where intellectual rigor and creativity collide. This comes from a flexible academic curriculum that emphasizes an interdisciplinary approach. The campus community is generally relaxed, accepting, a bit outdoorsy, and usually bundled up under eight layers of clothing to get through the New Hampshire winters. What students learn outside the classroom is often as meaningful as what they learn inside. All incoming freshmen live in residential housing clusters located throughout the campus, and more than 80 percent of upperclassmen choose to do so as well. Almost all of the student body comes from outside the college's New Hampshire base. Greek groups add to the social mix because everyone is welcome to attend fraternity and sorority parties and events. Intramural athletics are insanely popular on campus as well.

BANG FOR YOUR BUCK

Dartmouth's approximately 4,300 undergraduate students enjoy the college's strong reputation as a member of the Ivy League, as well as its high-quality academics through twenty-nine departments and ten multidisciplinary programs. Academics at New Hampshire's preeminent college, comparable with other Ivy League schools, are demanding, but Dartmouth students feel they are up to the challenge. Unlike many of the other Ivies, though, the

Dartmouth College

Financial Aid: 603-646-2451 • Website: www.dartmouth.edu

student-faculty ratio of 7:1 favors the undergrads, who find graduate assistants in their classes to have the same open willingness to help them learn as the regular professors do.

STUDENT LIFE

Dartmouth students are continually on the go and they "wouldn't have it any other way." As one senior shares, "After attending classes in the morning, we run from meetings to debates to the library and finally to Frat Row. It is a relentless, fast-paced cycle, but it is so unbelievably fun and rewarding." More specifically, undergrads can enjoy "movies playing at our arts center . . . activities night (games, movies, etc. . . .), performance groups (dance troupes, a cappella groups, plays), outdoor activities (skiing, camping, hiking, sailing, etc.), and much more." We're told that "a very large percentage" of the student body chooses to go Greek. Fortunately, it's a "unique and VERY welcoming [scene] and much more low key than at other schools." And, of course, these undergrads love participating in Dartmouth traditions like "running around a giant three-story bonfire hundreds of times or streaking the green or singing karaoke with a milkshake close by."

CAREER

A Dartmouth degree and professional success typically go hand-in-hand. After all, according to PayScale.com, the median starting salary for Dartmouth grads is an impressive $71,500. Some of this success can indeed be attributed to the college's extensive alumni network. As one grateful psych major shares, "Alumni are...a HUGE resource; they love to stay involved with the college and are often willing to talk to current students about careers (and many have been known to give internships and jobs to Dartmouth students)." Certainly, students can also turn to the fantastic Center for Professional Development as well. Undergrads may use the office to find

ACADEMICS
Academic Rating	92
% students returning for sophomore year	97
% students graduating within 4 years	88
% students graduating within 6 years	96
Calendar	Quarter
Student/faculty ratio	7:1
Profs interesting rating	85
Profs accessible rating	96
Most classes have 10–19 students.	

MOST POPULAR MAJORS
Psychology, General; Economics, General; Political Science and Government, General

SELECTIVITY
Admissions Rating	98
# of applicants	22,033
% of applicants accepted	9
% of acceptees attending	61
# offered a place on the wait list	1,925
% accepting a place on wait list	67
% admitted from wait list	0
# of early decision applicants	2,269
% accepted early decision	25

funding for unpaid internships, receive graduate and professional school advising and even get help finding housing for when they head out into the world. And, perhaps most important, the center hosts numerous recruiting sessions throughout the year.

GENERAL INFO

Activities: Campus Ministries; Choral groups; Concert band; Dance; Drama/theater; International Student Organization; Jazz band; Literary magazine; Marching band; Model UN; Music ensembles; Musical theater; Opera; Pep band; Radio station; Student government; Student newspaper; Student-run film society; Symphony orchestra; Television station; Yearbook. 350 registered organizations, 4 honor societies, 24 religious organizations, 17 fraternities, 11 sorority, on campus. **Athletics (Intercollegiate):** *Men:* baseball, basketball, crew/rowing, cross-country, diving, equestrian sports, fencing, football, golf, ice hockey, lacrosse, sailing, skiing (downhill/alpine), skiing nordic cross-country, soccer, squash, swimming, tennis, track/field (outdoor), track/field (indoor). *Women:* basketball, crew/rowing, cross-country, diving, equestrian sports, fencing, field hockey, golf, ice hockey, lacrosse, sailing, skiing (downhill/alpine), skiing nordic cross-country, soccer, softball, squash, swimming, tennis, track/field (outdoor), track/field (indoor), volleyball. **On-Campus Highlights:** Hopkins Center for Creative and Performing Arts, Hood Museum of Art, Murals by Jose Clemente Orozco, Ten library system, all open to visitors, Ledyard Canoe Club, oldest in the country. **Environmental Initiatives:** As part of our commitment to reduce greenhouse gas emissions, Dartmouth commissioned an energy audit for the buildings that collectively use 75% of the energy on campus. Based on the results of this audit, the Trustees invested $12.5 million in 250 energy conservation and efficiency projects in existing buildings, which are now underway.

Dartmouth College

FINANCIAL AID

Students should submit: Business/Farm Supplement; CSS/Financial Aid PROFILE; FAFSA; Noncustodial PROFILE. Priority filing deadline is 2/1. The Princeton Review suggests that all financial aid forms be submitted as soon as possible after October 1. *Need-based scholarships/grants offered*: College/university scholarship or grant aid from institutional funds; Federal Pell; Private scholarships; SEOG; State scholarships/grants. *Loan aid offered*: Direct PLUS loans; Direct Subsidized Stafford Loans; Direct Unsubsidized Stafford Loans. Applicants will be notified of awards on or about 4/2. Federal Work-Study Program available. Institutional employment available.

BOTTOM LINE

To enjoy an Ivy League education with a nod to the New England collegiate experience, incoming freshmen at Dartmouth can expect to pay about $55,605 in tuition and roughly another $2,017 in required fees. On-campus room and board totals more than $16,374. Over half of Dartmouth students receive financial aid to help defray these costs, as the school maintains the philosophy that no one should hesitate to apply for fear they won't be able to afford it. A recent graduate shares her experience: "The administration is great to work with. Opportunities for funding to travel and do research, internships, volunteer, etc. are AMAZING."

FINANCIAL FACTS	
Financial Aid Rating	94
Annual tuition	$55,605
Room and board	$16,374
Required fees	$2,017
Books and supplies	$1,100
Average frosh need-based scholarship	$52,542
Average UG need-based scholarship	$51,118
% needy frosh rec. need-based scholarship or grant aid	94
% needy UG rec. need-based scholarship or grant aid	96
% needy frosh rec. non-need-based scholarship or grant aid	0
% needy UG rec. non-need-based scholarship or grant aid	0
% needy frosh rec. need-based self-help aid	90
% needy UG rec. need-based self-help aid	92
% frosh rec. any financial aid	50
% UG rec. any financial aid	51
% UG borrow to pay for school	49
Average cumulative indebtedness	$18,903
% frosh need fully met	100
% ugrads need fully met	100
Average % of frosh need met	100
Average % of ugrad need met	100

CAREER INFORMATION FROM PAYSCALE.COM	
ROI Rating	94
Bachelors and No Higher	
Median starting salary	$71,500
Median mid-career salary	$130,900
At Least Bachelors	
Median starting salary	$73,100
Median mid-career salary	$152,700
Alumni with high job meaning	50%
Degrees awarded in STEM subjects	35%

Dartmouth College

Denison University

100 W. College St., Granville, OH 43023 • Admissions: 740-587-6276 • Fax: 740-587-6306

#64 BEST VALUE COLLEGE

CAMPUS LIFE

Quality of Life Rating	90
Fire Safety Rating	96
Green Rating	96
Type of school	Private
Environment	Village

STUDENTS

Total undergrad enrollment	2,368
% male/female	46/54
% from out of state	74
% frosh from public high school	67
% frosh live on campus	100
% ugrads live on campus	99
# of fraternities	
(% ugrad men join)	9 (48)
# of sororities	
(% ugrad women join)	9 (27)
% African American	6
% Asian	4
% Caucasian	63
% Hispanic	9
% Native American	0
% Pacific Islander	<1
% Two or more races	3
% Race and/or ethnicity unknown	2
% international	12
# of countries represented	37

ABOUT THE SCHOOL

Ohio's Denison University is a liberal arts college that prioritizes "connections…between students, faculty, alumni, and the community [at large.]" Many undergrads remark that the school "feel[s] like home." Academics here are "rigorous," but, thankfully, there's plenty of "support available." For example, students can take advantage of amazing "tutor[ing] services," and they can turn to "the Writing Center and the library [for assistance with] researching and writing." "Small class size[s]" are a staple of a Denison education, which guarantees that students will encounter "engaged professors who love teaching undergraduates." Denison routinely hires instructors who are "expert[s] in their field" and who maintain "very high expectations for student performance and push students to produce their best work." These "very accessible" professors are "usually very excited to help when students have questions and…eager to meet…outside the classroom."

BANG FOR YOUR BUCK

Denison is steadfast in its commitment to remain affordable for students with financial need. And many undergrads here remark on their "generous" aid packages. Of course, that should be expected considering every year the university awards over $60 million in both need and merit-based aid. It's also important to mention that less than half of Denison's undergraduates incur any debt. (The average amount of loan debt per graduate is $28,833.) All accepted students are considered for merit scholarships with awards that generally range from $5,000 to full tuition coverage. Even better, they are all renewable. Students are selected based on superior academic achievement, leadership potential, and commitment to community.

Denison University

Financial Aid: 800-336-4766 • E-mail: admissions@denison.edu • Website: www.denison.edu

SCHOOL LIFE

Rest assured, at Denison "there's never an absence of things to do outside of classes and work." In fact, some students suggest that "the school is actually over programmed, since so much goes on." You can always find a "concert, a speaker or a club/organization event" to attend. Additionally, "movie nights" and "student run comedy [shows]" always yield a big crowd. Intramural sports are also rather "popular." And many individuals enjoy participating in "arcade game night, galas [and] food truck festivals." We're also told that "if it's a Wednesday, Friday or Saturday, there are parties around campus in suites or senior apartments." These are typically "hosted by fraternities." When students need a little bit of breather, they often "explore downtown Granville" or head to "nearby Columbus," just thirty miles from campus.

CAREER

Undergrads at Denison receive a tremendous amount of "career support…[from] the college." And they are quick to sing the praises of the Knowlton Center, which "offers a variety of help with career decisions." Here, students "practice interviews, [get] career coaching, résumé building, and more." The center also runs some innovative programs such as First Looks, which helps students at the start of their professional journey to gain a better understanding of certain jobs and industries via information sessions, networking opportunities, and company tours. Through these events, undergrads connect with industry insiders to ask questions about company culture, daily responsibilities, and individual career paths. Ideally, this kind of information and early networking helps students clarify their own dreams and ambitions.

ACADEMICS

Academic Rating	92
% students returning for sophomore year	89
% students graduating within 4 years	82
% students graduating within 6 years	85
Calendar	Semester
Student/faculty ratio	10:1
Profs interesting rating	92
Profs accessible rating	95
Most classes have 10–19 students.	

MOST POPULAR MAJORS

Biology, General; Psychology, General; Economics, General

SELECTIVITY

Admissions Rating	93
# of applicants	8,042
% of applicants accepted	34
% of acceptees attending	24
# offered a place on the wait list	1,555
% accepting a place on wait list	14
% admitted from wait list	11
# of early decision applicants	506
% accepted early decision	65

GENERAL INFO

Activities: Campus Ministries; Choral groups; Dance; Drama/theater; International Student Organization; Jazz band; Literary magazine; Music ensembles; Musical theater; Radio station; Student government; Student newspaper; Student-run film society; Television station; Yearbook. 175 registered organizations, 8 honor societies, 10 religious organizations, 9 fraternities, 9 sororities, on campus. **Athletics (Intercollegiate):** *Men:* baseball, basketball, cross-country, diving, football, golf, lacrosse, soccer, swimming, tennis, track/field (outdoor), track/field (indoor). *Women:* basketball, cross-country, diving, field hockey, golf, lacrosse, soccer, softball, swimming, tennis, track/field (outdoor), track/field (indoor), volleyball. **On-Campus Highlights:** Samson Talbot Hall of Biological Science, Bryant Arts Center, Mitchell Recreation and Athletics Center, Michael D. Eisner Center for the Performing Arts, F.W. Olin Science Hall. **Environmental Initiatives:** The signing of the ACUPCC and the development of a standing Campus Sustainability Committee as part of the campus governance system.

FINANCIAL AID

Students should submit: CSS/Financial Aid PROFILE; FAFSA; Noncustodial PROFILE. Priority filing deadline is 1/15. The Princeton Review suggests that all financial aid forms be submitted as soon as possible after October 1. *Need-based scholarships/grants offered:* College/university scholarship or grant aid from institutional funds; Federal Pell; Private scholarships; SEOG; State scholarships/grants. *Loan aid offered:* Direct PLUS loans; Direct Subsidized Stafford Loans; Direct Unsubsidized Stafford Loans. Applicants will be notified of awards on or about 3/15. Federal Work-Study Program available. Institutional employment available.

Denison University

BOTTOM LINE

Tuition at Denison University currently costs $52,620. The school charges another $13,050 for room and board and another $1,210 in required fees. Denison estimates that undergraduates will need another $1,000 for books and classroom supplies.

CAREER INFORMATION FROM PAYSCALE.COM	
ROI Rating	91
Bachelors and No Higher	
Median starting salary	$54,400
Median mid-career salary	$104,800
At Least Bachelors	
Median starting salary	$55,800
Median mid-career salary	$116,100
Alumni with high job meaning	48%
Degrees awarded in STEM subjects	22%

FINANCIAL FACTS	
Financial Aid Rating	94
Annual tuition	$52,620
Room and board	$13,050
Required fees	$1,210
Books and supplies	$1,000
Average frosh need-based scholarship	$41,158
Average UG need-based scholarship	$41,138
% needy frosh rec. need-based scholarship or grant aid	100
% needy UG rec. need-based scholarship or grant aid	100
% needy frosh rec. non-need-based scholarship or grant aid	17
% needy UG rec. non-need-based scholarship or grant aid	15
% needy frosh rec. need-based self-help aid	80
% needy UG rec. need-based self-help aid	84
% frosh rec. any financial aid	93
% UG rec. any financial aid	95
% UG borrow to pay for school	53
Average cumulative indebtedness	$31,551
% frosh need fully met	89
% ugrads need fully met	63
Average % of frosh need met	100
Average % of ugrad need met	96

Denison University

Duke University

2138 Campus Drive, Box 90586, Durham, NC 27708-0586 • Admissions: 919-684-3214

CAMPUS LIFE

Quality of Life Rating	85
Fire Safety Rating	60*
Green Rating	60*
Type of school	Private
Affiliation	Methodist
Environment	City

STUDENTS

Total undergrad enrollment	6,548
% male/female	50/50
% from out of state	85
% frosh from public high school	65
% frosh live on campus	100
% ugrads live on campus	81
# of fraternities	
(% ugrad men join)	21 (29)
# of sororities	
(% ugrad women join)	14 (42)
% African American	10
% Asian	21
% Caucasian	44
% Hispanic	9
% Native American	1
% Pacific Islander	<1
% Two or more races	2
% Race and/or ethnicity unknown	3
% international	10
# of countries represented	89

#19 BEST VALUE COLLEGE

ABOUT THE SCHOOL

Duke University offers students a word-class education and freedom in choosing the academic path that best meets their needs. The school's research expenditures rank in the top ten nationally, the library system is extensive, and the school's Division I sports teams are legendary. Still, the undergraduate experience is the heart and soul of the school. Students are required to live on campus for three years. First-year students live together on East Campus, where about a quarter of them participate in FOCUS, a living/learning program organized around academic themes, which gives them access to faculty mentoring and a smaller community of students they get to know well. Maybe it's the mild North Carolina climate, but the students say their campus is way more laid-back than what you'd find at any of the Ivy League schools. It's also breathtakingly beautiful, featuring soaring Gothic buildings, modern teaching and research facilities, accessible athletic fields and recreational spaces, and a lush botanical garden. It's true that Duke students are focused on academics, but they are just as enthusiastic about attending campus events, participating in Greek functions, or cheering on the teams at Duke sporting events, especially when it's the school's top-ranked basketball team that's playing.

BANG FOR YOUR BUCK

Duke is dedicated to making its outstanding education affordable. More than half of undergraduates receive some sort of financial assistance, including need-based aid, and merit or athletic scholarships. Students

Duke University

Financial Aid: 919-684-6225 • E-mail: undergrad-admissions@duke.edu • Website: www.duke.eduwww.duke.edu

are evaluated for admission without regard to their ability to pay. If admitted, Duke pledges to meet 100 percent of need. There are no loans or parental contributions required for families with incomes under $40,000. Families with incomes under $60,000 are not required to make a parental contribution, and the school offers capped loans for eligible families with incomes of more than $100,000. The biggest value is the academic experience. One student explains, "Every single one of my professors actually knows me very well. They know where I'm from; they know what I actually find funny in class; they know when I'm sick and are incredibly parental in making sure that I get all of my work done and stay healthy; they know ME. How many other students can say that in any university?" Another student adds, "I wanted a medium college that was not too large but had research opportunities. I liked the culture at Duke and the choice was easy because they also gave me the best financial package."

ACADEMICS

Academic Rating	90
% students returning for sophomore year	97
% students graduating within 6 years	95
Calendar	Semester
Student/faculty ratio	6:1
Profs interesting rating	75
Profs accessible rating	74

Most classes have 10–19 students. Most lab/discussion sessions have 10–19 students.

MOST POPULAR MAJORS
Psychology, General; Public Policy Analysis, General; Economics, General

SELECTIVITY

Admissions Rating	98
# of applicants	33,077
% of applicants accepted	10
% of acceptees attending	48
# of early decision applicants	3,451
% accepted early decision	25

STUDENT LIFE

Life involves "getting a ton of work done first and then finding time to play and have fun," and the typical student here wears five or more hats: "He/she is studious but social, athletic but can never be seen in the gym, job hunting but not worrying, and so on and so forth." Of course, "Duke basketball games are a must" and sorority/fraternity life is popular but not necessary. The school has an on-campus movie theater and events happening all the time, and students also can just do their own thing, such as "exploring, going skiing or to the beach for a weekend, [or] making a bonfire in the forest." No matter what your weekend plan is, "people will be hitting the books on Sundays (all-nighters are common) in order to maintain their grades."

CAREER

Duke students "are focused on graduating and obtaining a lucrative and prosperous career." The "engaged Career Center" provides a range of services (such as seminars, workshops, and online databases) that help students fine-tune their skills. Career fairs are held throughout the year (including the "Just-in-Time" Career Fair in the spring, for employers who have immediate openings for graduating students. Drop-in advising is always available. Fifty-three percent of Duke graduates who visited PayScale.com reported feeling their jobs had a meaningful impact on the world. The median starting salary for Duke grads is $71,100.

GENERAL INFO

Activities: Campus Ministries; Choral groups; Concert band; Dance; Drama/theater; International Student Organization; Jazz band; Literary magazine; Marching band; Model UN; Music ensembles; Musical theater; Opera; Pep band; Radio station; Student government; Student newspaper; Student-run film society; Symphony orchestra; Television station. 200 registered organizations, 10 honor societies, 25 religious organizations, 21 fraternity, 14 sororities, on campus. **Athletics (Intercollegiate):** *Men:* baseball, basketball, cross-country, diving, fencing, football, golf, lacrosse, soccer, swimming, tennis, track/field (outdoor), track/field (indoor), volleyball, wrestling. *Women:* basketball, crew/rowing, cross-country, diving, fencing, field hockey, golf, lacrosse, soccer, swimming, tennis, track/field (outdoor), track/field (indoor), volleyball. **On-Campus Highlights:** Duke Chapel, Primate Center, Sarah P. Duke Gardens, Duke Forest, Levine Science Research Center. **Environmental Initiatives:** Duke has signed the ACUPCC and made a commitment to make Duke a climate neutral institution.

Duke University

FINANCIAL AID

Students should submit: Business/Farm Supplement; CSS/Financial Aid PROFILE; FAFSA; Noncustodial PROFILE. Priority filing deadline is 2/1. The Princeton Review suggests that all financial aid forms be submitted as soon as possible after October 1. *Need-based scholarships/grants offered*: College/university scholarship or grant aid from institutional funds; Federal Pell; Private scholarships; SEOG; State scholarships/grants. *Loan aid offered*: Direct PLUS loans; Direct Subsidized Stafford Loans; Direct Unsubsidized Stafford Loans. Federal Work-Study Program available. Institutional employment available.

BOTTOM LINE

Total estimated cost of attendance for Duke University comes to $78,608. That is a very large sum of money. But 52 percent of students do not pay that sticker price. The average need based grant award is $47,556. Combining that with work study and merit aid results in an average debt of $23,819 upon graduation. Also a large sum of money. But the theme of large sums continues with a median starting salary of $71,100. A great place to start to pay back that debt. 54% of Duke grads attribute high meaning to their jobs.

FINANCIAL FACTS

Financial Aid Rating	91
Annual tuition	$55,880
Room and board	$15,588
Required fees	$2,051
Books and supplies	$1,260
Average frosh need-based scholarship	$49,174
Average UG need-based scholarship	$47,556
% needy frosh rec. need-based scholarship or grant aid	96
% needy UG rec. need-based scholarship or grant aid	95
% needy frosh rec. non-need-based scholarship or grant aid	6
% needy UG rec. non-need-based scholarship or grant aid	9
% needy frosh rec. need-based self-help aid	82
% needy UG rec. need-based self-help aid	85
% UG borrow to pay for school	33
Average cumulative indebtedness	$23,819
% frosh need fully met	100
% ugrads need fully met	100
Average % of frosh need met	100
Average % of ugrad need met	100

CAREER INFORMATION FROM PAYSCALE.COM

ROI Rating	94
Bachelors and No Higher	
Median starting salary	$71,100
Median mid-career salary	$132,100
At Least Bachelors	
Median starting salary	$73,500
Median mid-career salary	$146,600
Alumni with high job meaning	54%
Degrees awarded in STEM subjects	26%

Duke University

Emory University

1390 Oxford Road NE, Atlanta, GA 30322 • Admissions: 404-727-6036 • Fax: 404-727-6039

CAMPUS LIFE

Quality of Life Rating	98
Fire Safety Rating	65
Green Rating	96
Type of school	Private
Affiliation	Methodist
Environment	City

STUDENTS

Total undergrad enrollment	6,975
% male/female	40/60
% from out of state	79
% frosh from public high school	56
% frosh live on campus	99
% ugrads live on campus	63
# of fraternities	
(% ugrad men join)	17 (28)
# of sororities	
(% ugrad women join)	15 (25)
% African American	8
% Asian	21
% Caucasian	40
% Hispanic	10
% Native American	<1
% Pacific Islander	<1
% Two or more races	4
% Race and/or ethnicity unknown	1
% international	16

#46 BEST VALUE COLLEGE

ABOUT THE SCHOOL

Emory University, just 15 minutes outside of Atlanta in Decatur, Georgia, is known for its excellent pre-professional programs, academic rigor, and strong focus on research. Students say the university's emphasis on community-building shapes a culture that prizes non-competitive achievement and a balance of challenging coursework with an engaged life on the "gorgeous" campus. The business and pre-med schools are top-rated, and students are given opportunities from freshman year onward to form close relationships with faculty, "renowned experts in their fields" who are generally "accessible and supportive" and include President Jimmy Carter, Salman Rushdie, and the Dalai Lama. Students appreciate that they are "encouraged to pursue their interests, both in the classroom and outside of it, and to pave their own paths." Emory has recently eliminated some of their liberal arts majors (journalism, visual arts, and education), to focus on core programs and growing areas.

BANG FOR YOUR BUCK

Emory offers generous financial aid packages and pledges a "commit[ment] to meeting 100 percent of demonstrated financial need for all accepted domestic students." In 2016–17, the average student received $42,277 in financial aid. Twenty percent of students receive federal Pell grants. All students who apply for need-based aid will automatically be considered for Emory Advantage funding, "available to students from families with annual total incomes of $100,000 or less." The Loan Replacement Grant "replaces loans for dependent undergraduate students whose families' annual

Emory University

Financial Aid: 404-727-6039 • E-mail: admission@emory.edu • Website: www.emory.edu

total incomes are $50,000 or less," and the Loan Cap Program caps federal loans at 15,000 for any student whose family's income is between $50,000 and $100,000.

STUDENT LIFE

Students can get involved in wealth of campus activities, including Greek life (who throw most of the weekend's parties), intramural and varsity sports, and downtown Atlanta offers all the restaurants, shopping, arts and culture students could ask for. Downtown Decatur has a shopping district, as well. There's a farmer's market every Tuesday, and "Wonderful Wednesdays" are a "favorite Emory tradition," showcasing student clubs and providing free food, music, and the occasional quirky event (i.e. petting zoo). Students also "play nighttime soccer on McDonough Field," play video games at the Cox Computing Center, or write for The Emory Wheel, the college newspaper. "I love the fact that Emory's school spirit is not solely wrapped around athletics," one student says. "At Emory, all events are well attended and respected by all students. Community is something that Emory strives accomplished from day one, utilizing the orientation and residence life programs."

ACADEMICS

Academic Rating	94
% students returning for sophomore year	95
% students graduating within 4 years	83
% students graduating within 6 years	90
Calendar	Semester
Student/faculty ratio	9:1
Profs interesting rating	95
Profs accessible rating	89

Most classes have 10–19 students. Most lab/discussion sessions have 10–19 students.

MOST POPULAR MAJORS

Biology/Biological Sciences, General; Registered Nursing/Registered Nurse; Business Administration and Management, General

SELECTIVITY

Admissions Rating	98
# of applicants	27,559
% of applicants accepted	19
% of acceptees attending	28
# offered a place on the wait list	4,983
% accepting a place on wait list	53
% admitted from wait list	0
# of early decision applicants	2,680
% accepted early decision	26

CAREER

As a leading research university, Emory gives students ample opportunity to get hands-on experience working with renowned scholars, as well as internships and training "…at the Emory University Hospital, the Center for Disease Control, the Carter Center, and other organizations that Emory partners with…including the Tibet Science program with our honorary faculty member, the Dalai Lama." Pre-med and pre-nursing students have valuable access to the lauded Woodruff Health Sciences Center, comprised of

FRESHMAN PROFILE

Range SAT EBRW	660–730
Range SAT Math	690–790
Range ACT Composite	31–34
# submitting SAT scores	748
% submitting SAT scores	52
# submitting ACT scores	683
% submitting ACT scores	48
Average HS GPA	3.8
% graduated top 10% of class	84
% graduated top 25% of class	98
% graduated top 50% of class	100

DEADLINES

Early decision	
Deadline	11/1
Notification	12/15
Other ED Deadline	1/1
Other ED Notification	2/15
Regular	
Deadline	1/1
Notification	4/1
Nonfall registration?	No

the School of Medicine, the Nell Hodgson Woodruff School of Nursing, the Rollins School of Public Health, the Winship Cancer Institute, and the Yerkes National Primate Research Center. According to PayScale.com, 50 percent of Emory University alumni report that their work makes the world a better place. The median yearly starting salary is $62,000.

GENERAL INFO

Activities: Campus Ministries; Choral groups; Concert band; Dance; Drama/theater; International Student Organization; Jazz band; Literary magazine; Model UN; Music ensembles; Musical theater; Opera; Radio station; Student government; Student newspaper; Student-run film society; Symphony orchestra; Television station. 161 registered organizations, 28 honor societies, 26 religious organizations, 17 fraternities, 12 sororities, on campus. **Athletics (Intercollegiate):** *Men:* baseball, basketball, cross-country, diving, golf, soccer, swimming, tennis, track/field (outdoor). *Women:* basketball, cross-country, diving, soccer, softball, swimming, tennis, track/field (outdoor), volleyball. **On-Campus Highlights:** Michael C. Carlos Museum, Lullwater Park, Clifton Health Sciences Corridor, 10th Floor of the Woodruff Library, Candler Library Reading Room. **Environmental Initiatives:** Emory has among the highest number of square feet of LEED-certified space of any campus in America. Emory constructed the first LEED-certified building in the Southeast in the 1990's, the first Good LEED-EB in the U.S., and since 2001 all new and future construction must be LEED (with Silver currently the minimum). Emory is also auditing and retrofitting exisiting buildings—roughly 1 million square feet are currently underway with an additional 1 million in planning phase.

FINANCIAL AID

Students should submit: CSS/Financial Aid PROFILE; FAFSA; Noncustodial PROFILE. Priority filing deadline is 2/15. The Princeton Review suggests that all financial aid forms be submitted as soon as possible after October 1. *Need-based scholarships/grants offered*: College/university scholarship or grant aid from institutional funds; Federal Pell; Private scholarships; SEOG; State scholarships/grants. *Loan aid offered*: Direct PLUS loans; Direct Subsidized Stafford Loans; Direct Unsubsidized Stafford Loans. Applicants will be notified of awards on or about 4/1. Federal Work-Study Program available. Institutional employment available.

BOTTOM LINE

Students studying business and the sciences will benefit from expert faculty and well-funded departments. Emory estimates the total costs of attendance in 2017–18 at $70,000, including $53,070 in tuition and $14,972 in room and board. Lower-income to middle-class students, however, are aided by the Emory Advantage funding, which leaves students in far less debt upon graduation.

FINANCIAL FACTS	
Financial Aid Rating	95
Annual tuition	$53,070
Room and board	$14,972
Required fees	$734
Books and supplies	$1,224
Average frosh need-based scholarship	$44,463
Average UG need-based scholarship	$41,583
% needy frosh rec. need-based scholarship or grant aid	94
% needy UG rec. need-based scholarship or grant aid	95
% needy frosh rec. non-need-based scholarship or grant aid	35
% needy UG rec. non-need-based scholarship or grant aid	23
% needy frosh rec. need-based self-help aid	88
% needy UG rec. need-based self-help aid	91
% frosh rec. any financial aid	66
% UG rec. any financial aid	61
% UG borrow to pay for school	34
Average cumulative indebtedness	$29,658
% frosh need fully met	100
% ugrads need fully met	98
Average % of frosh need met	100
Average % of ugrad need met	100

CAREER INFORMATION FROM PAYSCALE.COM	
ROI Rating	92
Bachelors and No Higher	
Median starting salary	$62,000
Median mid-career salary	$110,800
At Least Bachelors	
Median starting salary	$64,000
Median mid-career salary	$123,800
Alumni with high job meaning	50%
Degrees awarded in STEM subjects	20%

Emory University

Florida State University

PO Box 3062400, Tallahassee, FL 32306-2400 • Admissions: 850-644-6200 • Fax: 850-644-0197

#67 BEST VALUE COLLEGE

CAMPUS LIFE

Quality of Life Rating	90
Fire Safety Rating	90
Green Rating	60*
Type of school	Public
Environment	City

STUDENTS

Total undergrad enrollment	32,072
% male/female	43/57
% from out of state	11
% frosh from public high school	79
% frosh live on campus	82
% ugrads live on campus	21
# of fraternities	
(% ugrad men join)	24 (14)
# of sororities	
(% ugrad women join)	24 (24)
% African American	9
% Asian	2
% Caucasian	60
% Hispanic	21
% Native American	<1
% Pacific Islander	<1
% Two or more races	4
% Race and/or ethnicity unknown	1
% international	2
# of countries represented	103

ABOUT THE SCHOOL

Located in sunny Tallahassee, Florida State University is a pre-eminent research university that offers its 32,000 undergraduates the choice of more than one hundred majors. This range means that "research opportunities are endless," and in fact the university spends around $200 million on research each year. In all, roughly a quarter of all FSU students assist a mentoring professor, which gets them "meaningful insight to the learning environment both in class and out of class." Even those not involved directly in research will find "many support systems like tutoring and counseling" with which to avail themselves. Overall, "Florida State is constantly growing," and the school has been able to "seamlessly implement techniques including virtual discussion boards, touchscreens, and many new modes to teach," which means that "every class is a bit different, and it definitely helps to keep things interesting." As one student shares, "No matter how successful a college or program is at Florida State, it never stays stagnant."

BANG FOR YOUR BUCK

Florida residents pay a bargain of an in-state tuition at around $4,640 a year. And while the majority of the student body hails from in-state, there are a select number of Out-of-State Tuition Waiver Scholarships available to reduce the additional cost for non-Florida residents. Further aid is available through both the college and numerous state funds such as the Bright Futures Scholarship Program. The financial aid office maintains an online scholarship platform called FS4U (Finding Scholarships for You) that helps students identify scholarships for which they are eligible, as well as a listing of private donors that have awarded grants to FSU students in the past.

Florida State University

Financial Aid: 850-644-5716 • E-mail: admissions@admin.fsu.edu • Website: www.fsu.edu

STUDENT LIFE

FSU "does a great job of trying to make the school feel smaller" by creating "cohorts within majors or residence halls and encouraging students to be involved on campus to meet students with similar interests." The sense of community is encouraged by the "absolutely beautiful" campus, as "many students like to lay out on Landis [Green] between classes, throw their Frisbees, or take long walks," which gives plenty of time for socialization. That extends to sporting events as well: "The weekends during football season are spent at football games and tailgates." The school also "owns its own reservation off campus where students can go swimming, paddle boarding, relaxing, or climbing on the ropes course," as well as "an entire complex just off campus that is specifically for Intramurals." Off-campus, "there is always something to do in Tallahassee."

CAREER

The Career Center is FSU's centralized resource for linking students with jobs, internships, and mentors, and it hosts regular job fairs, workshops, and Résumé Cafés to help students along the way. "Our career fairs and internship fairs are incredible and attended by a large amount of employers," says a student. The school encourages students to document and plan for their future careers through its online Career Portfolio tool, and given that "opportunities like undergraduate research are extremely accessible," it is easy for students to flesh those out. The faculty "also help assist students in career opportunities and bring companies in to speak." The school's dedication to lifelong learning even continues past when a student graduates through the Center for Academic & Professional Development, which offers certification programs, continuing education, and online courses. As one student sums up it up: "With a little bit of confidence and networking, the opportunities are limitless."

ACADEMICS

Academic Rating	82
% students returning for sophomore year	93
% students graduating within 4 years	66
% students graduating within 6 years	83
Calendar	Semester
Student/faculty ratio	21:1
Profs interesting rating	83
Profs accessible rating	83

Most classes have 10–19 students. Most lab/discussion sessions have 20–29 students.

MOST POPULAR MAJORS

Psychology, General; Criminal Justice/ Safety Studies; Finance, General

SELECTIVITY

Admissions Rating	92
# of applicants	50,314
% of applicants accepted	37
% of acceptees attending	34

GENERAL INFO

Activities: Campus Ministries; Choral groups; Concert band; Dance; Drama/theater; International Student Organization; Jazz band; Literary magazine; Marching band; Model UN; Music ensembles; Musical theater; Opera; Pep band; Radio station; Student government; Student newspaper; Student-run film society; Symphony orchestra; Television station; Yearbook. 550 registered organizations, 23 honor societies, 45 religious organizations, 24 fraternities, 24 sororities, on campus. **Athletics (Intercollegiate):** *Men:* baseball, basketball, cheerleading, cross-country, diving, football, golf, swimming, tennis, track/field (outdoor), track/field (indoor). *Women:* basketball, cheerleading, cross-country, diving, golf, soccer, softball, swimming, tennis, track/field (outdoor), track/field (indoor), volleyball. **On-Campus Highlights:** Suwannee Dining Hall, Bobby E. Leach Student Recreation Center, Bobby Bowden Field at Doak Campbell Stadium, National High Magnetic Field Laboratory, FSU Reservation. **Environmental Initiatives:** Creation of the FSU Office of Sustainability and the hiring of a full-time Director of Campus Sustainability to help build a comprehensive sustainable campus program.

Florida State University

FINANCIAL AID

Students should submit: FAFSA; State aid form. The Princeton Review suggests that all financial aid forms be submitted as soon as possible after October 1. *Need-based scholarships/grants offered*: College/university scholarship or grant aid from institutional funds; Federal Pell; Private scholarships; SEOG; State scholarships/grants; United Negro College Fund. *Loan aid offered*: Direct PLUS loans; Direct Subsidized Stafford Loans; Direct Unsubsidized Stafford Loans. Applicants will be notified of awards on a rolling basis beginning 4/5. Federal Work-Study Program available. Institutional employment available.

BOTTOM LINE

Annual tuition and fees for a resident of the Sunshine State student will run just over $6,500 for fall 2019. A true deal when considering the size and scope of an institution with 16 colleges ranging from Arts and Sciences to Physician Assistant Practice. 92 percent of undergraduates received some form of aid for fall 2018 with an average need-based scholarship of $13,227.

FINANCIAL FACTS

Financial Aid Rating	85
Annual in-state tuition	$4,640
Annual out-of-state tuition	$19,806
Room and board	$10,666
Required fees	$1,877
Books and supplies	$1,000
Average frosh need-based scholarship	$14,597
Average UG need-based scholarship	$13,227
% needy frosh rec. need-based scholarship or grant aid	96
% needy UG rec. need-based scholarship or grant aid	90
% needy frosh rec. non-need-based scholarship or grant aid	81
% needy UG rec. non-need-based scholarship or grant aid	55
% needy frosh rec. need-based self-help aid	46
% needy UG rec. need-based self-help aid	59
% frosh rec. any financial aid	98
% UG rec. any financial aid	92
% UG borrow to pay for school	49
Average cumulative indebtedness	$22,840
% frosh need fully met	21
% ugrads need fully met	17
Average % of frosh need met	81
Average % of ugrad need met	76

CAREER INFORMATION FROM PAYSCALE.COM

ROI Rating	91
Bachelors and No Higher	
Median starting salary	$50,800
Median mid-career salary	$92,700
At Least Bachelors	
Median starting salary	$52,100
Median mid-career salary	$98,900
Alumni with high job meaning	51%
Degrees awarded in STEM subjects	18%

Florida State University

Georgia Institute of Technology

Georgia Institute of Technology, Atlanta, GA 30332-0320 • Admissions: 404-894-4154 • Fax: 404-894-9511

CAMPUS LIFE

Quality of Life Rating	89
Fire Safety Rating	96
Green Rating	96
Type of school	Public
Environment	Metropolis

STUDENTS

Total undergrad enrollment	15,212
% male/female	62/38
% from out of state	39
% frosh live on campus	97
% ugrads live on campus	43
# of fraternities	
(% ugrad men join)	40 (26)
# of sororities	
(% ugrad women join)	15 (30)
% African American	7
% Asian	22
% Caucasian	48
% Hispanic	7
% Native American	<1
% Pacific Islander	<1
% Two or more races	4
% Race and/or ethnicity unknown	4
% international	8
# of countries represented	113

#11 BEST VALUE COLLEGE

ABOUT THE SCHOOL

One of the nation's top-ranked public research universities, Georgia Tech offers its 15,500 undergraduate students "a technologically focused education" that emphasizes critical inquiry and dynamic problem solving. Despite the rigor of its engineering, science, computing, business, and liberal arts programs, "there isn't a sense of cut-throat academic rivalry; everyone is…helpful and supportive of one another," notes one student. Described as "driven, passionate, and relentless," the students here are "constantly striving to pursue academic excellence, as well as technological advancement." Georgia Tech professors are leaders in their fields and are "truly passionate about what they're teaching," making themselves "highly approachable outside of classroom time." A shared sense of purpose unites this diverse student body, who feel that Georgia Tech is helping them become "better able to work together to solve the world's problems."

BANG FOR YOUR BUCK

Georgia Tech is a public institution that is committed not only to ensuring that education is as affordable as possible, but also, through its many co-op and internship programs, that students are exceedingly prepared for the job market. There are numerous scholarships and grants available, including those that are merit and need-based. In addition, the school's highly-rated study-abroad and international internship programs help make students "ideal for competitive positions in today's global economy." The university's Center for Career Discovery and Development is considered one of the

Georgia Institute of Technology

Financial Aid: 404-894-4160 • E-mail: admission@gatech.edu • Website: www.gatech.edu

nation's best in helping place students in competitive jobs and fostering recruitment opportunities. As one student puts it, "Georgia Tech has great job placement…it gives you the tools to get wherever you want to go."

STUDENT LIFE

Asked to describe their peers, many students point out that "people here are diverse, fun, friendly." While the academic environment at Georgia Tech is rigorous, "everybody has time to unwind," says one student. There are plenty of opportunities for extracurricular activities; the fitness-minded go to the school's state-of-the-art sports and recreation center, and there are over 500 clubs and societies to take part in. As one student puts it, "There is always something going on or an event I want to attend." Greek life here is vibrant, too, and a great deal of the student community rallies around the school's Division I football team; "if it's game day, the campus goes nuts" notes one fan. Located in Atlanta, many attending Georgia Tech love that they can experience the city while living in a "lush, green, bustling campus." The students here "make their best efforts to show goodwill toward [each] other…and generally strive to better their community."

CAREER

A Georgia Tech education is widely considered an excellent investment, with graduates earning a median starting salary of $72,700, and 48 percent of alumni noting their work has "high meaning" to them. Since it's located in Atlanta, students at the school have access to countless internships, co-ops, and other career-advancement opportunities with local companies. The university also emphasizes partnerships with business and engineering communities through its VentureLab and Advanced Technology

ACADEMICS

Academic Rating	85
% students returning for sophomore year	97
% students graduating within 4 years	40
% students graduating within 6 years	87
Calendar	Semester
Student/faculty ratio	21:1
Profs interesting rating	80
Profs accessible rating	79

Most classes have 20–29 students.
Most lab/discussion sessions have 10–19 students.

MOST POPULAR MAJORS

Computer and Information Sciences, General; Mechanical Engineering; Industrial Engineering

SELECTIVITY

Admissions Rating	97
# of applicants	35,611
% of applicants accepted	23
% of acceptees attending	39
# offered a place on the wait list	3,511
% accepting a place on wait list	65
% admitted from wait list	3

Development Center, two of the country's most successful and dynamic innovation incubators. Not only that, Georgia Tech's Center for Career Discovery and Development offers a range of programs to help students become more competitive in the job market, including resume and cover letter coaching as well as career fairs. Through it all, as one student puts it, "Georgia Tech is about producing competitive students with valuable and unique research, job, and international experiences in order to lead them to successful careers."

GENERAL INFO

Activities: Campus Ministries; Choral groups; Concert band; Dance; Drama/theater; International Student Organization; Jazz band; Literary magazine; Marching band; Model UN; Music ensembles; Musical theater; Pep band; Radio station; Student government; Student newspaper; Student-run film society; Symphony orchestra; Television station; Yearbook. 533 registered organizations, 16 honor societies, 36 religious organizations, 40 fraternities, 15 sororities, on campus. **Athletics (Intercollegiate):** *Men:* baseball, basketball, cheerleading, cross-country, diving, football, golf, swimming, tennis, track/field (outdoor), track/field (indoor). *Women:* basketball, cheerleading, cross-country, diving, softball, swimming, tennis, track/field (outdoor), track/field (indoor), volleyball. **On-Campus Highlights:** Tech Square-Bookstore/Hotel, Olympic Aquatic Center/Campus Recreation, The Hill/Tech Tower, Student Center Commons and the Library, Ferst Center for the Arts. **Environmental Initiatives:** Education: Over 200 courses are offered across all of the colleges with the goal that every student who graduates has taken at least one sustainability course. Many degree programs at the undergraduate and graduate levels, and many continuing education and certificate programs focus on sustainability and major areas of sustainability. Sustainability has been included in the Institute Mission Statement and Strategic Plan since 1994. Our office updated the Sustainability Strategic Plan in 2010, and in 2018 reached the final stages. The Institute's Serve*Learn*Sustain has incorporated the UN's "Grand Challenges" in the Strategic Plan to align with, "Improving the Human Condition and a Sustainable Global Economy."

Georgia Institute of Technology

FINANCIAL AID

Students should submit: CSS/Financial Aid PROFILE; FAFSA; Institution's own financial aid form. Priority filing deadline is 1/31. The Princeton Review suggests that all financial aid forms be submitted as soon as possible after October 1. *Need-based scholarships/grants offered*: College/university scholarship or grant aid from institutional funds; Federal Pell; Private scholarships; SEOG; State scholarships/grants; United Negro College Fund. *Loan aid offered*: Direct PLUS loans; Direct Subsidized Stafford Loans; Direct Unsubsidized Stafford Loans. Applicants will be notified of awards on or about 4/1. Federal Work-Study Program available. Institutional employment available.

BOTTOM LINE

Tuition for Georgia residents is $10,258 a year with out-of-state students paying $31,370. Annual room and board costs are $12,090, and books and other supplies run about $800. That said, the university offers several scholarships and grants, with the average undergraduate need-based scholarship totaling $12,571.

FINANCIAL FACTS	
Financial Aid Rating	82
Annual in-state tuition	$10,258
Annual out-of-state tuition	$31,370
Room and board	$12,090
Required fees	$2,424
Books and supplies	$800
Average frosh need-based scholarship	$14,630
Average UG need-based scholarship	$12,581
% needy frosh rec. need-based scholarship or grant aid	90
% needy UG rec. need-based scholarship or grant aid	88
% needy frosh rec. non-need-based scholarship or grant aid	68
% needy UG rec. non-need-based scholarship or grant aid	42
% needy frosh rec. need-based self-help aid	46
% needy UG rec. need-based self-help aid	54
% frosh rec. any financial aid	76
% UG rec. any financial aid	67
% UG borrow to pay for school	36
Average cumulative indebtedness	$32,760
% frosh need fully met	29
% ugrads need fully met	24
Average % of frosh need met	66
Average % of ugrad need met	57

CAREER INFORMATION FROM PAYSCALE.COM	
ROI Rating	95
Bachelors and No Higher	
Median starting salary	$72,700
Median mid-career salary	$133,400
At Least Bachelors	
Median starting salary	$73,700
Median mid-career salary	$138,700
Alumni with high job meaning	48%
Degrees awarded in STEM subjects	80%

Georgia Institute of Technology

Grinnell College

1103 Park Street, Grinnell, IA 50112 • Admissions: 641-269-3600 • Fax: 641-269-4800

CAMPUS LIFE
Quality of Life Rating	83
Fire Safety Rating	93
Green Rating	76
Type of school	Private
Environment	Village

STUDENTS
Total undergrad enrollment	1,677
% male/female	45/55
% from out of state	92
% frosh live on campus	100
% ugrads live on campus	88
# of fraternities	0
# of sororities	0
% African American	5
% Asian	8
% Caucasian	50
% Hispanic	8
% Native American	0
% Pacific Islander	0
% Two or more races	5
% Race and/or ethnicity unknown	5
% international	19
# of countries represented	44

#40 BEST VALUE COLLEGE

ABOUT THE SCHOOL

Grinnell College is a smorgasbord of intellectual delights in a tiny, quintessential Iowa town that is surrounded by cornfields. The arts and sciences facilities here are world-class. The academic atmosphere is extremely challenging and stressful. Classes are hard and demanding. The ability to handle a lot of reading and writing is vital. Key features at Grinnell are its "open curriculum [and] low faculty-to-student ratio," which provide both academic freedom and better access to professors, in turn allowing students to push themselves further. Undergrads here often complete work that would be considered graduate-level at other institutions. At the same time, there isn't much in the way of competition; students bring the pressure on themselves. Classes are small and intimate. Professors are crazy accessible. The curriculum is completely open except for a freshman tutorial—a writing-intensive course that introduces academic thinking and research. Beyond that, there are no subject- matter requirements for obtaining a degree from Grinnell, as the school "encourages liberal arts academic exploration." Students are free to design their own paths to graduation. Mentored advanced projects provide a chance to work closely with a faculty member on scholarly research or the creation of a work of art. Fifty to 60 percent of every graduating class is accepted onto a wide range of off-campus study programs both domestic and abroad. On campus, Scholars' Convocation enriches the college's academic community by bringing notable speakers to campus.

Grinnell College

Financial Aid: 641-269-3250 • E-mail: askgrin@grinnell.edu • Website: www.grinnell.edu

BANG FOR YOUR BUCK

Grinnell was founded by a group of Iowa pioneers in 1843, and that pioneering spirit still informs the college's approach to education. Grinnell's endowment these days is in the range of a billion dollars. That's billion, with a B, so admission here is in no way contingent on your economic situation. If you can get admitted here (no small feat), Grinnell will meet 100 percent of your financial need. The college is even moving to meet the full demonstrated institutional need of select international students. In a typical year, Grinnell awards over ten times more in grants than in loans. As part of the culture of alumni support, the college also raises specific funds from alumni to reduce, at the time of graduation, the indebtedness of seniors who have demonstrated a solid work ethic both academically and cocurricularly. Eligible students may designate one summer devoted to either an approved Grinnell-sponsored internship or summer research at Grinnell. In return, the expected summer earnings contribution of $2,500 will be eliminated for that one summer only. One student notes that "on-campus employment is virtually guaranteed."

STUDENT LIFE

Undergrads here seem to live at fairly frenzied clip. Indeed, "Grinnellians pride themselves on working hard, but also playing hard." And, thankfully, there's plenty of fun to be had. To begin with, "every weekend there are movies, concerts, and parties planned and run by students all going on in addition to other events planned by the college." Additionally, "a lot of students volunteer for fun at the animal shelter or our Liberal Arts in Prison program, or they join an organization to learn something new or change the world." Moreover, Grinnell definitely has a party scene, one that is viewed as "thriving, quirky, welcoming, and casual." And "even [when it does get] raucous...you will

ACADEMICS

Academic Rating	98
% students returning for sophomore year	93
% students graduating within 4 years	78
% students graduating within 6 years	84
Calendar	Semester
Student/faculty ratio	9:1
Profs interesting rating	99
Profs accessible rating	98

Most classes have 10–19 students. Most lab/discussion sessions have fewer than 10 students.

MOST POPULAR MAJORS

Biology/Biological Sciences, General; Economics, General; Political Science and Government, General

SELECTIVITY

Admissions Rating	96
# of applicants	7,349
% of applicants accepted	24
% of acceptees attending	26
# offered a place on the wait list	1,447
% accepting a place on wait list	50
% admitted from wait list	5
# of early decision applicants	353
% accepted early decision	58

FRESHMAN PROFILE	
Range SAT EBRW	670–745
Range SAT Math	700–785
Range ACT Composite	30–34
# submitting SAT scores	223
% submitting SAT scores	48
# submitting ACT scores	240
% submitting ACT scores	52
% graduated top 10% of class	68
% graduated top 25% of class	90
% graduated top 50% of class	99

DEADLINES	
Early decision	
Deadline	11/15
Notification	mid Dec
Other ED Deadline	1/1
Other ED Notification	late Jan
Early action	
Deadline	Notification
Regular	
Deadline	1/15
Notification	4/1
Nonfall registration?	No

[still] find people discussing 17th century literature or debating hot political topics." Overall, Grinnell provides "an amazing mix of silly times and very smart people."

CAREER

Grinnell undergrads do pretty well for themselves. Indeed, according to PayScale.com, the median starting salary for these students is $53,400. Students are thankful that the "Grinnell College alumni...are very proactive in providing students with assistance in the form of...employment, or mentorship." And, even if undergrads are unable to hook up with an alum, they can always turn to the Center for Careers, Life and Service (CLS). Besides interview prep, job shadowing programs, and on-campus recruiting, the center also houses the Service Learning and Civic Engagement Program, which helps students find co-curricular service learning opportunities. Grinnellink internships are specific (and paid!) opportunities with college alumni and friends and are open exclusively to Grinnell students. Off-campus study experiences, whether abroad like Grinnell-in-London, or at a U.S. location like Grinnell-in Washington, offer more ways for experiential learning to complement coursework.

GENERAL INFO

Activities: Campus Ministries; Choral groups; Concert band; Dance; Drama/theater; International Student Organization; Jazz band; Literary magazine; Model UN; Music ensembles; Musical theater; Pep band; Radio station; Student government; Student newspaper; Student-run film society; Symphony orchestra; Yearbook. 105 registered organizations, 2 honor societies, 5 religious organizations, 0 fraternities, 0 sororities, on campus. **Athletics (Intercollegiate):** *Men:* baseball, basketball, cross-country, diving, football, golf, soccer, swimming, tennis, track/field (outdoor), track/field (indoor). *Women:* basketball, cross-country, diving, golf, soccer, softball, swimming, tennis, track/field (outdoor), track/field (indoor), volleyball. **On-Campus Highlights:** Two buildings on campus are listed on the National Register of Historic Places: Mears Cottage and Goodnow Hall, Faulconer Gallery, Joe Rosenfield '25 Center, Bucksbaum Center for the Arts, Charles Benson Bear '39 Recreation and Athletic Center. **Environmental Initiatives:** All new buildings are LEED certified.

Grinnell College

FINANCIAL AID

Students should submit: CSS/Financial Aid PROFILE; FAFSA; Noncustodial PROFILE. Priority filing deadline is 1/15. The Princeton Review suggests that all financial aid forms be submitted as soon as possible after October 1. *Need-based scholarships/grants offered*: College/university scholarship or grant aid from institutional funds; Federal Pell; Private scholarships; SEOG; State scholarships/grants. *Loan aid offered*: Direct PLUS loans; Direct Subsidized Stafford Loans; Direct Unsubsidized Stafford Loans. Applicants will be notified of awards on or about 4/1. Federal Work-Study Program available. Institutional employment available.

BOTTOM LINE

The tab for tuition, room and board, fees, and books and supplies at Grinnell comes to about $68,546. About 86 percent of Grinnell's first-year students receive some form of financial aid, though. On average, need-based financial aid packages for undergrads includes a $43,783 scholarship.

FINANCIAL FACTS	
Financial Aid Rating	99
Annual tuition	$53,872
Room and board	$13,292
Required fees	$482
Books and supplies	$900
Average frosh need-based scholarship	$45,007
Average UG need-based scholarship	$43,783
% needy frosh rec. need-based scholarship or grant aid	100
% needy UG rec. need-based scholarship or grant aid	100
% needy frosh rec. non-need-based scholarship or grant aid	13
% needy UG rec. non-need-based scholarship or grant aid	12
% needy frosh rec. need-based self-help aid	87
% needy UG rec. need-based self-help aid	88
% frosh rec. any financial aid	86
% UG rec. any financial aid	86
% UG borrow to pay for school	60
Average cumulative indebtedness	$18,694
% frosh need fully met	100
% ugrads need fully met	100
Average % of frosh need met	100
Average % of ugrad need met	100

CAREER INFORMATION FROM PAYSCALE.COM	
ROI Rating	92
Bachelors and No Higher	
Median starting salary	$53,400
Median mid-career salary	$96,500
At Least Bachelors	
Median starting salary	$56,300
Median mid-career salary	$110,700
Alumni with high job meaning	52%
Degrees awarded in STEM subjects	41%

Grinnell College

Hamilton College

Office of Admission, Clinton, NY 13323 • Admissions: 315-859-4421 • Fax: 315-859-4457

CAMPUS LIFE
Quality of Life Rating	86
Fire Safety Rating	92
Green Rating	60*
Type of school	Private
Environment	Rural

STUDENTS
Total undergrad enrollment	1,905
% male/female	47/53
% from out of state	71
% frosh from public high school	56
% frosh live on campus	100
% ugrads live on campus	100
# of fraternities	
(% ugrad men join)	8 (17)
# of sororities	
(% ugrad women join)	4 (8)
% African American	4
% Asian	7
% Caucasian	63
% Hispanic	10
% Native American	<1
% Pacific Islander	0
% Two or more races	5
% Race and/or ethnicity unknown	5
% international	7
# of countries represented	46

#45 BEST VALUE COLLEGE

ABOUT THE SCHOOL

Founded more than two centuries ago, upstate New York's Hamilton College offers forty-three majors (called concentrations) to its 1,850 undergraduates, each featuring an "emphasis on effective communication" and independent thinking. That emphasis is encouraged through an open curriculum that lets students "jump right into the fields they are interested in without having to fulfill meaningless distribution requirements." The guiding principles of a Hamilton education just require students to pass at least three writing-intensive courses, to pass a quantitative and symbolic reasoning course, and to complete a Senior Project in their concentration. Along the way, "class trips, study abroad, and experiential learning are all big focuses for Hamilton," and "professors also often give students an opportunity to present and teach the class." Additionally, "every course is designed with an emphasis on teaching either written or oral communication," so "classes are very small and discussion based." One student sums it up: "Learning in an environment where risk-taking and unconventional thinking are not only permitted, but encouraged, is a liberating experience." Another adds, "Hamilton's best trait is its ability to foster bold choice [on the part of] its students."

BANG FOR YOUR BUCK

Hamilton considers itself a "school of opportunity" and it wants to make sure that such an education is accessible and affordable. So, around half of all students receive financial aid, and the school meets the full demonstrated

Hamilton College

Financial Aid: 800-859-4413 • E-mail: admission@hamilton.edu • Website: www.hamilton.edu

need for a student's entire four years. Though Hamilton does not offer merit-based scholarships, it does prioritize need-based aid, and Hamilton endowed scholarships (which come from alumni and friends of the college) account for about 40 percent of the $46 million scholarship budget. Students with need receive this money automatically, without any further work required beyond their application. These "amazing financial aid … resources" extend beyond traditional allotment: "I received extremely generous financial aid, and whenever I couldn't afford books for my classes or my medical bills, I reached out to Hamilton's student fund committee and they covered these costs, no questions asked," says a student.

STUDENT LIFE

Hamilton students keep busy: "A lot of people have on-campus jobs or club meetings or sports" due to the "endless amount of activities ranging from athletics to music to anything imaginable." People will often "hang out in their residence hall common rooms, or Cafe Opus, to do work and catch up with their friends." When the weather cooperates, students will "sit outside for meals or in Adirondack chairs scattered around campus doing work." As it's located in a small town, Hamilton's isolation can "sometimes feel like a drawback," but mostly "breeds a tight-knit community" where "all the activities you need are on school grounds." If you're "looking for a bigger adventure, you can take a trip somewhere else," such as the nearby Adirondacks.

CAREER

The Career Center (and its more than seventy student employees) is available for general advising as well as résumé and cover letter guidance. The center also hosts specialized programs all throughout the years, including a regular table set up on campus that offers free donuts in exchange for information

ACADEMICS

Academic Rating	95
% students returning for sophomore year	94
% students graduating within 4 years	88
% students graduating within 6 years	93
Calendar	Semester
Student/faculty ratio	9:1
Profs interesting rating	94
Profs accessible rating	95

Most classes have 10–19 students. Most lab/discussion sessions have 10–19 students.

MOST POPULAR MAJORS
Economics; Mathematics; Government

SELECTIVITY

Admissions Rating	97
# of applicants	6,240
% of applicants accepted	21
% of acceptees attending	36
# offered a place on the wait list	1,406
% accepting a place on wait list	54
% admitted from wait list	4
# of early decision applicants	581
% accepted early decision	42

FRESHMAN PROFILE

Range SAT EBRW	670–740
Range SAT Math	680–770
Range ACT Composite	31–34
# submitting SAT scores	243
% submitting SAT scores	51
# submitting ACT scores	205
% submitting ACT scores	43
% graduated top 10% of class	81
% graduated top 25% of class	98
% graduated top 50% of class	100

DEADLINES

Early decision	
Deadline	11/15
Notification	12/15
Other ED Deadline	1/1
Other ED Notification	2/15
Regular	
Deadline	1/1
Notification	4/1
Nonfall registration?	Yes

about students' latest internships. And the students always have something to share in that regard: "Everyone gets internships here, and there are a lot of workshops … to help you find and apply to all sorts of jobs and programs," says one. Indeed, 83 percent of seniors graduate with experience from at least two internships. Professors are also helpful in achieving that number, providing "a lot of opportunities to network and work on career-building skills," and their focus on thinking critically and developing meaningful connections are "raw skills [that] will carry anyone who capitalizes on [them] to success."

GENERAL INFO

Activities: Campus Ministries; Choral groups; Dance; Drama/theater; International Student Organizations; Jazz band; Literary magazine; Model UN; Music ensembles; Musical theater; Radio station; Student government; Student newspaper; Student-run film society; Symphony orchestra; Yearbook. 218 registered organizations, 8 honor societies, 8 religious organizations, 8 fraternities, 4 sororities, on campus. **Athletics (Intercollegiate):** *Men:* baseball, basketball, crew/rowing, cross-country, diving, football, golf, ice hockey, lacrosse, soccer, squash, swimming, tennis, track/field (outdoor), track/field (indoor). *Women:* basketball, crew/rowing, cross-country, diving, field hockey, golf, ice hockey, lacrosse, soccer, softball, squash, swimming, tennis, track/field (outdoor), track/field (indoor), volleyball. **On-Campus Highlights:** Kennedy Center for Theatre and the Studio Arts (2014), Blood Fitness and Dance Center (2006), Wellin Museum of Art (2012), Sadove Student Center (2010), Root Glen/Outdoor Leadership Center (2006), Johnson Center for Health and Wellness (2019).

Hamilton College

FINANCIAL AID

Students should submit: CSS/Financial Aid PROFILE; FAFSA; Institution's own financial aid form; Noncustodial PROFILE. Priority filing deadline is 1/15. The Princeton Review suggests that all financial aid forms be submitted as soon as possible after October 1. *Need-based scholarships/grants offered*: College/university scholarship or grant aid from institutional funds; Federal Pell; Private scholarships; SEOG; State scholarships/grants. *Loan aid offered*: Direct PLUS loans; Direct Subsidized Stafford Loans; Direct Unsubsidized Stafford Loans. Applicants will be notified of awards on or about 4/1. Federal Work-Study Program available. Institutional employment available.

BOTTOM LINE

Hamilton College is one of the nation's top liberal arts colleges, and you certainly get what you pay for here. The total cost of tuition, room and board, and everything else adds up to about $71,890 per year. Hamilton is need-blind and pledges to meet 100 percent of students' demonstrated need.

FINANCIAL FACTS	
Financial Aid Rating	97
Annual tuition	$55,970
Room and board	$14,360
Required fees	$560
Books and supplies	$1,000
Average frosh need-based scholarship	$45,196
Average UG need-based scholarship	$43,434
% needy frosh rec. need-based scholarship or grant aid	100
% needy UG rec. need-based scholarship or grant aid	100
% needy frosh rec. non-need-based scholarship or grant aid	0
% needy UG rec. non-need-based scholarship or grant aid	0
% needy frosh rec. need-based self-help aid	79
% needy UG rec. need-based self-help aid	78
% frosh rec. any financial aid	56
% UG rec. any financial aid	52
% UG borrow to pay for school	44
Average cumulative indebtedness	$20,582
% frosh need fully met	100
% ugrads need fully met	100
Average % of frosh need met	100
Average % of ugrad need met	100

CAREER INFORMATION FROM PAYSCALE.COM	
ROI Rating	92
Bachelors and No Higher	
Median starting salary	$62,600
Median mid-career salary	$108,100
At Least Bachelors	
Median starting salary	$63,700
Median mid-career salary	$116,400
Alumni with high job meaning	51%
Degrees awarded in STEM subjects	25%

Hamilton College

Harvard College

86 Brattle Street, Cambridge, MA 02138 • Admissions: 617-495-1551 • Fax: 617-495-8821

CAMPUS LIFE

Quality of Life Rating	79
Fire Safety Rating	60*
Green Rating	60*
Type of school	Private
Environment	City

STUDENTS

Total undergrad enrollment	6,722
% male/female	51/49
% from out of state	84
% frosh from public high school	58
% frosh live on campus	100
% ugrads live on campus	97
# of fraternities	0
# of sororities	0
% African American	9
% Asian	21
% Caucasian	39
% Hispanic	11
% Native American	<1
% Pacific Islander	<1
% Two or more races	7
% Race and/or ethnicity unknown	2
% international	12
# of countries represented	100

#8 BEST VALUE COLLEGE

ABOUT THE SCHOOL

At Harvard College you will find a faculty of academic rock stars, intimate classes, a cosmically vast curriculum, world-class facilities (including what is arguably the best college library in the United States), a diverse student body from across the country and around the world ("The level of achievement is unbelievable"), and a large endowment that allows the college to support undergraduate and faculty research projects. When you graduate, you'll have unlimited bragging rights and the full force and prestige of the Harvard brand working for you for the rest of your life. All first-year students live on campus, and Harvard guarantees housing to its students for all four years. All freshmen also eat in the same place, Annenberg Hall, and there are adult residential advisers living in the halls to help students learn their way around the vast resources of this "beautiful, fun, historic, and academically alive place." Social and extracurricular activities at Harvard are pretty much unlimited: "Basically, if you want to do it, Harvard either has it or has the money to give to you so you can start it." With more than 400 student organizations on campus, whatever you are looking for, you can find it here. The off-campus scene is hopping, too. Believe it or not, Harvard kids do party, and "there is a vibrant social atmosphere on campus and between students and the local community," with Cambridge offering art and music, not to mention more than a couple of great bars. Downtown Boston and all of its attractions is just a short ride across the Charles River on the "T" (subway).

Harvard College

Financial Aid: 617-495-1581 • E-mail: college@fas.harvard.edu • Website: www.college.harvard.edu

BANG FOR YOUR BUCK

Harvard is swimming in cash, and financial need simply isn't a barrier to admission. In fact, the admissions staff here often looks especially favorably upon applicants who have stellar academic and extracurricular records despite having to overcome considerable financial obstacles. About 90 percent of the students who request financial aid qualify for it. If you qualify, 100 percent of your financial need will be met. Just so we're clear: by aid, we mean free money—not loans. Harvard doesn't do loans. Instead, Harvard asks families that qualify for financial aid to contribute somewhere between zero and 10 percent of their annual income each year. If your family income is less than $65,000, the odds are very good that you and your family won't pay a dime for you to attend. It's also worth noting that Harvard extends its commitment to full financial aid for all four undergraduate years. Families with higher incomes facing unusual financial challenges may also qualify for need–based scholarship assistance. Home equity is no longer considered in Harvard's assessment of the expected parent contribution.

ACADEMICS

Academic Rating	81
% students returning for sophomore year	98
% students graduating within 4 years	87
% students graduating within 6 years	98
Calendar	Semester
Student/faculty ratio	7:1
Profs interesting rating	61
Profs accessible rating	61

Most classes have fewer than 10 students. Most lab/discussion sessions have 20–29 students.

MOST POPULAR MAJORS

Social Sciences, General; Economics, General; Political Science and Government, General

SELECTIVITY

Admissions Rating	99
# of applicants	42,749
% of applicants accepted	5
% of acceptees attending	82
# offered a place on the wait list	0

STUDENT LIFE

As you might expect, ambition and achievement are the ties that bind at Harvard. Most every student can be summed up in three bullet points: "Works really hard. Doesn't sleep. Involved in a million extracurriculars." Diversity is found in all aspects of life, from ethnicities to religion to ideology, and "there is a lot of tolerance and acceptance at Harvard for individuals of all races, religions, socioeconomic backgrounds, life styles, etc." Campus on the Charles River is a "beautiful, fun, historic, and academically alive place," with close to 400 student organizations to stoke your interests. "Arts First Week" annually showcases the talents of the arts and culture groups, and students gather each June (in Connecticut) for the Harvard-Yale Regatta. Nearby Cambridge and Boston are quintessential college towns, so students

Range SAT EBRW	720–780
Range SAT Math	740–800
Range ACT Composite	33–35
# submitting SAT scores	1,146
% submitting SAT scores	69
# submitting ACT scores	772
% submitting ACT scores	47
Average HS GPA	4.2
% graduated top 10% of class	94
% graduated top 25% of class	99
% graduated top 50% of class	100

DEADLINES

Early action	
Deadline	11/1
Notification	12/15
Regular	
Deadline	1/1
Notification	4/1
Nonfall registration?	No

never lack for options. As one satisfied undergrad puts it, "Boredom does not exist here. There are endless opportunities and endless passionate people to do them with."

CAREER

As befits a school known for graduating presidents, CEOs, and literary legends, Harvard's Office of Career Service is tireless in working to educate, connect, and advise students about their options and opportunities. At its three locations, OCS offers specialized resources for finding internships, jobs, global opportunities, research and funding opportunities, or just getting your foot in the door of the field of your choice. Crimson Careers lists jobs and internships tailored for Harvard students only, including listings posted by alumni, and an impressive career fair and expo lineup ensures students always have access to hiring companies. Alumni who visited PayScale.com report a median starting salary of $74,800 and 57 percent believe their work makes the world a better place.

GENERAL INFO

Activities: Campus Ministries; Choral groups; Concert band; Dance; Drama/theater; International Student Organization; Jazz band; Literary magazine; Marching band; Model UN; Music ensembles; Musical theater; Opera; Pep band; Radio station; Student government; Student newspaper; Student-run film society; Symphony orchestra; Television station; Yearbook. 451 registered organizations, 1 honor society, 25 religious organizations, 0 fraternities, 0 sororities, on campus. **Athletics (Intercollegiate):** *Men:* baseball, basketball, crew/rowing, cross-country, diving, fencing, football, golf, ice hockey, lacrosse, sailing, skiing (downhill/alpine), skiing nordic cross-country, soccer, squash, swimming, tennis, track/field (outdoor), track/field (indoor), volleyball, water polo, wrestling. *Women:* basketball, crew/rowing, cross-country, diving, fencing, field hockey, golf, ice hockey, lacrosse, sailing, skiing (downhill/alpine), skiing nordic cross-country, soccer, softball, squash, swimming, tennis, track/field (outdoor), track/field (indoor), volleyball, water polo. **On-Campus Highlights:** Widener Library, Harvard Yard, Fogg Museum, Annenburg/Memorial Hall, Science Center. **Environmental Initiatives:** Campus-wide Sustainability Principles that provide a broad vision to guide University operations and planning (adopted in 2004) and an

Harvard College

established University-wide Office for Sustainability (green.harvard.edu) that oversees implementation of Harvard's GHG reduction goal and sustainability commitments. The University has had a formal sustainability office for a decade, initially created by a faculty and staff initiative with strong student involvement.

FINANCIAL AID

Students should submit: Business/Farm Supplement; CSS/Financial Aid PROFILE; FAFSA; Noncustodial PROFILE. Priority filing deadline is 2/1. The Princeton Review suggests that all financial aid forms be submitted as soon as possible after October 1. *Need-based scholarships/grants offered*: College/university scholarship or grant aid from institutional funds; Federal Pell; Private scholarships; SEOG; State scholarships/grants. *Loan aid offered*: Direct PLUS loans; Direct Subsidized Stafford Loans; Direct Unsubsidized Stafford Loans. Applicants will be notified of awards on or about 4/1. Federal Work-Study Program available. Institutional employment available.

BOTTOM LINE

The sticker price to attend Harvard is as exorbitant as its opportunities. Tuition, fees, room and board, and expenses cost about $63,025 a year. However, financial aid here is so unbelievably ample and generous that you just shouldn't worry about that. The hard part about going to Harvard is getting in. If you can accomplish that, Harvard will help you find a way to finance your education. Period.

FINANCIAL FACTS	
Financial Aid Rating	92
Annual tuition	$46,340
Room and board	$17,160
Required fees	$4,080
Books and supplies	$1,000
Average frosh need-based scholarship	$56,771
Average UG need-based scholarship	$54,001
% needy frosh rec. need-based scholarship or grant aid	100
% needy UG rec. need-based scholarship or grant aid	100
% needy frosh rec. non-need-based scholarship or grant aid	0
% needy UG rec. non-need-based scholarship or grant aid	0
% needy frosh rec. need-based self-help aid	77
% needy UG rec. need-based self-help aid	85
% frosh rec. any financial aid	71
% UG rec. any financial aid	65
% UG borrow to pay for school	17
Average cumulative indebtedness	$13,372
% frosh need fully met	100
% ugrads need fully met	100
Average % of frosh need met	100
Average % of ugrad need met	100

CAREER INFORMATION FROM PAYSCALE.COM	
ROI Rating	96
Bachelors and No Higher	
Median starting salary	$74,800
Median mid-career salary	$146,800
At Least Bachelors	
Median starting salary	$77,700
Median mid-career salary	$156,500
Alumni with high job meaning	57%
Degrees awarded in STEM subjects	19%

Harvard College

Harvey Mudd College

301 Platt Boulevard, 301 Platt Blvd, Claremont, CA 91711-5990 • Admissions: 909-621-8011 • Fax: 909-621-8360

#3 BEST VALUE COLLEGE

CAMPUS LIFE

Quality of Life Rating	89
Fire Safety Rating	84
Green Rating	86
Type of school	Private
Environment	Town

STUDENTS

Total undergrad enrollment	889
% male/female	51/49
% from out of state	56
% frosh from public high school	67
% frosh live on campus	100
% ugrads live on campus	98
# of fraternities	0
# of sororities	0
% African American	3
% Asian	19
% Caucasian	31
% Hispanic	20
% Native American	<1
% Pacific Islander	<1
% Two or more races	11
% Race and/or ethnicity unknown	6
% international	10
# of countries represented	26

ABOUT THE SCHOOL

A member of the Claremont Consortium, Harvey Mudd shares resources with Pitzer, Scripps, Claremont McKenna, and Pomona Colleges. It is the "techie" school of the bunch and focuses on educating future scientists, engineers, and mathematicians. "Mudd is a place where everyone is literate in every branch of science." The college offers four-year degrees in chemistry, mathematics, physics, computer science, biology, and engineering, as well as interdisciplinary degrees in mathematical and computational biology, and a few joint majors for students seeking extra challenges. Harvey Mudd is "small, friendly, and tough. Professors and other students are very accessible. The honor code is an integral part of the college." The honor code is so entrenched in campus culture that the college entrusts the students to twenty-four-hour-per-day access to many buildings, including some labs, and permits take-home exams, specified either as open-book or closed-book, timed or untimed. "Our honor code really means something," insists one student. "It isn't just a stray sentence or two that got put into the student handbook; it's something that the students are really passionate about." Academics at Harvey Mudd may seem "excessive [and] soul-crushing," but there are "great people and community," nonetheless. In order to ensure that all students receive a well-rounded education, students enrolled at Harvey Mudd are required to take a core component of humanities courses. Research opportunities are literally limitless. The Clinic program is open to students of all majors, who collaborate to satisfy the requests of an actual company. Best of all, these opportunities are available without the cutthroat competition of other similar schools.

Harvey Mudd College

Financial Aid: 909-621-8055 • E-mail: admission@hmc.edu • Website: www.hmc.edu

BANG FOR YOUR BUCK

Harvey Mudd believes that college choice is more about fit than finances. That's why the college offers a robust program of need-based and merit-based awards to help insure that a Harvey Mudd education is accessible to all who qualify. Eighty-two percent of students receive financial aid, and 40 percent qualify for merit-based awards. In determining who will receive merit-based awards, the Office of Admission looks primarily at academic achievement—financial need is not considered. While these awards are granted independent of financial need, students who receive a merit-based award and are also eligible for need-based aid. Standout programs include the Harvey S. Mudd Merit Award, in which students receive a $40,000 scholarship distributed annually in the amount of $10,000 per year. The President's Scholars Program is a renewable, four-year, full-tuition scholarship that promotes excellence and diversity at Harvey Mudd by recognizing outstanding young men and women from populations that are traditionally underrepresented at HMC.

STUDENT LIFE

Mudders say they are united by "a brimming passion for science and a love of knowledge for its own sake." "All students are exceptionally intelligent and are able to perform their work in a professional manner." Beyond that, there's "a really diverse group of personalities" at Mudd, who are "not afraid to show their true colors" and who all have "a unique sense of humor." Students say they "are all friendly, smart, and talented, which brings us together. Upperclassmen look out for underclassmen, and students tend to bond together easily over difficult homework." In such a welcoming community, "students primarily fit in by not fitting in—wearing pink pirate hats, or skateboarding while playing harmonica, or practicing unicycle jousting are

ACADEMICS

Academic Rating	97
% students returning for sophomore year	97
% students graduating within 4 years	86
% students graduating within 6 years	96
Calendar	Semester
Student/faculty ratio	8:1
Profs interesting rating	98
Profs accessible rating	99

Most classes have fewer than 10 students. Most lab/discussion sessions have 10–19 students.

MOST POPULAR MAJORS

Computer and Information Sciences, General; Engineering, General; Physical Sciences, General

SELECTIVITY

Admissions Rating	98
# of applicants	4,101
% of applicants accepted	15
% of acceptees attending	39
# offered a place on the wait list	509
% accepting a place on wait list	64
% admitted from wait list	0
# of early decision applicants	465
% accepted early decision	19

all good ways to fit in perfectly," though it should be noted that several student have "never seen a dorm swordfight." The speed of the Wi-Fi network on campus has been deemed "great."

CAREER

Harvey Mudd College graduates who visit PayScale. com report a median starting salary of $88,800, and 55 percent of graduates feel their jobs have a lot of meaning in the world. Students feel that at Mudd, "the Office of Career Services finds more than enough summer internships," and one student in particular notes that one dedicated adviser "worked very hard to help me find a summer internship, calling many of his friends and passing around my resume." Students especially feel that their professors have been very helpful about finding them jobs and internships, and that Mudd provides "first-rate preparation for graduate study or (especially for the engineering major) success in the job market."

GENERAL INFO

Activities: Campus Ministries; Choral groups; Concert band; Dance; Drama/theater; International Student Organization; Jazz band; Literary magazine; Music ensembles; Radio station; Student government; Student newspaper; Symphony orchestra; Yearbook. 123 registered organizations, 4 honor societies, 6 religious organizations, 0 fraternities, 0 sororities, on campus. **Athletics (Intercollegiate):** *Men:* baseball, basketball, cross-country, diving, football, golf, soccer, swimming, tennis, track/field (outdoor), water polo. *Women:* basketball, cross-country, diving, golf, lacrosse, soccer, softball, swimming, tennis, track/field (outdoor), volleyball, water polo. **On-Campus Highlights:** Dorm Lounges, Platt Campus Center Living Room, Hoch Shanahan Dining Hall, Jay's Pizza Place, Linde Student Activities Center. **Environmental Initiatives:** In February 2008 Harvey Mudd College President Maria Klawe signed the American College & University Presidents' Climate Commitment and Harvey Mudd College Board of Trustees adopted HMC Sustainability Policy Statement. Additionally, the Board of Trustees passed a resolution where the standard for new buildings will be at least U.S. Green Building Council LEED Silver standard or equivalent and premium rated or ENERGY STAR certified products are purchased for use on campus where possible.

Harvey Mudd College

FINANCIAL AID

Students should submit: Business/Farm Supplement; CSS/Financial Aid PROFILE; FAFSA; Noncustodial PROFILE; State aid form. Priority filing deadline is 2/1. The Princeton Review suggests that all financial aid forms be submitted as soon as possible after October 1. *Need-based scholarships/grants offered*: College/university scholarship or grant aid from institutional funds; Federal Pell; Private scholarships; SEOG; State scholarships/grants. *Loan aid offered*: Direct PLUS loans; Direct Subsidized Stafford Loans; Direct Unsubsidized Stafford Loans. Applicants will be notified of awards on or about 4/1. Federal Work-Study Program available. Institutional employment available.

BOTTOM LINE

The retail price for tuition, room and board, and fees at Harvey Mudd ends up being a little more than $74,753 a year. Financial aid is plentiful here, though, so please don't let cost scare you away from applying. The average need-based scholarship is $42,182, and some students report receiving "excellent financial aid packages," including a "full-tuition scholarship."

FINANCIAL FACTS	
Financial Aid Rating	95
Annual tuition	$56,331
Room and board	$18,127
Required fees	$295
Books and supplies	$800
Average frosh need-based scholarship	$45,244
Average UG need-based scholarship	$42,182
% needy frosh rec. need-based scholarship or grant aid	96
% needy UG rec. need-based scholarship or grant aid	98
% needy frosh rec. non-need-based scholarship or grant aid	49
% needy UG rec. non-need-based scholarship or grant aid	43
% needy frosh rec. need-based self-help aid	99
% needy UG rec. need-based self-help aid	67
% frosh rec. any financial aid	74
% UG rec. any financial aid	71
% UG borrow to pay for school	46
Average cumulative indebtedness	$31,594
% frosh need fully met	100
% ugrads need fully met	100
Average % of frosh need met	100
Average % of ugrad need met	100

CAREER INFORMATION FROM PAYSCALE.COM	
ROI Rating	98
Bachelors and No Higher	
Median starting salary	$88,800
Median mid-career salary	$158,200
At Least Bachelors	
Median starting salary	$90,700
Median mid-career salary	$161,800
Alumni with high job meaning	55%
Degrees awarded in STEM subjects	85%

Harvey Mudd College

Haverford College

370 Lancaster Avenue, Haverford, PA 19041 • Admissions: 610-896-1350 • Fax: 610-896-1338

#34 BEST VALUE COLLEGE

CAMPUS LIFE

Quality of Life Rating	92
Fire Safety Rating	89
Green Rating	84
Type of school	Private
Environment	Town

STUDENTS

Total undergrad enrollment	1,305
% male/female	49/51
% from out of state	86
% frosh from public high school	60
% frosh live on campus	100
% ugrads live on campus	98
# of fraternities	0
# of sororities	0
% African American	7
% Asian	13
% Caucasian	53
% Hispanic	10
% Native American	<1
% Pacific Islander	0
% Two or more races	3
% Race and/or ethnicity unknown	3
% international	11
# of countries represented	36

ABOUT THE SCHOOL

Haverford College prides itself on the type of student that it draws. Academically minded and socially conscious are two words that often describe the typical Haverford student. Many are drawn to the college because of the accessibility of the professors and attention each student receives in the classroom. They don't have to fight for attention in a large lecture hall, since the most common class size is around fourteen students, and most professors live on or around campus and regularly invite students over for a lively talk over dinner or tea. There is also a larger sense of community on campus that is proliferated by the much-lauded honor code, which, according to one surprised student, "really works, and we actually do have things like closed-book, timed, take-home tests." Many find that the honor code (which includes proctorless exams) brings a certain type of student looking for a mature academic experience that helps prepare students by treating them as intellectual equals. In fact, even comparing grades with other students is discouraged, which tends to limit competitiveness and creates a greater sense of community. This sense of togetherness is prevalent throughout campus. Students are actively involved in student government since they have Plenary twice a year, where at least two-thirds of students must be present to make any changes to documents such as the student constitution and the honor code.

BANG FOR YOUR BUCK

Students with family income below $60,000/year will not have loans included in their financial aid package; loan levels for incomes above this line range from $1,500–$3,000 each year. Though they don't offer any merit-based aid, the school does meet the demonstrated need of

Haverford College

Financial Aid: 610-896-1350 • E-mail: admissions@haverford.edu • Website: www.haverford.edu

all students who were deemed eligible according to the college. Many students are able to find on-campus jobs to help support themselves. Haverford also encourages students to take internships through one of its three Academic Centers, which connect students with opportunities for paid research or internship experiences. The Center for Peace and Global Citizenship, for example, helps Haverfordians find fields that are simpatico with the college's ideals of trust and creating civically minded adults. The Center for Career and Professional Advising also has numerous programs that coordinate with alumni and help students expand their networking abilities and create job opportunities for when they graduate.

STUDENT LIFE

Many students describe themselves as a little "nerdy" or "quirky," but in the best possible way. "For the most part, Haverfordians are socially awkward, open to new friends, and looking for moral, political, [or] scholarly debate." As for the honor code in place at Haverford—"students who are not fully committed to abiding by Haverford's academic and social honor code will feel out of place. Students here are really in love with the atmosphere the honor code creates and feel uncomfortable with those who feel differently." Most are "liberal-minded" and "intellectual" and "want to save the world after they graduate." Some students found that "a lot of people were actually way more mainstream than I expected—not everyone is an awkward nerd with no social skills!" and in addition, "the party scene is open to everyone, and generally consists of music provided by student DJs, some dancing, the options to drink hard alcohol or beer (or soft drinks) and a generally fun environment."

ACADEMICS

Academic Rating	95
% students returning for sophomore year	97
% students graduating within 4 years	88
% students graduating within 6 years	92
Calendar	Semester
Student/faculty ratio	9:1
Profs interesting rating	87
Profs accessible rating	90

Most classes have fewer than 10 students. Most lab/discussion sessions have 10–19 students.

MOST POPULAR MAJORS

English Language and Literature, General; Biology/Biological Sciences, General; Psychology, General

SELECTIVITY

Admissions Rating	98
# of applicants	4,672
% of applicants accepted	19
% of acceptees attending	41
# offered a place on the wait list	1,349
% accepting a place on wait list	45
% admitted from wait list	2
# of early decision applicants	444
% accepted early decision	44

School Profiles ■ 139

CAREER

The typical Haverford College graduate has a median starting salary of around $59,300. Students feel that Haverford offers a great deal of internship opportunities, especially ones with financial support. Koshland Integrated Natural Sciences Center and the Hurford Center for Arts and Humanities act as grant-making organizations to fund internships and research experiences on-campus, locally in the city of Philadelphia, across the U.S. and abroad. The Integrated Natural Science Center offers "plenty of internship opportunities." The Center for Career and Professional Advising, with a mission to "empower" past and enrolled students to "translate their Haverford liberal arts education into a rewarding life," offers several job boards like CareerConnect as well as other helpful resources.

GENERAL INFO

Activities: Campus Ministries; Choral groups; Dance; Drama/theater; International Student Organization; Literary magazine; Music ensembles; Musical theater; Student government; Student newspaper; Yearbook. 145 registered organizations, 1 honor society, 14 religious organizations, 0 fraternities, 0 sororities, on campus. **Athletics (Intercollegiate):** *Men:* baseball, basketball, cross-country, fencing, lacrosse, soccer, squash, tennis, track/field (outdoor), track/field (indoor). *Women:* basketball, cross-country, fencing, field hockey, lacrosse, soccer, softball, squash, tennis, track/field (outdoor), track/field (indoor), volleyball. **On-Campus Highlights:** Integrated Natural Sciences Center, John Whitehead Campus Center, Cantor Fitzgerald Gallery, Arboretum, Douglas B. Gardner Athletic Center. **Environmental Initiatives:** The athletic center is the 1st gold LEED certified recreation center in the US (opened in 2005).

Haverford College

FINANCIAL AID

Students should submit: Business/Farm Supplement; CSS/Financial Aid PROFILE; FAFSA; Noncustodial PROFILE. Priority filing deadline is 2/1. The Princeton Review suggests that all financial aid forms be submitted as soon as possible after October 1. *Need-based scholarships/grants offered*: College/university scholarship or grant aid from institutional funds; Federal Pell; SEOG; State scholarships/grants. *Loan aid offered*: Direct PLUS loans; Direct Subsidized Stafford Loans; Direct Unsubsidized Stafford Loans. Applicants will be notified of awards on or about 3/25. Federal Work-Study Program available. Institutional employment available.

BOTTOM LINE

Though the annual tuition is $54,100 per year, Haverford offers more than half of its students financial aid. The average cumulative indebtedness is around $11,000. The price may seem high on paper, but Haverford helps its students afford the education.

FINANCIAL FACTS

Financial Aid Rating	95
Annual tuition	$54,100
Room and board	$16,402
Required fees	$492
Average frosh need-based scholarship	$51,777
Average UG need-based scholarship	$51,198
% needy frosh rec. need-based scholarship or grant aid	100
% needy UG rec. need-based scholarship or grant aid	100
% needy frosh rec. non-need-based scholarship or grant aid	0
% needy UG rec. non-need-based scholarship or grant aid	0
% needy frosh rec. need-based self-help aid	92
% needy UG rec. need-based self-help aid	93
% frosh rec. any financial aid	48
% UG rec. any financial aid	47
% UG borrow to pay for school	36
Average cumulative indebtedness	$11,000
% frosh need fully met	100
% ugrads need fully met	100
Average % of frosh need met	100
Average % of ugrad need met	100

CAREER INFORMATION FROM PAYSCALE.COM

ROI Rating	93
Bachelors and No Higher	
Median starting salary	$59,300
Median mid-career salary	$112,300
At Least Bachelors	
Median starting salary	$60,700
Median mid-career salary	$137,300
Alumni with high job meaning	57%
Degrees awarded in STEM subjects	36%

Haverford College

Johns Hopkins University

Office of Undergraduate Admissions, Mason Hall, 3400 N. Charles Street, Baltimore, MD 21218 • Admissions: 410-516-8171

#37 BEST VALUE COLLEGE

CAMPUS LIFE	
Quality of Life Rating	90
Fire Safety Rating	98
Green Rating	94
Type of school	Private
Environment	Metropolis

STUDENTS	
Total undergrad enrollment	5,304
% male/female	48/52
% from out of state	90
% frosh from public high school	56
% frosh live on campus	99
% ugrads live on campus	51
# of fraternities	
(% ugrad men join)	11 (18)
# of sororities	
(% ugrad women join)	13 (27)
% African American	7
% Asian	27
% Caucasian	30
% Hispanic	15
% Native American	<1
% Pacific Islander	<1
% Two or more races	6
% Race and/or ethnicity unknown	6
% international	10
# of countries represented	65

ABOUT THE SCHOOL

Without a doubt, Johns Hopkins University's reputation for academic rigor and its wide array of programs in the sciences and humanities make it a magnet for its top-notch students. In addition to its lauded biochemical engineering, international studies, and writing programs, this research university also offers opportunities for its students to study at its other divisions, including the Peabody Conservatory, the Nitze School of Advanced International Studies, the Carey Business School, and the Bloomberg School of Public Health. Students appreciate the school's flexible curriculum, small class size, and emphasis on academic exploration and hands-on learning. Around two-thirds of the students are involved in some kind of research opportunity, and an equal amount of students complete internships. Many of the distinguished professors at Johns Hopkins often serve as mentors and collaborators on these research projects. According to one student, "Johns Hopkins puts you shoulder-to-shoulder with some of the greatest minds in the world while promoting a work ethic that forces you to push yourself to your intellectual limits."

BANG FOR YOUR BUCK

To apply for financial aid, students must submit the FAFSA. Johns Hopkins distributes more than 90 percent of its financial aid awards on the basis of need and also provides need- and merit-based scholarships, including the Hodson Trust Scholarship, Bloomberg Scholarship, Clark Scholarship for engineers, and the Daniels-Rosen First Generation Scholarship. Along with financial aid, students receive a lot of support from the school's Career Center

Johns Hopkins University

Fax: 410-516-6025 • Financial Aid: 410-516-8028 • E-mail: gotojhu@jhu.edu • Website: www.jhu.edu

and Office of Pre-Professional Programs and Advising, as well as the extensive and loyal alumni network, to help them tackle their career-development and postgraduation goals.

STUDENT LIFE

For some reason, Hopkins developed a reputation as a school where "studies are more important than having fun." However, many undergrads here balk at that notion and insist that it couldn't be further from the truth. Indeed, while the academics are certainly rigorous there's also plenty of fun to be had. As one international studies major asserts, "There's never a dull moment at Johns Hopkins: you just have to step outside your room and look for five seconds." For starters, there are plenty of "free on-campus movies, plays, dance and a cappella performances" to catch. Additionally, the MSE symposium "always has interesting speakers (like Will Ferrell)." Moreover, about "one fourth of the school population is involved in Greek life." Of course, should students (temporarily) grow weary of campus life, Hodson Trust Scholarship, Bloomberg Scholarship, Clark Scholarship for engineers, and the Daniels-Rosen First Generation Scholarship. And, as an added bonus, D.C. and Philadelphia are both roughly an hour away.

CAREER

If you asked Hopkins undergrads to summarize their career services office in one word, it would likely be "awesome." And that's no surprise. After all, when the median starting salary for graduates is $67,200 (according to PayScale.com), you know the school is doing something right. The Career Center truly bends over backwards to help students prepare for the job market. With Career Academies in arts, media, and marketing;

ACADEMICS

Academic Rating	95
% students returning for sophomore year	98
% students graduating within 4 years	88
% students graduating within 6 years	94
Calendar	4-1-4
Student/faculty ratio	7:1
Profs interesting rating	82
Profs accessible rating	82
Most classes have 10–19 students.	

MOST POPULAR MAJORS

Bioengineering and Biomedical Engineering; Neuroscience; Public Health, General

SELECTIVITY

Admissions Rating	99
# of applicants	29,129
% of applicants accepted	11
% of acceptees attending	43
# offered a place on the wait list	3,555
% accepting a place on wait list	61
% admitted from wait list	9
# of early decision applicants	2,023
% accepted early decision	30

consulting; finance; health sciences; nonprofit and government; and STEM and innovation, the Career Center provides students with employer connections and industry-specific knowledge. Impressively, undergrads can request customized workshops on any career-related topic they deem important. They can also participate in programs and internships during intersession, the university's winter semester. Locally, some popular internships are at Baltimore-based Under Armour as well as T. Rowe Price and the Baltimore Sun newspaper. In addition, undergrads can receive more traditional guidance such as resume and cover letter writing, mock interviews, and networking opportunities.

GENERAL INFO

Activities: Campus Ministries; Choral groups; Concert band; Dance; Drama/theater; International Student Organization; Jazz band; Literary magazine; Model UN; Music ensembles; Musical theater; Opera; Pep band; Radio station; Student government; Student newspaper; Student-run film society; Symphony orchestra; Yearbook. 422 registered organizations, 13 honor societies, 16 religious organizations, 11 fraternity, 13 sororities, on campus. **Athletics (Intercollegiate):** *Men:* baseball, basketball, cross-country, diving, fencing, football, lacrosse, soccer, swimming, tennis, track/field (outdoor), track/field (indoor), water polo, wrestling. *Women:* basketball, cross-country, diving, fencing, field hockey, lacrosse, soccer, swimming, tennis, track/field (outdoor), track/field (indoor), volleyball. **On-Campus Highlights:** Brody Learning Commons, Gilman Hall, Undergraduate Teaching Labs, Ralph S. O'Connor Recreation Center, Fresh Food Cafe. **Environmental Initiatives:** Comprehensive climate commitment includes reaching a 51% reduction in GHG by 2025, investing over $73 million in GHG reduction projects, and seed grants for climate researchers.

FINANCIAL AID

Students should submit: CSS/Financial Aid PROFILE; FAFSA; Noncustodial PROFILE. Priority filing deadline is 1/15. The Princeton Review suggests that all financial aid forms be submitted as soon as possible after October 1. *Need-based scholarships/ grants offered*: College/university scholarship or grant aid from institutional funds; Federal Pell; Private scholarships; SEOG; State scholarships/grants. *Loan aid offered*: Direct PLUS loans; Direct Subsidized Stafford Loans; Direct Unsubsidized Stafford Loans. Applicants will be notified of awards on or about 4/1. Federal Work-Study Program available. Institutional employment available.

BOTTOM LINE

Johns Hopkins tuition fees hover at the $53,740 mark, with an additional $15,836 for room and board. This does not include books, supplies, personal expenses, or transportation. The average undergraduate need-based scholarship totals $44,147.

FINANCIAL FACTS	
Financial Aid Rating	94
Annual tuition	$53,740
Room and board	$15,836
Required fees	$500
Books and supplies	$1,240
Average frosh need-based scholarship	$47,492
Average UG need-based scholarship	$44,147
% needy frosh rec. need-based scholarship or grant aid	100
% needy UG rec. need-based scholarship or grant aid	99
% needy frosh rec. non-need-based scholarship or grant aid	16
% needy UG rec. non-need-based scholarship or grant aid	14
% needy frosh rec. need-based self-help aid	83
% needy UG rec. need-based self-help aid	87
% frosh rec. any financial aid	67
% UG rec. any financial aid	62
% UG borrow to pay for school	46
Average cumulative indebtedness	$25,697
% frosh need fully met	100
% ugrads need fully met	100
Average % of frosh need met	100
Average % of ugrad need met	100

CAREER INFORMATION FROM PAYSCALE.COM	
ROI Rating	93
Bachelors and No Higher	
Median starting salary	$67,200
Median mid-career salary	$117,100
At Least Bachelors	
Median starting salary	$70,500
Median mid-career salary	$126,900
Alumni with high job meaning	59%
Degrees awarded in STEM subjects	31%

John Hopkins University

Lafayette College

118 Markle Hall, Easton, PA 18042 • Admissions: 610-330-5100 • Fax: 610-330-5355

#53 BEST VALUE COLLEGE

CAMPUS LIFE

Quality of Life Rating	86
Fire Safety Rating	91
Green Rating	91
Type of school	Private
Environment	City

STUDENTS

Total undergrad enrollment	2,616
% male/female	48/52
% from out of state	81
% frosh from public high school	53
% frosh live on campus	100
% ugrads live on campus	92
# of fraternities	
(% ugrad men join)	3 (24)
# of sororities	
(% ugrad women join)	6 (34)
% African American	5
% Asian	4
% Caucasian	66
% Hispanic	7
% Native American	0
% Pacific Islander	0
% Two or more races	3
% Race and/or ethnicity unknown	5
% international	10
# of countries represented	57

ABOUT THE SCHOOL

Thinking across disciplines has defined the Lafayette College experience since its founding in 1826. With a total student body of 2,500, the focus is exclusively on undergraduates at this top liberal arts college. Lafayette graduates are well-trained in cross-disciplinary thinking and practical application. Here's what that looks like in real terms: computer science, art, biology, and neuroscience students might work together on brain research. A team of engineering, economics, psychology, and English students might take on a consulting project to redesign a new arts and cultural center in New Orleans. Lafayette sees the world through this interdisciplinary lens, and an ability to pursue those intersections in a practical way is a big reason Lafayette students land top research, academic, and employment opportunities. Students love that "even though the school is a small liberal arts college, its strengths in math, science, and engineering give it a very practical feel," and students also "think our greatest strength is our academic diversity." Undergrads are quite pleased to discover that "classes are mostly small and even our lecture classes don't get bigger than roughly seventy-five students." The small student-to-teacher ratio allows students to build a relationship with their professors and, according to a contented undergrad, "creates a spectacular class dynamic and sense of trust."

BANG FOR YOUR BUCK

Lafayette College is part of a very small group of colleges and universities throughout the United States that provide reduced-loan or no-loan financial aid awards to lower- and middle-income students who gain admission

Lafayette College

Financial Aid: 610-330-5055 • E-mail: admissions@lafayette.edu • Website: www.lafayette.edu

and seek financial assistance. Scholarships are also offered to top applicants (no additional application needed). There are two major merit-based programs: The Marquis Fellowship, worth $40,000 per year and the Marquis Scholarship, worth $24,000 per year. The majority of Marquis winners are selected solely on the merits presented in their application. Both awards come with special mentoring activities with faculty and other campus scholars, and an additional $4,000 scholarship for an off-campus course during the interim period (in winter or summer). These awards are based on superior academic performance and evidence of leadership and major contribution to school or community activities. Said one thankful student, "I was lucky enough to be chosen as a Marquis Scholar, giving me ample opportunity to study abroad."

STUDENT LIFE

Life at Lafayette "is everything you make it. There are as many or as few social opportunities as any one person can handle." With 250 registered student organizations—at a school with only roughly 2,500 students—there really is something for everyone. Greek life plays a role in the social scene, with six sororities and four fraternities on campus. Roughly 34 percent of women join a sorority and 23 percent of men join a fraternity. According to one Mathematics major, "Greek life and [Division I] sports teams dominate the social scene after freshmen year." Lafayette students "work hard...but also know how to have a good time" and "tend to go to a lot of events on campus[,] whether it be musicians or comedians." There is "very little to do in Easton itself," so most students stick to campus activities sponsored by the school, various sports teams, or one of the Greek houses.

ACADEMICS

Academic Rating	94
% students returning for sophomore year	93
% students graduating within 4 years	86
% students graduating within 6 years	90
Calendar	Semester
Student/faculty ratio	10:1
Profs interesting rating	89
Profs accessible rating	94

Most classes have 10–19 students. Most lab/discussion sessions have 10–19 students.

MOST POPULAR MAJORS
Mechanical Engineering; Biology/ Biological Sciences, General; Economics, General

SELECTIVITY

Admissions Rating	94
# of applicants	9,237
% of applicants accepted	29
% of acceptees attending	27
# offered a place on the wait list	2,332
% accepting a place on wait list	41
% admitted from wait list	0
# of early decision applicants	772
% accepted early decision	52

FRESHMAN PROFILE

Range SAT EBRW	620–700
Range SAT Math	630–735
Range ACT Composite	27–32
# submitting SAT scores	512
% submitting SAT scores	70
# submitting ACT scores	300
% submitting ACT scores	41
Average HS GPA	3.5
% graduated top 10% of class	52
% graduated top 25% of class	78
% graduated top 50% of class	96

DEADLINES

Early decision	
Deadline	11/15
Notification	12/15
Other ED Deadline	2/1
Other ED Notification	2/15
Regular	
Deadline	1/15
Notification	4/1
Nonfall registration?	No

CAREER

The median starting salary for a Lafayette graduate is roughly $66,500, according to PayScale.com, which also reports that 43 percent of Lafayette graduates consider their careers to be in keeping with making the world a better place. Popular jobs after graduation include project engineer, civil engineer, and marketing coordinator, with the most popular majors being Mechanical Engineering, Economics, and Civil Engineering. "Career counseling services start freshman year and are readily available to any student who wants to utilize them," says one Government/Law and Spanish double major. The Office of Career Services is "proud to be a national leader in career development," according to the school's website, and is ranked as one of the top twenty higher education career services offices. Students are encouraged to join Gateway, the school's four-year individualized career exploration program, and Lafayette's website reports that 85 percent of each undergraduate class signs up. A Psychology and Government double major praises the school's "strong career services program that provides excellent opportunities and...works closely with alumni to provide career exposure opportunities even to first year students."

GENERAL INFO

Activities: Campus Ministries; Choral groups; Concert band; Dance; Drama/theater; International Student Organization; Jazz band; Literary magazine; Model UN; Music ensembles; Musical theater; Pep band; Radio station; Student government; Student newspaper; Student-run film society; Symphony orchestra; Yearbook. 250 registered organizations, 17 honor societies, 8 religious organizations, 3 fraternities, 6 sororities, on campus. **Athletics (Intercollegiate):** *Men:* baseball, basketball, cheerleading, crew/rowing, cross-country, diving, equestrian sports, fencing, football, golf, gymnastics, ice hockey, lacrosse, soccer, softball, swimming, tennis, track/field (outdoor), track/field (indoor), volleyball, wrestling. *Women:* basketball, cheerleading, crew/rowing, cross-country, diving, equestrian sports, fencing, field hockey, golf, gymnastics, softball, swimming, tennis, track/field (outdoor), track/field (indoor), volleyball. **On-Campus Highlights:** Skillman and Kirby Libraries, Farinon College Center, Williams Center for the Arts, Kirby Sports Center, Williams Visual Arts Building (downtown). **Environmental Initiatives:** In addition to signing American College

Lafayette College

and University Presidents' Climate Commitment, three undertakings summarize the College's efforts towards responsible stewardship of the environment: Waste Reduction-Recycling, including composting.- Purchases of materials/goods made from recycled materials and/or virgin material that is recyclable and produced from renewable sources.

FINANCIAL AID

Students should submit: CSS/Financial Aid PROFILE; FAFSA; Noncustodial PROFILE. Priority filing deadline is 1/15. The Princeton Review suggests that all financial aid forms be submitted as soon as possible after October 1. *Need-based scholarships/ grants offered*: College/university scholarship or grant aid from institutional funds; Federal Pell; Private scholarships; SEOG; State scholarships/grants. *Loan aid offered*: Direct PLUS loans; Direct Subsidized Stafford Loans; Direct Unsubsidized Stafford Loans. Applicants will be notified of awards on or about 4/1. Federal Work-Study Program available. Institutional employment available.

BOTTOM LINE

The tab for tuition, fees, and room and board at Lafayette College comes to about $71,266 per year. Fortunately, Lafayette's strong endowment enables the college to aggressively offset costs for students. Financial aid packages are generous and the average need-based scholarship is $45,231. Students thoroughly understand and appreciate the value of a Lafayette College education. "It's no secret that the education is expensive, but I feel like I'm really getting my money's worth from Lafayette."

CAREER INFORMATION FROM PAYSCALE.COM	
ROI Rating	92
Bachelors and No Higher	
Median starting salary	$66,500
Median mid-career salary	$122,500
At Least Bachelors	
Median starting salary	$68,000
Median mid-career salary	$134,700
Alumni with high job meaning	43%
Degrees awarded in STEM subjects	47%

Lehigh University

27 Memorial Drive West, Bethlehem, PA 18015 • Admissions: 610-758-3100 • Fax: 610-758-4361

CAMPUS LIFE

Quality of Life Rating	89
Fire Safety Rating	97
Green Rating	95
Type of school	Private
Environment	City

STUDENTS

Total undergrad enrollment	5,030
% male/female	54/46
% from out of state	73
% frosh live on campus	99
% ugrads live on campus	63
# of fraternities	
(% ugrad men join)	14 (30)
# of sororities	
(% ugrad women join)	10 (39)
% African American	3
% Asian	8
% Caucasian	63
% Hispanic	10
% Native American	<1
% Pacific Islander	<1
% Two or more races	3
% Race and/or ethnicity unknown	4
% international	9
# of countries represented	70

#31 BEST VALUE COLLEGE

ABOUT THE SCHOOL

Rigorous academics, a low student-to-faculty ratio, and a host of traditions are just a few of the many advantages at Lehigh University. A private research university in Bethlehem, Pennsylvania, the school's 100+ majors include more than twenty interdisciplinary programs spread across its colleges and departments. Around 87 percent of students graduate with at least one internship or co-op under their belts and nearly half study abroad. Lehigh's flexible curriculum lets students explore their interests and tailor a major, and the school encourages students to work side-by-side with faculty in research endeavors. The coursework is "difficult, keeping even the brightest students on their toes," but "the kinship formed through the struggle and triumph are irreplaceable," and students can even enroll in graduate classes while undergrads to get a head start. "Different colleges easily mix and can blend together," and professors are "always willing to help with any concerns or confusions about class matters or those outside of the classroom as well."

BANG FOR YOUR BUCK

According to students, "Lehigh is limitless." Though the school is known for engineering, "all programs and organizations are extremely dedicated to what they do" and "there are myriad opportunities available in all fields." "Make sure to get to know [professors] outside of the classroom since they often give out career advice," says a student. There are "so many research, internship, study abroad, and community service opportunities. Even though tuition is high, help is available. Students are considered for most

Lehigh University

Financial Aid: 610-758-3181 • E-mail: admissions@lehigh.edu • Website: www.lehigh.edu

merit-based scholarships just by applying to Lehigh, but some require an additional application. Dean's Scholarships are given for academic and leadership achievement to the tune of $12,000 per year; full tuition is given via Founder's and Trustees' Scholars to top students in the applicant pool.

STUDENT LIFE

Many students from Lehigh come from the states in proximity to Pennsylvania, though "there is a growing environment of diverse individuals from around the country (and other countries)." This group does it all. They are "hard working, smart, motivated, career-driven" who "spend countless hours in the library and still go out on average 3 to 4 times a week." "You are constantly doing school work and going out. It is nuts," says a student. Lehigh is big into Greek life, which "is a primary component to a lot of students"; the school's sixteen themed residential communities also help smaller subsets form. There is a "prevalence of the arts on campus," many students enjoy volunteering, and "most people hit the gym daily." The school throws Lehigh after Dark events, as well as "gym nights, music events, and cultural events where they always have food."

CAREER

Lehigh University's priority "is giving students the best chance for professional success." The Center for Career & Professional Development works with students on their individual plan at every step of the way, and 95 percent of students fulfill ones of the outcomes they had laid out, whether that be employment, graduate school, or other opportunities. Fall and spring career expos help students make connections, career coaches are embedded in each of the undergraduate colleges, and the alumni network "always reaches out to the school and are willing to help out

ACADEMICS

Academic Rating	93
% students returning for sophomore year	94
% students graduating within 4 years	72
% students graduating within 6 years	87
Calendar	Semester
Student/faculty ratio	9:1
Profs interesting rating	79
Profs accessible rating	73

Most classes have 10–19 students. Most lab/discussion sessions have 10–19 students.

MOST POPULAR MAJORS
Mechanical Engineering; Accounting; Finance, General

SELECTIVITY

Admissions Rating	96
# of applicants	15,622
% of applicants accepted	22
% of acceptees attending	37
# offered a place on the wait list	7,737
% accepting a place on wait list	43
% admitted from wait list	2
# of early decision applicants	1,178
% accepted early decision	60

current students." Currently, the school has over 21,000 full-time positions and internships posted on the CCPD's job board. Of the Lehigh University alumni visiting PayScale.com, 48 percent report that they derive a high level of meaning from their jobs.

GENERAL INFO

Activities: Campus Ministries; Choral groups; Concert band; Dance; Drama/theater; International Student Organization; Jazz band; Literary magazine; Marching band; Model UN; Music ensembles; Musical theater; Pep band; Radio station; Student government; Student newspaper; Student-run film society; Symphony orchestra; Yearbook. 150 registered organizations, 18 honor societies, 14 religious organizations, 14 fraternities, 10 sororities, on campus. **Athletics (Intercollegiate):** *Men:* baseball, basketball, cross-country, diving, football, golf, lacrosse, soccer, swimming, tennis, track/field (outdoor), track/field (indoor), wrestling. *Women:* basketball, crew/rowing, cross-country, diving, field hockey, golf, lacrosse, soccer, softball, swimming, tennis, track/field (outdoor), track/field (indoor), volleyball. **On-Campus Highlights:** Linderman Library, University Center, Wilbur Powerhouse, Taylor Gymnasium, Zoellner Arts Center.

Lehigh University

FINANCIAL AID

Students should submit: CSS/Financial Aid PROFILE; FAFSA; Noncustodial PROFILE. Priority filing deadline is 2/1. The Princeton Review suggests that all financial aid forms be submitted as soon as possible after October 1. *Need-based scholarships/grants offered*: College/university scholarship or grant aid from institutional funds; Federal Pell; Private scholarships; SEOG; State scholarships/grants. *Loan aid offered*: Direct PLUS loans; Direct Subsidized Stafford Loans; Direct Unsubsidized Stafford Loans. Applicants will be notified of awards on or about 3/30. Federal Work-Study Program available. Institutional employment available.

BOTTOM LINE

Tuition is a steep $52,480, with room and board costing another $13,600. The school caps loans at $5,000 per year to reduce student debt at graduation, and around half of all students receive some form of financial aid.

FINANCIAL FACTS

Financial Aid Rating	98
Annual tuition	$52,480
Room and board	$13,600
Required fees	$450
Books and supplies	$1,000
Average frosh need-based scholarship	$44,745
Average UG need-based scholarship	$44,210
% needy frosh rec. need-based scholarship or grant aid	92
% needy UG rec. need-based scholarship or grant aid	95
% needy frosh rec. non-need-based scholarship or grant aid	12
% needy UG rec. non-need-based scholarship or grant aid	17
% needy frosh rec. need-based self-help aid	90
% needy UG rec. need-based self-help aid	93
% frosh rec. any financial aid	59
% UG rec. any financial aid	58
% UG borrow to pay for school	50
Average cumulative indebtedness	$35,109
% frosh need fully met	75
% ugrads need fully met	79
Average % of frosh need met	97
Average % of ugrad need met	98

CAREER INFORMATION FROM PAYSCALE.COM

ROI Rating	93
Bachelors and No Higher	
Median starting salary	$69,500
Median mid-career salary	$134,100
At Least Bachelors	
Median starting salary	$70,500
Median mid-career salary	$143,700
Alumni with high job meaning	48%
Degrees awarded in STEM subjects	52%

Lehigh University

Massachusetts Institute of Technology

77 Massachusetts Avenue, Cambridge, MA 02139 • Admissions: 617-253-3400 • Fax: 617-258-8304

CAMPUS LIFE

Quality of Life Rating	91
Fire Safety Rating	91
Green Rating	60*
Type of school	Private
Environment	City

STUDENTS

Total undergrad enrollment	4,550
% male/female	53/47
% from out of state	91
% frosh from public high school	70
% frosh live on campus	100
% ugrads live on campus	92
# of fraternities	
(% ugrad men join)	28 (43)
# of sororities	
(% ugrad women join)	10 (28)
% African American	6
% Asian	28
% Caucasian	32
% Hispanic	15
% Native American	<1
% Pacific Islander	<1
% Two or more races	7
% Race and/or ethnicity unknown	2
% international	10
# of countries represented	103

ABOUT THE SCHOOL

The essence of Massachusetts Institute of Technology is its appetite for problems. Students here tend to be game-changers, capable of finding creative solutions to the world's big, intractable, complicated problems. A chemical engineering major says that "MIT is different from many schools in that its goal is not to teach you specific facts in each subject. MIT teaches you how to think, not about opinions but about problem-solving. Facts and memorization are useless unless you know how to approach a tough problem." While MIT is a research university committed to world-class inquiry in math, science, and engineering, MIT has equally distinguished programs in architecture, the humanities, management, and the social sciences. No matter what their field, almost all MIT students get involved in research during their undergraduate career, making contributions in fields as diverse as biochemistry, artificial intelligence, and urban planning. "Research opportunities for undergrads with some of the nation's leading professors" is a real highlight for students here. The school also operates an annual Independent Activities Period during the month of January, during which MIT faculty offer hundreds of noncredit activities and short for-credit classes, from lecture and film series to courses like Ballroom Dance or Introduction to Weather Forecasting (students may also use this period to work on research or independent projects). Students are frequently encouraged to unite MIT's science and engineering excellence with public service. Recent years have focused on projects using alternative forms of energy, and machines that could be used for sustainable agriculture. MIT's D-Lab, Poverty Action Lab, and Public Service Center all support students and professors in the

Massachusetts Institute of Technology

Financial Aid: 617-258-4917 • E-mail: admissions@mit.edu • Website: web.mit.edu

research and implementation of culturally sensitive and environmentally responsible technologies and programs that alleviate poverty.

BANG FOR YOUR BUCK

Aid from all sources totals more than $115.6 million, and 72 percent of that total is provided by MIT Scholarships. Sixty-two percent of undergraduates qualify for need-based MIT Scholarships, and the average scholarship award exceeds $32,000. MIT is one of only a few number of institutions that have remained wholly committed to need-blind admissions and need-based aid. (There are no purely merit-based scholarships.) What truly sets MIT apart, however, is the percentage of students from lower-income households. Twenty-eight percent of MIT undergraduates are from families earning less than $75,000 a year, and 19 percent qualify for a federal Pell Grant. MIT also educates a high proportion of first-generation college students, including 16 percent of the current freshman class.

STUDENT LIFE

"As soon as you arrive on campus," students say, "you are bombarded with choices." Extracurricular options range from "building rides" (recent projects have included a motorized couch and a human-sized hamster wheel) "to partying at fraternities to enjoying the largest collection of science fiction novels in the United States at the MIT Science Fiction Library." Students occasionally find time to "pull a hack," which is an ethical prank, like changing digital construction signs on Mass Ave to read "Welcome to Bat Country," or building a "life-size Wright brothers' plane that appeared on top of the Great Dome for the 100th anniversary of flight." Luckily, "there actually isn't one typical student at MIT," students here assure us. "The one thing students all have in common is that they are insanely smart and love to learn. Pretty much anyone can find the perfect group of friends to hang out with at MIT."

ACADEMICS

Academic Rating	92
% students returning for sophomore year	98
% students graduating within 4 years	85
% students graduating within 6 years	94
Calendar	4-1-4
Student/faculty ratio	3:1
Profs interesting rating	72
Profs accessible rating	74

Most classes have fewer than 10 students. Most lab/discussion sessions have 10–19 students.

MOST POPULAR MAJORS

Computer Science; Mechanical Engineering; Mathematics, General

SELECTIVITY

Admissions Rating	99
# of applicants	21,706
% of applicants accepted	7
% of acceptees attending	76
# offered a place on the wait list	460
% accepting a place on wait list	83
% admitted from wait list	0

CAREER

MIT's Global Education & Career Development "seeks to empower" students and alumni by taking a holistic approach to career services. A few offerings (among many) include career counseling and mock interviews, study abroad informational sessions, and graduate school advising. Frequent career fairs connect undergrads with potential employers (and the Career Fair Online Workshop will help you make the most of your time with them) or you can also peruse job and internship listings on CareerBridge. Students definitely get a hand-up from the rock-solid alumni network, and the surrounding areas of Cambridge and Boston abound with tech and research companies, offering students abundant opportunities for networking and internships. Alumni who visited PayScale.com reported starting salaries at about $86,300 and 58 percent felt that they do meaningful work.

GENERAL INFO

Activities: Campus Ministries; Choral groups; Concert band; Dance; Drama/theater; International Student Organization; Jazz band; Literary magazine; Marching band; Model UN; Music ensembles; Musical theater; Radio station; Student government; Student newspaper; Student-run film society; Symphony orchestra; Television station; Yearbook. 500 registered organizations, 9 honor societies, 24 religious organizations, 28 fraternities, 10 sororities, on campus. **Athletics (Intercollegiate):** *Men:* baseball, basketball, crew/rowing, cross-country, diving, fencing, football, golf, gymnastics, lacrosse, pistol, riflery, sailing, skiing (downhill/alpine), skiingnordiccross-country, soccer, squash, swimming, tennis, track/field (outdoor), track/field (indoor), volleyball, water polo, wrestling. *Women:* basketball, crew/rowing, cross-country, diving, fencing, field hockey, gymnastics, ice hockey, lacrosse, pistol, riflery, sailing, skiing (downhill/alpine), skiingnordiccross-country, soccer, softball, swimming, tennis, track/field (outdoor), track/field (indoor), volleyball. **On-Campus Highlights:** Ray and Maria Stata Center, Zesiger Sports and Fitness Center, Killian Court, The Infinite Corridor, The Student Center (W20). **Environmental Initiatives:** In 2013, MIT created a new Office of Sustainability reporting directly to our Executive Vice President, which is the highest administrative for operations office. This creates an office at the highest level with a new director to scale up MIT's already robust sustainability programs. MIT has also launched a new Sustainability Executive Committee (comprised of the Provost, Directors of MIT's top sustainability research programs, Chancellor, and Vice President for Research)

Massachusetts Institute of Technology

and a Campus Sustainability Task Force (comprised of respresentatives of all 5 schools, and key operational areas and students) to coordinate implementation of MIT's sustainability plans.

FINANCIAL AID

Students should submit: CSS/Financial Aid PROFILE; FAFSA; Noncustodial PROFILE. Priority filing deadline is 2/15. The Princeton Review suggests that all financial aid forms be submitted as soon as possible after October 1. *Need-based scholarships/grants offered*: College/university scholarship or grant aid from institutional funds; Federal Pell; Private scholarships; SEOG; State scholarships/grants; United Negro College Fund. *Loan aid offered*: Direct PLUS loans; Direct Subsidized Stafford Loans; Direct Unsubsidized Stafford Loans. Applicants will be notified of awards on or about 3/15. Federal Work-Study Program available. Institutional employment available.

BOTTOM LINE

For the fall and spring terms, MIT tuition is about $53,450. Room and board averages about $14,720 per academic year, though those costs vary depending on a student's living situation. Books run about $1,000. MIT admits students without regard to their familys' circumstances and awards financial aid to students solely on the basis of need. The school is very clear that its sticker price not scare away applicants; approximately 70 percent of undergrads receive some form of aid. They also try to limit the amount of aid provided in loan form, aiming to meet the first $6,000 of need with loans or on-campus work, and covering the remainder of a student's demonstrated need with a scholarship.

FINANCIAL FACTS	
Financial Aid Rating	92
Annual tuition	$53,450
Room and board	$16,390
Required fees	$340
Books and supplies	$820
Average frosh need-based scholarship	$49,010
Average UG need-based scholarship	$48,562
% needy frosh rec. need-based scholarship or grant aid	98
% needy UG rec. need-based scholarship or grant aid	98
% needy frosh rec. non-need-based scholarship or grant aid	3
% needy UG rec. non-need-based scholarship or grant aid	3
% needy frosh rec. need-based self-help aid	63
% needy UG rec. need-based self-help aid	70
% frosh rec. any financial aid	83
% UG rec. any financial aid	70
% UG borrow to pay for school	29
Average cumulative indebtedness	$22,696
% frosh need fully met	100
% ugrads need fully met	100
Average % of frosh need met	100
Average % of ugrad need met	100

CAREER INFORMATION FROM PAYSCALE.COM	
ROI Rating	99
Bachelors and No Higher	
Median starting salary	$86,300
Median mid-career salary	$155,200
At Least Bachelors	
Median starting salary	$89,900
Median mid-career salary	$159,400
Alumni with high job meaning	58%
Degrees awarded in STEM subjects	69%

Massachusetts Institute of Technology

Middlebury College

The Emma Willard House, Middlebury, VT 05753-6002 • Admissions: 802-443-3000 • Fax: 802-443-2056

CAMPUS LIFE

Quality of Life Rating	94
Fire Safety Rating	96
Green Rating	99
Type of school	Private
Environment	Village

STUDENTS

Total undergrad enrollment	2,551
% male/female	47/53
% from out of state	94
% frosh live on campus	100
% ugrads live on campus	95
# of fraternities	0
# of sororities	0
% African American	4
% Asian	7
% Caucasian	62
% Hispanic	10
% Native American	<1
% Pacific Islander	<1
% Two or more races	5
% Race and/or ethnicity unknown	2
% international	11
# of countries represented	67

ABOUT THE SCHOOL

Home to "smart people who enjoy Aristotelian ethics and quantum physics, but aren't too stuck up to go sledding in front of Mead Chapel at midnight," Middlebury College is a small, exclusive liberal arts school with "excellent foreign language programs" as well as standout offerings in environmental studies, the sciences, theatre, and writing. The successful Middlebury candidate excels in a variety of areas, including academics, athletics, the arts, leadership, and service to others. These strengths and interests permit students to grow beyond their traditional comfort zones and conventional limits. The classrooms are as varied as the Green Mountains, the Metropolitan Museum of Art, or the great cities of Russia and Japan. Outside the classroom, students informally interact with professors in activities such as intramural basketball games and community service. At Middlebury, students develop critical-thinking skills, enduring bonds of friendship, and the ability to challenge themselves. Middlebury offers majors and programs in forty-five different fields, with particular strengths in languages, international studies, environmental studies, literature and creative writing, and the sciences. Opportunities for engaging in individual research with faculty abound at Middlebury.

BANG FOR YOUR BUCK

Distribution requirements and other general requirements ensure that a Middlebury education "is all about providing students with a complete college experience, including excellent teaching, exposure to many other cultures, endless opportunities for growth and success, and a challenging (yet relaxed) environment." Its "small class size and friendly yet competitive

Middlebury College

E-mail: admissions@middlebury.edu • Website: www.middlebury.edu

atmosphere make for the perfect college experience," as do "the best facilities of a small liberal arts college in the country." A new squash center and new field house recently opened. Students are grateful for the stellar advantages the school is able to provide them with. "I think that even if I didn't have classes or homework, I wouldn't be able to take advantage of all of the opportunities available on campus on a day-to-day basis." "The academics here are unbeatable. I'd come here over an Ivy League school any day."

STUDENT LIFE

Middlebury students are, in three words: "Busy, friendly, and busy." Everyone "will talk about how stressed they are, but it's not just from preparing for a Chinese exam while also trying to finish up a lab report for biology; it's doing both of those while also playing a club or a varsity sport and finding time to enjoy long meals in the cafeteria with friends." Weekends are for much-deserved relaxation: hiking or skiing (the school has its own ski mountain, the Snow Bowl, and cross-country ski area, Rikert Nordic Center), attending shows and concerts, film screenings, dance parties, and parties are put on by sports teams and other clubs on campus. The student activity board "does a pretty good job, but if you don't like it, you are always welcome to apply to be on the board." Many here are politically active in some way, and "the environment is big for most."

CAREER

Middlebury students "know how to take advantage of resources that aid their success." The Center for Careers & Internships helps students to find internships or even develop their own, and the online resources include a comprehensive series of Five-Minute Workshops. Funding is even available for unpaid internships, conferences, service projects, international

ACADEMICS

Academic Rating	97
% students returning for sophomore year	96
% students graduating within 4 years	83
% students graduating within 6 years	91
Calendar	4-1-4
Student/faculty ratio	8:1
Profs interesting rating	93
Profs accessible rating	89

Most classes have 10–19 students.

MOST POPULAR MAJORS

Economics; Computer Science; Neuroscience; Environmental Studies

SELECTIVITY

Admissions Rating	97
# of applicants	9,227
% of applicants accepted	17
% of acceptees attending	41
# offered a place on the wait list	1,215
% accepting a place on wait list	43
% admitted from wait list	2
# of early decision applicants	853
% accepted early decision	47

volunteer programs, and local public service projects. Experiential learning is a heavy focus of the college, and there are numerous centers for students to enhance academic work, or explore possible career paths. Middlebury College graduates who visited PayScale.com had an average starting salary of $60,400; 56 percent said they felt their job had a meaningful impact on the world.

GENERAL INFO

Activities: Campus Ministries; Choral groups; Dance; Drama/theater; International Student Organization; Jazz band; Literary magazine; Model UN; Music ensembles; Musical theater; Pep band; Radio station; Student government; Student newspaper; Student-run film society; Symphony orchestra; Yearbook. 150 registered organizations, 0 fraternities, 0 sororities, on campus. **Athletics (Intercollegiate):** *Men:* baseball, basketball, cross-country, diving, football, golf, ice hockey, lacrosse, skiing (downhill/alpine), skiingnordiccross-country, soccer, swimming, tennis, track/field (outdoor), track/field (indoor). *Women:* basketball, cross-country, diving, field hockey, golf, ice hockey, lacrosse, skiing (downhill/alpine), skiingnordiccross-country, soccer, softball, squash, swimming, tennis, track/field (outdoor), track/field (indoor), volleyball. **On-Campus Highlights:** Science-Bicentennial Hall, The Center for the Arts, Athletic Facilities, The Commons System, Middlebury College Snow Bowl (Ski Area). **Environmental Initiatives:** Student initiated effort that led to Trustees resolution in 2007 charging the entire college community to work together to achieve carbon neutrality by 2016. A similar effort modeled on this one is also in progress with regard to divesting the college endowment from fossil fuel related companies. Thus far, it has led to new proxy voting policies in support of open and transparent governance and environmental and social responsibility, a student member of the Advisory Committee on Socially Responsible Investing has been appointed to the Investment Committee of the Board, and the question of divesting from fossil fuels is currently being given full and open consideration by the Trustees with significant community involvement in the discussion.

Middlebury College

FINANCIAL AID

Students should submit: CSS/Financial Aid PROFILE; FAFSA; Institution's own financial aid form; Noncustodial PROFILE. Priority filing deadline is 11/15. The Princeton Review suggests that all financial aid forms be submitted as soon as possible after October 1. *Need-based scholarships/grants offered*: College/university scholarship or grant aid from institutional funds; Federal Pell; Private scholarships; SEOG; State scholarships/grants. *Loan aid offered*: Direct PLUS loans; Direct Subsidized Stafford Loans; Direct Unsubsidized Stafford Loans. Applicants will be notified of awards on or about 4/1. Federal Work-Study Program available. Institutional employment available.

BOTTOM LINE

Middlebury College is not the most expensive institution in the country, but it is a substantial investment. Fortunately, the opportunity for financial aid and other support is provided for needy students. Tuition is $60,400 per year, and Middlebury meets full demonstrated need for all admitted students. About 46 percent of enrollees receive some form of financial aid. Forty-five percent of students borrow to help offset the cost of their education and, upon graduating, are looking at a total loan debt of under $18,736; extremely reasonable for an education of the caliber provided by Middlebury.

FINANCIAL FACTS	
Financial Aid Rating	**95**
Annual tuition	$55,790
Room and board	$16,032
Required fees	$426
Books and supplies	$1,000
Average frosh need-based scholarship	$48,993
Average UG need-based scholarship	$49,003
% needy frosh rec. need-based scholarship or grant aid	100
% needy UG rec. need-based scholarship or grant aid	98
% needy frosh rec. non-need-based scholarship or grant aid	0
% needy UG rec. non-need-based scholarship or grant aid	0
% needy frosh rec. need-based self-help aid	91
% needy UG rec. need-based self-help aid	91
% frosh rec. any financial aid	51
% UG rec. any financial aid	46
% UG borrow to pay for school	50
Average cumulative indebtedness	$18,955
% frosh need fully met	100
% ugrads need fully met	100
Average % of frosh need met	100
Average % of ugrad need met	100

CAREER INFORMATION FROM PAYSCALE.COM	
ROI Rating	92
Bachelors and No Higher	
Median starting salary	$60,400
Median mid-career salary	$109,800
At Least Bachelors	
Median starting salary	$62,400
Median mid-career salary	$125,200
Alumni with high job meaning	56%
Degrees awarded in STEM subjects	19%

Middlebury College

North Carolina State University

Box 7103, Raleigh, NC 27695 • Admissions: 919-515-2434 • Fax: 919-515-5039

CAMPUS LIFE

Quality of Life Rating	90
Fire Safety Rating	95
Green Rating	99
Type of school	Public
Environment	Metropolis

STUDENTS

Total undergrad enrollment	23,658
% male/female	53/47
% from out of state	9
% frosh from public high school	84
% frosh live on campus	97
% ugrads live on campus	38
# of fraternities	
(% ugrad men join)	30 (13)
# of sororities	
(% ugrad women join)	20 (17)
% African American	6
% Asian	7
% Caucasian	69
% Hispanic	6
% Native American	<1
% Pacific Islander	<1
% Two or more races	4
% Race and/or ethnicity unknown	4
% international	4
# of countries represented	86

ABOUT THE SCHOOL

Science and technology are big at North Carolina State University, a major research university and the largest four-year institution in its state. While the College of Engineering and the College of Sciences form the backbone of the academic program, the school also boasts nationally reputable majors in architecture, design, textiles, management, agriculture, humanities and social sciences, education, natural resources, and veterinary medicine, providing "big-school opportunity with a small-school feel." The "vicinity to top-of-the-line research" is palpable, as more than 70 percent of NC State's faculty is involved in sponsored research, and the school is "an incubator for outstanding engineering and scientific research." For undergraduates, many of whom grew up wanting to attend the school, this opportunity to participate in important research is a major advantage. It makes sense, given that NC State "is all about developing skills in school that will help you throughout your professional career." In addition, an education at NC State includes many opportunities for students to get a head start on a real-world job, and the school also has "a great [Exploratory Studies] for students . . . who aren't sure what major they want to go into." The university's co-op program is one of the largest in the nation, with more than 1,000 work rotations a year, all due to the school's excellent reputation. "I want my degree to pack a punch when people see it, without having to be ridiculously rich or a prodigy of some sort," says a student of his decision to go to NC State.

North Carolina State University

Financial Aid: 919-515-2421 • E-mail: undergrad_admissions@ncsu.edu • Website: www.ncsu.edu

BANG FOR YOUR BUCK

NC State continues to be a best value for North Carolina residents. Offering financial assistance to qualified students is an integral part of NC State's history. In 2017, NC State awarded $3,520,520 in institutional scholarships.

STUDENT LIFE

North Carolina State offers a lot for students to do both on and off campus. Though students report that they spend a great deal of time studying, social life is very big as well: "Everyone manages to have some fun doing what they want to do while maintaining their GPA. And there is something for everyone here at State." "The school offers various activities throughout each semester that are usually lots of fun, and the best part is they're free," says a student. "There are also a lot of club events. Outdoor Adventures usually does something about every weekend, involving a trip to the mountains or something. There's always a lot of support for the sports teams and tons of school spirit." In addition to attending sporting events, "it's easy to get out and play yourself" through a variety of intramural teams and clubs. For those looking to venture out at night, "students love to go to downtown Raleigh to have fun in clubs or wander Hillsborough Street. There is opportunity to do just about anything in the area."

CAREER

Students at NC State work hard in order to be prepared for their future careers, and most feel that the school prepares them very well for life after college. The Career Development Center offers one-on-one academic advising and career planning; job and internship search resources; career fairs and on-campus recruiting in many different fields; and help with resume

ACADEMICS

Academic Rating	83
% students returning for sophomore year	94
% students graduating within 4 years	54
% students graduating within 6 years	81
Calendar	Semester
Student/faculty ratio	14:1
Profs interesting rating	77
Profs accessible rating	83

Most classes have 10–19 students. Most lab/discussion sessions have 20–29 students.

MOST POPULAR MAJORS

Engineering, General; Biology/Biological Sciences, General; Business Administration and Management, General

SELECTIVITY

Admissions Rating	91
# of applicants	30,193
% of applicants accepted	47
% of acceptees attending	34
# offered a place on the wait list	4,133
% accepting a place on wait list	100
% admitted from wait list	0

building, job interviews, and other professional skills. The school also offers a Cooperative Education program that allows students to pursue paid work in their field while studying for their degree. "I have had several good academic advisors that have helped me decide what courses I should take based on the different career paths I have been considering," says a student. "Also, all of my professors always wish to do whatever they can in order to help out the students." Out of NC State alumni visiting PayScale.com, 53 percent report that they derive a high level of meaning from their jobs.

GENERAL INFO

Activities: Campus Ministries; Choral groups; Concert band; Dance; Drama/theater; International Student Organization; Jazz band; Literary magazine; Marching band; Model UN; Music ensembles; Musical theater; Pep band; Radio station; Student government; Student newspaper; Student-run film society; Symphony orchestra; Yearbook. 630 registered organizations, 20 honor societies, 39 religious organizations, 30 fraternities, 20 sororities, on campus. **Athletics (Intercollegiate):** *Men:* baseball, basketball, cheerleading, cross-country, diving, football, golf, riflery, soccer, swimming, tennis, track/field (outdoor), track/field (indoor), wrestling. *Women:* basketball, cheerleading, cross-country, diving, golf, gymnastics, riflery, soccer, softball, swimming, tennis, track/field (outdoor), track/field (indoor), volleyball. **On-Campus Highlights:** Hunt Library, Gregg Museum of Art and Design, Carter Finley Stadium / PNC Center, Talley Student Union, University Theatre. **Environmental Initiatives:** NC State students become leaders in sustainability through the NC State Stewards campus sustainability ambassadors, the Social Innovation Fellows entrepreneurial leaders program and the B Corp Clinic, which pairs student consultants with local businesses seeking to improve sustainability.

North Carolina State University

FINANCIAL AID

Students should submit: FAFSA. Priority filing deadline is 3/1. The Princeton Review suggests that all financial aid forms be submitted as soon as possible after October 1. *Need-based scholarships/grants offered*: College/university scholarship or grant aid from institutional funds; Federal Pell; Private scholarships; SEOG; State scholarships/grants; United Negro College Fund. *Loan aid offered*: Direct PLUS loans; Direct Subsidized Stafford Loans; Direct Unsubsidized Stafford Loans. Applicants will be notified of awards on a rolling basis beginning 4/1. Federal Work-Study Program available. Institutional employment available.

BOTTOM LINE

Annual tuition and fees for North Carolina residents are $9,100. For nonresidents, tuition and fees reach $28,444. For both residents and nonresidents, room and board runs about $11,078 per year, while books and supplies average just over $1,000 annually. Around 54 percent of all NC State students take out loans—students who borrow money graduate with an average loan debt of roughly $24,002.

FINANCIAL FACTS	
Financial Aid Rating	86
Annual in-state tuition	$6,535
Annual out-of-state tuition	$25,878
Room and board	$11,078
Required fees	$2,566
Books and supplies	$1,082
Average frosh need-based scholarship	$10,104
Average UG need-based scholarship	$9,944
% needy frosh rec. need-based scholarship or grant aid	93
% needy UG rec. need-based scholarship or grant aid	92
% needy frosh rec. non-need-based scholarship or grant aid	16
% needy UG rec. non-need-based scholarship or grant aid	11
% needy frosh rec. need-based self-help aid	66
% needy UG rec. need-based self-help aid	69
% frosh rec. any financial aid	90
% UG rec. any financial aid	70
% UG borrow to pay for school	51
Average cumulative indebtedness	$24,002
% frosh need fully met	23
% ugrads need fully met	21
Average % of frosh need met	73
Average % of ugrad need met	74

CAREER INFORMATION FROM PAYSCALE.COM	
ROI Rating	92
Bachelors and No Higher	
Median starting salary	$57,300
Median mid-career salary	$106,500
At Least Bachelors	
Median starting salary	$58,600
Median mid-career salary	$112,000
Alumni with high job meaning	52%
Degrees awarded in STEM subjects	47%

North Carolina State University

Pomona College

333 North College Way, Claremont, CA 91711-6312 • Admissions: 909-621-8134 • Fax: 909-621-8952

#17 BEST VALUE COLLEGE

ABOUT THE SCHOOL

Students here are among the most happy and comfortable in the nation. To help ease the transition to college life, first-year students are assigned to sponsor groups of ten to twenty fellow first-years who live in adjacent rooms, with two or three sophomore sponsors who help them learn the ropes of college life. Students rave that the sponsor program is "the single best living situation for freshmen." It "makes you feel welcome the second you step on campus as a new student" and is "amazing at integrating the freshmen into the community smoothly." Greek life is almost nonexistent, but you'll never hear a complaint about a lack of (usually free and awesome) things to do. There's virtually always an event or a party happening either on campus or just a short walk away on one of the other Claremont campuses (Scripps, Pitzer, Claremont McKenna, and Harvey Mudd). Students say that the Claremont Consortium offers "an abundance of nightlife that you wouldn't expect at a small elite liberal arts school." There are also quite a few quirky traditions here throughout the academic year. If you find yourself craving some big-city life, Los Angeles is just a short train ride away.

BANG FOR YOUR BUCK

The financial aid program here is exceedingly generous and goes beyond just covering tuition, room and board, and fees, for which Pomona can and does meet 100 percent of students' demonstrated financial need. The financial aid packages consist wholly of grants and scholarships, along with a campus job that you work maybe ten hours a week. For students on financial aid who wish to participate in study abroad, Pomona ensures that

Pomona College

Financial Aid: 909-621-8205 • E-mail: admissions@pomona.edu • Website: www.pomona.edu

cost is not a barrier. All programs carry academic credit and no extra cost for tuition or room and board. To ensure that all Pomona students are able to participate in the college's internship program, funding is provided on a competitive basis in the form of a stipend for semester-long internships, making it possible for students to take unpaid positions. The Career Development Office (CDO) also subsidizes transportation to and from internships. In addition, the college offers funding, based on need, to students with job interviews on the East Coast during the Winter Break Recruiting Days program.

STUDENT LIFE

Because of its location in Southern California, "life [at Pomona] consists of a lot of school work but always done out in the beautiful sun. I think most people love it here." "People usually are athletic or at least interested in outdoor activities like hiking, camping, and rock climbing." For those with access to cars "the beach, the mountains, and Joshua Tree National Park are other popular locations for a day or weekend," and many students will venture into nearby Los Angeles for fun. However it's not necessary to get away to have a good time, as "at Pomona, there's usually so much happening on campus that you don't need to venture out." "While partying is a big deal—as it is at almost any college—it certainly isn't the only deal. There are movie nights all over campus, music festivals, plays, impromptu games of Frisbee going on at all times of the year." Many students also say that talking the night away with their friends is one of the things they love about Pomona. "Deep conversations" are a frequent occurrence and "people engage in AMAZING conversations about EVERYTHING." "Whatever you like to do for fun," students say, "there's a good chance that you'll find others who like to do the same."

ACADEMICS

Academic Rating	92
% students returning for sophomore year	97
% students graduating within 4 years	89
% students graduating within 6 years	94
Calendar	Semester
Student/faculty ratio	8:1
Profs interesting rating	90
Profs accessible rating	90

Most classes have 10–19 students.
Most lab/discussion sessions have 10–19 students.

MOST POPULAR MAJORS
Economics; Mathematics; Computer Science

SELECTIVITY

Admissions Rating	98
# of applicants	10,245
% of applicants accepted	8
% of acceptees attending	53
# offered a place on the wait list	826
% accepting a place on wait list	64
% admitted from wait list	13
# of early decision applicants	1,364
% accepted early decision	15

CAREER

Pomona's Career Development Office offers advising and counseling to help students explore their interests and discover careers to which they might be suited; hosts career fairs and recruiting events; and provides resources for networking job searches. It also hosts a Prestigious Scholarships and Fellowships Expo that brings representatives from foundations and universities to discuss post-graduate opportunities. However despite the number of offerings, many students list the Career Office as an area that "could definitely be better" and say that the school needs "more resources for internships and career development." On the other hand, several students cite their professors as a helpful resource to "get the internships and jobs that we want or need for our desired careers," and more than 200 students conduct mentored research, with a stipend, each summer. Overall, students say that Pomona provides "a diverse education that will prepare students for whatever they choose to do afterward" and out of alumni visiting PayScale.com, 53 percent report that they derive meaning from their career.

GENERAL INFO

Activities: Campus Ministries; Choral groups; Concert band; Dance; Drama/theater; International Student Organization; Jazz band; Literary magazine; Model UN; Music ensembles; Musical theater; Pep band; Radio station; Student government; Student newspaper; Student-run film society; Symphony orchestra; intramural sports. 280 registered organizations, 8 honor societies, 5 religious organizations, 3 fraternities, 0 sororities, on campus. **Athletics (Intercollegiate):** *Men:* baseball, basketball, cross-country, diving, football, golf, soccer, swimming, tennis, track/field (outdoor), water polo. *Women:* basketball, cross-country, diving, golf, lacrosse, soccer, softball, swimming, tennis, track/field (outdoor), volleyball, water polo. **On-Campus Highlights:** Smith Campus Center, Sontag Greek Theater, Skyspace, The Coop, The Farm, Benton Museum of Art at Pomona College (opening fall 2020). **Environmental Initiatives:** Pomona's Environmental Analysis Program incorporates sustainability across the curriculum in a variety of disciplines. The program offers tracks within its major, the most popular being Sustainability and the

Pomona College

Built Environment, allowing students to focus on sustainability in a variety of natural science, social science, and humanities subjects. Sustainability is well incorporated across the curriculum.

FINANCIAL AID

Students should submit: CSS Profile for primary and secondary households; FAFSA; State aid form. Priority filing deadline is 1/15. The Princeton Review suggests that all financial aid forms be submitted as soon as possible after October 1. *Need-based scholarships/grants offered*: College/university scholarship or grant aid from institutional funds; Federal Pell Grant; Federal SEOG Grant; Private scholarships; State scholarships/grants. *Loan aid offered*: Direct PLUS loans; Direct Subsidized Stafford Loans; Direct Unsubsidized Stafford Loans. Applicants will be notified of awards on or about 4/1. Federal Work-Study Program available. Institutional employment available.

BOTTOM LINE

Tuition, fees, and room and board at Pomona run about $71,980 for a year. At the same time, the mantra here is that no one should hesitate to apply because of the cost. Pomona College has need-blind admissions and meets the full, demonstrated financial aid need of every accepted student with scholarships and work-study. Students say that Pomona "has a reputation of providing great financial aid packages."

FINANCIAL FACTS	
Financial Aid Rating	99
Annual tuition	$54,380
Room and board	$17,218
Required fees	$382
Books and supplies	$1,000
Average frosh need-based scholarship	$54,404
Average UG need-based scholarship	$53,123
% needy frosh rec. need-based scholarship or grant aid	100
% needy UG rec. need-based scholarship or grant aid	100
% needy frosh rec. non-need-based scholarship or grant aid	0
% needy UG rec. non-need-based scholarship or grant aid	0
% needy frosh rec. need-based self-help aid	100
% needy UG rec. need-based self-help aid	100
% frosh rec. any financial aid	59
% UG rec. any financial aid	57
% UG borrow to pay for school	30
Average cumulative indebtedness	$17,303
% frosh need fully met	100
% ugrads need fully met	100
Average % of frosh need met	100
Average % of ugrad need met	100

CAREER INFORMATION FROM PAYSCALE.COM	
ROI Rating	94
Bachelors and No Higher	
Median starting salary	$63,800
Median mid-career salary	$117,200
At Least Bachelors	
Median starting salary	$66,700
Median mid-career salary	$136,400
Alumni with high job meaning	53%
Degrees awarded in STEM subjects	37%

Pomona College

Princeton University

PO Box 430, Admission Office, Princeton, NJ 08542-0430 • Admissions: 609-258-3060 • Fax: 609-258-6743

CAMPUS LIFE

Quality of Life Rating	89
Fire Safety Rating	94
Green Rating	88
Type of school	Private
Environment	Town

STUDENTS

Total undergrad enrollment	5,246
% male/female	51/49
% from out of state	82
% frosh from public high school	60
% frosh live on campus	100
% ugrads live on campus	96
# of fraternities	0
# of sororities	0
% African American	8
% Asian	21
% Caucasian	43
% Hispanic	10
% Native American	<1
% Pacific Islander	<1
% Two or more races	4
% Race and/or ethnicity unknown	1
% international	12
# of countries represented	99

#1 BEST VALUE COLLEGE

ABOUT THE SCHOOL

Princeton offers its 5,000 undergraduate students a top-notch liberal arts education, taught by some of the best minds in the world. The university is committed to undergraduate teaching, and all faculty, including the president, teach undergraduates. "You get the attention you deserve—if you seek it," says a student. Supporting these efforts are exceptional academic and research resources, including the world-class Firestone Library, the new Frick Chemistry Laboratory that emphasizes hands-on learning in teaching labs, a genomics institute, the Woodrow Wilson School of Public and International Affairs that trains leaders in public service, and an engineering school that enrolls more than 900 undergraduates. Freshman seminars take students into a variety of settings, such as to theaters on Broadway, geological sites in the West, art museums, and more. Princeton students can choose between more than seventy-five fields of concentration (majors) and interdisciplinary certificate programs, of which history, political science, economics, and international affairs are among the most popular. The school's excellent faculty-student ratio of five to one means that many classes are discussion-based, giving students a direct line to their brilliant professors, and "once you take upper-level courses, you'll have a lot of chances to work closely with professors and study what you are most interested in." All "unfailingly brilliant, open, and inspirational" faculty members also work closely with undergraduates in the supervision of junior-year independent work and senior theses. "Professors love teaching, and there are many fantastic lecturers," giving students a chance "to meet and take classes from some of the most brilliant academic minds in the world." Even before they start taking Princeton classes, select students each year are chosen for the Bridge Year Program, which provides funding for

Princeton University

Financial Aid: 609-258-3330 • E-mail: uaoffice@princeton.edu • Website: www.princeton.edu

students to engage in public-service opportunities in one of four countries: India, Peru, Ghana, or Serbia. There are "pools of resources available for students for all sorts of nonacademic or extracurricular pursuits."

BANG FOR YOUR BUCK

Princeton operates need-blind admissions, as well as one of the strongest need-based financial aid programs in the country. Once a student is admitted, Princeton meets 100 percent of each student's demonstrated financial need. One of the first schools in the country to do so, Princeton has eliminated all loans for students who qualify for aid—it is possible to graduate from this Ivy League school without debt. Financial awards come in the form of grants, which do not need to be repaid. About 60 percent of Princeton students receive financial aid, with an average grant of about $44,890. No need to pinch yourself, you're not dreaming. In recent years, the amount of grant aid available at Princeton has outpaced the annual increase in school fees. Good news for international students: Financial aid packages extend to international admits as well.

STUDENT LIFE

"Academics come first" at this hallowed Ivy, but an "infinite number of clubs" on campus means that "almost everyone at Princeton is involved with something other than school about which they are extremely passionate." Students "tend to participate in a lot of different activities from varsity sports (recruits), intramural sports (high school athletes)...[to] Engineers Without Borders, and the literary magazine." If you need to relax, "sporting events, concerts, recreational facilities," "a movie theater that frequently screens current films for free," and "arts and crafts at the student center" will help you de-stress. Others enjoy Princeton's eating clubs—private houses that service as social clubs and cafeterias for upperclassmen. Campus is located in a quaint little bubble of a New Jersey

ACADEMICS

Academic Rating	90
% students returning for sophomore year	98
% students graduating within 4 years	89
% students graduating within 6 years	97
Calendar	Semester
Student/faculty ratio	5:1
Profs interesting rating	77
Profs accessible rating	69

Most classes have 10–19 students. Most lab/discussion sessions have 10–19 students.

MOST POPULAR MAJORS

Computer Engineering, General; Public Administration; Economics, General

SELECTIVITY

Admissions Rating	99
# of applicants	31,056
% of applicants accepted	6
% of acceptees attending	66
# offered a place on the wait list	1,168
% accepting a place on wait list	71
% admitted from wait list	12

FRESHMAN PROFILE

Range SAT EBRW	710–780
Range SAT Math	720–790
Range ACT Composite	32–35
# submitting SAT scores	854
% submitting SAT scores	65
# submitting ACT scores	709
% submitting ACT scores	54
Average HS GPA	3.9
% graduated top 10% of class	94
% graduated top 25% of class	99
% graduated top 50% of class	100

DEADLINES

Early action	
Deadline	11/1
Notification	12/15
Regular	
Deadline	1/1
Notification	4/1
Nonfall registration?	No

town and is full of traditions (some dating back hundreds of years), but if you crave some city-life "there's NJ transit if you want to go to New York, Philly, or even just the local mall."

CAREER

As one student tells us, "Princeton is a place that prepares you for anything and everything, providing you with a strong network every step of the way." Career Services lends a hand the moment students arrive on campus by guiding undergrads through self-assessments, educating about majors and careers, updating HireTigers—which holds hundreds of listings for jobs, fellowships, and internships—and, of course, strategize regarding resumes, cover letters, and online profiles. "Princeternships" allow students to experience "a day in the life" by shadowing an alumnus at their workplace for a few days. According to PayScale.com, the average starting salary for recent grads is $75,200.

GENERAL INFO

Activities: Campus Ministries; Choral groups; Concert band; Dance; Drama/theater; International Student Organization; Jazz band; Literary magazine; Marching band; Model UN; Music ensembles; Musical theater; Opera; Pep band; Radio station; Student government; Student newspaper; Student-run film society; Symphony orchestra; Television station; Yearbook. 250 registered organizations, 30 honor societies, 28 religious organizations, 0 fraternities, 0 sororities, on campus. **Athletics (Intercollegiate):** *Men:* baseball, basketball, crew/rowing, cross-country, diving, fencing, football, golf, ice hockey, lacrosse, light weight football, soccer, squash, swimming, tennis, track/field (outdoor), track/field (indoor), volleyball, water polo, wrestling. *Women:* basketball, crew/rowing, cross-country, diving, fencing, field hockey, golf, ice hockey, lacrosse, soccer, softball, squash, swimming, tennis, track/field (outdoor), track/field (indoor), volleyball, water polo. **On-Campus Highlights:** Nassau Hall, Firestone Library, McCarter Theater, University Art Museum, University Chapel. **Environmental Initiatives:** Greenhouse Gas reduction goal: 1990 levels by 2020 through local verifiable action, while adding more than 1 million gross square feet of built area, and without the purchase of offsets. 5.3 megawatt solar PV installation installed on campus.

Princeton University

FINANCIAL AID

Students should submit: FAFSA; Institution's own financial aid form. Priority filing deadline is 2/1. The Princeton Review suggests that all financial aid forms be submitted as soon as possible after October 1. *Need-based scholarships/grants offered*: College/university scholarship or grant aid from institutional funds; Federal Pell; Private scholarships; SEOG; State scholarships/grants. *Loan aid offered*: Direct PLUS loans; Direct Subsidized Stafford Loans; Direct Unsubsidized Stafford Loans. Applicants will be notified of awards on or about 4/1. Federal Work-Study Program available. Institutional employment available.

BOTTOM LINE

If you can afford it, Princeton is far from cheap. A year's tuition is $47,140, plus about $15,610 in room and board. These figures are nothing to scoff at. However, if you qualify for aid, you'll be granted the amount you need, without loans.

FINANCIAL FACTS	
Financial Aid Rating	99
Annual tuition	$47,140
Room and board	$15,610
Books and supplies	$1,050
Average frosh need-based scholarship	$52,800
Average UG need-based scholarship	$51,365
% needy frosh rec. need-based scholarship or grant aid	100
% needy UG rec. need-based scholarship or grant aid	100
% needy frosh rec. non-need-based scholarship or grant aid	0
% needy UG rec. non-need-based scholarship or grant aid	0
% needy frosh rec. need-based self-help aid	100
% needy UG rec. need-based self-help aid	100
% frosh rec. any financial aid	60
% UG rec. any financial aid	60
% UG borrow to pay for school	18
Average cumulative indebtedness	$9,005
% frosh need fully met	100
% ugrads need fully met	100
Average % of frosh need met	100
Average % of ugrad need met	100

CAREER INFORMATION FROM PAYSCALE.COM	
ROI Rating	99
Bachelors and No Higher	
Median starting salary	$75,200
Median mid-career salary	$139,400
At Least Bachelors	
Median starting salary	$76,800
Median mid-career salary	$154,300
Alumni with high job meaning	53%
Degrees awarded in STEM subjects	48%

Purdue University—West Lafayette

1080 Schleman Hall, West Lafayette, IN 47907-2050 • Admissions: 765-494-1776 • Fax: 765-494-0544

#49 BEST VALUE COLLEGE

CAMPUS LIFE

Quality of Life Rating	90
Fire Safety Rating	96
Green Rating	60*
Type of school	Public
Environment	Town

STUDENTS

Total undergrad enrollment	30,831
% male/female	57/43
% from out of state	36
% frosh live on campus	94
% ugrads live on campus	41
# of fraternities	
(% ugrad men join)	30 (18)
# of sororities	
(% ugrad women join)	25 (22)
% African American	3
% Asian	8
% Caucasian	63
% Hispanic	5
% Native American	<1
% Pacific Islander	<1
% Two or more races	3
% Race and/or ethnicity unknown	2
% international	16
# of countries represented	123

ABOUT THE SCHOOL

Located in rural Indiana, Purdue University, with close to 30,000 students, is one of the most educationally and ethnically diverse universities in the United States. Purdue has rich tradition and has one of the oldest colleges of agriculture in the nation. "An institution filled with brain power and immense achievement, yet at the same time exceedingly humble and saturated with the warm-hearted hospitality of the Midwest," a contented undergrad tells us. Academics are taken seriously here. Purdue is research-intensive but retains great faculty-student interaction inside and outside of the classroom. "It allows undergraduates to enter laboratory research very early in their college career," says one student excitedly. Purdue has excellent research opportunities that are open to almost anyone who shows interest and dedication, and prides itself on being strong in STEM (science, technology, engineering, and math) education, with heavy emphasis on real-world practical research and knowledge. When combined with an emphasis on innovation and creative thinking, Purdue becomes a great choice for anyone looking to have a successful future. A well-networked university, that is incorporated into the surrounding town through collaborative learning, field experiences, and service opportunities, allows students to learn in and out of the classroom.

BANG FOR YOUR BUCK

One student describes the value of a Purdue education by saying, "I considered the problem mathematically. Math + science + social skills = engineering. Engineering + Midwest = Purdue." Others add, "I knew that I would be

Purdue University—West Lafayette

Financial Aid: 765-494-0998 • E-mail: admissions@purdue.edu • Website: www.purdue.edu

receiving an excellent education and that I would be prepared for my chosen career field," and explain that Purdue offers "a great education that will prepare you for a career, and it won't break the bank," and "tries its hardest to ensure everyone comes out of college with a job lined up." Purdue also draws a lot of employers for internships and full-time positions at many of their career fairs; the school produces marketable graduates who are in high demand by a number of top employers. Students are not hesitant with their praise. "I love Purdue and all of the doors it has opened for me in terms of engineering jobs and opportunities." The school's "emphasis on real-world practical research and knowledge, combined with an emphasis on innovation and creative thinking, make Purdue a great choice for anyone looking to have a successful future." High expectations ensure that the students at Purdue are well prepared for the future. "Nurturing a strong work ethic and high moral accountability" is important at Purdue, one student tells us. "It's been extremely tough, and a lot of work, but I feel like a much better engineer than I would have been had I gone anywhere else," says another appreciative enrollee.

ACADEMICS

Academic Rating	86
% students returning for sophomore year	92
% students graduating within 4 years	51
% students graduating within 6 years	79
Calendar	Semester
Student/faculty ratio	13:1
Profs interesting rating	75
Profs accessible rating	87

Most classes have 10–19 students. Most lab/discussion sessions have 20–29 students.

MOST POPULAR MAJORS
Computer Science; Mechanical Engineering; Mechanical Engineering/ Mechanical Technology/Technician

SELECTIVITY

Admissions Rating	89
# of applicants	48,912
% of applicants accepted	57
% of acceptees attending	27
# offered a place on the wait list	3,664
% accepting a place on wait list	61
% admitted from wait list	4

STUDENT LIFE

"Students do work hard in the classroom throughout the week because we know that we are getting an outstanding education here. Come weekend time though, we definitely like to cut loose." Football and basketball games are major draws at the school, and "a lot of people on our campus think about when the next sporting event is. Big Ten Sports are huge here on campus. But not so huge that those who are uninterested in sports feel left out." When students are looking for ways to unwind that don't involve either sporting events or parties, they can choose from "so many different organizations" that are designed to "meet whatever your interests are whether it be sports, music, art, or may be even medieval jousting." A student raves that "Lafayette has plenty of restaurants, movie theatres, bowling, shopping,

Range SAT EBRW	570–670
Range SAT Math	580–710
Range ACT Composite	25–31
# submitting SAT scores	5,253
% submitting SAT scores	69
# submitting ACT scores	4,529
% submitting ACT scores	60
Average HS GPA	3.8
% graduated top 10% of class	44
% graduated top 25% of class	78
% graduated top 50% of class	97

DEADLINES

Early action	
Deadline	11/1
Notification	12/12
Regular	
Priority	2/1
Notification	4/15
Nonfall registration?	Yes

etc....Chicago and Indianapolis are also near enough for day trips! I am so busy on campus because there are so many great organizations to join! I could be busy every night, if I wanted!" General consensus about life at Purdue seems to be that "there's always something going on on-campus, no one can TRULY say they have NOTHING to do."

CAREER

"The programs to help people out with career development are countless. That's definitely a strength at Purdue," raves one student, and students definitely seem to feel that the school leaves them well prepared to navigate life after graduation. The Center for Career Opportunities offers counseling on academic majors and career paths, networking and recruiting opportunities, resources for job and internship searches, and coaching on résumés, cover letters, and interviews. Overall, "Purdue has an outstanding reputation for developing difference makers, role models, and individuals who can think outside the box." Out of Purdue alumni visiting PayScale.com, 49 percent report feeling as though they derive a high level of meaning from their careers.

GENERAL INFO

Activities: Campus Ministries; Choral groups; Concert band; Dance; Drama/theater; International Student Organization; Jazz band; Literary magazine; Marching band; Model UN; Music ensembles; Pep band; Radio station; Student government; Student newspaper; Symphony orchestra; Television station. 919 registered organizations, 42 honor societies, 47 religious organizations, 30 fraternities, 25 sororities, on campus. **Athletics (Intercollegiate):** *Men:* baseball, basketball, cross-country, diving, football, golf, swimming, tennis, track/field (outdoor), track/field (indoor), wrestling. *Women:* basketball, cross-country, diving, golf, soccer, softball, swimming, tennis, track/field (outdoor), track/field (indoor), volleyball. **On-Campus Highlights:** Purdue Memorial Union, Recreational Sports Center, Neil Armstrong Hall of Engineering, Marriott Hall (hospitality and tourism management program), Pao Hall for Visual and Performing Arts. **Environmental Initiatives:** Friday Night Lights (FNL) was launched as a collaborative partnership between the Student Sustainability Council, Office of University Sustainability, Building Services, Building Deputies, Purdue Police Department, and numerous student volunteers. Every Friday

Purdue University—
West Lafayette

evening participants volunteer an hour of their time to turn off lights in classrooms of targeted academic buildings so they will not be left on over the weekend. Not only does this program reduce Purdue's energy use and carbon footprint, it also increases social capital among those on campus and, ultimately, trims Purdue's bottom line.

FINANCIAL AID

Students should submit: FAFSA. Priority filing deadline is 3/1. The Princeton Review suggests that all financial aid forms be submitted as soon as possible after October 1. *Need-based scholarships/grants offered*: College/university scholarship or grant aid from institutional funds; Federal Pell; Private scholarships; SEOG; State scholarships/grants. *Loan aid offered*: Direct PLUS loans; Direct Subsidized Stafford Loans; Direct Unsubsidized Stafford Loans. Applicants will be notified of awards on or about 4/15. Federal Work-Study Program available. Institutional employment available.

BOTTOM LINE

Tuition is about $9,200 for in-state students, with those from other states looking at a substantial increase to over $28,000. Room, board, books, and fees will increase this amount by another $12,000.

FINANCIAL FACTS	
Financial Aid Rating	85
Annual in-state tuition	$9,208
Annual out-of-state tuition	$28,010
Room and board	$10,030
Required fees	$784
Books and supplies	$1,160
Average frosh need-based scholarship	$12,990
Average UG need-based scholarship	$12,782
% needy frosh rec. need-based scholarship or grant aid	68
% needy UG rec. need-based scholarship or grant aid	73
% needy frosh rec. non-need-based scholarship or grant aid	37
% needy UG rec. non-need-based scholarship or grant aid	30
% needy frosh rec. need-based self-help aid	53
% needy UG rec. need-based self-help aid	60
% frosh rec. any financial aid	74
% UG rec. any financial aid	77
% UG borrow to pay for school	42
Average cumulative indebtedness	$27,617
% frosh need fully met	38
% ugrads need fully met	32
Average % of frosh need met	76
Average % of ugrad need met	77

"The financial aid package was the best offered to me, along with a very good scholarship." Purdue is "cheaper than a private school but it is a world-renowned engineering school at the same time." One student reports, "[Purdue] gave me a very generous scholarship package."

CAREER INFORMATION FROM PAYSCALE.COM	
ROI Rating	92
Bachelors and No Higher	
Median starting salary	$60,900
Median mid-career salary	$110,000
At Least Bachelors	
Median starting salary	$63,000
Median mid-career salary	$113,000
Alumni with high job meaning	50%
Degrees awarded in STEM subjects	38%

Purdue University—
West Lafayette

Rensselaer Polytechnic Institute

110 Eighth Street, Troy, NY 12180-3590 • Admissions: 518-276-6000 • Fax: 518-276-4072

#66 BEST VALUE COLLEGE

CAMPUS LIFE

Quality of Life Rating	84
Fire Safety Rating	94
Green Rating	60*
Type of school	Private
Environment	City

STUDENTS

Total undergrad enrollment	6,590
% male/female	68/32
% from out of state	66
% frosh from public high school	70
% frosh live on campus	100
% ugrads live on campus	57
# of fraternities	
(% ugrad men join)	29 (30)
# of sororities	
(% ugrad women join)	5 (16)
% African American	4
% Asian	14
% Caucasian	51
% Hispanic	9
% Native American	<1
% Pacific Islander	<1
% Two or more races	6
% Race and/or ethnicity unknown	1
% international	15
# of countries represented	44

ABOUT THE SCHOOL

As the first technological research university in the country, Rensselaer Polytechnic Institute has some legs to stand on in the higher education world. Though primarily an engineering institution, RPI offers degrees through five schools and encourages its students to take part in interdisciplinary programs that combine work from different areas of study. A focus on bringing the skills and technology from the lab to the real world has kept the school current and provided many a career showpiece for students. For instance, according to the school, in the last thirty years RPI has helped launch almost 300 start-up companies, many of which grew out of class projects. Classes are sized so that students can get to know their professors, who "make it a point to be accessible to students, either personally or through other venues like phone or email."

BANG FOR YOUR BUCK

Ninety-three percent of Rensselaer students receive need-based financial aid, and the school meets an average of 77 percent of need. The school offers numerous merit-based scholarships and grants, most prominently the Rensselaer Leadership Award for academic and personal achievements, and the Rensselaer Medal, which offers a $25,000 per year to students who have distinguished themselves in mathematics and science. A relatively large number of RPI students receive the Rensselaer Medal (13 percent of the most recently admitted class). International students are not eligible to receive financial aid outside of the Medal.

Rensselaer Polytechnic Institute

Financial Aid: 518-276-6813 • E-Mail: admissions@rpi.edu • Website: www.rpi.edu

STUDENT LIFE

RPI draws a significant portion (nearly one-third) of its "very diverse" students from outside of the northeast. The typical student "may be considered 'nerdy' by the liberal arts world, but being a nerd is totally cool here," says a student. "Everyone has quirks that are appreciated here, and people with similar quirks tend to flock together." There "is always something going on, especially with all the student clubs," of which there are over 180, and the intramural sports (hockey is especially big at Rensselaer), and most people stay on campus over the weekends (even those who are local) since it is "packed full of concerts, sporting events, plays, and club events." Students often split up the weekend with some homework and pick and choose which events to attend; they "are really focused and goal-oriented, but know when and how to have a good time."

CAREER

RPI is all about ensuring every student gets legitimate experience in his or her field of study as soon as possible, and looks to "equip each student with the skills needed to be a valuable member of any research team or company." The focus on problem-solving and "opportunities to be involved in hands-on research" are just two of the ways the school accomplishes this, and "the research buildings are amazing." The RPI name has a great reputation with science and tech employers, and many take part in co-ops throughout the academic year. The Center for Career & Professional Development maintains JobLink, an online job recruiting and posting system, offers career programming tailored to your class year, and hosts a Spring Career Fair. Forty-eight percent of the RPI graduates who visited PayScale.com reported feeling that their jobs had a high level of meaningful impact on the world, and brought in an average starting salary of $71,000.

ACADEMICS

Academic Rating	83
% students returning for sophomore year	92
% students graduating within 4 years	62
% students graduating within 6 years	86
Calendar	Semester
Student/faculty ratio	13:1
Profs interesting rating	65
Profs accessible rating	77

MOST POPULAR MAJORS

Computer Engineering, General; Electrical and Electronics Engineering; Business/Commerce, General

SELECTIVITY

Admissions Rating	95
# of applicants	20,402
% of applicants accepted	43
% of acceptees attending	20
# offered a place on the wait list	5,769
% accepting a place on wait list	67
% admitted from wait list	0
# of early decision applicants	1,197
% accepted early decision	47

GENERAL INFO

Activities: Campus Ministries; Choral groups; Concert band; Dance; Drama/theater; International Student Organization; Jazz band; Literary magazine; Music ensembles; Musical theater; Pep band; Radio station; Student government; Student newspaper; Student-run film society; Symphony orchestra; Television station; Yearbook. 229 registered organizations, 40 honor societies, 11 religious organization, 29 fraternities, 5 sororities, on campus. **Athletics (Intercollegiate):** *Men:* baseball, basketball, cross-country, diving, football, golf, ice hockey, lacrosse, soccer, swimming, tennis, track/field (outdoor), track/field (indoor). *Women:* basketball, cross-country, diving, field hockey, ice hockey, lacrosse, soccer, softball, swimming, tennis, track/field (outdoor), track/field (indoor). **On-Campus Highlights:** Rensselaer Union, Mueller Fitness Center, Experimental Media & Performing Arts Ctr, Houston Field House (hockey arena), ECAV. **Environmental Initiatives:** Student Sustainability Task Force.

FINANCIAL AID

Students should submit: CSS/Financial Aid PROFILE; FAFSA. Priority filing deadline is 2/1. The Princeton Review suggests that all financial aid forms be submitted as soon as possible after October 1. *Need-based scholarships/grants offered*: College/university scholarship or grant aid from institutional funds; Federal Pell; Private scholarships; SEOG; State scholarships/grants. *Loan aid offered*: Direct PLUS loans; Direct Subsidized Stafford Loans; Direct Unsubsidized Stafford Loans. Applicants will be notified of awards on or about 3/15. Federal Work-Study Program available. Institutional employment available.

Rensselaer Polytechnic Institute

BOTTOM LINE

Tuition runs a hefty $54,000, with an additional $15,260 needed for room and board. With fees and supplies added in the estimated cost of attendance is $73,813, but the vast majority of students receive aid so as not to pay the sticker price. The average need-based scholarship award is $37,236.

CAREER INFORMATION FROM PAYSCALE.COM	
ROI Rating	91
Bachelors and No Higher	
Median starting salary	$71,300
Median mid-career salary	$134,100
At Least Bachelors	
Median starting salary	$73,200
Median mid-career salary	$138,600
Alumni with high job meaning	50%
Degrees awarded in STEM subjects	78%

FINANCIAL FACTS

Financial Aid Rating	81
Annual tuition	$54,000
Room and board	$15,580
Required fees	$1,375
Books and supplies	$2,858
Average frosh need-based scholarship	$38,861
Average UG need-based scholarship	$37,236
% needy frosh rec. need-based scholarship or grant aid	100
% needy UG rec. need-based scholarship or grant aid	100
% needy frosh rec. non-need-based scholarship or grant aid	18
% needy UG rec. non-need-based scholarship or grant aid	12
% needy frosh rec. need-based self-help aid	99
% needy UG rec. need-based self-help aid	97
% frosh rec. any financial aid	83
% UG rec. any financial aid	86
% UG borrow to pay for school	63
% frosh need fully met	21
% ugrads need fully met	16
Average % of frosh need met	82
Average % of ugrad need met	78

Rensselaer Polytechnic Institute

Rhodes College

2000 North Parkway, Memphis, TN 38112 • Admissions: 901-843-3700 • Fax: 901-843-3631

#52 BEST VALUE COLLEGE

CAMPUS LIFE

Quality of Life Rating	94
Fire Safety Rating	87
Green Rating	75
Type of school	Private
Affiliation	Presbyterian
Environment	Metropolis

STUDENTS

Total undergrad enrollment	1,985
% male/female	44/56
% from out of state	71
% frosh from public high school	46
% frosh live on campus	97
% ugrads live on campus	69
# of fraternities	
(% ugrad men join)	8 (34)
# of sororities	
(% ugrad women join)	7 (40)
% African American	9
% Asian	6
% Caucasian	69
% Hispanic	6
% Native American	<1
% Pacific Islander	<1
% Two or more races	5
% Race and/or ethnicity unknown	1
% international	4
# of countries represented	26

ABOUT THE SCHOOL

Located in the heart of Memphis, Tennessee, Rhodes College was founded in 1848 by Freemasons, but came to be affiliated with the Presbyterian Church. This private liberal arts college encourages students to study "as many different disciplines as possible in order to gain a broader understanding of the world." Rhodes students can expect small classes—averaging ten to nineteen students—and "rigorous" academics. Students who put in the work can expect to succeed: "Most people here work hard and see it academically pay off." The school's "very dedicated professors" "really care about their students and make an effort to get to know us and help us succeed." One student proudly explains that "Rhodes offers a close, personalized environment where teachers and faculty are not just willing, but enthusiastic to help you find your unique path to achievement." The school's 110-acre campus, situated right in the middle of historic Memphis, is known for its "beautiful" grounds and architecture. Over a dozen of Rhodes's buildings are listed in the National Register of Historic Places. The campus is located near Overton Park and the Memphis Zoo, and a short walk to many entertainment, internship, and research opportunities, including institutions such as St. Jude Children's Research Hospital and the National Civil Rights Museum.

BANG FOR YOUR BUCK

"Memphis is a city with character, and Rhodes is an institution [that] helps foster it," one student explains. The city of Memphis offers it all to students, from internships to "great restaurants" and weekend activities. Despite being located in a city, the college provides a secluded college atmosphere for those who want it. The professors are "great and helpful," and with a student-to-

Rhodes College

Financial Aid: 901-843-3810 • E-mail: adminfo@rhodes.edu • Website: www.rhodes.edu

faculty ratio of 10:1, they are easily accessible. The student body is "actually really diverse and tends to have some great opportunities for students to learn about other cultures and countries."

STUDENT LIFE

"Stereotypically, Rhodes is a white, private college full of men in sweater-vests and women in pearls. But, there is an incredible diversity at Rhodes between upper socioeconomic backgrounds to lower socioeconomic backgrounds, between different races, between different ethnic backgrounds, between political backgrounds, and between genders. There are 'preppy' students, 'hippies,' 'punks,' and 'nerds.' The one thing that unites us all is that, on the inside, we're all just a bunch of geeks who love to learn and want to broaden our horizons." The school is full of hard workers ("academic but not full of nerds") and its honor code is taken very seriously. One thing is for certain—students here are "busy" in all areas of their life: studying, taking advantage of the "countless service opportunities," arts, athletics, and Greek life. At Rhodes, "there is an emphasis on academics, a friendly atmosphere, and plenty of extra-curriculars to get involved in."

CAREER

The typical Rhodes College graduate has a starting salary of around $51,900, and 47 percent report that their job has a great deal of meaning. Students feel that Rhodes "is the epitome of opportunity: from service to sports to academics to internships and jobs to career services and professors. Rhodes has it all." A Biochemistry major notes that "I get to do cutting edge biomedical Cancer research at St. Jude Children's Research hospital. This is an invaluable internship I got through Rhodes." Many students feel that the internship opportunities at Rhodes are not only "invaluable," but the sort of things that "helped pull us here."

ACADEMICS

Academic Rating	95
% students returning for sophomore year	90
% students graduating within 4 years	82
% students graduating within 6 years	85
Calendar	Semester
Student/faculty ratio	10:1
Profs interesting rating	98
Profs accessible rating	99
Most classes have 10–19 students.	
Most lab/discussion sessions have 20–29 students.	

MOST POPULAR MAJORS

English Language and Literature, General; Biology/Biological Sciences, General; Business Administration and Management, General

SELECTIVITY

Admissions Rating	93
# of applicants	5,093
% of applicants accepted	45
% of acceptees attending	24
# offered a place on the wait list	1,253
% accepting a place on wait list	24
% admitted from wait list	14
# of early decision applicants	155
% accepted early decision	63

DEADLINES

Early decision	
Deadline	11/1
Notification	12/1
Other ED Deadline	1/1
Other ED Notification	2/1
Early action	
Deadline	11/15
Notification	1/15
Regular	
Priority	1/15
Nonfall registration?	Yes

GENERAL INFO

Activities: Campus Ministries; Choral groups; Dance; Drama/theater; International Student Organization; Jazz band; Literary magazine; Model UN; Music ensembles; Musical theater; Pep band; Radio station; Student government; Student newspaper; Student-run film society; Symphony orchestra; Television station; Yearbook. 131 registered organizations, 15 honor societies, 7 religious organizations, 8 fraternities, 7 sororities, on campus. **Athletics (Intercollegiate):** *Men:* baseball, basketball, cross-country, football, golf, soccer, swimming, tennis, track/field (outdoor). *Women:* basketball, cross-country, field hockey, golf, soccer, softball, swimming, tennis, track/field (outdoor), volleyball. **On-Campus Highlights:** Paul Barret, Jr. Library, The Middle Ground (coffee shop), Burrow Refectory (Cafeteria), Bryan Campus Life Center (athletic facility), Lynx Lair (Bar and Cafe). **Environmental Initiatives:** $500,000 Andrew W. Mellon Foundation grant to expand Environmental Studies initiatives through community partnerships.

FINANCIAL AID

Students should submit: FAFSA; Noncustodial PROFILE. Priority filing deadline is 3/1. The Princeton Review suggests that all financial aid forms be submitted as soon as possible after October 1. *Need-based scholarships/grants offered*: College/university scholarship or grant aid from institutional funds; Federal Pell; Private scholarships; SEOG; State scholarships/grants. *Loan aid offered*: Direct PLUS loans; Direct Subsidized Stafford Loans; Direct Unsubsidized Stafford Loans. Federal Work-Study Program available. Institutional employment available.

Rhodes College

BOTTOM LINE

Annual tuition at Rhodes is $47,580 to which a student should expect to add another $12,838 for living and other school expenses. However, in addition to working hard to meet students with financial needs—a full 93 percent of undergraduates receive aid—the school offers many merit-based scholarships. The Rhodes Student Associate Program is a unique work program that matches students with "meaningful employment that requires advanced skills and dedication." The program currently offers more than 100 positions in a variety of both academic and administrative departments. Rhodes also facilitates many off-campus student employment opportunities with local non-profits.

CAREER INFORMATION FROM PAYSCALE.COM	
ROI Rating	92
Bachelors and No Higher	
Median starting salary	$51,900
Median mid-career salary	$97,800
At Least Bachelors	
Median starting salary	$54,500
Median mid-career salary	$115,800
Alumni with high job meaning	47%
Degrees awarded in STEM subjects	25%

FINANCIAL FACTS	
Financial Aid Rating	**93**
Annual tuition	$47,580
Room and board	$11,403
Required fees	$310
Books and supplies	$1,125
Average frosh need-based scholarship	$32,532
Average UG need-based scholarship	$33,275
% needy frosh rec. need-based scholarship or grant aid	99
% needy UG rec. need-based scholarship or grant aid	99
% needy frosh rec. non-need-based scholarship or grant aid	49
% needy UG rec. non-need-based scholarship or grant aid	35
% needy frosh rec. need-based self-help aid	53
% needy UG rec. need-based self-help aid	63
% frosh rec. any financial aid	95
% UG rec. any financial aid	93
% UG borrow to pay for school	48
Average cumulative indebtedness	$24,187
% frosh need fully met	51
% ugrads need fully met	43
Average % of frosh need met	93
Average % of ugrad need met	90

Rhodes College

Rice University

MS 17, PO Box 1892, Houston, TX 77251-1892 • Admissions: 713-348-7423 • Fax: 713-348-5952

CAMPUS LIFE

Quality of Life Rating	98
Fire Safety Rating	95
Green Rating	92
Type of school	Private
Environment	Metropolis

STUDENTS

Total undergrad enrollment	3,962
% male/female	52/48
% from out of state	53
% frosh from public high school	72
% frosh live on campus	99
% ugrads live on campus	72
# of fraternities	0
# of sororities	0
% African American	7
% Asian	26
% Caucasian	33
% Hispanic	16
% Native American	<1
% Pacific Islander	<1
% Two or more races	4
% Race and/or ethnicity unknown	2
% international	12
# of countries represented	55

#14 BEST VALUE COLLEGE

ABOUT THE SCHOOL

Houston's Rice University is a leading interdisciplinary research university that boasts a 6:1 student-to-faculty ratio, more than fifty majors, and dozens of research centers. That mix offers students "a diverse array of opportunities so there's something for everyone" and a lot of chances "to participate in hands-on learning and research," all of which is enabled by "generous, flexible funding." Students here "are challenged and encouraged to learn as much as possible," starting with first-year writing seminars that feature "lots of discussions and different types of group work." And later on, "many academically-oriented competitions" give students a chance to let their hard work and studies shine. Those studies are aided by professors who "understand the material incredibly well, structure their courses well, [and] are always willing to help. Those teachers are even "great at letting you help shape the curriculum to make sure you cover what will help you in the future." And if students ever feel professors are falling short, the university also has a "comprehensive evaluation of teachers done by the students at the end of each semester to ensure that all professors are performing to the standards of Rice."

BANG FOR YOUR BUCK

Rice was originally founded as a tuition-free university, so it's no surprise that it retains a strong commitment to affordability through The Rice Investment. Under this initiative, students from families who make under $65,000 a year receive full assistance with their tuition, fees, and room and board. Those from families making between $65,000 and $130,000 receive full assistance with their tuition. The school meets 100 percent of demonstrated financial need,

Rice University

Financial Aid: 713-348-4958 • E-mail: admi@rice.edu • Website: www.rice.edu

and merit scholarships are all determined through the application process without any further paperwork needed on the part of the student. As for on-campus projects, there is an "abundance of resources" at Rice, and "students have a lot of say in where most of the money is spent." As one student shares, "The faculty and endowment support the students in whichever endeavors they want to involve themselves in."

STUDENT LIFE

Rice's eleven residential colleges help break it down into smaller communities and "enable ... students to create strong, meaningful relationships with hundreds of people" as they live, dine, and share space with the same group of students throughout their four years. The school also "does an excellent job making sure that their students are happy, healthy, and have tons of resources to ensure their wellbeing." That includes a great deal of student autonomy, and the administration "allows the students to run their own dorm governments, businesses, Honor Council, and many other organizations integral to campus life." But the school also recognizes the importance of letting off some steam, so they throw a party almost every weekend at different residential colleges; these "are large, loud, themed parties that many people find fun and safe." Off-campus, the "unique and vibrant city of Houston" has "a relatively mild and warm climate year round," and people will go to concerts and the nearby museum district. They'll also venture into town to "eat out quite often."

CAREER

The Center for Career Development offers résumé reviews, mock interviews, and internship and externship exploration for any student by appointment. In addition to the weekly newsletter it sends to all students, it also offers advising, alumni mentorship, career workshops, and campus recruiting events for all undergraduates. The center also utilizes a roadmap called the ProfessionOwl

ACADEMICS

Academic Rating	91
% students returning for sophomore year	97
% students graduating within 4 years	83
% students graduating within 6 years	91
Calendar	Semester
Student/faculty ratio	6:1
Profs interesting rating	85
Profs accessible rating	87
Most classes have 10–19 students.	

MOST POPULAR MAJORS

Computer Science; Chemical Engineering; Economics

SELECTIVITY

Admissions Rating	98
# of applicants	20,923
% of applicants accepted	11
% of acceptees attending	41
# offered a place on the wait list	3,296
% accepting a place on wait list	65
% admitted from wait list	1
# of early decision applicants	1,675
% accepted early decision	22

Plan (POP), which helps students identify, build, and associate their skills with relevant career goals. The Houston location is also great career-wise, being "very beneficial [with] so many resources around ... for internships and research." One student claims, "There are more internships available than there are students on campus." But this kind of assistance doesn't end with graduation: The School of Continuing Studies is also available to all lifelong learners who wish to continue personal and professional development even after they've left the university.

GENERAL INFO

Activities: Campus Ministries; Choral groups; Concert band; Dance; Drama/theater; International Student Organization; Jazz band; Literary magazine; Marching band; Music ensembles; Musical theater; Opera; Pep band; Radio station; Student government; Student newspaper; Student-run film society; Symphony orchestra; Television station; Yearbook. 280 registered organizations, 11 honor society, 14 religious organizations, 0 fraternities, 0 sororities, on campus. **Athletics (Intercollegiate):** *Men:* baseball, basketball, cross-country, football, golf, tennis, track/field (outdoor), track/field (indoor). *Women:* basketball, cross-country, soccer, swimming, tennis, track/field (outdoor), track/field (indoor), volleyball. **On-Campus Highlights:** Rice Memorial Center, Baker Institute for Public Policy, Brochstein Pavilion (cafe), Shepherd School of Music, Reckling Park-baseball stadium. **Environmental Initiatives:** Green Building. At present, we have roughly 1,000,000 square feet of facilities on campus that are under construction that will receive some level of LEED certification, including the student dormitory Duncan College which is targeted for LEED-Gold. In addition, an off-campus child care center is pursuing LEED certification. Also, an off-campus graduate student apartment complex has been designed to LEED standards although it will not be formally submitted for certification. With this complex, we anticipate savings in energy of about 30% and water savings of 20%. Further, the complex was constructed in an area with excellent pedestrian access, and it includes extensive bicycle storage along with shuttle bus service to campus and to major nearby grocery stores. Our campus standard for on-campus LEED certification for new buildings is LEED-Silver as a minimum. The University has also enjoyed significant successes with construction waste recycling, with many of our largest projects to date logging diversion rates of 85-90% to recycling.

Rice University

FINANCIAL AID

Students should submit: CSS/Financial Aid PROFILE; FAFSA; Noncustodial PROFILE. Priority filing deadline is 2/15. The Princeton Review suggests that all financial aid forms be submitted as soon as possible after October 1. *Need-based scholarships/grants offered*: College/university scholarship or grant aid from institutional funds; Federal Pell; Private scholarships; SEOG; State scholarships/grants. *Loan aid offered*: Direct PLUS loans; Direct Subsidized Stafford Loans; Direct Unsubsidized Stafford Loans. Applicants will be notified of awards on or about 4/1. Federal Work-Study Program available. Institutional employment available.

BOTTOM LINE

Tuition comes in at $48,330; the total cost, including $14,140 for room and board and $782 in mandatory fees, is $62,352. Rice meets the full need of admitted students, and 72% of students graduate without debt. Beginning in fall 2019 under the school's new initiative, The Rice Investment, middle-income families with demonstrated need and typical assets will receive grant aid to cover full tuition if they earn up to $130,000 per year, and half tuition for families earning between $130,001–$200,000. Students with family incomes below $65,000 and typical assets will receive grant aid covering not only their full tuition, but also mandatory fees and room and board. Students receiving aid under The Rice Investment will have all demonstrated need met without any loans.

FINANCIAL FACTS

Financial Aid Rating	99
Annual tuition	$48,330
Room and board	$14,140
Required fees	$782
Books and supplies	$1,200
Average frosh need-based scholarship	$44,044
Average UG need-based scholarship	$43,174
% needy frosh rec. need-based scholarship or grant aid	100
% needy UG rec. need-based scholarship or grant aid	100
% needy frosh rec. non-need-based scholarship or grant aid	13
% needy UG rec. non-need-based scholarship or grant aid	6
% needy frosh rec. need-based self-help aid	44
% needy UG rec. need-based self-help aid	57
% frosh rec. any financial aid	56
% UG rec. any financial aid	54
% UG borrow to pay for school	24
Average cumulative indebtedness	$24,635
% frosh need fully met	100
% ugrads need fully met	100
Average % of frosh need met	100
Average % of ugrad need met	100

CAREER INFORMATION FROM PAYSCALE.COM

ROI Rating	95
Bachelors and No Higher	
Median starting salary	$71,000
Median mid-career salary	$129,500
At Least Bachelors	
Median starting salary	$72,200
Median mid-career salary	$135,700
Alumni with high job meaning	51%
Degrees awarded in STEM subjects	45%

Rose-Hulman Institute of Technology

5500 Wabash Ave., Terra Haute, IN 47803 • Admissions: 812-877-8213 • Fax: 812-877-8941

#20 BEST VALUE COLLEGE

CAMPUS LIFE

Quality of Life Rating	92
Fire Safety Rating	96
Green Rating	80
Type of school	Private
Environment	Town

STUDENTS

Total undergrad enrollment	2,085
% male/female	75/25
% from out of state	65
% frosh from public high school	63
% frosh live on campus	98
% ugrads live on campus	55
# of fraternities	
(% ugrad men join)	8 (37)
# of sororities	
(% ugrad women join)	3 (26)
% African American	3
% Asian	6
% Caucasian	66
% Hispanic	5
% Native American	<1
% Pacific Islander	<1
% Two or more races	5
% Race and/or ethnicity unknown	1
% international	15
# of countries represented	9

ABOUT THE SCHOOL

Though ostensibly dedicated to the study of engineering, science and mathematics, the Rose-Hulman Institute of Technology seeks to create a "collaborative rather than competitive" environment that sends its graduates into the real world with the tools needed to secure employment. "Everyone from the housekeepers and residence life to professors and staff truly wants you to succeed, academically and at life in general," says a student. The professors in the small classes "genuinely care about your learning and advancing you in your career path," the "accommodating" administration creates an "intimate family atmosphere," and there is an open door policy that extends "from your fellow students all the way up to the president." Additionally, there are many resources for students who are struggling, and the school makes it a point to encourage students to take advantage of the artwork and cultural opportunities available at the school (including the Rose-Hulman art collection, drama club productions, and the Performing Arts Series).

BANG FOR YOUR BUCK

Almost every single student attending Rose-Hulman receives aid of some sort, and the college makes the application process as ingrained with the admissions process as possible. In addition to federal grants and scholarships, there are several institutional scholarships available. Rose-Hulman Merit Scholarships are based on both academic and non-academic measures (such as extracurricular activities, leadership and community service), and all admitted students are automatically considered. Rose-Hulman Named

Rose-Hulman Institute of Technology

Financial Aid: 812-877-8259 • E-mail: admissions@rose-hulman.edu • Website: www.rose-hulman.edu

Scholarships are more limited in number and have specific restrictions placed on them by the donor; all students are also considered upon admission.

STUDENT LIFE

Students at this 2,100 strong school "are time- and efficiency-oriented" and while they may put a lot of hours into school, they all "choose a few extracurriculars with which to get very involved." Rose-Hulman "is a sort of social oasis for the kids that knew everything in high school" and "we are all proud to be nerds together," beams a student. "Students are pretty goofy and creative" so "random games like 'owling' and fruit golf pop up," says one. The excellent residential life program means that "floor residents become extremely close and participate in many events together" and people call it the "Rose bubble" because "life on campus is amazing (although unrealistic to the outside world because of how nice everyone is)." Indeed, there's so much to do on campus that people leave very rarely: "If we aren't busy studying or getting homework done, we are out participating in intramurals, varsity athletics, community service, religious groups, gaming groups, campus jobs, greek life...the list goes on and on," says a student.

CAREER

This is one of the top undergraduate engineering schools in the country, and "the job placement rate and average starting salary are amazing." The importance is set strictly on academics and employers recognize that, and "the opportunities for gaining experience in your field of study are endless." Career Services brings in numerous companies to help provide jobs, co-ops, and internships to students, and sets up mock interviews, résumé reviews, and numerous career and graduate school fairs to help the job hunt process

ACADEMICS

Academic Rating	94
% students returning for sophomore year	92
% students graduating within 4 years	67
% students graduating within 6 years	81
Calendar	Quarter
Student/faculty ratio	11:1
Profs interesting rating	96
Profs accessible rating	99

Most classes have 20–29 students. Most lab/discussion sessions have 10–19 students.

MOST POPULAR MAJORS
Computer Science; Chemical Engineering; Mechanical Engineering

SELECTIVITY

Admissions Rating	92
# of applicants	4,471
% of applicants accepted	68
% of acceptees attending	16
# offered a place on the wait list	357
% accepting a place on wait list	38
% admitted from wait list	36

run smoothly. Fifty-one percent of Rose-Hulman graduates who visited PayScale.com felt their job had a meaningful impact on the world; an average starting salary of $75,000 was reported.

GENERAL INFO

Activities: Choral groups; Concert band; Dance; Drama/theater; International Student Organization; Jazz band; Music ensembles; Musical theater; Pep band; Radio station; Student government; Student newspaper; Symphony orchestra. 104 registered organizations, 7 honor societies, 2 religious organizations, 8 fraternities, 3 sororities, on campus. **Athletics (Intercollegiate):** *Men:* baseball, basketball, cross-country, diving, football, golf, riflery, soccer, swimming, tennis, track/field (outdoor), track/field (indoor). *Women:* basketball, cross-country, diving, golf, riflery, soccer, softball, swimming, tennis, track/field (outdoor), track/field (indoor), volleyball. **On-Campus Highlights:** Sports and Recreation Center, Hatfield Hall, White Chapel, Branam Innovation Center. **Environmental Initiatives:** Signing of the American College & University Presidents' Climate Commitment.

FINANCIAL AID

Students should submit: FAFSA. Priority filing deadline is 3/10. The Princeton Review suggests that all financial aid forms be submitted as soon as possible after October 1. *Need-based scholarships/grants offered*: College/university scholarship or grant aid from institutional funds; Federal Pell; SEOG; State scholarships/grants. *Loan aid offered*: Direct PLUS loans; Direct Subsidized Stafford Loans; Direct Unsubsidized Stafford Loans. Applicants will be notified of awards on or about 3/10. Federal Work-Study Program available. Institutional employment available.

Rose-Hulman Institute of Technology

BOTTOM LINE

Tuition rings in at $46,641, with another $14,766 going towards room and board. Fortunately, 100 percent of undergraduates receive financial aid. Of the 58 percent of students who borrow through a loan program, the average debt upon graduation is $43,459. About 60 percent of Rose-Hulman students also participate in Federal Work-Study or Work Opportunity to help offset costs while they are at school.

CAREER INFORMATION FROM PAYSCALE.COM	
ROI Rating	94
Bachelors and No Higher	
Median starting salary	$75,000
Median mid-career salary	$135,800
At Least Bachelors	
Median starting salary	$76,200
Median mid-career salary	$138,800
Alumni with high job meaning	51%
Degrees awarded in STEM subjects	96%

FINANCIAL FACTS	
Financial Aid Rating	93
Annual tuition	$46,641
Room and board	$14,766
Required fees	$930
Books and supplies	$1,500
Average frosh need-based scholarship	$30,676
Average UG need-based scholarship	$28,385
% needy frosh rec. need-based scholarship or grant aid	99
% needy UG rec. need-based scholarship or grant aid	99
% needy frosh rec. non-need-based scholarship or grant aid	68
% needy UG rec. non-need-based scholarship or grant aid	74
% needy frosh rec. need-based self-help aid	76
% needy UG rec. need-based self-help aid	78
% frosh rec. any financial aid	100
% UG rec. any financial aid	100
% UG borrow to pay for school	58
Average cumulative indebtedness	$43,459
% frosh need fully met	20
% ugrads need fully met	17
Average % of frosh need met	65
Average % of ugrad need met	62

Rose-Hulman Institute of Technology

Smith College

Seven College Lane, Northampton, MA 01063 • Admissions: 413-585-2500 • Fax: 413-585-2527

#65 BEST VALUE COLLEGE

CAMPUS LIFE

Quality of Life Rating	92
Fire Safety Rating	84
Green Rating	97
Type of school	Private
Environment	Town

STUDENTS

Total undergrad enrollment	2,484
% male/female	0/100
% from out of state	81
% frosh from public high school	62
% frosh live on campus	100
% ugrads live on campus	95
# of sororities	0
% African American	7
% Asian	9
% Caucasian	48
% Hispanic	12
% Native American	<1
% Pacific Islander	<1
% Two or more races	5
% Race and/or ethnicity unknown	6
% international	14
# of countries represented	70

ABOUT THE SCHOOL

Located in western Massachusetts in the idyllic college town of Northampton, Smith College boasts "extremely challenging academics" in a setting where "women come first." Along with the school's "global and interdisciplinary focus," women at Smith enjoy an "excellent academic atmosphere, close-knit community, small class size, top-notch professors, [and] fantastic resources" in a "beautiful New England" setting. Smith's "open curriculum" "doesn't have course requirements," and the school boasts "lots of unique traditions that make it enjoyable." Smith professors are "strikingly committed to their students." Students routinely attend "class dinners with professors," where mentors "volunteer to read drafts, and help with research." As one student attests, "not only that, but [professors] always get excited when you visit office hours—the one-on-one is not only available here, but encouraged." Another incoming freshman recalls, "Walking onto Smith College campus was like a breath of fresh air. The old brick buildings (mixed in with the newer ones), the gorgeous campus (designed by Fredrick Law Olmsted), and atmosphere pulled me in. The academics were superb and the people welcoming." In a nutshell, this highly prestigious women's college is "all about being socially aware and making a positive impact in the environment, economy, politics, and everyday life."

BANG FOR YOUR BUCK

One of the cornerstones of a Smith education is the ability to design your own academic experience within a plethora of curricular opportunities. Students here are routinely engaged in one-on-one research as undergraduates, with professors in the arts, humanities, sciences, and social sciences. There are no required courses

Smith College

Financial Aid: 413-585-2530 • E-mail: admission@smith.edu • Website: www.smith.edu

outside of the freshman year writing-intensive seminar. In addition, students have the added benefit of the larger academic community of the Five Colleges Consortium, which includes Amherst, Hampshire, Mount Holyoke, and the University of Massachusetts Amherst. Smith has the largest and oldest women-only ABET-accredited Engineering program in the country, and more than 43 percent of Smithies major in the hardcore sciences. Praxis, Smith's unique internship program, guarantees all students access to at least one college-funded internship during their four years at the college.

STUDENT LIFE

Undergrads at Smith certainly cultivate full and varied lives. Of course, it helps that "a range of social activities" abound. The student government continually sponsors a number of events "like movie showings, outdoor activities [and] bowling nights." As you might expect, these ladies are also incredibly politically savvy. Hence, there's also "a lot of involvement in community service and activism for global issues, women's rights, LGBTQ rights, the environment, and pretty much anything that fights oppression." Further, during the weekend "there are always house parties on campus and students can go to other college parties at surrounding campuses." Additionally, "downtown Northampton [is] always bustling with events. Indeed, "there are...concerts, restaurants, and cute shops...to provide us with distractions."

CAREER

Hands down, "Smith provides so many opportunities for [undergrads]!" Indeed, from "on-campus resources to internship and job opportunities—Smith gives students the means to thrive in the world." To begin with, it's definitely not uncommon for professors to "[go] out of their way to help [students] find contacts and resources for jobs." What's more, according

ACADEMICS

Academic Rating	92
% students returning for sophomore year	93
% students graduating within 4 years	83
% students graduating within 6 years	89
Calendar	Semester
Student/faculty ratio	8:1
Profs interesting rating	86
Profs accessible rating	83
Most classes have 10–19 students.	

MOST POPULAR MAJORS

Psychology, General; Economics, General; Political Science and Government, General

SELECTIVITY

Admissions Rating	97
# of applicants	5,780
% of applicants accepted	31
% of acceptees attending	34
# offered a place on the wait list	923
% accepting a place on wait list	50
% admitted from wait list	15
# of early decision applicants	578
% accepted early decision	49

Range SAT EBRW	670–750
Range SAT Math	670–770
Range ACT Composite	31–34
# submitting SAT scores	262
% submitting SAT scores	43
# submitting ACT scores	185
% submitting ACT scores	30
Average HS GPA	4.0
% graduated top 10% of class	72
% graduated top 25% of class	96
% graduated top 50% of class	100

DEADLINES

Early decision	
Deadline	11/15
Notification	12/15
Other ED Deadline	1/1
Other ED Notification	late January
Regular	
Deadline	1/15
Notification	4/1
Nonfall registration?	No

to a grateful American studies major, "The Career Development Office will do everything in its power to help you get a job/internship." With its myriad of workshops, Preparing for Finance Interviews or Marketing Your Study Abroad Experience for example, Smith students can confidently enter the job market. They can visit the office to get assistance in tweaking their resumes and cover letters or to gain insight in the grad school admissions process. And they may definitely take advantage of the career fairs the college hosts. Organizations in attendance have included the Peace Corps, Bloomingdale's, Verizon Wireless and Teach for America.

GENERAL INFO

Activities: Campus Ministries; Choral groups; Concert band; Dance; Drama/theater; International Student Organization; Jazz band; Literary magazine; Model UN; Music ensembles; Musical theater; Radio station; Student government; Student newspaper; Symphony orchestra; Television station; Yearbook. 100 registered organizations, 3 honor societies, 9 religious organizations, 0 fraternities, 0 sororities, on campus. **Athletics (Intercollegiate):** *Women:* basketball, crew/rowing, cross-country, diving, equestrian sports, field hockey, lacrosse, skiing (downhill/alpine), soccer, softball, squash, swimming, tennis, track/field (outdoor), track/field (indoor), volleyball. **On-Campus Highlights:** Smith Art Museum, The Botanical Gardens, Campus Center, Mendenhall Center for Performing Arts, Ford Hall (Engineering, science). **Environmental Initiatives:** A new natural gas fired cogeneration facility went online in October 2008, which generates most campus electric use and schieves 80% efficiency with new absorption chillers.

FINANCIAL AID

Students should submit: CSS/Financial Aid PROFILE; FAFSA; Institution's own financial aid form; Noncustodial PROFILE. Priority filing deadline is 1/25. The Princeton Review suggests that all financial aid forms be submitted as soon as possible after October 1. *Need-based scholarships/grants offered*: College/university scholarship or grant aid from institutional funds; Federal

Smith College

Pell; Private scholarships; SEOG; State scholarships/ grants. *Loan aid offered*: Direct PLUS loans; Direct Subsidized Stafford Loans; Direct Unsubsidized Stafford Loans. Applicants will be notified of awards on or about 4/1. Federal Work-Study Program available. Institutional employment available.

BOTTOM LINE

Smith makes no bones about its commitment to finding inroads to making a serious private education available to women of all stripes, no matter their financial background. Though the cost of education here doesn't come at a discount—annual tuition is currently $53,940, with room and board tallying an additional $18,130—according to our recent statistics, over the past several years Smith has boasted a 100 percent success rate when it comes to meeting not just freshman financial need but financial need across all four years. The average student indebtedness after four years totals $22,083, with 62 percent of undergraduates receiving some form of need-based financial aid.

FINANCIAL FACTS	
Financial Aid Rating	**93**
Annual tuition	$53,940
Room and board	$18,130
Required fees	$284
Books and supplies	$800
Average frosh need-based scholarship	$50,491
Average UG need-based scholarship	$52,924
% needy frosh rec. need-based scholarship or grant aid	96
% needy UG rec. need-based scholarship or grant aid	97
% needy frosh rec. non-need-based scholarship or grant aid	3
% needy UG rec. non-need-based scholarship or grant aid	2
% needy frosh rec. need-based self-help aid	90
% needy UG rec. need-based self-help aid	93
% frosh rec. any financial aid	70
% UG rec. any financial aid	71
% UG borrow to pay for school	58
Average cumulative indebtedness	$22,083
% frosh need fully met	100
% ugrads need fully met	100
Average % of frosh need met	100
Average % of ugrad need met	100

CAREER INFORMATION FROM PAYSCALE.COM	
ROI Rating	91
Bachelors and No Higher	
Median starting salary	$52,700
Median mid-career salary	$98,200
At Least Bachelors	
Median starting salary	$54,100
Median mid-career salary	$113,100
Alumni with high job meaning	52%
Degrees awarded in STEM subjects	26%

Smith College

St. Olaf College

1520 St. Olaf Avenue, Northfield, MN 55057 • Admissions: 507-786-3025 • Fax: 507-786-3832

CAMPUS LIFE

Quality of Life Rating	95
Fire Safety Rating	82
Green Rating	60*
Type of school	Private
Affiliation	Lutheran
Environment	Village

STUDENTS

Total undergrad enrollment	3,031
% male/female	43/57
% from out of state	53
% frosh from public high school	70
% frosh live on campus	100
% ugrads live on campus	94
# of fraternities	0
# of sororities	0
% African American	3
% Asian	7
% Caucasian	70
% Hispanic	7
% Native American	<1
% Pacific Islander	<1
% Two or more races	3
% Race and/or ethnicity unknown	1
% international	10
# of countries represented	80

#70 BEST VALUE COLLEGE

ABOUT THE SCHOOL

Located in Northfield, Minnesota, less than an hour drive from the Twin Cities, St. Olaf College boasts a combination of top-rated programs and academic rigor with an uncommon emphasis on community-building. Historically connected to the Evangelical Lutheran Church, the college offers a secular educational experience rooted in Norwegian traditions. The small class size allows for "strong relationships" between faculty and students, and professors are "passionate," "incredibly accessible," and "challenging." Along with the top-ranked, "incredible" study abroad program, its music program is highly prized and "nationally recognized." The mathematics/statistics and religion/theology programs are also highly ranked, and professors across disciplines receive "tens across the board." The clear majority of its approximately 3,000 students (nicknamed "Oles") live on the "beautiful" 300-acre campus, building a tight-knit community students call "inclusive" and true to the school's unofficial motto of "Never leave an Ole behind." "St. Olaf has this inherent spirit of possibility and collaboration that drew me in…" says one student. "There is a feeling that…everyone is there to work hard and achieve."

BANG FOR YOUR BUCK

St. Olaf's mission sets out "to be a globally engaged community" and "to explore meaningful vocation," a philosophy institutionalized in the Piper Center, which "works tirelessly to make sure Oles have the resources to land their dream internship, job, or service opportunity." Paired with the ample study abroad opportunities, students can expect to be prepared for life after St. Olaf, whether that means gaining full-time employment,

St. Olaf College

Financial Aid: 507-786-3019 • E-mail: admissions@stolaf.edu • Website: www.stolaf.edu

entering competitive graduate programs, or joining the large cohort of graduating seniors who become Fulbright Scholars. Over ninety percent of students receive institutional gift aid, averaging about $37,000 per student. Notably, students point out that the centrality of the school's music program to the campus means that they can "give scholarships in music to non-music majors."

STUDENT LIFE

The "highly residential" and dry campus help shape the culture on campus for students, which is described as a "busy…but fulfilled life." Most Oles engage in at least one extracurricular activity every day—and the offerings are vast. With "over 200 clubs," frequent dances at "The Pause," a campus hangout and concert venue, [and] student government-sponsored activities…" most students balance "a full course load, in addition to a music ensemble, club sport, or some other type of group—sometimes all of the above." The Tostrud Recreation Center—with its varied offerings that include a rock climbing wall—is a popular place to blow off steam, along with intramural sports teams and the "surrounding natural lands for…walks and de-stressing." The music program (including its celebrated St. Olaf Christmas Festival) is world renowned and deeply integrated into campus culture.

CAREER

Students say that one of St. Olaf's greatest strengths is its Piper Center for Vocation and Career. By maintaining "strategic relationships with employers, faculty, staff, alumni, parents, and donors," the center can "maximize opportunities for students and alumni." Furthermore, students say that the "vocational retreats, alumni luncheons, [and] one-on-one coaching…makes sure that all the hard work put into classes pays off." According to PayScale.com, over 50 percent of

ACADEMICS

Academic Rating	91
% students returning for sophomore year	91
% students graduating within 4 years	82
% students graduating within 6 years	86
Calendar	4-1-4
Student/faculty ratio	12:1
Profs interesting rating	92
Profs accessible rating	93

Most classes have 10–19 students.

MOST POPULAR MAJORS

Biology/Biological Sciences, General; Mathematics, General; Economics, General

SELECTIVITY

Admissions Rating	90
# of applicants	5,496
% of applicants accepted	50
% of acceptees attending	29
# offered a place on the wait list	911
% accepting a place on wait list	49
% admitted from wait list	11
# of early decision applicants	368
% accepted early decision	76

FRESHMAN PROFILE

Range SAT EBRW	600–700
Range SAT Math	590–710
Range ACT Composite	25–32
# submitting SAT scores	283
% submitting SAT scores	35
# submitting ACT scores	602
% submitting ACT scores	74
Average HS GPA	3.7
% graduated top 10% of class	41
% graduated top 25% of class	72
% graduated top 50% of class	96

DEADLINES

Early decision	
Deadline	11/15
Notification	12/15
Other ED Deadline	1/8
Other ED Notification	2/1
Regular	
Deadline	1/15
Notification	4/1
Nonfall registration?	No

St. Olaf alumni report that they derive a high level of meaning from their careers. The average "early career" (alumni with 0-5 years of experience) yearly salary is $54,100.

GENERAL INFO

Activities: Campus Ministries; Choral groups; Concert band; Dance; Drama/theater; International Student Organization; Jazz band; Literary magazine; Model UN; Music ensembles; Musical theater; Opera; Pep band; Radio station; Student government; Student newspaper; Student-run film society; Symphony orchestra. 221 registered organizations, 20 honor societies, 15 religious organizations, 0 fraternities, 0 sororities, on campus. **Athletics (Intercollegiate):** *Men:* baseball, basketball, cross-country, diving, football, golf, ice hockey, skiing (downhill/alpine), skiing nordic cross-country, soccer, swimming, tennis, track/field (outdoor), track/field (indoor), wrestling. *Women:* basketball, cross-country, diving, golf, ice hockey, skiing (downhill/alpine), skiing nordiccross-country, soccer, softball, swimming, tennis, track/field (outdoor), track/field (indoor), volleyball. **On-Campus Highlights:** Fireside Lounge, Buntrock Commons, The Lion's Pause (student-run nightclub), Tostrud Recreation Center.

St. Olaf College

FINANCIAL AID

Students should submit: CSS/Financial Aid PROFILE; FAFSA; Noncustodial PROFILE. Priority filing deadline is 1/15. The Princeton Review suggests that all financial aid forms be submitted as soon as possible after October 1. *Need-based scholarships/grants offered*: College/university scholarship or grant aid from institutional funds; Federal Pell; Private scholarships; SEOG; State scholarships/grants. *Loan aid offered*: Direct Subsidized Stafford Loans; Direct Unsubsidized Stafford Loans. Applicants will be notified of awards on or about 4/1. Federal Work-Study Program available. Institutional employment available.

BOTTOM LINE

If you are seeking a small, community-oriented, academically rigorous environment with an emphasis on social values and cooperation, St. Olaf fits the bill. The $49,710 tuition and $11,270 room and board costs are offset by St. Olaf's commitment to providing a financially manageable education: its financial aid packages meet 95 percent of undergraduate need across all four years.

FINANCIAL FACTS	
Financial Aid Rating	97
Annual tuition	$49,710
Room and board	$11,270
Books and supplies	$1,000
Average frosh need-based scholarship	$36,531
Average UG need-based scholarship	$35,236
% needy frosh rec. need-based scholarship or grant aid	100
% needy UG rec. need-based scholarship or grant aid	100
% needy frosh rec. non-need-based scholarship or grant aid	35
% needy UG rec. non-need-based scholarship or grant aid	26
% needy frosh rec. need-based self-help aid	90
% needy UG rec. need-based self-help aid	96
% frosh rec. any financial aid	97
% UG rec. any financial aid	97
% UG borrow to pay for school	64
Average cumulative indebtedness	$29,907
% frosh need fully met	95
% ugrads need fully met	76
Average % of frosh need met	100
Average % of ugrad need met	95

CAREER INFORMATION FROM PAYSCALE.COM	
ROI Rating	91
Bachelors and No Higher	
Median starting salary	$54,100
Median mid-career salary	$101,900
At Least Bachelors	
Median starting salary	$55,500
Median mid-career salary	$111,500
Alumni with high job meaning	53%
Degrees awarded in STEM subjects	30%

St. Olaf College

Stanford University

Undergraduate Admission, Montag Hall, 355 Galvez Street, Stanford, CA 94305-6106 • Admission: 650-723-2091

CAMPUS LIFE

Quality of Life Rating	94
Fire Safety Rating	89
Green Rating	99
Type of school	Private
Environment	City

STUDENTS

Total undergrad enrollment	7,083
% male/female	50/50
% from out of state	65
% frosh from public high school	59
% frosh live on campus	100
% ugrads live on campus	97
# of fraternities	
(% ugrad men join)	15 (18)
# of sororities	
(% ugrad women join)	14 (24)
% African American	6
% Asian	22
% Caucasian	34
% Hispanic	16
% Native American	<1
% Pacific Islander	<1
% Two or more races	9
% Race and/or ethnicity unknown	<1
% international	10
# of countries represented	90

#4 BEST VALUE COLLEGE

ABOUT THE SCHOOL

Stanford University is widely recognized as one of the nation's most outstanding universities, considered by many to be the West Coast's answer to the Ivy League. Stanford alumni, who can be found in 143 countries, eighteen territories, and all fifty states, have distinguished themselves in many fields, from government service to innovation to business to arts and entertainment. Academics are simply top-notch, and despite the fact that this is a research-driven university, professors are seriously interested in getting to know their undergrads. Students say that teachers at Stanford are "wonderful resources for guidance and tutoring," and there is "an opportunity to engage with them on a regular basis." The classroom experience is discussion-oriented and otherwise awesome. There are tons of majors, and, if you don't like any of the ones on offer, it's a breeze to design your own. The dorms are like palaces. The administration runs the school like a finely tuned machine. There's very little not to like about this place. "The classes, campus, and faculty are amazing," reports one contented undergrad; another is happy to find that Stanford "has incredible resources, incredible people...and an unrivaled atmosphere of openness and collaboration."

BANG FOR YOUR BUCK

Like a handful of other spectacularly wealthy schools in the United States, Stanford maintains a wholly need-blind admission policy, and it demonstrates a serious commitment to making its world-class education available to talented and well-prepared students regardless of economic circumstances. All of Stanford's scholarship funds are need-based. For parents with total annual income and typical assets below $65,000, Stanford will not expect any parent contribution toward educational costs. For parents with total annual income and typical assets below $125,000, the expected parent contribution will be low enough to

Stanford University

Financial Aid: 650-723-3058 • E-mail: admission@stanford.edu • Fax: 650-725-2846 • Website: www.stanford.edu

ensure that all tuition charges are covered with need-based scholarship, federal and state grants, and/or outside scholarship funds. Families with incomes at higher levels (typically up to $200,000 or higher) may also qualify for assistance, especially if more than one family member is enrolled in college. The hard part is getting admitted. If you can do that, the school will make sure you have a way to pay. The vast majority of successful applicants will be among the strongest students (academically) in their secondary schools.

STUDENT LIFE

"People often use the duck metaphor to describe Stanford," says a student, "on the surface they are calm and serene, under the surface they are paddling really hard." But it's not all hard work and studying for the student body, as "life at Stanford has the potential to be both extremely stressful (due to the strenuous academics) and very carefree (due to the wide variety of 'releases' available to students)." "We aren't a typical party school, but about a third of the student body tries to party enough for everyone else." For the other two-thirds, "there are tons of ways to be involved" and "clubs for every type of person." "Some dance, some sing, some play instruments, some plan events" and "students constantly 'roll out' to whatever performance, sports event, or talk they can in order to support their fellow classmates and the hard work that is put in to it." And of course, students can turn to the beautiful natural surroundings when in need of a little relaxation. "Life at Stanford is like a vacation. The campus with its palm trees and surrounding foothills is the most beautiful in the world." But while "anything you could possibly need is pretty much on campus" getting away can be great too: "Only at Stanford can you go from snowy mountains, to sunny beaches, to bustling city life [in San Francisco] all in one day."

CAREER

As a top-notch school, Stanford can lead to "great job opportunities" for motivated students looking to enter a wide variety of careers. Stanford students tend to be very focused on the future, with "about a 50/50 divide of people who are planning for

ACADEMICS

Academic Rating	95
% students returning for sophomore year	99
% students graduating within 4 years	75
% students graduating within 6 years	94
Calendar	Quarter
Student/faculty ratio	5:1
Profs interesting rating	85
Profs accessible rating	87

Most classes have fewer than 10 students. Most lab/discussion sessions have fewer than 10 students.

MOST POPULAR MAJORS
Computer Science; Human Biology; Engineering, General

SELECTIVITY

Admissions Rating	99
# of applicants	47,452
% of applicants accepted	4
% of acceptees attending	82
# offered a place on the wait list	870
% accepting a place on wait list	78
% admitted from wait list	4

careers to make money and people who are planning for careers to 'make a difference.'" Stanford's Career Development Center provides standard services such as job fairs and recruiting events, resume critique, and one-on-one counseling. The Center also offers "career communities" in specific fields, and a special community devoted solely to the needs of underclassmen still a few years from their job search. Most agree that Stanford "provides a great opportunity to pursue greater careers with a wide array of resources and support." Out of Stanford alumni visiting PayScale.com, 61 percent report that they derive meaning from their jobs.

GENERAL INFO

Activities: Campus Ministries; Choral groups; Concert band; Dance; Drama/theater; International Student Organization; Jazz band; Literary magazine; Marching band; Model UN; Music ensembles; Musical theater; Opera; Pep band; Radio station; Student government; Student newspaper; Student-run film society; Symphony orchestra; Television station; Yearbook. 600 registered organizations, 35 religious organizations, 15 fraternities, 14 sororities, on campus. **Athletics (Intercollegiate):** *Men:* baseball, basketball, crew/rowing, cross-country, diving, fencing, football, golf, gymnastics, sailing, soccer, swimming, tennis, track/field (outdoor), volleyball, water polo, wrestling. *Women:* basketball, crew/rowing, cross-country, diving, fencing, field hockey, golf, gymnastics, lacrosse, sailing, soccer, softball, squash, swimming, synchronized swimming, tennis, track/field (outdoor), volleyball, water polo. **On-Campus Highlights:** Cantor Center for the Visual Arts, The Anderson Collection at Stanford University, Memorial Church, Tresidder Memorial Union, Bing Concert Hall. **Environmental Initiatives:** STANFORD ENERGY SYSTEM INNOVATIONS (SESI) Between 1987 and 2015, Stanford relied on a natural gas-fired combined heat and power (CHP) plant for virtually all its energy demand. Although efficient, its fossil-fuel based source caused the CHP to produce 90% of Stanford's GHG emissions and consume 25% of the campus' potable water supply. As a result, Stanford's GHG reduction strategy focused primarily on transforming the university's energy supply through a new Central Energy Facility (CEF). The new CEF, which came online in April 2015, includes three large water tanks for thermal energy storage and a high voltage substation that receives electricity from the grid. A key feature of the CEF is an innovative heat recovery system that takes advantage of Stanford's overlap in heating and cooling needs. In addition to the CEF, the SESI project converted the heat supply of all buildings from steam

Stanford University

to hot water. This new system is 70% more efficient than the CHP plant. The efficiencies gained from the new CEF and hot water conversion, along with the introduction of a 67 MW off-site solar plant and 4.5 MW of on-site solar, will reduce the university's overall GHG emissions by approximately 68% between 2011 and 2017.

FINANCIAL AID

Students should submit: CSS/Financial Aid PROFILE; FAFSA; Noncustodial PROFILE. Priority filing deadline is 2/16. The Princeton Review suggests that all financial aid forms be submitted as soon as possible after October 1. *Need-based scholarships/grants offered*: College/university scholarship or grant aid from institutional funds; Federal Pell; Private scholarships; SEOG; State scholarships/grants. *Loan aid offered*: Direct PLUS loans; Direct Subsidized Stafford Loans; Direct Unsubsidized Stafford Loans. Applicants will be notified of awards on a rolling basis beginning 4/1. Federal Work-Study Program available. Institutional employment available.

BOTTOM LINE

A year of tuition, fees, room and board, and basic expenses at Stanford costs about $71,207. While that figure is staggering, you have to keep in mind that few students pay anywhere near that amount. Financial packages here are very generous. Most aid comes with no strings attached. Only 19 percent of undergrads borrow to pay for school, and those who do walk away with an average of $21,348 in loan debt.

FINANCIAL FACTS	
Financial Aid Rating	98
Annual tuition	$52,857
Room and board	$16,433
Required fees	$672
Books and supplies	$1,245
Average frosh need-based scholarship	$52,453
Average UG need-based scholarship	$50,542
% needy frosh rec. need-based scholarship or grant aid	96
% needy UG rec. need-based scholarship or grant aid	96
% needy frosh rec. non-need-based scholarship or grant aid	3
% needy UG rec. non-need-based scholarship or grant aid	3
% needy frosh rec. need-based self-help aid	63
% needy UG rec. need-based self-help aid	73
% frosh rec. any financial aid	86
% UG rec. any financial aid	85
% UG borrow to pay for school	19
Average cumulative indebtedness	$21,348
% frosh need fully met	93
% ugrads need fully met	90
Average % of frosh need met	100
Average % of ugrad need met	100

CAREER INFORMATION FROM PAYSCALE.COM	
ROI Rating	98
Bachelors and No Higher	
Median starting salary	$79,000
Median mid-career salary	$145,200
At Least Bachelors	
Median starting salary	$83,500
Median mid-career salary	$161,400
Alumni with high job meaning	61%
Degrees awarded in STEM subjects	51%

Stanford University

Swarthmore College

500 College Avenue, Swarthmore, PA 19081 • Admissions: 610-328-8300 • Fax: 610-328-8580

#30 BEST VALUE COLLEGE

ABOUT THE SCHOOL

Swarthmore College is among the most renowned liberal arts schools in the country. The locus of Swarthmore's greatness lies in the quality and passion of its faculty ("Some of my professors have knocked me to the floor with their brilliance"). A student/faculty ratio of eight to one ensures that students have close, meaningful engagement with their professors. "It's where to go for a real education—for learning for the sake of truly learning, rather than just for grades," says a student. The college's Honors Program features small groups of dedicated and accomplished students working closely with faculty, with an emphasis on independent learning, and helps further the school's reputation as "a community where everyone pushes each other toward success." External examiners who are experts in their fields, such as theater professionals from the Tisch School at NYU and Google software engineers, evaluate seniors in the Honors Program through written and oral examinations. Swatties are a bright and creative lot "who don't get enough sleep because they're too busy doing all they want to do in their time here." Professors and administrators are extremely supportive and "view the students as responsible adults, and thus leave them to their own devices when they are out of class." Students also enjoy an expansive curriculum—about 600 course offerings each year. Swarthmore is part of the Tri-College Consortium (along with Bryn Mawr and Haverford), which means that students can take courses at those schools and use their facilities.

Swarthmore College

Financial Aid: 610-328-8358 • E-mail: admissions@swarthmore.edu • Website: www.swarthmore.edu

BANG FOR YOUR BUCK

Swarthmore College maintains a need-blind admission policy. Admission here is not contingent on your economic situation, and financial aid awards meet 100 percent of admitted students' demonstrated need. Financial aid is also available for some international students. Best of all, all Swarthmore financial aid awards are loan-free (though some students choose to borrow to cover their portion). In most cases, Swarthmore students may apply their financial aid toward the cost of participation in a study abroad program. Finally, the annual activity fee covers everything from digital printing to sports matches, campus movie screenings to lectures and dance performances, making for a cash-free campus.

STUDENT LIFE

Students are "not sure if there is a typical Swattie," but suspect that "the defining feature among us is that each person is brilliant at something: maybe dance, maybe quantum physics, maybe philosophy." One undergrad sums up, "While it is tough to generalize…one word definitely applies to us all: busy." Swarthmore's small size combined with its vast number of clubs and organizations provide opportunities to participate in pretty much whatever you want, and if not "you can start your own club." "There are student musical performances, drama performances, movies, speakers, and comedy shows," along with all kinds of school-sponsored events, so "there is almost always something to do on the weekend." When they can spare a couple of hours, many Swatties like to blow off steam in nearby Philadelphia, which is easily accessible by public transportation, including the train station located right on campus.

ACADEMICS	
Academic Rating	88
% students returning for sophomore year	98
% students graduating within 4 years	89
% students graduating within 6 years	94
Calendar	Semester
Student/faculty ratio	8:1
Profs interesting rating	88
Profs accessible rating	89

Most classes have fewer than 10 students. Most lab/discussion sessions have 10–19 students.

MOST POPULAR MAJORS
Biology/Biological Sciences, General; Economics, General; Political Science and Government, General

SELECTIVITY	
Admissions Rating	98
# of applicants	10,749
% of applicants accepted	9
% of acceptees attending	41
# of early decision applicants	860
% accepted early decision	13

FRESHMAN PROFILE

Range SAT EBRW	680–760
Range SAT Math	700–790
Range ACT Composite	31–34
# submitting SAT scores	256
% submitting SAT scores	62
# submitting ACT scores	179
% submitting ACT scores	43
% graduated top 10% of class	90
% graduated top 25% of class	99
% graduated top 50% of class	100

DEADLINES

Early decision	
Deadline	11/15
Notification	12/15
Other ED Deadline	1/1
Other ED Notification	2/15
Regular	
Deadline	1/1
Notification	4/1
Nonfall registration?	No

CAREER

Swarthmore's Career Services does its part to help students reach their fullest potential by offering a variety of useful resources. Personalized career counseling advises undergrads on their options for major selection, internships, externships, and graduate school applications. The Career Cafés engage the community on broad topics, like women in leadership or sustainable farming, that may have career implications. And, of course, a packed events calendar lets students network with alumni, attend panel discussions, and impress potential employers at recruiting consortiums. Take note of Swarthmore's extensive externship program. It matches students with alumni volunteers for week-long job-shadowing experiences in laboratories, museums, publishing companies, labor unions, leading think-tanks, and other places where you might like to work someday. Alumni who visited PayScale.com reported a median starting salary of $67,500, and 46 percent think their work makes the world a better place.

GENERAL INFO

Activities: Campus Ministries; Choral groups; Dance; Drama/theater; International Student Organization; Jazz band; Literary magazine; Music ensembles; Musical theater; Radio station; Student government; Student newspaper; Student-run film society; Symphony orchestra; Yearbook. 150 registered organizations, 3 honor societies, 14 religious organizations, 2 fraternities, 1 sorority, on campus. **Athletics (Intercollegiate):** *Men:* baseball, basketball, cross-country, golf, lacrosse, soccer, swimming, tennis, track/field (outdoor), track/field (indoor). *Women:* badminton, basketball, cross-country, field hockey, lacrosse, soccer, softball, swimming, tennis, track/field (outdoor), track/field (indoor), volleyball. **On-Campus Highlights:** Kohlberg & Eldridge Commons Coffee Bars, Parrish Beach (the central campus lawn), Scott Outdoor Amphitheater, The Matchbox (wellness center), Paces (student-run cafe). **Environmental Initiatives:** 100% of the College's electrical demands are met by renewable energy credits and the College has made the decision to burn natural gas as its primary fuel and convert the heat plant from #6 fuel oil to #2 fuel oil as its back-up reserve.

Swarthmore College

FINANCIAL AID

Students should submit: CSS/Financial Aid PROFILE; FAFSA; Noncustodial PROFILE; State aid form. Financial aid application deadline is 1/1. The Princeton Review suggests that all financial aid forms be submitted as soon as possible after October 1. *Need-based scholarships/grants offered*: College/university scholarship or grant aid from institutional funds; Federal Pell; Private scholarships; SEOG; State scholarships/grants. *Loan aid offered*: Direct PLUS loans; Direct Subsidized Stafford Loans; Direct Unsubsidized Stafford Loans. Applicants will be notified of awards at the same time they are notified of their admission decision. Federal Work-Study Program available. Institutional employment available.

BOTTOM LINE

Swarthmore has staggeringly generous financial aid resources, and it will meet 100 percent of your demonstrated need without loans. The average need-based financial aid award here is more than $45,000. Don't assume you won't receive aid because your family is too wealthy and definitely—please!—don't assume you can't afford Swarthmore because your family isn't wealthy enough.

FINANCIAL FACTS	
Financial Aid Rating	92
Annual tuition	$54,256
Room and board	$16,088
Required fees	$400
Books and supplies	$1,360
Average frosh need-based scholarship	$53,395
Average UG need-based scholarship	$51,079
% needy frosh rec. need-based scholarship or grant aid	100
% needy UG rec. need-based scholarship or grant aid	100
% needy frosh rec. non-need-based scholarship or grant aid	0
% needy UG rec. non-need-based scholarship or grant aid	0
% needy frosh rec. need-based self-help aid	98
% needy UG rec. need-based self-help aid	98
% frosh rec. any financial aid	58
% UG rec. any financial aid	55
% UG borrow to pay for school	24
Average cumulative indebtedness	$22,060
% frosh need fully met	100
% ugrads need fully met	100
Average % of frosh need met	100
Average % of ugrad need met	100

CAREER INFORMATION FROM PAYSCALE.COM	
ROI Rating	93
Bachelors and No Higher	
Median starting salary	$67,500
Median mid-career salary	$123,200
At Least Bachelors	
Median starting salary	$67,700
Median mid-career salary	$136,900
Alumni with high job meaning	46%
Degrees awarded in STEM subjects	45%

Swarthmore College

Thomas Aquinas College

10,000 Ojai Road, Santa Paula, CA 93060 • Admissions: 800-634-9797 • Fax: 805-421-5905

#75 BEST VALUE COLLEGE

ABOUT THE SCHOOL

Founded in 1971, California's Thomas Aquinas College is a small Catholic liberal arts school that follows a great books curriculum instead of using textbooks and lectures. With just four hundred students in attendance, classes are all Socratic-style conversations about the seminal books that have characterized Western civilization, including works by Homer, Shakespeare, and Plato. "Every single class is designed to be discussion-based, even Natural Science and Mathematics," shares one TAC undergrad. "We get to experience science first-hand by recreating many experiments that we read about in the lab," says a student. Here, all students graduate with the same bachelor of the arts degree, the result of a program students find to be "academically rigorous, challenging students to read the original words of history's greatest thinkers, and to ponder mankind's perennial questions." But if students ever feel that task is overwhelming, they can call on their tutors (TAC's word for professors) for help. And that's easy to do since they often "eat meals with students in the commons and are always available to talk." Plus, they are "very good at untangling discussions in class."

Thomas Aquinas College

Financial Aid: 800-634-9797 • E-mail: admissions@thomasaquinas.edu • Website: www.thomasaquinas.edu

BANG FOR YOUR BUCK

"Thanks to the help of donors and charitable foundations—the school receives no government or Church subsidies—TAC aims to help all accepted students get financial aid, regardless of need. Additionally, institutionally-funded work-study and grants are available, though merit-based scholarships are not. Still, the cost of tuition is relatively lower than many other private colleges, and students generally do not pay more than four years' tuition since the curriculum is uniform. Students also have no book expenses; they will receive one complimentary copy of each text required by a course.

STUDENT LIFE

The Mission-style campus is located about sixty-five miles north of Los Angeles in the foothills of the Topatopa Mountains, with easy access to beaches, nature trails, and urban centers. Students all live on campus unless they are married, and, as one student shares, "the strict rules of residence regarding alcohol and single-sex dorms makes the campus a very safe place." With "the atmosphere [being] Catholic, intellectual, and intimate," most students "[attend] Mass daily and [frequent] the sacraments." You'll also find that "the campus coffee shop and rec room are buzzing most nights." During the weekends students "do more recreational things, [such] as hiking, playing sports, [and] talking to friends at length," and there are also "many dances that the student body hosts, which are very-well liked and attended." As for sports, since there is no competition with other colleges, "the athletics program is open to all students regardless of skill."

ACADEMICS

Academic Rating	94
% students returning for sophomore year	91
% students graduating within 4 years	71
% students graduating within 6 years	86
Calendar	Semester
Student/faculty ratio	11:1
Profs interesting rating	99
Profs accessible rating	98
Most classes have 10–19 students.	

MOST POPULAR MAJORS
Liberal Arts and Sciences/Liberal Studies

SELECTIVITY

Admissions Rating	87
# of applicants	211
% of applicants accepted	78
% of acceptees attending	74
# offered a place on the wait list	57
% accepting a place on wait list	100
% admitted from wait list	67

CAREER

Thomas Aquinas College "has people only working for our well-being," and "is an academic launch pad into any field you can think of." Its reputation is well-known; graduates can "express themselves clearly, understand the causes of an issue, and … isolate and attend to them in a cordial and personal manner." Students find the academic structure allows you "to excel in whatever field you choose because of the habits of critical thinking that you've cultivated over the four years." Students here "take the intellectual life seriously, and the life of study continues outside the classroom": nearly 40 percent of students ultimately enroll in graduate or professional school, and 11 percent of alumni have entered the priesthood or religious life.

GENERAL INFO

Activities: Campus Ministries; Choral groups; Dance; Drama/theater; Literary magazine; Music ensembles; Musical theater. 0 honor societies, 3 religious organizations, 0 fraternities, 0 sororities, on campus. **On-Campus Highlights:** St. Joseph Commons, The Dumb Ox Coffee Shop, Dorm Commons, St. Bernardine Library, St. Cecilia's Performing Arts Hall.

Thomas Aquinas College

FINANCIAL AID

Students should submit: FAFSA; Institution's own financial aid form; State aid form. Priority filing deadline is 3/2. The Princeton Review suggests that all financial aid forms be submitted as soon as possible after October 1. *Need-based scholarships/grants offered*: College/university scholarship or grant aid from institutional funds; Federal Pell; Private scholarships; State scholarships/grants. *Loan aid offered*: Direct PLUS loans; Direct Subsidized Stafford Loans; Direct Unsubsidized Stafford Loans. Applicants will be notified of awards on a rolling basis beginning 2/1. Institutional employment available.

BOTTOM LINE

Thomas Aquinas College sets out a very simple and relatively low-cost structure. Tuition is $25,600 with no additional fees or charges tacked on. Students must live on campus (unless married) so room and board is a required additional $8,800. Admissions at Thomas Aquinas is completely need blind, there is no application fee, and books (a sometimes overlooked expense) are completely covered by tuition. Thomas Aquinas provides an education based on The Great Books. A copy of each required test is provided to all incoming students. Just make sure to keep track of them all four years and you will not spend an additional dime on books. 62 percent of alumni reported their current jobs mean a great deal to both themselves and to the world.

FINANCIAL FACTS	
Financial Aid Rating	99
Annual tuition	$25,600
Room and board	$8,800
Average frosh need-based scholarship	$14,623
Average UG need-based scholarship	$14,552
% needy frosh rec. need-based scholarship or grant aid	84
% needy UG rec. need-based scholarship or grant aid	82
% needy frosh rec. non-need-based scholarship or grant aid	0
% needy UG rec. non-need-based scholarship or grant aid	0
% needy frosh rec. need-based self-help aid	100
% needy UG rec. need-based self-help aid	100
% frosh rec. any financial aid	80
% UG rec. any financial aid	76
% UG borrow to pay for school	73
Average cumulative indebtedness	$18,317
% frosh need fully met	100
% ugrads need fully met	100
Average % of frosh need met	100
Average % of ugrad need met	100

CAREER INFORMATION FROM PAYSCALE.COM	
ROI Rating	90
Bachelors and No Higher	
Median starting salary	$51,700
Median mid-career salary	$93,300
At Least Bachelors	
Median starting salary	$52,200
Median mid-career salary	$95,600
Alumni with high job meaning	62%
Degrees awarded in STEM subjects	0%

Thomas Aquinas College

Trinity University

One Trinity Place, San Antonio, TX 78212-7200 • Admissions: 210-999-7207 • Fax: 210-999-8164

#60 BEST VALUE COLLEGE

CAMPUS LIFE

Quality of Life Rating	92
Fire Safety Rating	94
Green Rating	73
Type of school	Private
Affiliation	Presbyterian
Environment	Metropolis

STUDENTS

Total undergrad enrollment	2,477
% male/female	47/53
% from out of state	24
% frosh from public high school	68
% frosh live on campus	100
% ugrads live on campus	82
# of fraternities	
(% ugrad men join)	7 (8)
# of sororities	
(% ugrad women join)	7 (15)
% African American	4
% Asian	7
% Caucasian	57
% Hispanic	21
% Native American	1
% Pacific Islander	<1
% Two or more races	4
% Race and/or ethnicity unknown	2
% international	5
# of countries represented	61

ABOUT THE SCHOOL

This private school in San Antonio, Texas, gives students a "great environment, great people, [and a] great education." The small student body—roughly 2,428—and the requirement that undergraduates must live on campus for three years gives the school a small-town feel in a big state. Trinity is a "small, liberal arts college...that has the comfort of a small secluded area [with the added] wonders of a big city." One Communication major says, Trinity is "a close-knit university with high standards of excellence and competency that challenge students, while creating a comfortable environment." The student to teacher ratio of roughly 9:1 helps foster this sense of community and the professors "know all of their students by name and are extremely accessible outside of class." With more than 47 majors offered, Trinity has something for everyone: "Some of the best aspects of Trinity are its emphasis on academic goals, assistance in preparing students for life after college, and, most importantly, the sense of community it provides between students, faculty, and alumni."

BANG FOR YOUR BUCK

Trinity meets an average of 94 percent of its students' financial needs and scholarship options draw in many prospective students, including international ones, who are eligible for financial assistance. One French and art history double major notes that Trinity is "warm and supportive but challenging—kind of like San Antonio's weather. The plentiful scholarship money didn't hurt either." Ninety-eight percent of freshmen get some form of financial aid, and 92 percent of other undergraduates receive financial

Trinity University

Financial Aid: 210-999-8315 • E-mail: admissions@trinity.edu • Website: www.trinity.edu

assistance. A Political Science major says that Trinity's "financial aid packages are great so there are many middle-class students and with such a smorgasbord of ethnicities, economic statuses, and cultures," the students "all learn from one another." According to the school's website, "All Trinity scholarships are renewable on an annual basis for up to eight semesters of undergraduate study, as long as the recipient meets each award's specified criteria." Most of these scholarships are merit-based but there are some that combine merit with financial need.

STUDENT LIFE

While "it's not uncommon to hear students worrying about tests," they are also "often looking forward to some big event over the weekend" such as themed parties or fundraisers for local charities. The school's location in San Antonio—"we are about five minutes from downtown"—also affords students access to clubs and restaurants. On campus, Greek life plays a significant role: the school has seven sororities and seven fraternities, with roughly 32 percent of women joining a sorority and 19 percent of men joining a fraternity. Though "Greek life is a popular way of getting involved," students can find "almost any type of...group on campus," where there are more than 115 registered student organizations. Even though students like to kick back and have fun, "when it's time to study, people study hard" and it's "not considered anti-social to not hang out with your friends a couple of nights before a big test. Overall, Trinity's students are an accepting fun-loving lot."

ACADEMICS

Academic Rating	94
% students returning for sophomore year	91
% students graduating within 4 years	65
% students graduating within 6 years	76
Calendar	Semester
Student/faculty ratio	9:1
Profs interesting rating	93
Profs accessible rating	96

Most classes have 10–19 students.
Most lab/discussion sessions have 10–19 students.

MOST POPULAR MAJORS

Communication and Media Studies; Communication, General; Engineering Science; Business Administration and Management, General

SELECTIVITY

Admissions Rating	93
# of applicants	8,654
% of applicants accepted	34
% of acceptees attending	23
# offered a place on the wait list	876
% accepting a place on wait list	52
% admitted from wait list	2
# of early decision applicants	144
% accepted early decision	79

FRESHMAN PROFILE

Range SAT EBRW	630–710
Range SAT Math	630–720
Range ACT Composite	28–32
# submitting SAT scores	342
% submitting SAT scores	50
# submitting ACT scores	335
% submitting ACT scores	49
Average HS GPA	3.6
% graduated top 10% of class	42
% graduated top 25% of class	76
% graduated top 50% of class	96

DEADLINES

Early decision	
Deadline	11/1
Notification	12/1
Other ED Deadline	1/15
Other ED Notification	2/1
Early action	
Deadline	11/1
Notification	12/15
Regular	
Deadline	1/15
Notification	3/15
Nonfall registration?	Yes

CAREER

According to PayScale.com, 49 percent of Trinity graduates consider their careers to be instrumental in making the world a better place. The median starting salary for a Trinity graduate is roughly $54,900, and popular jobs include marketing manager, financial analyst, and executive director. Popular majors at Trinity include Communication, Business Administration, and Engineering Science. One Communication major singled out a grant the school received from AT&T that allowed Trinity to "renovate the...communications lab [so] that is has [state-of-the-art] equipment," which helps to "further [the] interests and careers of students going into a media field." According to the school's website, Career Services "fosters career advancement and contributes to the growth and success of Trinity graduates." The office's website offers students access to Hire a Tiger, the school's online recruitment system. The school's website emphasizes that "Career Services at Trinity is a comprehensive and centralized service that works with both students (from first-years to seniors) and alumni." Trinity's small size makes it so "everyone really knows everyone, even alumni, which is really great because it makes networking so much easier."

GENERAL INFO

Activities: Campus Ministries; Choral groups; Concert band; Dance; Drama/theater; International Student Organization; Jazz band; Literary magazine; Model UN; Music ensembles; Musical theater; Opera; Pep band; Radio station; Student government; Student newspaper; Student-run film society; Symphony orchestra; Television station; Yearbook. 92 registered organizations, 7 honor societies, 10 religious organizations, 7 fraternities, 7 sororities, on campus. **Athletics (Intercollegiate):** *Men:* baseball, basketball, cross-country, diving, football, golf, soccer, swimming, tennis, track/field (outdoor). *Women:* basketball, cross-country, diving, golf, soccer, softball, swimming, tennis, track/field (outdoor), volleyball. **On-Campus Highlights:** Center for the Sciences and Innovation, Stieren Theatre, Laurie Auditorium, Coates Library, Bell Athletic Center.

Trinity University

FINANCIAL AID

Students should submit: CSS/Financial Aid PROFILE; FAFSA. Priority filing deadline is 2/15. The Princeton Review suggests that all financial aid forms be submitted as soon as possible after October 1. *Need-based scholarships/grants offered*: College/university scholarship or grant aid from institutional funds; Federal Pell; Private scholarships; SEOG; State scholarships/grants. *Loan aid offered*: Direct PLUS loans; Direct Subsidized Stafford Loans; Direct Unsubsidized Stafford Loans. Applicants will be notified of awards on or about 3/15. Federal Work-Study Program available. Institutional employment available.

BOTTOM LINE

A year at Trinity costs roughly $55,824, including tuition, room and board. With the average need-based gift aid for undergraduates being approximately $32,078, 44 percent of the previous graduating class borrowed to finance their education with an average cumulative debt of $42,036.

FINANCIAL FACTS	
Financial Aid Rating	91
Annual tuition	$42,360
Room and board	$13,464
Required fees	$616
Books and supplies	$1,000
Average frosh need-based scholarship	$33,399
Average UG need-based scholarship	$32,162
% needy frosh rec. need-based scholarship or grant aid	100
% needy UG rec. need-based scholarship or grant aid	99
% needy frosh rec. non-need-based scholarship or grant aid	31
% needy UG rec. non-need-based scholarship or grant aid	19
% needy frosh rec. need-based self-help aid	55
% needy UG rec. need-based self-help aid	62
% frosh rec. any financial aid	99
% UG rec. any financial aid	97
% UG borrow to pay for school	44
Average cumulative indebtedness	$42,036
% frosh need fully met	66
% ugrads need fully met	43
Average % of frosh need met	98
Average % of ugrad need met	92

CAREER INFORMATION FROM PAYSCALE.COM	
ROI Rating	91
Bachelors and No Higher	
Median starting salary	$54,900
Median mid-career salary	$102,900
At Least Bachelors	
Median starting salary	$56,500
Median mid-career salary	$112,800
Alumni with high job meaning	49%
Degrees awarded in STEM subjects	27%

Trinity University

Tufts University

Bendetson Hall, Medford, MA 02155 • Admissions: 617-627-3170 • Fax: 617-627-3860

#68 BEST VALUE COLLEGE

ABOUT THE SCHOOL

Some of the reasons Tufts students love their school are the "beautiful campus," "international focus," "diverse community," "proximity to Boston," and the "really chill vibe." This is a university that wants students to be "exploring passions and relating them to the world today." The size of the school is "not too big, not too small," but just right for many students. "Tufts is well known for being very liberal, focused on internationalism and global citizenship," a Religion major states. This is a place where "people aren't afraid to study and be intellectual." Often regarded as a "Little Ivy," Tufts offers a world-class academic education. Tufts professors are "highly accessible," "engaging and knowledgeable." "Professors have the students best interest at heart, so they do all they can to make sure we succeed," one student reports. A Political Science major says that "at Tufts, you're surrounded by so many intelligent, engaged, and interesting people in a supportive, collaborative learning environment."

BANG FOR YOUR BUCK

Although Tufts tuition is not insignificant, there are many opportunities for aid, loans, and scholarships. "There are a lot of work study programs offered at Tufts and a lot of people on complete financial aid," an International Relations student confirms. The Student Employment Office helps students get jobs on-campus or off and regularly posts jobs to the JobX and TuftsLife websites. The school has forty-four Tufts-specific scholarships and awards for everything from Fine Arts and Social Justice to various STEM majors. Prospective applicants can view the entire list online. Prospective applicants

Tufts University

Financial Aid: 617-627-2000 • E-mail: admissions.inquiry@ase.tufts.edu • Website: www.tufts.edu

can also use the school's online Net Price Calculator to get an idea what kind of aid they can expect if accepted.

STUDENT LIFE

"The campus culture is thriving and alive," one student says, "and as such it really encourages students to merge their academic and social interests and pursue both in a passionate way." Your average student at Tufts is "fun, passionate," "geeky" and likely an "activist." "The variety of clubs and activities available is amazing" and most students get "involved in many clubs and activities, campaigns, grassroots organizing, athletic teams, volunteer organizations, jobs, etc." "The Tufts Dance Collective and Quidditch clubs are some of the most popular and fun," one student helpfully suggests. Unlike many universities, there are "not too many 'cliques'" here and students tend to get along with each other. "The best way to fit in at Tufts is to be yourself, even if that sounds cheesy." If there is a Tufts uniform, it's "skinny jeans, a vintage sweater, worn-in shoes, and framed glasses" along with a "MacBook Pro" softly playing indie music. On campus, there are "extensive" student-run events and many students show up "for theater, dance and musical performances." When students need to get off campus, Boston is "less than an hour" away.

CAREER

"The school's strong reputation has helped me get summer jobs and internships," one student reports. This is a common sentiment among Tufts students. The university's reputation and proximity to Boston provide students with many opportunities to get a head start on their post-college careers. The "great alumni network" also helps students find "jobs or internships after college." The school frequently holds events like the Career Carnival and Tufts Career Fair along with consulting sessions. Fully 91

ACADEMICS

Academic Rating	92
% students returning for sophomore year	97
% students graduating within 4 years	87
% students graduating within 6 years	93
Calendar	Semester
Student/faculty ratio	9:1
Profs interesting rating	89
Profs accessible rating	88

Most classes have 10–19 students. Most lab/discussion sessions have 10–19 students.

MOST POPULAR MAJORS
Computer Science; Economics; International Relations and Affairs

SELECTIVITY

Admissions Rating	97
# of applicants	21,101
% of applicants accepted	15
% of acceptees attending	45
# offered a place on the wait list	1,504
% accepting a place on wait list	42
% admitted from wait list	0

FRESHMAN PROFILE

Range SAT EBRW	700–760
Range SAT Math	710–780
Range ACT Composite	31–34
# submitting SAT scores	473
% submitting SAT scores	34
# submitting ACT scores	934
% submitting ACT scores	66

DEADLINES

Early decision	
Deadline	11/1
Notification	12/15
Other ED Deadline	1/1
Other ED Notification	2/15
Regular	
Deadline	1/1
Notification	4/1
Nonfall registration?	No

percent of the Class of 2013 had found full-time employment or were in graduate school by 2014. The website PayScale.com reports a median starting salary of $65,200 and a median midcareer salary of $118,110.

GENERAL INFO

Activities: Campus Ministries; Choral groups; Concert band; Dance; Drama/theater; International Student Organization; Jazz band; Literary magazine; Model UN; Music ensembles; Musical theater; Opera; Pep band; Radio station; Student government; Student newspaper; Student-run film society; Symphony orchestra; Television station; Yearbook. 325 registered organizations, 5 honor societies, 20 religious organizations, 9 fraternities, 4 sororities, on campus. **Athletics (Intercollegiate):** *Men:* baseball, basketball, crew/rowing, cross-country, diving, football, golf, ice hockey, lacrosse, sailing, soccer, squash, swimming, tennis, track/field (outdoor), track/field (indoor). *Women:* basketball, cheerleading, crew/rowing, cross-country, diving, fencing, field hockey, golf, lacrosse, sailing, soccer, softball, squash, swimming, tennis, track/field (outdoor), track/field (indoor), volleyball. **On-Campus Highlights:** The Aidekman Arts Center, Tisch Library, Edwin Ginn Library, Gantcher Family Sports and Convocation Center and Tisch Sports and Fitness, Granoff Music Center, Mayer Campus Center. **Environmental Initiatives:** Reduced green house gas emissions to below 1998 levels, working to further that with the creation of a new power plant that will decrease energy usage.

Tufts University

FINANCIAL AID

Students should submit: CSS/Financial Aid PROFILE; FAFSA; Noncustodial PROFILE. Priority filing deadline is 2/15. The Princeton Review suggests that all financial aid forms be submitted as soon as possible after October 1. *Need-based scholarships/grants offered*: College/university scholarship or grant aid from institutional funds; Federal Pell; Private scholarships; SEOG; State scholarships/grants. *Loan aid offered*: Direct PLUS loans; Direct Subsidized Stafford Loans; Direct Unsubsidized Stafford Loans. Applicants will be notified of awards on or about 4/1. Federal Work-Study Program available. Institutional employment available.

BOTTOM LINE

The baseline tuition at Tufts is $57,324. Room and board are an additional $15,086. Adding the various fees, a student can expect a bill of $73,664 before any aid or scholarships.

FINANCIAL FACTS	
Financial Aid Rating	95
Annual tuition	$57,324
Room and board	$15,086
Required fees	$1,254
Average frosh need-based scholarship	$44,967
Average UG need-based scholarship	$42,763
% needy frosh rec. need-based scholarship or grant aid	93
% needy UG rec. need-based scholarship or grant aid	94
% needy frosh rec. non-need-based scholarship or grant aid	3
% needy UG rec. non-need-based scholarship or grant aid	8
% needy frosh rec. need-based self-help aid	86
% needy UG rec. need-based self-help aid	89
% frosh rec. any financial aid	38
% UG rec. any financial aid	36
% UG borrow to pay for school	34
Average cumulative indebtedness	$27,367
% frosh need fully met	100
% ugrads need fully met	93
Average % of frosh need met	100
Average % of ugrad need met	100

CAREER INFORMATION FROM PAYSCALE.COM	
ROI Rating	91
Bachelors and No Higher	
Median starting salary	$65,200
Median mid-career salary	$118,100
At Least Bachelors	
Median starting salary	$66,700
Median mid-career salary	$136,100
Alumni with high job meaning	52%
Degrees awarded in STEM subjects	25%

Tufts University

Union College (NY)

Grant Hall, Schenectady, NY 12308 • Admissions: 518-388-6112 • Fax: 518-388-6986

#61 BEST VALUE COLLEGE

CAMPUS LIFE

Quality of Life Rating	85
Fire Safety Rating	92
Green Rating	94
Type of school	Private
Environment	Town

STUDENTS

Total undergrad enrollment	2,163
% male/female	53/47
% from out of state	62
% frosh from public high school	65
% frosh live on campus	99
% ugrads live on campus	90
# of fraternities	
(% ugrad men join)	11 (32)
# of sororities	
(% ugrad women join)	7 (41)
% African American	4
% Asian	6
% Caucasian	72
% Hispanic	7
% Native American	<1
% Pacific Islander	0
% Two or more races	3
% Race and/or ethnicity unknown	<1
% international	7
# of countries represented	37

ABOUT THE SCHOOL

Union College is a small, private institution located in upstate New York that operates on the trimester schedule. It offers more than forty majors, the most prominent of which are Biology, Economics, and Psychology, and a thriving study abroad program in which roughly 60 percent of students take part. Additionally, Union boasts a ten to one student-to-faculty ratio, with the most frequent class size coming in at between ten and nineteen students. Fifty-four percent of the student body is male, 46 percent is female, and 72 percent is white. A neuroscience major reports that "they give amazing scholarships, they have a great program for what I want to pursue, the atmosphere suited me extremely well, and I've never met friendlier people." Most students feel that "Union College is the perfect balance of the interdisciplinary liberal arts and engineering, where your extracurricular activities are just as important as academics," and also that there are "strong faculty-student interaction both in and out of the classroom," with one student noting "it is nice that the President of the school is willing to stop and talk with you, and knows your name." All students and faculty are assigned to one of seven Minerva Houses, community spaces which offer further opportunities for leadership, service, and faculty interaction. Overall, "Union is a work hard, play hard school with an active student body and accessible professors who are always willing to help."

Union College (NY)

Financial Aid: 518-388-6123 • E-mail: admissions@union.edu • Website: www.union.edu

BANG FOR YOUR BUCK

Tuition at Union College comes to $56,853, with the average aid package coming to around $44,649. Union meets the full demonstrated need of admitted students, and roughly 79 percent of students receive some form of aid. Students feel that "Union College is very generous with its financial aid and scholarship money," which is the sort of thing that practically anyone would want to hear. Multiple students report receiving full rides, and many others report receiving at least a partial merit scholarship. Union College also participates in academic opportunity programs like POSSE Scholars and Yellow Ribbon.

STUDENT LIFE

Every student on campus belongs to a Minerva House, and 39 percent of students of either gender are involved in Greek Life. The average Union student "comes from a upper middle class background in the northeast," and many find it remarkable that "students are able to have so much fun and do so well in their classes." It is noted that though there are students who are not from upper middle-class northeastern backgrounds, these students tend to fit in rather well. However, "while the rich New Englander is the 'typical' student, it is not saying that he isn't playing Dungeons and Dragons with the gaming kids." Drinking is a popular weekend activity, and yet there are atypical students in this aspect as well. Students feel that Union is making an effort to diversify the "typical" student body.

ACADEMICS

Academic Rating	94
% students returning for sophomore year	92
% students graduating within 4 years	79
% students graduating within 6 years	85
Calendar	Trimester
Student/faculty ratio	10:1
Profs interesting rating	96
Profs accessible rating	97
Most classes have 10–19 students.	
Most lab/discussion sessions have 10–19 students.	

MOST POPULAR MAJORS

Mechanical Engineering; Psychology, General; Economics, General

SELECTIVITY

Admissions Rating	93
# of applicants	6,676
% of applicants accepted	37
% of acceptees attending	23
# offered a place on the wait list	1,066
% accepting a place on wait list	49
% admitted from wait list	7
# of early decision applicants	408
% accepted early decision	63

FRESHMAN PROFILE

Range SAT EBRW	630–700
Range SAT Math	640–730
Range ACT Composite	29–32
# submitting SAT scores	214
% submitting SAT scores	38
# submitting ACT scores	211
% submitting ACT scores	37
Average HS GPA	3.4
% graduated top 10% of class	63
% graduated top 25% of class	88
% graduated top 50% of class	99

DEADLINES

Early decision	
Deadline	11/15
Notification	12/15
Other ED Deadline	1/15
Other ED Notification	2/8
Regular	
Deadline	1/15
Notification	3/25
Nonfall registration?	Yes

CAREER

Union College graduates report their median starting salary at around $63,300, and 54 percent report that their job has a great deal of meaning. Past that, students feel that "Union has an awesome career center that is always reaching out to students to help them with life after college with jobs, internships, resumes, etc. . . ." Others add that "there are so many resources available in terms of funding, internships, and leadership opportunities." Students report being thrilled about the "undergraduate research opportunities" like the Sophomore Research Seminar or those through National Science Foundation awards, and the annual Steinmetz Symposium allows them to present their work to the entire campus community. A distinctive Union institution, the Minerva House program has produced sixty-two fellows selected to spend a year after graduation working on a global service project.

GENERAL INFO

Activities: Campus Ministries; Choral groups; Concert band; Dance; Drama/theater; International Student Organization; Jazz band; Literary magazine; Model UN; Music ensembles; Pep band; Radio station; Student government; Student newspaper; Student-run film society; Symphony orchestra; Television station; Yearbook. 101 registered organizations, 14 honor societies, 11 religious organization, 11 fraternity, 7 sororities, on campus. **Athletics (Intercollegiate):** *Men:* baseball, basketball, crew/rowing, cross-country, diving, football, ice hockey, lacrosse, soccer, swimming, tennis, track/field (outdoor), track/field (indoor). *Women:* basketball, crew/rowing, cross-country, diving, field hockey, ice hockey, lacrosse, soccer, softball, swimming, tennis, track/field (outdoor), track/field (indoor), volleyball. **On-Campus Highlights:** The Nott Memorial, Schaffer Library, Reamer Campus Center, Jackson's Garden, Wold Center for Science and Engineering. **Environmental Initiatives:** Incorporation of Sustainability into Union College's Mission, Presidential Priority & Strategic Plan.

FINANCIAL AID

Students should submit: CSS/Financial Aid PROFILE; FAFSA; Noncustodial PROFILE; State aid form. Priority filing deadline is 1/15. The Princeton Review suggests that all financial aid forms be submitted as soon as possible after October 1. *Need-based scholarships/grants offered*: College/university scholarship or grant aid from institutional funds; Federal Pell; Private scholarships; SEOG; State scholarships/grants. *Loan aid offered*: Direct PLUS loans; Direct Subsidized Stafford Loans; Direct Unsubsidized Stafford Loans. Applicants will be notified of awards on or about 3/25. Federal Work-Study Program available. Institutional employment available.

BOTTOM LINE

The tuition at Union College comes to about $56,853. The average aid package comes to $44,649, with 79 percent of students receiving some aid. On average 100 percent of student demonstrated need is met. Union isn't cheap, but offers a great deal of financial aid to those who need it.

FINANCIAL FACTS	
Financial Aid Rating	96
Annual tuition	$56,853
Room and board	$14,061
Required fees	$471
Books and supplies	$1,500
Average frosh need-based scholarship	$37,841
Average UG need-based scholarship	$37,748
% needy frosh rec. need-based scholarship or grant aid	97
% needy UG rec. need-based scholarship or grant aid	100
% needy frosh rec. non-need-based scholarship or grant aid	8
% needy UG rec. non-need-based scholarship or grant aid	9
% needy frosh rec. need-based self-help aid	97
% needy UG rec. need-based self-help aid	97
% frosh rec. any financial aid	79
% UG rec. any financial aid	79
% UG borrow to pay for school	56
Average cumulative indebtedness	$34,221
% frosh need fully met	100
% ugrads need fully met	100
Average % of frosh need met	100
Average % of ugrad need met	100

CAREER INFORMATION FROM PAYSCALE.COM	
ROI Rating	91
Bachelors and No Higher	
Median starting salary	$63,300
Median mid-career salary	$117,500
At Least Bachelors	
Median starting salary	$65,000
Median mid-career salary	$132,400
Alumni with high job meaning	54%
Degrees awarded in STEM subjects	47%

Union College (NY)

University of California—Berkeley

110 Sproul Hall, #5800, Berkeley, CA 94720-5800 • Admissions: 510-642-3175 • Fax: 510-642-7333

CAMPUS LIFE

Quality of Life Rating	81
Fire Safety Rating	92
Green Rating	99
Type of school	Public
Environment	City

STUDENTS

Total undergrad enrollment	30,853
% male/female	47/53
% from out of state	16
% frosh live on campus	96
% ugrads live on campus	27
# of fraternities	
(% ugrad men join)	38 (10)
# of sororities	
(% ugrad women join)	19 (10)
% African American	2
% Asian	35
% Caucasian	25
% Hispanic	15
% Native American	<1
% Pacific Islander	<1
% Two or more races	6
% Race and/or ethnicity unknown	4
% international	13

#10 BEST VALUE COLLEGE

ABOUT THE SCHOOL

University of California—Berkeley enjoys a reputation for quality and value that few other colleges can match. Large, diverse, and highly regarded, Berkeley is often ranked among the top public institutions in the world. Berkeley offers around 350 undergraduate and graduate degree programs in a wide range of disciplines. Best known for research, the school counts Nobel laureates, MacArthur Fellowship recipients, and Pulitzer Prize and Academy Award winners among its faculty. With an "all-star faculty and resources," professors here are "intelligent [and] accessible," with many departments boasting "the best [academics] in their field." Needless to say, undergraduate education is first-rate. The school maintains a low student-to-teacher ratio, and opportunities to get in on cutting-edge research at Berkeley abound. In fact, approximately half of the school's undergraduates assist faculty in creative or research projects during their time here. As some students note, "you don't get the coddling that the private universities show. You don't have a billion counselors catering to your every need." Though students note that survey classes here can sometimes be "enormous," professors "make themselves very accessible via e-mail and office hours." Berkeley maintains an incredibly high number of nationally ranked programs; however, engineering, computer science, molecular and cell biology, and political science are the most popular majors for undergraduates.

University of California—Berkeley

Financial Aid: 510-642-6642 • Website: www.berkeley.edu

BANG FOR YOUR BUCK

Berkeley's Undergraduate Scholarships, Prizes and Honors unit of the Financial Aid Office administers three different scholarship programs. Twenty-five Berkeley Undergraduate Scholarships are awarded each year. The Regent's and Chancellor's Scholarship is Berkeley's most prestigious scholarship, and is awarded annually to approximately 200 incoming undergraduates. The by-invitation-only Cal Opportunity Scholarship is designed to attract high-achieving students who have overcome challenging socioeconomic circumstances. Award amounts vary for each of these scholarship programs, and are often based on financial need. All applicants to Berkeley are automatically considered for these scholarship programs. As a public institution, UC Berkeley's low in-state tuition makes this school very affordable. With a low cost and an active financial aid program, Berkeley is an ideal choice for high-achieving students from low-income families. More than 30 percent of Berkeley undergraduates are eligible for Pell Grants. The Blue and Gold Opportunity Plan helps middle-class families keep debt down by capping the parents' contribution.

ACADEMICS

Academic Rating	84
% students returning for sophomore year	97
% students graduating within 4 years	75
% students graduating within 6 years	91
Calendar	Semester
Student/faculty ratio	20:1
Profs interesting rating	78
Profs accessible rating	73

Most classes have 10–19 students.
Most lab/discussion sessions have 20–29 students.

MOST POPULAR MAJORS

Computer Engineering General; Economics; Political Science; Business

SELECTIVITY

Admissions Rating	98
# of applicants	89,621
% of applicants accepted	15
% of acceptees attending	45
# offered a place on the wait list	7,824
% accepting a place on wait list	53
% admitted from wait list	37

STUDENT LIFE

At Berkeley "you are free to express yourself." "Conversations vary from the wicked party last night" to "debates about the roles of women in Hindu mythology." To simply label this school as "diverse" seems like an oversimplification. Here, people "think about everything." Students regard fellow students as "passionate" and "intelligent." Full of their signature optimism, they believe that "life at Berkeley has no limits"; they "study and hear obscure languages, meet famous scientists, engage with brilliant students, eat delicious food, and just relax with friends daily." Student life includes taking advantage of everything San Francisco has to offer across the bay, but even when remaining on campus, "there are clubs and classes that cater to everybody's needs and such a diverse group of people that it would be hard to not fit in."

CAREER

"Berkeley's greatest strengths are the amount of resources and opportunities it provides to students not only to allow them to explore numerous academic fields but to engage them in the community, in the country, and in the world." "There are internship opportunities for students from all disciplines, both on campus and in the surrounding cities of Berkeley, Oakland, and San Francisco." "Research opportunities are abundant" and "the career center is amazing." There are "endless options for student involvement" and employers like the school's "prestigious" reputation. According to the website PayScale.com, the median starting salary for graduates is $70,700 and 51 percent of alumni find their jobs to be highly meaningful.

GENERAL INFO

Activities: Campus Ministries; Choral groups; Concert band; Dance; Drama/theater; International Student Organization; Jazz band; Literary magazine; Marching band; Model UN; Music ensembles; Musical theater; Pep band; Radio station; Student government; Student newspaper; Student-run film society; Symphony orchestra; Television station; Yearbook. 300 registered organizations, 6 honor societies, 28 religious organizations, 38 fraternities, 19 sororities, on campus. **Athletics (Intercollegiate):** *Men:* baseball, basketball, crew/rowing, cross-country, diving, football, golf, gymnastics, rugby, sailing, soccer, swimming, tennis, track/field (outdoor), water polo. *Women:* basketball, crew/rowing, cross-country, diving, field hockey, golf, gymnastics, lacrosse, sailing, soccer, softball, swimming, tennis, track/field (outdoor), volleyball, water polo. **On-Campus Highlights:** Botanical Gardens, Lawrence Hall of Science, Museum of Anthropology, Museum of Art. **Environmental Initiatives:** Voluntary target to reduce greenhouse gas emissions (GHG) to 1990 levels ahead of UC Policy and State of California guidelines which call for this level of reduction by the year 2020. We have reduced our emissions and met our first target by: Investing in energy efficiency and sustainable transportation practices. Since 2006, the campus has saved 20 million kWh of electricity through building retrofits and reduced fuel use by more than 1 million gallons by increasing

University of California—Berkeley

the number of bicycle, pedestrian and mass-transit commuters. Buying Greener Power: The campus is using electricity that includes more solar and wind energy and less coal through purchases from Pacific Gas & Electric, a utility that is required by state law to provide power that by 2020 will include 33 percent renewable energy. Improving Data and Methods: UC Berkeley has improved the accuracy of its emissions inventory profile by using the best data available about campus energy use and by staying current with the best reporting methods.

FINANCIAL AID

Students should submit: FAFSA; State aid form. Priority filing deadline is 3/2. The Princeton Review suggests that all financial aid forms be submitted as soon as possible after October 1. *Need-based scholarships/ grants offered*: College/university scholarship or grant aid from institutional funds; Federal Pell; Private scholarships; SEOG; State scholarships/grants. *Loan aid offered*: Direct PLUS loans; Direct Subsidized Stafford Loans; Direct Unsubsidized Stafford Loans. Applicants will be notified of awards on or about 3/31. Federal Work-Study Program available. Institutional employment available.

FINANCIAL FACTS	
Financial Aid Rating	84
Annual in-state tuition	$11,442
Annual out-of-state tuition	$41,196
Room and board	$17,220
Required fees	$2,811
Books and supplies	$870
Average frosh need-based scholarship	$23,542
Average UG need-based scholarship	$21,662
% needy frosh rec. need-based scholarship or grant aid	92
% needy UG rec. need-based scholarship or grant aid	94
% needy frosh rec. non-need-based scholarship or grant aid	3
% needy UG rec. non-need-based scholarship or grant aid	2
% needy frosh rec. need-based self-help aid	67
% needy UG rec. need-based self-help aid	69
% UG borrow to pay for school	34
Average cumulative indebtedness	$18,225
% frosh need fully met	30
% ugrads need fully met	31
Average % of frosh need met	83
Average % of ugrad need met	83

BOTTOM LINE

For California residents, Berkeley is a great deal, ringing in at $11,442 annually for tuition. In addition, the school estimates expenditures of $870 for books and supplies, though these costs vary by major. Nonresident tuition alone is $41,196 annually.

CAREER INFORMATION FROM PAYSCALE.COM	
ROI Rating	95
Bachelors and No Higher	
Median starting salary	$70,700
Median mid-career salary	$131,800
At Least Bachelors	
Median starting salary	$72,100
Median mid-career salary	$143,300
Alumni with high job meaning	51%
Degrees awarded in STEM subjects	36%

University of California—Berkeley

University of California—Davis

550 Alumni Lane, One Shields Ave, Davis, CA 95616 • Admissions: 530-752-2971 • Fax: 530-752-1280

CAMPUS LIFE

Quality of Life Rating	91
Fire Safety Rating	97
Green Rating	60*
Type of school	Public
Environment	Town

STUDENTS

Total undergrad enrollment	30,636
% male/female	40/60
% from out of state	5
% frosh from public high school	84
% frosh live on campus	92
% ugrads live on campus	25
# of fraternities	28
# of sororities	21
% African American	2
% Asian	27
% Caucasian	24
% Hispanic	21
% Native American	<1
% Pacific Islander	<1
% Two or more races	5
% Race and/or ethnicity unknown	2
% international	17
# of countries represented	121

ABOUT THE SCHOOL

"A top-tier research institution," University of California—Davis is a school that "provides... tremendous opportunities." Undergrads are enamored with the "beautiful" campus and value the UC Davis focus on "green energy." Students can study virtually any academic discipline here, many call out the university's "top ranked" animal science and agriculture programs. Just as critical, students appreciate that they can make their "voices...heard." As one undergrad explains, "When we want change or we are upset about the way the school is being run, the Dean or Chancellor addresses it." This praise also extends to the "awesome" professors who are typically "world-renowned in their field." Not only do they want their students to "learn the material," they work diligently to ensure said students understand how to "apply" that knowledge. Further, their "passion" for their subject matter is often infectious. And while the "course load is heavy," the professors here make sure that they're "very accessible and helpful outside of the classroom."

BANG FOR YOUR BUCK

UC Davis really does an admirable job in providing an affordable education. Impressively, 52 percent of their students graduate debt free. Even better, approximately 75 percent of the aid offered comes in the form of grants, scholarships and work-study. California residents can take advantage of a handful of plans meant to ease the financial burden for low- and middle-income families. For example, the Blue and Gold Opportunity Plan covers UC tuition as well as the student services fee for undergrads whose parents earn $80,000 or less. And the Aggie Grant Plan awards up to $3,771 annually

University of California—Davis

Financial Aid: 530-752-2390 • E-mail: undergraduateadmissions@ucdavis.edu • Website: www.ucdavis.edu

to students whose annual family income ranges from $80,000 to 120,000. Thankfully, there are also plenty of merit scholarships for which all students can be considered. In fact, Davis doles out over $17 million in scholarships every year.

STUDENT LIFE

There's no shortage of extracurricular options at Davis. After all, the university offers "800+ clubs… including 66 Greek organizations." It's also quite common to find people simply "playing Frisbee or throwing a football on the quad, with students reading and eating lunch on the grass beside them." Many undergrads also enjoy participating in "intramural sports [as a] fun way to [take a break] from studying." As one student shares, "Volleyball and inner-tube water polo are some of my favorites." There is also a party scene but we're told that mostly takes place at "people's houses" and these events are relatively "discreet." When students need a little break from campus life, they can easily head "to neighboring cities [like] Sacramento, San Francisco [and] Tahoe."

ACADEMICS

Academic Rating	78
% students returning for sophomore year	92
Calendar	Differs By Program
Student/faculty ratio	19:1
Profs interesting rating	78
Profs accessible rating	78

Most classes have 20–29 students.
Most lab/discussion sessions have 20–29 students.

MOST POPULAR MAJORS

Psychology, General; Economics, General; Managerial Economics

SELECTIVITY

Admissions Rating	90
# of applicants	76,647
% of applicants accepted	41
% of acceptees attending	20
# offered a place on the wait list	9,213
% accepting a place on wait list	35
% admitted from wait list	1

CAREER

Without a doubt, UC Davis provides students with "numerous career and internship resources." Undergrads have easy access to an outstanding Internship and Career Center that assists with all aspects of career planning. Students can use the office to explore career paths associated with various majors, find opportunities for job shadowing, and connect with various professional associations. Students can receive individual counseling on everything from how to conduct a job search to interview techniques and salary negotiation. UC Davis also does a tremendous job of attracting top companies to recruit on campus. The university hosts multiple career fairs throughout the year allowing undergrads to network with hundreds of employers.

GENERAL INFO

Activities: Campus Ministries; Choral groups; Concert band; Dance; Drama/theater; International Student Organization; Jazz band; Literary magazine; Marching band; Model UN; Music ensembles; Musical theater; Pep band; Radio station; Student government; Student newspaper; Student-run film society; Symphony orchestra; Television station; Yearbook. 800+ registered organizations, 26 honor societies, 50 religious organizations, 66 Greek life organizations on campus. **Athletics (Intercollegiate):** *Men:* baseball, basketball, cross-country, football, golf, soccer, tennis, track/field (outdoor), water polo. *Women:* basketball, beach volleyball, cross-country, diving, field hockey, golf, gymnastics, lacrosse, soccer, softball, swimming, tennis, track/field (outdoor), track/field (indoor), volleyball, water polo. **On-Campus Highlights:** Mondavi Center for the Performing Arts, Memorial Union/Coffee House, Activities and Recreation Center (The ARC), Manetti Shrem Museum of Art, The UC Davis Arboretum. **Environmental Initiatives:** With a long history of sustainability achievements, UC Davis helps lead the state and the world in climate change and sustainability science and action. In the past year, the campus's faculty research inspired the launch of the UC Million LED Challenge, informed California's Fourth Climate Change Assessment, led to a new partnership with Mexico's Ministry of Energy for the Centro de Tecnología de Iluminación and launched OneClimate, a new campus initiative designed to leverage UC Davis's unique blend of cross-disciplinary problem-solving into scalable, repeatable networks of solutions—from the campus to the world.

From the Learning by Leading program to the Unitrans bus system run by student drivers, mechanics and dispatchers to myriad project-based classes, such as Professor Lloyd Knox's Physics 150/250: Pathways to Climate Neutrality in California, students actively learn at UC Davis using the campus as their classroom.

University of California—Davis

FINANCIAL AID

Students should submit: FAFSA; State aid form. Priority filing deadline is 3/2. The Princeton Review suggests that all financial aid forms be submitted as soon as possible after October 1. *Need-based scholarships/grants offered*: College/university scholarship or grant aid from institutional funds; Federal Pell; Private scholarships; SEOG; State scholarships/grants. *Loan aid offered*: Direct PLUS loans; Direct Subsidized Stafford Loans; Direct Unsubsidized Stafford Loans. Applicants will be notified of awards on a rolling basis beginning 3/10.

BOTTOM LINE

UC Davis charges California residents $14,495 for its annual tuition (and fees). Undergraduates hailing from out of state can expect to pay an additional $29,754. All students will likely spend around $1,159 for books and supplies. Undergrads living on campus will pay another $15,863 for room and board. UC Davis suggests that students budget $1,399 for personal expenses and $487 for transportation. Students who opt to get health insurance through the university will spend $2,628.

FINANCIAL FACTS	
Financial Aid Rating	82
Annual in-state tuition	$11,442
Annual out-of-state tuition	$41,196
Room and board	$15,863
Required fees	$3,053
Books and supplies	$1,159
Average frosh need-based scholarship	$21,402
Average UG need-based scholarship	$19,236
% needy frosh rec. need-based scholarship or grant aid	98
% needy UG rec. need-based scholarship or grant aid	98
% needy frosh rec. non-need-based scholarship or grant aid	2
% needy UG rec. non-need-based scholarship or grant aid	2
% needy frosh rec. need-based self-help aid	54
% needy UG rec. need-based self-help aid	51
% UG rec. any financial aid	58
% UG borrow to pay for school	48
Average cumulative indebtedness	$18,575
% frosh need fully met	24
% ugrads need fully met	22
Average % of frosh need met	83
Average % of ugrad need met	81

CAREER INFORMATION FROM PAYSCALE.COM	
ROI Rating	91
Bachelors and No Higher	
Median starting salary	$61,500
Median mid-career salary	$112,600
At Least Bachelors	
Median starting salary	$62,500
Median mid-career salary	$123,300
Alumni with high job meaning	53%
Degrees awarded in STEM subjects	35%

University of California—Davis

University of California—Los Angeles

405 Hilgard Avenue, Los Angeles, CA 90095-1405 • Admissions: 310-825-3101 • Fax: 310-206-1206

#36 BEST VALUE COLLEGE

CAMPUS LIFE

Quality of Life Rating	87
Fire Safety Rating	92
Green Rating	75
Type of school	Public
Environment	Metropolis

STUDENTS

Total undergrad enrollment	31,577
% male/female	42/58
% from out of state	13
% frosh from public high school	74
% frosh live on campus	98
% ugrads live on campus	48
# of fraternities	
(% ugrad men join)	35 (11)
# of sororities	
(% ugrad women join)	35 (13)
% African American	3
% Asian	28
% Caucasian	27
% Hispanic	22
% Native American	<1
% Pacific Islander	<1
% Two or more races	6
% Race and/or ethnicity unknown	2
% international	12
# of countries represented	116

ABOUT THE SCHOOL

In a word, the University of California—Los Angeles is about diversity—in what you can study, in what you can do with your free time, in ethnicity, in gender and sexuality, in everything. With more than 200 undergraduate and graduate degree programs on offer for its 40,000 students, there truly is something for everyone. The technology and research resources here are dreamy. There is comprehensive quality across the broad range of disciplines. There are almost 7,500 undergraduate and graduate courses. You can take classes here in pretty much any academic endeavor, and you will likely run across some of the best and brightest professors in the world. Brushes with fame are common here—with a location near Hollywood and a world-famous film and television school, the UCLA campus has attracted film productions for decades. That being said, you should be aware that bigness and breadth have their limitations (lots of teaching assistants, big classes, anonymity). But if you don't mind being a small fish in a big pond, chances are you'll have a great experience here. And with just a little bit of initiative, you might even make a splash. Perhaps more notable, "UCLA is the kind of school that pushes you to work hard academically but reminds you that interaction with people outside of the classroom is just as important."

BANG FOR YOUR BUCK

Even in a time of rising fees, UCLA remains far below most of the other top research universities in total costs for undergraduate study. A little more than half of the student population here receives need-based financial aid. This school prizes its diversity, and that definitely includes economic diversity. UCLA ranks at the top among major research universities in the percentage of its students that receive Pell Grants (which is free government money for low-income students). The university also offers the prestigious Regents Scholarship, intended to reward extraordinary

University of California—Los Angeles

Financial Aid: 310-206-0400 • E-mail: ugadm@saonet.ucla.edu • Website: www.ucla.edu

academic excellence and exemplary leadership and community service accomplishments. Also, the career-planning operation here is first-rate, and there are extensive opportunities for internships with local employers. UCLA Financial Aid and Scholarships has both advisors and counselors available to help students complete financial aid applications, and to provide guidance throughout the process. In-person appointments can be scheduled, but the office also has walk-in hours. The UCLA website also provides access to certain scholarship opportunities, but the school also has a resource center on campus. The Scholarship Resource Center opened in 1996 to provide scholarship information, resources, and support services to all UCLA students, regardless of financial aid eligibility.

STUDENT LIFE

"UCLA is the mold that fits to you," says a happy student. "There is no 'typical student,' and everyone can easily find a group of students to fit in with. The benefits of 30,000 students and over 1,000 student groups!" The school has an extremely large campus and a very diverse student body, but it fosters an environment where everyone can find a place in the community: "Whether it be in Greek life, a club or organization, everybody has somewhere they can go to relax and have some fun. The apartments are close to campus, so nearly everybody lives in a small area with close proximity." And the benefits of going to school in a big, busy city are manifold: "LA is a vibrant and multicultural city. You have the beach to the west and the deserts/mountains to the east. EVERYTHING is accessible here in this city. If you want to go surf during the week it's ten minutes away. The food here is amazing and brings out the inner foodie in everyone!" One student puts the student experience at UCLA very succinctly: "I, like most people here, love [my] life."

CAREER

"UCLA is about getting a top notch education at a (currently) affordable price that will start your career off on an excellent path," is a popular sentiment regarding how the school equips students for their future. The Career Center

ACADEMICS

Academic Rating	79
% students returning for sophomore year	97
% students graduating within 4 years	77
% students graduating within 6 years	90
Calendar	Quarter
Student/faculty ratio	18:1
Profs interesting rating	63
Profs accessible rating	62

Most classes have 10–19 students. Most lab/discussion sessions have 20–29 students.

MOST POPULAR MAJORS

Biology/Biological Sciences, General; Psychology, General; Business/Managerial Economics

SELECTIVITY

Admissions Rating	98
# of applicants	113,761
% of applicants accepted	14
% of acceptees attending	39

offers standard services like advising and counseling; job fairs; on-campus recruiting; job and internship search tools; resources for those applying to grad school or looking for international opportunities; and "JumpStart" workshops covering professional development topics in a wide variety of fields. Students seem very satisfied with what the school affords them: "Networking and marketing, you're always told of a ton of activities, internships, resource opportunities—there are constant career fairs and activities. Also, location-wise, L.A. is a huge cosmopolitan city, you've got the opportunity to work in anything." Out of UCLA alumni visiting PayScale.com, 47 percent report that they derive a high level of meaning from their job.

GENERAL INFO

Activities: Campus Ministries; Choral groups; Concert band; Dance; Drama/theater; International Student Organization; Jazz band; Literary magazine; Marching band; Model UN; Music ensembles; Musical theater; Opera; Pep band; Radio station; Student government; Student newspaper; Student-run film society; Symphony orchestra; Television station; Yearbook. 850 registered organizations, 21 honor society, 35 fraternities, 35 sororities, on campus. **Athletics (Intercollegiate):** *Men:* baseball, basketball, cross-country, football, golf, soccer, tennis, track/field (outdoor), track/field (indoor), volleyball, water polo. *Women:* basketball, crew/rowing, cross-country, diving, golf, gymnastics, soccer, softball, swimming, tennis, track/field (outdoor), track/field (indoor), volleyball, water polo. **On-Campus Highlights:** UCLA Library, Fowler Museum of Cultural History, Hammer Museum, Royce Hall, Pauley Pavilion & Sports Hall of Fame. **Environmental Initiatives:** The University of California and state legislation set a target of reducing greenhouse gas emissions to 1990 levels by 2020. UCLA's comprehensive Climate Action Plan catalogs the steps the university has taken in the past and contains a detailed financial feasibility analysis for the initiatives that the university will undertake in energy and transportation to reduce greenhouse gas emissions. The initiatives outlined in the Climate Action Plan, in addition to addressing a critical environmental issue, will also conserve university resources and result in significant cost reductions. The energy initiatives have an average payback period of less than 5 years, with some lighting initiatives paying back through cost savings in less than a year. By demonstrating that it is possible to address climate change through concrete verifiable emissions reductions even in the toughest budget situation, UCLA is setting an example for the rest of California and the nation. The plan also catalogs academic and research initiatives at UCLA focused on climate change and sustainability. UCLA is a living laboratory for climate and sustainability research. Undergraduate and graduate students engage with staff and faculty to pilot new technologies and policies on the university campus. With over 25 research centers focused on climate and sustainability, UCLA is creating the

University of California—
Los Angeles

technology and training the leaders of tomorrow, while leading by example in our own operations.

FINANCIAL AID

Students should submit: FAFSA. Priority filing deadline is 3/2. The Princeton Review suggests that all financial aid forms be submitted as soon as possible after October 1. *Need-based scholarships/grants offered*: College/university scholarship or grant aid from institutional funds; Federal Nursing Scholarships; Federal Pell; Private scholarships; SEOG; State scholarships/grants; United Negro College Fund. *Loan aid offered*: Direct PLUS loans; Direct Subsidized Stafford Loans; Direct Unsubsidized Stafford Loans. Applicants will be notified of awards on a rolling basis beginning 3/15. Federal Work-Study Program available. Institutional employment available.

BOTTOM LINE

For Californians, the cumulative price tag to attend UCLA for a year—when you add up fees, room and board, and basic expenses—is somewhere around $29,128. Your living arrangements can make a noticeable difference. If you can't claim residency in the Golden State, the cost totals $58,120. Almost all students who demonstrate need receive some form of aid, and the average cumulative indebtedness, at just $22,390, is relatively reasonable.

FINANCIAL FACTS	
Financial Aid Rating	82
Annual in-state tuition	$11,442
Annual out-of-state tuition	$40,434
Room and board	$15,902
Required fees	$1,784
Books and supplies	$1,450
Average frosh need-based scholarship	$20,953
Average UG need-based scholarship	$20,489
% needy frosh rec. need-based scholarship or grant aid	96
% needy UG rec. need-based scholarship or grant aid	96
% needy frosh rec. non-need-based scholarship or grant aid	3
% needy UG rec. non-need-based scholarship or grant aid	2
% needy frosh rec. need-based self-help aid	56
% needy UG rec. need-based self-help aid	59
% frosh rec. any financial aid	53
% UG rec. any financial aid	54
% UG borrow to pay for school	43
Average cumulative indebtedness	$22,390
% frosh need fully met	28
% ugrads need fully met	26
Average % of frosh need met	83
Average % of ugrad need met	83

CAREER INFORMATION FROM PAYSCALE.COM	
ROI Rating	93
Bachelors and No Higher	
Median starting salary	$62,000
Median mid-career salary	$116,100
At Least Bachelors	
Median starting salary	$63,900
Median mid-career salary	$127,100
Alumni with high job meaning	51%
Degrees awarded in STEM subjects	31%

University of California—
Los Angeles

University of California—Riverside

3106 Student Services Building, Riverside, CA 92521 • Admissions: 951-827-3411 • Fax: 951-827-6344

CAMPUS LIFE	
Quality of Life Rating	86
Fire Safety Rating	99
Green Rating	98
Type of school	Public
Environment	City

STUDENTS	
Total undergrad enrollment	20,562
% male/female	45/55
% from out of state	1
% frosh from public high school	90
% frosh live on campus	72
% ugrads live on campus	30
# of fraternities	
(% ugrad men join)	15 (4)
# of sororities	
(% ugrad women join)	21 (7)
% African American	3
% Asian	34
% Caucasian	11
% Hispanic	42
% Native American	<1
% Pacific Islander	<1
% Two or more races	6
% Race and/or ethnicity unknown	1
% international	3
# of countries represented	60

#74 BEST VALUE COLLEGE

ABOUT THE SCHOOL

Committed to promoting a top-notch research and academic environment, the University of California—Riverside (UCR), part of the esteemed University of California system, is on the rise. With plans in place to expand faculty and facilities, this school is looking to further build on its established record as an accessible and vibrant campus. Alongside one of the country's best undergraduate business administration programs, UCR's engineering and sciences programs are highly regarded by students. The university's inland, southern California location makes it ideal for the study of "air, water, energy, biodiversity, sustainability, land use, [and] the habitat/agriculture interface." The campus is very diverse, and, as one student puts it, it is truly "a place where everyone will feel at home and welcomed." Despite a sizable undergraduate body of about 20,000, professors here are more than willing to provide individualized attention and mentorship. While many students commute, several on-campus clubs and events help foster a distinct sense of community.

BANG FOR YOUR BUCK

A state school with a demonstrated commitment to making higher education accessible and attainable, UCR offers eligible students a wide range of scholarship and grant opportunities. California students from families making less than $80,000 are eligible for The Blue and Gold Opportunity Plan, which, by combining applicable scholarships and grants, ensures they do not pay out of pocket for tuition and fees. In addition, merit-based scholarships, such as the Regent's and Chancellor's Scholarship, are always an option. Eighty-six percent of incoming full-time students

University of California—Riverside

Financial Aid: 951-827-3878 • E-mail: admin@ucr.edu • Website: www.ucr.edu

receive some sort of aid. UCR also has a robust internship program and regularly works with major companies to help students to gain real, on-the-job experience prior to graduation. Not only that, the school regularly organizes career fairs and professional coaching sessions to help students enter the workforce smoothly and successfully.

STUDENT LIFE

Asked about the atmosphere at UCR, most students report "studying" being a focus, but according to one, "if you are looking to get involved, meet like-minded individuals, and learn outside of the classroom, it is very easy to do so at UCR." Even though most students live off-campus, there's a distinct culture; as one student notes, "there are over 400 clubs... many of which organize their own activities." The Student Recreation Center is well-liked and features "a rock wall, assorted sport courts, [and] Olympic-style pool." Popular as well are concerts and parties organized by the school. "Every week there is a mini-concert in the middle of campus," one student says. Not only that, many students join fraternities and sororities, and there are plenty of opportunities to "attend a party" or "hang out at the restaurants or bars near campus." More outdoorsy types are also in the right place because of UCR's "1,200-acre, park-like campus" featuring the stunning Botanic Gardens.

CAREER

UCR students are known for being driven and focused, so it's no wonder that most graduate feeling well-prepared for their careers. The university offers numerous resources for those looking to enter the job market with their feet on the ground, and one student notes the school "takes pride in preparing students for jobs by encouraging them to dive into research and internships." For engineers and those going into sciences, UCR's centers

ACADEMICS

Academic Rating	81
% students returning for sophomore year	89
% students graduating within 4 years	55
% students graduating within 6 years	75
Calendar	Quarter
Student/faculty ratio	21:1
Profs interesting rating	77
Profs accessible rating	77

Most classes have 20–29 students. Most lab/discussion sessions have 20–29 students.

MOST POPULAR MAJORS

Biological and Biomedical Sciences, Other; Psychology, General; Business Administration and Management, General

SELECTIVITY

Admissions Rating	93
# of applicants	49,082
% of applicants accepted	51
% of acceptees attending	18
# offered a place on the wait list	11,058
% accepting a place on wait list	61
% admitted from wait list	17

FRESHMAN PROFILE

Range SAT EBRW	560–650
Range SAT Math	550–680
Range ACT Composite	23–29
# submitting SAT scores	4,172
% submitting SAT scores	92
# submitting ACT scores	1,911
% submitting ACT scores	42
Average HS GPA	3.8
% graduated top 10% of class	94
% graduated top 25% of class	100
% graduated top 50% of class	100

DEADLINES

Regular	
Deadline	11/30
Nonfall registration?	No

and institutes such as the Center for Environmental Research and Technology and the Agricultural Experimentation Station provide ample opportunities for students to gain research experience. The Career Center further helps by organizing fairs and offering training in professional skills, and their SCOTjobs online database lists numerous internships and job opportunities. It certainly pays off: graduates enter their careers making an average of $55,900 per year, with 48 percent reporting that their work as "high meaning."

GENERAL INFO

Activities: Campus Ministries; Choral groups; Comedic acting/improv; Concert band; Dance; Drama/theater; International Student Organization; Jazz band; Literary magazine; Model UN; Music ensembles; Pep band; Public service; Radio station; Student government; Student newspaper; Student-run film society; Symphony orchestra. 480 registered organizations, 21 honor societies, 24 religious organizations, 15 fraternities, 21 sororities, on campus. **Athletics (Intercollegiate):** *Men:* baseball, basketball, cross-country, golf, soccer, tennis, track/field (outdoor), track/field (indoor), volleyball. *Women:* basketball, cross-country, golf, soccer, softball, tennis, track/field (outdoor), track/field (indoor), volleyball. **On-Campus Highlights:** The Highlander Union Building (HUB), Student Recreation Center, Coffee Bean and Tea Leaf, Marketplace at Glen Mor, Residence Halls. **Environmental Initiatives:** UCR has a funded non-restrictive Office of Sustainability charged with coordinating sustainability initiatives throughout the campus supported by the Chancellor's Committee on Sustainability with the Chancellor serving as chair.

University of California—Riverside

FINANCIAL AID

Students should submit: FAFSA; State aid form. Priority filing deadline is 3/2. The Princeton Review suggests that all financial aid forms be submitted as soon as possible after October 1. *Need-based scholarships/grants offered*: College/university scholarship or grant aid from institutional funds; Federal Pell; Private scholarships; SEOG; State scholarships/grants. *Loan aid offered*: Direct PLUS loans; Direct Subsidized Stafford Loans; Direct Unsubsidized Stafford Loans; Federal Perkins Loans; University loans; Private loans. Applicants will be notified of awards on a rolling basis beginning 3/1. Federal Work-Study Program available. Institutional employment available.

BOTTOM LINE

In-state tuition and fees for UCR is only $13,853 per year, making it a very affordable institution of higher learning. Out-of-state students, however, pay considerably more: $43,607. For those opting to live in dorms, room and board is $16,100 a year. Books and supplies typically add $1,450 in annual cost for both in-state and out-of-state students.

FINANCIAL FACTS	
Financial Aid Rating	86
Annual in-state tuition	$11,442
Annual out-of-state tuition	$41,196
Room and board	$16,100
Required fees	$2,411
Books and supplies	$1,450
Average frosh need-based scholarship	$21,119
Average UG need-based scholarship	$18,195
% needy frosh rec. need-based scholarship or grant aid	97
% needy UG rec. need-based scholarship or grant aid	95
% needy frosh rec. non-need-based scholarship or grant aid	2
% needy UG rec. non-need-based scholarship or grant aid	2
% needy frosh rec. need-based self-help aid	80
% needy UG rec. need-based self-help aid	67
% frosh rec. any financial aid	76
% UG rec. any financial aid	77
% UG borrow to pay for school	62
Average cumulative indebtedness	$21,500
% frosh need fully met	17
% ugrads need fully met	16
Average % of frosh need met	86
Average % of ugrad need met	83

CAREER INFORMATION FROM PAYSCALE.COM	
ROI Rating	91
Bachelors and No Higher	
Median starting salary	$55,900
Median mid-career salary	$106,900
At Least Bachelors	
Median starting salary	$57,200
Median mid-career salary	$118,400
Alumni with high job meaning	48%
Degrees awarded in STEM subjects	31%

University of California—Riverside

University of California—San Diego

9500 Gilman Drive, 0021, La Jolla, CA 92093-0021 • Admissions: 858-534-4831 • Fax: 858-534-5723

CAMPUS LIFE

Quality of Life Rating	83
Fire Safety Rating	85
Green Rating	95
Type of school	Public
Environment	Metropolis

STUDENTS

Total undergrad enrollment	30,165
% male/female	50/50
% from out of state	6
% frosh live on campus	89
% ugrads live on campus	39
# of fraternities	
(% ugrad men join)	16 (14)
# of sororities	
(% ugrad women join)	12 (14)
% African American	3
% Asian	37
% Caucasian	19
% Hispanic	19
% Native American	<1
% Pacific Islander	<1
% Two or more races	0
% Race and/or ethnicity unknown	3
% international	19
# of countries represented	111

#39 BEST VALUE COLLEGE

ABOUT THE SCHOOL

Mathematics and the sciences reign supreme at the University of California—San Diego, and the school has an excellent reputation, huge research budgets, and an idyllic climate that have helped it attract eight Nobel laureates to its faculty. While research and graduate study garner most of the attention, undergraduates still receive a solid education that results in an impressive degree. The division of the undergraduate program into six smaller colleges helps take some of the edge off UC San Diego's big-school vibe (roughly 23,000 undergraduates) and allows students easier access to administrators. A quarterly academic calendar also keeps things moving. Campus life is generally pretty quiet. Students are divided on whether this school in scenic but sleepy La Jolla has a boring social scene or whether one simply has to look hard to find recreation. "There is always something to do on campus, and it is always changing! I never get bored!" But one thing is certain: some students work way too hard to afford the luxury of a social life. Students are often too busy with schoolwork to spend a lot of time partying, and when they have free time, they find hometown La Jolla a little too tiny for most college students. Also, the town won't sanction a frat row, so Greek life doesn't include raucous parties. Those students who remain in their dorms, however, can rest easy knowing that the 1,000-bed Village at Torrey Pines, built especially for transfer students, is one of the most environmentally sustainable student housing structures in the nation. Students also spend a lot of time at the beach or enjoying the school's intramural sports programs. One student summed up the dichotomy perfectly: "My school is all about science and the beach." Trying to study the hard sciences despite the distraction of the

University of California—San Diego

Financial Aid: 858-534-4480 • E-mail: admissionsinfo@ucsd.edu • Website: www.ucsd.edu

Pacific only a few blocks away is a mammoth task. And a fine public transit system makes downtown San Diego very accessible.

BANG FOR YOUR BUCK

More than half of UC San Diego's undergraduate students receive need-based support. The University of California's Blue and Gold Opportunity Plan (B&G) will cover students' UC fees if they are California residents and their families earn $80,000 or less and the student also qualifies for UC financial aid. For needy middle-class families earning up to $120,000, UC offers additional grant money that offsets half of any UC fee increase. In response to California's current economic climate, UC San Diego launched the $50 million Invent the Future student-support fundraising campaign, which will help fund scholarships and fellowships for all who need them.

STUDENT LIFE

A handful of undergrads seem to continually gripe that UC San Diego is "socially dead." However, plenty of students counter that there are definitely good times to be had, you simply have to "take control of your own college experience" and not just "go to class and [then retreat] to your room." For starters, San Diego offers "beautiful scenery and the perfect weather to go outside and play sports, chill at the beach or just hang out." Indeed, many undergrads tell us that there's a "huge surfing community." Additionally, students can typically find "small concerts or raves going on every week." The residence counsels also host lots of "fun programs such as Jell-o Fight, drive-in movies, casino nights, and much more." And there are a number of "spectacular" dance and play performances "that happen on campus."

ACADEMICS

Academic Rating	73
% students returning for sophomore year	95
% students graduating within 4 years	62
% students graduating within 6 years	86
Calendar	Quarter
Student/faculty ratio	19:1
Profs interesting rating	62
Profs accessible rating	62

Most classes have 10–19 students.
Most lab/discussion sessions have 10–19 students.

MOST POPULAR MAJORS

Biological and Biomedical Sciences;
Biology/Biological Sciences, General;
Mathematics and Statistics; Economics

SELECTIVITY

Admissions Rating	97
# of applicants	95,037
% of applicants accepted	30
% of acceptees attending	23

FRESHMAN PROFILE

Range SAT EBRW	550–680
Range SAT Math	610–750
# submitting SAT scores	5,751
% submitting SAT scores	86
# submitting ACT scores	2,645
% submitting ACT scores	39
Average HS GPA	4.1
% graduated top 10% of class	100
% graduated top 25% of class	100
% graduated top 50% of class	100

DEADLINES

Regular	
Deadline	11/30
Nonfall registration?	No

CAREER

Professional success is practically synonymous with UCSD. Indeed, according to PayScale.com, the median starting salary for San Diego grads is $63,400. Students looking to jumpstart their search can easily turn to the Career Services Center. Here undergrads have the opportunity to meet with advisors to explore the breadth of career options, conduct assessments and research various industries. Most importantly, the Center hosts job fairs and networking events every quarter. These present great opportunities for undergrads to learn about internships, part-time gigs and full-time positions. Companies that have recently attended include Amazon, Boeing, Apple, Chevron Corporation, California State Auditor, Hulu, Groupon, Intel Corporation, and the Peace Corps.

GENERAL INFO

Activities: Campus Ministries; Choral groups; Concert band; Dance; Drama/theater; International Student Organization; Jazz band; Literary magazine; Marching band; Model UN; Music ensembles; Musical theater; Opera; Pep band; Radio station; Student government; Student newspaper; Student-run film society; Symphony orchestra; Television station; Yearbook. 436 registered organizations, 4 honor societies, 36 religious organizations, 16 fraternities, 12 sororities, on campus. **Athletics (Intercollegiate):** *Men:* baseball, basketball, crew/rowing, cross-country, diving, fencing, golf, soccer, swimming, tennis, track/field (outdoor), volleyball, water polo. *Women:* basketball, crew/rowing, cross-country, diving, fencing, soccer, softball, swimming, tennis, track/field (outdoor), volleyball, water polo. **On-Campus Highlights:** Geisel Library, Stuart Art (sculpture) Gallery, Sun God Statue, Ocean Cliffs-Torrey Pines State Reserve, Stephen Birch Aquarium and Museum. **Environmental Initiatives:** The LEED Gold Certified Sustainability Resource Center (SRC), completed November 20, 2009 was constructed to provide a centralized, collaborative space in which to realize the common goals of maximizing campus environmental, social, and economic stewardship and sustainability; reducing the campus impact on the environment; maximizing campus and local outreach and participation; and, establishing a model for contributing to local, national, and global sustainability.

University of California— San Diego

FINANCIAL AID

Students should submit: FAFSA; State aid form. Priority filing deadline is 3/2. The Princeton Review suggests that all financial aid forms be submitted as soon as possible after October 1. *Need-based scholarships/ grants offered*: College/university scholarship or grant aid from institutional funds; Federal Pell; Private scholarships; SEOG; State scholarships/grants. *Loan aid offered*: Direct PLUS loans; Direct Subsidized Stafford Loans; Direct Unsubsidized Stafford Loans. Applicants will be notified of awards on a rolling basis beginning 3/15. Federal Work-Study Program available. Institutional employment available.

BOTTOM LINE

California residents attending UC San Diego full-time pay roughly $14,170 in tuition and fees. Room and board costs come to about $13,788, not to mention additional costs for transportation, books, and personal expenses. Nonresidents pay more than $40,400 in tuition alone.

FINANCIAL FACTS	
Financial Aid Rating	82
Annual in-state tuition	$11,442
Annual out-of-state tuition	$40,434
Room and board	$13,788
Required fees	$2,728
Books and supplies	$1,101
Average frosh need-based scholarship	$50,567
Average UG need-based scholarship	$19,929
% needy frosh rec. need-based scholarship or grant aid	91
% needy UG rec. need-based scholarship or grant aid	94
% needy frosh rec. non-need-based scholarship or grant aid	3
% needy UG rec. non-need-based scholarship or grant aid	1
% needy frosh rec. need-based self-help aid	71
% needy UG rec. need-based self-help aid	73
% frosh rec. any financial aid	77
% UG rec. any financial aid	63
% UG borrow to pay for school	48
Average cumulative indebtedness	$21,430
% frosh need fully met	34
% ugrads need fully met	41
Average % of frosh need met	88
Average % of ugrad need met	88

CAREER INFORMATION FROM PAYSCALE.COM	
ROI Rating	92
Bachelors and No Higher	
Median starting salary	$63,400
Median mid-career salary	$123,700
At Least Bachelors	
Median starting salary	$65,100
Median mid-career salary	$135,500
Alumni with high job meaning	55%
Degrees awarded in STEM subjects	58%

University of California— San Diego

University of California—Santa Barbara

Office of Admissions, 1210 Cheadle Hall, Santa Barbara, CA 93106-2014 • Admissions: 805-893-2881

#23 BEST VALUE COLLEGE

CAMPUS LIFE

Quality of Life Rating	91
Fire Safety Rating	95
Green Rating	98
Type of school	Public
Environment	City

STUDENTS

Total undergrad enrollment	22,186
% male/female	46/54
% from out of state	4
% frosh from public high school	80
% frosh live on campus	95
% ugrads live on campus	38
# of fraternities	
(% ugrad men join)	12 (4)
# of sororities	
(% ugrad women join)	20 (8)
% African American	2
% Asian	21
% Caucasian	34
% Hispanic	26
% Native American	<1
% Pacific Islander	<1
% Two or more races	6
% Race and/or ethnicity unknown	1
% international	8
# of countries represented	82

ABOUT THE SCHOOL

UCSB's beautiful campus is located 100 miles north of Los Angeles, with views of the ocean and the mountains, and typically benevolent Southern California weather. Perched above the Pacific coast, the University of California—Santa Barbara is a top-ranked public university with a multitude of world-class academic, extracurricular, and social opportunities. University of California–Santa Barbara is "a beautiful, laid-back learning institute on the beach," yet students say it's much more than a great place to get a tan. This prestigious public school is "one of the best research universities in the country," which "attracts many excellent professors" as well as a cadre of dedicated students. Maybe it's the sunny weather, but "professors here are more accessible than [at] other universities," and they are "genuinely interested in helping the students learn." This large university offers more than 200 major programs, of which business, economics, biology, communications, psychology, and engineering are among the most popular. Students agree that the competent and enthusiastic faculty is one of the school's greatest assets. Teaching assistants are also noted for being dedicated and helpful, especially in leading small discussion sessions to accompany large lecture courses. There are six Nobel laureates on the UCSB faculty, and the school offers many opportunities for undergraduates to participate in research.

BANG FOR YOUR BUCK

As a part of the prestigious University of California system, UCSB fuses good value and strong academics. It is a state school with over 20,000 students enrolled, so many classes are large. But with all the resources

University of California—Santa Barbara

Fax: 805-893-2676 • Financial Aid: 805-893-2118 • E-mail: admissions@sa.ucsb.edu • Website: www.ucsb.edu

of a major research school at your fingertips, it's a definite bargain. The University of California operates the Blue and Gold Opportunity Plan. For in-state students with household incomes of less than the state median of $80,000, the Blue and Gold Opportunity plan will fully cover the mandatory UC fees for four years. California residents are also eligible for Cal Grants, a grant program administered by the state and open to college students that meet certain minimum GPA requirements. In addition to state and federal aid, there are a number of scholarships available to UCSB undergraduates. New freshmen with outstanding academic and personal achievement may be awarded the prestigious Regents Scholarship. There are additional merit awards offered through each of the university's four colleges, as well as through the alumni association.

STUDENT LIFE

University of California—Santa Barbara is "a place for strong academics, excellent research opportunities, all with a laid-back and vibrant student life." With its large student body—there are over 20,000 undergraduates—there's something for everyone. Students note that outdoor activities are popular, from surfing to hiking, and underscore that UCSB has "a beach on campus." There are about 500 registered student organizations on campus and students participate in activities as varied as "a Shakespeare flash mob group" and "aerial dancing class." The Greek system is also a mainstay of campus life, with the school housing eighteen sororities and seventeen fraternities. Roughly 12 percent of women join a sorority, with 8 percent of men joining a fraternity. The school strikes a balance, though, according to one Literature major, who describes the population at UCSB as "lots of Greeks [and] lots of geeks." For another student, the number of "clubs, internships, research opportunities, and avenues to create...your own extracurricular activities is almost intimidating."

ACADEMICS

Academic Rating	86
% students returning for sophomore year	92
% students graduating within 4 years	70
% students graduating within 6 years	87
Calendar	Quarter
Student/faculty ratio	17:1
Profs interesting rating	84
Profs accessible rating	85

Most classes have fewer than 10 students. Most lab/discussion sessions have 20–29 students.

MOST POPULAR MAJORS

Biology/Biological Sciences, General; Psychology, General; Economics, General; Sociology

SELECTIVITY

Admissions Rating	96
# of applicants	80,319
% of applicants accepted	33
% of acceptees attending	17
# offered a place on the wait list	6,650
% accepting a place on wait list	60
% admitted from wait list	24

CAREER

According to PayScale.com, the median starting salary for a UCSB graduate is roughly $59,700 and popular careers include software engineer, mechanical engineer, and marketing manager. The most popular majors for UCSB students are Communication, Economics, and Sociology. While one Biochemistry major laments there are "basically too many students, and not enough open positions," other students praise the range of internship and post-graduation career opportunities, with one describing UCSB as "a springboard for the greatest young minds to launch into highly successful research and careers." The Career Services department at UCSB encourages students to take advantage of "GauchoLink," a frequently updated database of job and internship opportunities that also lists upcoming career-oriented events hosted by the school or by potential employers. Students are also able to store letters of recommendation with the Career Services department so as to streamline the process of applying for internships or jobs during their school tenure or after graduation.

GENERAL INFO

Activities: Campus Ministries; Choral groups; Concert band; Dance; Drama/theater; International Student Organization; Jazz band; Literary magazine; Model UN; Music ensembles; Musical theater; Opera; Pep band; Radio station; Student government; Student newspaper; Student-run film society; Symphony orchestra; Television station; Yearbook. 404 registered organizations, 13 honor societies, 16 religious organizations, 12 fraternities, 20 sororities, on campus. **Athletics (Intercollegiate):** *Men:* baseball, basketball, cross-country, diving, golf, gymnastics, soccer, swimming, tennis, track/field (outdoor), volleyball, water polo. *Women:* basketball, cross-country, diving, gymnastics, soccer, softball, swimming, tennis, track/field (outdoor), volleyball, water polo. **On-Campus Highlights:** Storke Tower Plaza/University Center, University Art Museum, UCSB Davidson Library, Recreation Center, Career and Counseling Services Center. **Environmental Initiatives:** Green buildings: minimum silver and strive for gold LEED certification—six buildings are currently certified, including San Clemente Villages Graduate Housing—one of the largest Gold certified housing projects in the US—and Bren Hall—the first building in the US to receive two Platinum ratings for new construction and existing buildings. Plus, 24 additional existing buildings scheduled to be certified in the next couple years through the USGBC Portfolio Program. UCSB has the most LEED EB buildings in the UC System. It created a Low Environmental Impact Cleaning Policy for the campus custodial services. All cleaning products and soaps used by the custodial staff are Green Seal certified. Plus toilet tissue, seat covers, and brown paper towels have 100% recycled content. Housing & Residential Services, supports solar water heating providing hot water for dorms, recycling used cooking oil from dining commons for biofuel, extensive recycling program including composting of food waste, purchasing local and/or organic foods for dining commons, using Green Seal cleaning products for custodial duties.

FINANCIAL AID

Students should submit: FAFSA. Priority filing deadline is 3/2. The Princeton Review suggests that all financial aid forms be submitted as soon as possible after October 1. *Need-based scholarships/grants offered*: College/university scholarship or grant aid from institutional funds; Federal Pell; SEOG; State scholarships/grants. *Loan aid offered*: Direct PLUS loans; Direct Subsidized Stafford Loans; Direct Unsubsidized Stafford Loans. Federal Work-Study Program available. Institutional employment available.

FINANCIAL FACTS	
Financial Aid Rating	83
Annual in-state tuition	$12,570
Annual out-of-state tuition	$42,324
Room and board	$15,111
Required fees	$1,875
Books and supplies	$1,143
Average frosh need-based scholarship	$21,491
Average UG need-based scholarship	$18,698
% needy frosh rec. need-based scholarship or grant aid	94
% needy UG rec. need-based scholarship or grant aid	93
% needy frosh rec. non-need-based scholarship or grant aid	1
% needy UG rec. non-need-based scholarship or grant aid	1
% needy frosh rec. need-based self-help aid	62
% needy UG rec. need-based self-help aid	60
% frosh rec. any financial aid	61
% UG rec. any financial aid	59
% UG borrow to pay for school	56
Average cumulative indebtedness	$20,978
% frosh need fully met	15
% ugrads need fully met	15
Average % of frosh need met	80
Average % of ugrad need met	79

BOTTOM LINE

Depending on where you live and what you study, the cost of attending UC Santa Barbara fluctuates. For California residents, the school estimates that total expenses come to about $30,699 annually. For out-of-state residents, the estimated annual cost comes to $60,453.

CAREER INFORMATION FROM PAYSCALE.COM	
ROI Rating	93
Bachelors and No Higher	
Median starting salary	$59,700
Median mid-career salary	$116,300
At Least Bachelors	
Median starting salary	$60,700
Median mid-career salary	$128,600
Alumni with high job meaning	49%
Degrees awarded in STEM subjects	29%

University of California—
Santa Barbara

The University of Chicago

1101 E 58th Street, Rosenwald Hall Suite 105, Chicago, IL 60637 • Admissions: 773-702-8650 • Fax: 773-702-4199

CAMPUS LIFE

Quality of Life Rating	89
Fire Safety Rating	97
Green Rating	89
Type of school	Private
Environment	Metropolis

STUDENTS

Total undergrad enrollment	6,552
% male/female	51/49
% from out of state	81
% frosh live on campus	100
% ugrads live on campus	55
% African American	5
% Asian	19
% Caucasian	39
% Hispanic	14
% Native American	<1
% Pacific Islander	<1
% Two or more races	6
% Race and/or ethnicity unknown	2
% international	14
# of countries represented	77

#29 BEST VALUE COLLEGE

ABOUT THE SCHOOL

The University of Chicago has a reputation as a favorite destination of the true intellectual: students here are interested in learning for learning's sake, and they aren't afraid to express their opinions. A rigorous, intellectually challenging, and world-renowned research university, the University of Chicago continues to offer a community where students thrive and ideas matter. Here, an attitude of sharp questioning seems to be the focus, rather than the more relaxed inquiry and rumination approach at some schools of equal intellectual repute. Many find welcome challenges in the debates and discussions that define the campus atmosphere; the typical Chicago student is task-oriented, intellectually driven, sharp, vocal, and curious. As one student surveyed said, "There is nothing more exciting, challenging, and rewarding than the pursuit of knowledge in all of its forms." The undergraduate program at Chicago emphasizes critical thinking through a broad-based liberal arts curriculum. At the heart of the experience is the Common Core, the foundation for any major and all future endeavors. No lecture courses here—Core courses are discussion-based, and enrollment is limited to twenty. Chicago's numerous major programs range from religious studies to linguistics, history, economics, and molecular engineering.

BANG FOR YOUR BUCK

The University of Chicago operates a need-blind admissions process, admitting qualified students regardless of their financial situation. Once admitted, the school guarantees to meet 100 percent of a student's demonstrated financial need. Under a program called "No Barriers,"

The University of Chicago

Financial Aid: 773-702-8655 • E-mail: collegeadmissions@uchicago.edu• Website: www.uchicago.edu

grants replace student loans for every student's need-based financial aid package. Highly qualified freshman candidates may also be considered for competitive merit scholarships. Scholarships are awarded to applicants on the basis of outstanding academic and extracurricular achievement, demonstrated leadership, and commitment to their communities. Notable merit scholarships include: the Odyssey Scholarship, a renewable scholarship and guaranteed summer internship for students from low- and moderate-income families; and University Scholarships, which are guaranteed for four years of study. There are also scholarship programs for first-generation students, children of police officers and firefighters, and a partnershp with the Posse Foundation's Veterans Program.

STUDENT LIFE

Students rejoice! The "social scene at UChicago is truly vibrant and encompasses a very wide spectrum." Indeed, it "allows you to dabble in a variety of groups; one weekend you can hang out at a frat playing flip cup or pong, while another weekend you can go out in downtown Chicago, drink wine with your sorority sisters, discuss Marx and Smith at an apartment party, or just simply watch a movie with your roommates." There are also "tons of [clubs to join], from numerous different martial arts to gymnastics to multiple magazines to event planning for the school to tutoring kids and community service to cultural groups to a vegan society." And, of course, the city of Chicago also helps to guarantee boredom will be kept at bay. There is "always something to do like going to festivals, trying new restaurants, shopping, seeing a performance, listening to a concert, visiting museums, or experiencing a different culture."

ACADEMICS

Academic Rating	97
% students returning for sophomore year	99
% students graduating within 4 years	89
% students graduating within 6 years	94
Calendar	Quarter
Student/faculty ratio	5:1
Profs interesting rating	86
Profs accessible rating	85

Most classes have fewer than 10 students. Most lab/discussion sessions have 10–19 students.

MOST POPULAR MAJORS

Biology/Biological Sciences, General; Mathematics, General; Economics, General

SELECTIVITY

Admissions Rating	99
# of applicants	32,283
% of applicants accepted	7
% of acceptees attending	77

CAREER

Without a doubt, a University of Chicago education means that students will "enter a competitive job market prepared." This sentiment is supported by the fact that 94 percent of students have jobs or post-grad plans soon after leaving school. In fact, the median starting salary (according to PayScale. com) for recent UChicago grads is $64,000. The school's Career Advancement office maintains some unique programs to help ensure this success. For example, students can participate in the Jeff Metcalf Internship Program, which provides more than 2,500 paid internships each year throughout the country and abroad, or the Alumni Board Job Shadowing Program where they can shadow an accomplished professional.

GENERAL INFO

Activities: Campus Ministries; Choral groups; Concert band; Dance; Drama/theater; International Student Organization; Jazz band; Literary magazine; Model UN; Music ensembles; Musical theater; Opera; Pep band; Radio station; Student government; Student newspaper; Student-run film society; Symphony orchestra; Television station. 388 registered organizations, 2 honor societies, 22 religious organizations, on campus. **Athletics (Intercollegiate):** *Men:* baseball, basketball, cross-country, diving, football, soccer, swimming, tennis, track/field (outdoor), track/field (indoor), volleyball, wrestling. *Women:* basketball, cross-country, diving, soccer, softball, swimming, tennis, track/field (outdoor), track/field (indoor), volleyball. **On-Campus Highlights:** Logan Arts Center, Joseph Regenstein Library, Robie House, Gerald Ratner Athletics Center, Rockefeller Memorial Chapel.

FINANCIAL AID

Students should submit: FAFSA; Institution's own financial aid form or CSS/Financial Aid PROFILE. Priority filing deadline is 2/15. The Princeton Review suggests that all financial aid forms be submitted as soon as possible after October 1. *Need-based scholarships/grants offered*: College/university scholarship or grant aid from institutional funds; Federal Pell; Private scholarships; SEOG; State scholarships/grants. *Loan aid offered*: Direct PLUS loans; Direct Subsidized Stafford Loans; Direct Unsubsidized Stafford Loans. Applicants will be notified of awards on or about 3/15. Federal Work-Study Program available. Institutional employment available.

BOTTOM LINE

Yearly tuition to University of Chicago is a little more than $55,425, plus an additional $1,581 in mandatory fees. For campus residents, room and board is about $16,350 per year. Once you factor in personal expenses, transportation, books, and supplies, an education at University of Chicago costs about $77,331 per year. At University of Chicago, all demonstrated financial need is met through financial aid packages.

FINANCIAL FACTS	
Financial Aid Rating	97
Annual tuition	$55,425
Room and board	$16,350
Required fees	$1,581
Books and supplies	$1,800
Average frosh need-based scholarship	$51,679
Average UG need-based scholarship	$50,697
% needy frosh rec. need-based scholarship or grant aid	100
% needy UG rec. need-based scholarship or grant aid	100
% needy frosh rec. need-based self-help aid	83
% needy UG rec. need-based self-help aid	69
% frosh rec. any financial aid	56
% UG rec. any financial aid	57
% UG borrow to pay for school	29
Average cumulative indebtedness	$19,817
% frosh need fully met	100
% ugrads need fully met	100
Average % of frosh need met	100
Average % of ugrad need met	100

CAREER INFORMATION FROM PAYSCALE.COM	
ROI Rating	93
Bachelors and No Higher	
Median starting salary	$64,000
Median mid-career salary	$114,200
At Least Bachelors	
Median starting salary	$66,000
Median mid-career salary	$126,200
Alumni with high job meaning	46%
Degrees awarded in STEM subjects	22%

University of Florida

201 Criser Hall, Gainesville, FL 32611-4000 • Admissions: 352-392-1365 • Fax: 352-392-3987

#42 BEST VALUE COLLEGE

ABOUT THE SCHOOL

The University of Florida is the prototypical large state school that "provides its students with a well-rounded experience: an excellent education coated in incomparable school camaraderie." With a total enrollment of just over 56,000, this school is among the five largest universities in the nation, proffering "first class amenities, athletics, academics, campus, and students." Those students hail from all fifty states and more than 150 countries, all of whom are looking for more than your standard academic fare. UF certainly doesn't disappoint, as the school has "a great reputation and…great academic programs for the tuition price." The campus is home to more than 100 undergraduate degree programs, and undergraduates interested in conducting research with faculty can participate in UF's University Scholars Program. One unique learning community, Innovation Academy, pulls together students from thirty majors who share a common minor in innovation. The Career Connection Center (CCC) is a major centralized service that helps students prepare for their post-graduation experiences—UF "seeks to graduate academically ahead and 'real-world-prepared' alumni"—and organized career fairs are conducted regularly and the university is very successful in attracting top employers nationally to recruit on campus.

BANG FOR YOUR BUCK

The cost of attending University of Florida is well below the national average for four-year public universities. Annual tuition and fees are $6,381 (based on a typical schedule of thirty credit hours per year), while campus room and board will run you another $9,000-plus. Overall, Florida residents

University of Florida

Financial Aid: 352-392-6684 • Website: www.ufl.edu

are the main benefactors of this great value. Out-of-state undergraduates pay a little over $22,000 more in tuition and fees and must also factor in higher transportation costs. The school prides itself on providing prospective students with financial aid packages that will help lower educational costs through a variety of "Gator Aid" options. Their website offers a net price calculator to help students and their families get a better idea of exactly how much it would cost to attend the school. In-state students should be sure to check out the Florida Bright Futures Scholarship Program, which offers scholarships based on high school academic achievement. The program has different award levels, each with its own eligibility criteria and award amounts.

STUDENT LIFE

Though students at UF study hard and things can get very serious during finals and midterms, fun abounds at school. "A lot of UF culture is based around sports. We are always going to or watching something," is a sentiment expressed by many students. "The sporting events are top notch and everyone [can] find a sport to cheer for because we are great at them all! Our intramural program and gym are also amazing." With sports tend to come parties, but while "many activities revolve around drinking and partying (especially during football season)," there are lots of other ways to enjoy yourself at school. "GatorNights are always fun," says a student. "Every Friday, there are different events from wax hands to comedians to sand candy and a lot more. Also, the clubs are great here. They have so many clubs, from Software Development to Aerial Dance and everything in between." There are opportunities to get away as well: "Occasionally when looking for a change of scenery we embrace the nature around us and float down...Ginnie Springs or go to the school's lake." So no matter how you like to spend your time, UF should have something to offer.

ACADEMICS

Academic Rating	81
% students returning for sophomore year	97
% students graduating within 4 years	68
% students graduating within 6 years	90
Calendar	Semester
Student/faculty ratio	18:1
Profs interesting rating	74
Profs accessible rating	79

Most classes have 10–19 students.
Most lab/discussion sessions have 10–19 students.

MOST POPULAR MAJORS

Biology/Biological Sciences, General; Psychology, General; Finance, General

SELECTIVITY

Admissions Rating	95
# of applicants	38,905
% of applicants accepted	39
% of acceptees attending	45

CAREER

Students widely feel that UF does a great job at preparing them for life after school, from the first-rate academics to the "excellent" career services. The Career Resource Center offers an abundance of services, including academic advising and career planning, job fairs and recruiting events, resume critique and mock interviews, and resources for job and internship searches. Gator Shadow Day allows student to learn about careers by shadowing a professional at work. The Center also offers a program called Gator Launch to provide "underrepresented" students in the science and technology fields with special mentoring opportunities. All in all, students seem to leave happy. Of University of Florida alumni visiting PayScale.com, 52 percent report that they derive a high level of meaning from their jobs.

GENERAL INFO

Activities: Campus Ministries; Choral groups; Concert band; Dance; Drama/theater; International Student Organization; Jazz band; Literary magazine; Marching band; Model UN; Music ensembles; Musical theater; Opera; Pep band; Radio station; Student government; Student newspaper; Student-run film society; Symphony orchestra; Television station; Yearbook. 1,050 registered organizations, 43 honor societies, 50 religious affiliated organizations, 38 fraternities, 27 sororities, on campus. **Athletics (Intercollegiate):** *Men:* baseball, basketball, cross-country, diving, football, golf, swimming, tennis, track/field (outdoor), track/field (indoor). *Women:* basketball, cross-country, diving, golf, gymnastics, lacrosse, soccer, softball, swimming, tennis, track/field (outdoor), track/field (indoor), volleyball. **On-Campus Highlights:** Southwest Recreation Center, Plaza of Americas, Library West, Ben Hill Griffin Stadium, J. Wayne Reitz Student Union, and Newell Hall Learning Commons. **Environmental Initiatives:** As a result of Dr. Machen's goal for Zero Waste by 2015, UF now recycles over 6,500 tons of material annually, approximately 43% of the waste stream. Additionally, UF strives to recycle at least 75% of its deconstruction debris and has instituted an Electronics Reuse/Recycling Policy and accompanying step-by-step guide for disposal and recycling. Indoor collection of paper, cans & bottles is institution-wide. UF initiated a Tail-gator recycling program for home game days in 2006 and the program has diverted more than 350,000 pounds of recyclables from the landfill since then. This program continues to grow through self-service stations and other outreach

University of Florida

on campus and within the stadium. In 2013, UF began composting efforts on campus by taking the stadium "zero waste" through the football season—diverting an additional 200,000 pounds of organic waste from the landfill. UF researchers recycle Helium on campus and the Veterinary Medical Center repurposes animal waste through a composting partnership with the Forestry Service.

FINANCIAL AID

Students should submit: FAFSA. Priority filing deadline is 12/15. The Princeton Review suggests that all financial aid forms be submitted as soon as possible after October 1. *Need-based scholarships/grants offered*: College/university scholarship or grant aid from institutional funds; Federal Pell; Private scholarships; SEOG; State scholarships/grants; United Negro College Fund. *Loan aid offered*: Federal Perkins Loans; College/university loans from institutional funds; Direct PLUS loans; Direct Subsidized Stafford Loans; Direct Unsubsidized Stafford Loans. Applicants will be notified of awards on a rolling basis beginning 2/22. Federal Work-Study Program available. Institutional employment available.

FINANCIAL FACTS	
Financial Aid Rating	83
Annual in-state tuition	$6,381
Annual out-of-state tuition	$28,658
Room and board	$10,220
Required fees	$1,904
Books and supplies	$850
Average frosh need-based scholarship	$9,083
Average UG need-based scholarship	$8,476
% needy frosh rec. need-based scholarship or grant aid	53
% needy UG rec. need-based scholarship or grant aid	62
% needy frosh rec. non-need-based scholarship or grant aid	88
% needy UG rec. non-need-based scholarship or grant aid	68
% needy frosh rec. need-based self-help aid	28
% needy UG rec. need-based self-help aid	41
% frosh rec. any financial aid	98
% UG rec. any financial aid	98
% UG borrow to pay for school	38
Average cumulative indebtedness	$21,800
% frosh need fully met	29
% ugrads need fully met	24
Average % of frosh need met	99
Average % of ugrad need met	98

BOTTOM LINE

With relatively low tuition and a strong scholarship program for in-state students, UF is an especially good value for Florida residents. The Machen Florida Opportunity Scholars (MFOS) is a scholarship program for first-generation college freshmen from economically disadvantaged backgrounds. The scholarship provides a full grant scholarship aid package for up to four years of undergraduate education.

CAREER INFORMATION FROM PAYSCALE.COM	
ROI Rating	92
Bachelors and No Higher	
Median starting salary	$55,800
Median mid-career salary	$102,800
At Least Bachelors	
Median starting salary	$58,000
Median mid-career salary	$108,800
Alumni with high job meaning	52%
Degrees awarded in STEM subjects	29%

University of Florida

University of Michigan—Ann Arbor

1220 Student Activities Building, Ann Arbor, MI 48109-1316 • Admissions: 734-764-7433

CAMPUS LIFE

Quality of Life Rating	92
Fire Safety Rating	88
Green Rating	90
Type of school	Public
Environment	City

STUDENTS

Total undergrad enrollment	30,079
% male/female	50/50
% from out of state	41
% frosh live on campus	98
% ugrads live on campus	31
# of fraternities	
(% ugrad men join)	30 (12)
# of sororities	
(% ugrad women join)	27 (25)
% African American	4
% Asian	15
% Caucasian	59
% Hispanic	6
% Native American	<1
% Pacific Islander	<1
% Two or more races	4
% Race and/or ethnicity unknown	5
% international	7
# of countries represented	92

#59 BEST VALUE COLLEGE

ABOUT THE SCHOOL

The University of Michigan—Ann Arbor is a big school with big opportunities, and we do mean big. The university has a multibillion-dollar endowment and one of the largest research expenditures of any American university, also in the billions. Its physical campus includes more than 34 million square feet of building space, and its football stadium is the largest college football stadium in the country. With nearly 31,000 undergraduates, the scale of the University of Michigan's stellar offerings truly is overwhelming. But for those students who can handle the "first-class education in a friendly, competitive atmosphere," there are a lot of advantages to attending a university of this size and stature, and they will find "a great environment both academically and socially." You get an amazing breadth of classes, excellent professors, a "wide range of travel abroad opportunities," unparalleled research opportunities, and inroads into an alumni network that can offer you entry into any number of postgraduate opportunities. The school "provides every kind of opportunity at all times to all people," and students here get "the opportunity to go far within their respective concentrations."

BANG FOR YOUR BUCK

UM spent $423 million in 2017–18 on total undergraduate need-based and merit-aid. That is truly staggering and reflects an amount more than the total endowment of many schools. Students who are Pell-grant eligible may benefit from UM's debt-elimination programs. All in-state students can expect to have 100 percent of their demonstrated need met. The Go Blue Guarantee will cover full tuition for students whose family income is less than $65,000.

University of Michigan—Ann Arbor

Fax: 734-936-0740 • Financial Aid: 734-763-6600 • Website: www.umich.edu

The university's schools, colleges, and departments administer their own scholarship programs, so you should feel free to check with them directly. UM's Office of Financial Aid also administers a variety of scholarship programs that recognize superior academic achievement, leadership qualities, and potential contribution to the scholarly community. The majority of these scholarships are awarded automatically to eligible students. A full list of UM scholarships is available on the university's website. In addition to the scholarship programs offered by the school, there are also private scholarships available to prospective students. These are offered by a variety of corporate, professional, trade, governmental, civic, religious, social and fraternal organizations. While these applications can be time consuming, they can be worth it. Some are worth thousands of dollars. The University of Michigan has a full list of these scholarships—and their deadlines—on their website. The school is dedicated to helping prospective students gain a better understanding of how to pay for their education by providing access to financial aid counselors. Their website also features an application called M-Calc, a net price calculator, which allows students and their families to access an early estimate of the full-time cost of attendance the University of Michigan.

ACADEMICS

Academic Rating	84
% students returning for sophomore year	97
% students graduating within 4 years	77
% students graduating within 6 years	92
Calendar	Trimester
Student/faculty ratio	15:1
Profs interesting rating	67
Profs accessible rating	69

Most classes have 10–19 students. Most lab/discussion sessions have 20–29 students.

MOST POPULAR MAJORS

Computer Science; Business Administration and Management, General; Economics

SELECTIVITY

Admissions Rating	96
# of applicants	64,917
% of applicants accepted	23
% of acceptees attending	45
# offered a place on the wait list	14,783
% accepting a place on wait list	41
% admitted from wait list	7

STUDENT LIFE

The Michigan student body is "hugely diverse," which "is one of the things Michigan prides itself on." There is a place for everyone here, because "there are hundreds of mini-communities within the campus, made of everything from service fraternities to political organizations to dance groups." As one undergrad puts it, "That's part of the benefit of 40,000-plus students!" Students also rave about "great programs like UMix...phenomenal cultural opportunities in Ann Arbor especially music and movies," and "the hugely popular football Saturdays. The sense of school spirit here is impressive." With over 1,200 registered student organizations on campus, "if you have an interest, you can find a group of people who enjoy the same thing."

CAREER

The Career Center offers a wealth of resources to students learning to be advocates for themselves post-graduation. The massive fall Career Fair jumpstarts the process for job-seekers (the Career Center even offers a smartphone App for navigating the floor plan), and the semester schedule is packed with programs and workshops like Career Crawls, which focus on themes such as choosing a major, or Immersions, a program which hosts half-day visits to an organization's workplace. Career Center Connector lists tons of job and internship opportunities while Alumni Profiles provide glimpses into grad's career choices and job search strategies. Other structured programs, like the Public Service Intern Program, link students with internship openings in the U.S. and abroad. Graduates who visited PayScale.com report an average starting salary of $65,600, and 49 percent believe that their jobs make the world a better place.

GENERAL INFO

Activities: Campus Ministries; Choral groups; Concert band; Dance; Drama/theater; International Student Organization; Jazz band; Literary magazine; Marching band; Model UN; Music ensembles; Musical theater; Opera; Pep band; Radio station; Student government; Student newspaper; Student-run film society; Symphony orchestra; Television station; Yearbook. 1,500 registered organizations, 38 honor societies, 99 religious organizations, 30 fraternities, 27 sororities, on campus. **Athletics (Intercollegiate):** *Men:* baseball, basketball, cheerleading, cross-country, diving, football, golf, gymnastics, ice hockey, swimming, tennis, track/field (outdoor), track/field (indoor), wrestling. *Women:* basketball, cheerleading, crew/rowing, cross-country, diving, field hockey, golf, gymnastics, soccer, softball, swimming, tennis, track/field (outdoor), track/field (indoor), volleyball, water polo. **On-Campus Highlights:** Michigan Stadium, Michigan Union, Diag, Campus Recreation Buildings, Wave Field. **Environmental Initiatives:** Establishment and tracking of Campus Sustainability goals. sustainability. umich.edu/ocs/goals

University of Michigan— Ann Arbor

FINANCIAL AID

Students should submit: CSS/Financial Aid PROFILE; FAFSA. Priority filing deadline is 3/31. The Princeton Review suggests that all financial aid forms be submitted as soon as possible after October 1. *Need-based scholarships/grants offered*: College/university scholarship or grant aid from institutional funds; Federal Pell; Private scholarships; SEOG; State scholarships/grants. *Loan aid offered*: Direct PLUS loans; Direct Subsidized Stafford Loans; Direct Unsubsidized Stafford Loans. Applicants will be notified of awards on a rolling basis beginning 1/15. Federal Work-Study Program available. Institutional employment available.

BOTTOM LINE

UM's top-of-the-line education and comparatively low tuition make this school the definition of a best value. For Michigan residents, the estimated total cost of attendance for one year is about $29,584, including tuition, fees, room and board, books and supplies. For nonresidents, the price is roughly double the in-state rate at $66,041.

FINANCIAL FACTS	
Financial Aid Rating	86
Annual in-state tuition	$16,212
Annual out-of-state tuition	$52,669
Room and board	$11,996
Required fees	$328
Books and supplies	$1,048
Average frosh need-based scholarship	$19,145
Average UG need-based scholarship	$20,108
% needy frosh rec. need-based scholarship or grant aid	77
% needy UG rec. need-based scholarship or grant aid	81
% needy frosh rec. non-need-based scholarship or grant aid	70
% needy UG rec. non-need-based scholarship or grant aid	67
% needy frosh rec. need-based self-help aid	70
% needy UG rec. need-based self-help aid	75
% frosh rec. any financial aid	69
% UG rec. any financial aid	61
% UG borrow to pay for school	37
Average cumulative indebtedness	$27,224
% frosh need fully met	71
% ugrads need fully met	76
Average % of frosh need met	91
Average % of ugrad need met	93

CAREER INFORMATION FROM PAYSCALE.COM	
ROI Rating	91
Bachelors and No Higher	
Median starting salary	$63,500
Median mid-career salary	$112,200
At Least Bachelors	
Median starting salary	$65,600
Median mid-career salary	$118,500
Alumni with high job meaning	49%
Degrees awarded in STEM subjects	38%

University of Michigan—
Ann Arbor

The University of North Carolina at Chapel Hill

Campus Box #2200, Chapel Hill, NC 27599-2200 • Admissions: 919-966-3621 • Fax: 919-962-3045

#21 BEST VALUE COLLEGE

CAMPUS LIFE

Quality of Life Rating	91
Fire Safety Rating	97
Green Rating	96
Type of school	Public
Environment	Town

STUDENTS

Total undergrad enrollment	18,968
% male/female	41/59
% from out of state	15
% frosh from public high school	82
% frosh live on campus	100
% ugrads live on campus	51
# of fraternities	
(% ugrad men join)	36 (20)
# of sororities	
(% ugrad women join)	24 (20)
% African American	8
% Asian	11
% Caucasian	60
% Hispanic	8
% Native American	1
% Pacific Islander	<1
% Two or more races	5
% Race and/or ethnicity unknown	4
% international	3
# of countries represented	101

ABOUT THE SCHOOL

The University of North Carolina at Chapel Hill is the country's first public university and the flagship campus of the UNC system. The school offers its nearly 19,000 undergraduates 77 majors to choose from. Each of those majors features "rigorous academics" from professors who are "extremely enthusiastic and excited to teach." Even when classes are large, faculty members "do their best to get students involved in the conversation by requiring recitations," which are smaller, discussion-based versions of the class. Students feel "this is a great technique that fosters true, more hands-on learning." A UNC education "is more about learning how to think and write than memorizing facts"; for example, professors often take advantage of the campus' Ackland Art Museum, "creating assignments around the artwork on display—not just art classes, but language, drama, and history classes." The school's Making Connections Curriculum includes an Experiential Education (EE) requirement, which "could range from visiting geological anomalies to completing an internship," and there are many "project-based classes where students have the opportunity to propose the specific topic ... which they work on in a class."

BANG FOR YOUR BUCK

More than half of all students who attend UNC receive financial aid, and the Carolina Covenant is a promise that aims to make sure that eligible low-income students (from families making less than 200 percent of the federal poverty level) have the opportunity to graduate debt-free via grants, scholarships, and work-study. Scholarships without any need

The University of North Carolina at Chapel Hill

Financial Aid: 919-962-8396 • E-mail: unchelp@admissions.unc.edu • Website: www.unc.edu

requirements are also available with 7 percent of first-year students receiving them. Among these are the Pogue Scholarships which offers $10,000 for North Carolina residents, or tuition, fees, and room and board for out-of-state students, with a demonstrated commitment to diversity, while the Chancellor's Science Scholarship focuses on preparing students for scientific leadership in STEM subjects. "All of my financial needs were met and I have multiple resources and people to direct and advise me on my journey here," says a student.

STUDENT LIFE

Expect "a lot of studying and hours spent in the library," but also recognize that "game days are always big." Students are active both in club sports and in "catching various sporting events on campus," and for those not athletically inclined, "there's lots to do on Franklin Street [a neighborhood just blocks from the campus], and there are always activities on campus." But when they want a quick getaway, students can often be found taking "weekend excursions to the cities of Chapel Hill, Durham, and Raleigh for parties, amusement parks, or restaurants." There are "lots of places for day hikes somewhat close to campus," and this active student body also enjoys "going to the gym or on a run." The school also "holds fun events ... such as stargazing nights at the Planetarium."

CAREER

University Career Services (UCS) offers a slew of resources to students looking for advising, internships, and jobs, as well as workshops on job-seeking skills. Plus, "there are so many professors at this school that will go the extra mile to ensure you are comfortable and have a plan to maximize your potential." The campus' location in the Research Triangle "creates a wealth of opportunities for finding internships, jobs, shadowing, and/

ACADEMICS

Academic Rating	87
% students returning for sophomore year	97
% students graduating within 4 years	82
% students graduating within 6 years	90
Calendar	Semester
Student/faculty ratio	13:1
Profs interesting rating	84
Profs accessible rating	82

Most classes have 20–29 students.
Most lab/discussion sessions have 10–19 students.

MOST POPULAR MAJORS

Biology/Biological Sciences, General; Psychology, General; Economics, General

SELECTIVITY

Admissions Rating	97
# of applicants	43,473
% of applicants accepted	22
% of acceptees attending	45
# offered a place on the wait list	4,977
% accepting a place on wait list	46
% admitted from wait list	1

FRESHMAN PROFILE

Range SAT EBRW	640–720
Range SAT Math	630–750
Range ACT Composite	27–33
# submitting SAT scores	2,931
% submitting SAT scores	68
# submitting ACT scores	3,243
% submitting ACT scores	75
Average HS GPA	4.7
% graduated top 10% of class	78
% graduated top 25% of class	96
% graduated top 50% of class	99

DEADLINES

Early action	
Deadline	1/15
Notification	1/31
Regular	
Deadline	10/15
Notification	3/31
Nonfall registration?	No

or extracurricular activities," and since UNC is the nation's eleventh largest research university, there is "a colossal amount of ongoing research projects at the university," which students can often become involved in. And they're big believers in doing so: "The research is what has made me a better thinker and a better person," says one student.

GENERAL INFO

Activities: Campus Ministries; Choral groups; Concert band; Dance; Drama/theater; International Student Organization; Jazz band; Literary magazine; Marching band; Model UN; Music ensembles; Musical theater; Opera; Pep band; Radio station; Student government; Student newspaper; Student-run film society; Symphony orchestra; Television station; Yearbook. 822 registered organizations, 30 honor societies, 55 religious organizations, 36 fraternities, 24 sororities, on campus. **Athletics (Intercollegiate):** *Men:* baseball, basketball, cross-country, diving, fencing, football, golf, lacrosse, soccer, swimming, tennis, track/field (outdoor), track/field (indoor), wrestling. *Women:* basketball, crew/rowing, cross-country, diving, fencing, field hockey, golf, gymnastics, lacrosse, soccer, softball, swimming, tennis, track/field (outdoor), track/field (indoor), volleyball. **On-Campus Highlights:** The Pit, McCorkle Place, Polk Place, Dean Smith Center, Student Union. **Environmental Initiatives:** Partnered with Orange (County) Water and Sewer Authority (OWASA) to install a water reclamation and reuse system that replaced 218 million gallons of potable water in FY 2016. Started in summer 2009, the system provides makeup water at campus cooling towers, irrigates athletic fields and grounds, and flushes toilets in new buildings adjacent to the distribution network.

The University of North Carolina at Chapel Hill

FINANCIAL AID

Students should submit: CSS/Financial Aid PROFILE; FAFSA. Priority filing deadline is 3/1. The Princeton Review suggests that all financial aid forms be submitted as soon as possible after October 1. *Need-based scholarships/grants offered*: College/university scholarship or grant aid from institutional funds; Federal Pell; Private scholarships; SEOG; State scholarships/grants. *Loan aid offered*: Direct PLUS loans; Direct Subsidized Stafford Loans; Direct Unsubsidized Stafford Loans; Institutional loans. Applicants will be notified of awards on a rolling basis beginning 1/31. Federal Work-Study Program available. Institutional employment available.

BOTTOM LINE

The cost of attending Carolina is a real bargain—especially if your home state is North Carolina. In-state students can expect to pay about $8,986 in tuition and fees. Out-of-state students have it pretty good too; they can expect to cough up about $36,165 for the cost of tuition and fees for one year. Cost of living in Chapel Hill is pretty cheap too—you can expect room and board to run you just $11,526 per year.

The University of North Carolina at Chapel Hill

University of Notre Dame

220 Main Building, Notre Dame, IN 46556 • Admissions: 574-631-7505 • Fax: 574-631-8865

#71 BEST VALUE COLLEGE

ABOUT THE SCHOOL

As a private school with traditions of excellence in academics, athletics, and service, and with a vast, faithful alumni base that provides ample resources, the University of Notre Dame draws on its Catholic values to provide a well-rounded, world-class education. One student is thrilled to attend, noting that "as an Irish Catholic, Notre Dame is basically the equivalent of Harvard. I've always viewed the school as an institution with rigorous academics as well as rich tradition and history—and a symbol of pride for my heritage." Not all are Catholic here, although it seems that most undergrads "have some sort of spirituality present in their daily lives" and have a "vibrant social and religious life." Total undergraduate enrollment is just more than 8,000 students. ND is reportedly improving in diversity concerning economic backgrounds, according to members of the student body here. An incredible 90 percent are from out-of-state, and ninety countries are now represented throughout the campus. Undergrads say they enjoy "a college experience that is truly unique," "combining athletics and academics in an environment of faith." "It's necessary to study hard and often, [but] there's also time to do other things." Academics are widely praised, and one new student is excited that even "large lectures are broken down into smaller discussion groups once a week to help with class material and...give the class a personal touch."

University of Notre Dame

Financial Aid: 574-631-6436 • E-mail: admissions@nd.edu • Website: www.nd.edu

BANG FOR YOUR BUCK

Notre Dame is one of the most selective colleges in the country. Almost everyone who enrolls is in the top 10 percent of their graduating class and possesses test scores in the highest percentiles. But, as the student respondents suggest, strong academic ability isn't enough to get you in here. The school looks for students with other talents and seems to have a predilection for athletic achievement. Each residence hall is home to students from all classes; most will live in the same hall for all their years on campus. An average of 93 percent of entering students will graduate within five years. Students report that "the administration tries its best to stay on top of the students' wants and needs." The school is also extremely community-oriented, and Notre Dame has some of the strongest alumni support nationwide.

STUDENT LIFE

Undergrads at Notre Dame report "the vast majority" of their peers are "very smart" "white kids from upper to middle-class backgrounds from all over the country, especially the Midwest and Northeast." The typical student "is a type-A personality that studies a lot, yet is athletic and involved in the community. They are usually the outstanding seniors in their high schools," the "sort of people who can talk about the BCS rankings and Derrida in the same breath." Additionally, something like "85 percent of Notre Dame students earned a varsity letter in high school." "ND is slowly improving in diversity concerning economic backgrounds, with the university's policy to meet all demonstrated financial need." As things stand now, those who "don't tend to fit in with everyone else hang out in their own groups made up by others like them (based on ethnicity, sexual orientation, etc.)."

ACADEMICS

Academic Rating	80
% students returning for sophomore year	98
% students graduating within 4 years	94
% students graduating within 6 years	97
Calendar	Semester
Student/faculty ratio	10:1
Profs interesting rating	65
Profs accessible rating	70

Most classes have 10–19 students.

MOST POPULAR MAJORS

Psychology, General; Political Science and Government, General; Finance, General

SELECTIVITY

Admissions Rating	98
# of applicants	20,371
% of applicants accepted	18
% of acceptees attending	57
# offered a place on the wait list	1,450
% accepting a place on wait list	63
% admitted from wait list	2

School Profiles ■ 267

Range SAT EBRW	690–760
Range SAT Math	710–790
Range ACT Composite	33–35
# submitting SAT scores	822
% submitting SAT scores	40
# submitting ACT scores	1,248
% submitting ACT scores	60
% graduated top 10% of class	89
% graduated top 25% of class	98
% graduated top 50% of class	100

DEADLINES

Early action	
Deadline	11/1
Notification	12/15
Regular	
Deadline	1/1
Notification	2/15
Nonfall registration?	Yes

CAREER

At Notre Dame, The Career Center's mantra to students is "YOU must take ownership of your future." But, of course, career counselors and staff are there to support and assist students every step of the way. To that end, experiential career opportunities abound for freshmen and seniors alike: students can complete a Wall Street externship, shadow an alum at work, or be matched to a mentor in the industry of their choice. The Career Center funding program will even support students who need financial assistance to participate in a full-time summer internship. The university hosts several career and internship fairs each semester, along with networking programs like a Civil Engineering Luncheon or Consulting Night. Finally, Students visit Go IRISH, the center's primary recruiting database, for information about interviewing opportunities, employer information sessions, or opportunities that specifically seek a ND student or alum.

GENERAL INFO

Activities: Campus Ministries; Choral groups; Concert band; Dance; Drama/theater; International Student Organization; Jazz band; Literary magazine; Marching band; Model UN; Music ensembles; Musical theater; Opera; Pep band; Radio station; Student government; Student newspaper; Student-run film society; Symphony orchestra; Television station; Yearbook. 440 registered organizations, 10 honor societies, 9 religious organizations, 0 fraternities, 0 sororities, on campus. **Athletics (Intercollegiate):** *Men:* baseball, basketball, cross-country, diving, fencing, football, golf, ice hockey, lacrosse, soccer, swimming, tennis, track/field (outdoor). *Women:* basketball, crew/rowing, cross-country, diving, fencing, golf, lacrosse, soccer, softball, swimming, tennis, track/field (outdoor), volleyball. **On-Campus Highlights:** Grotto, The Golden Dome (Main Building), Basilica of the Sacred Heart, Notre Dame Stadium, Eck Center. **Environmental Initiatives:** Expansion of Office of Sustainability to include 3 full time staff and 7 interns; development of metrics and quantitative goals in 7 key sustainability areas.

University of Notre Dame

FINANCIAL AID

Students should submit: CSS/Financial Aid PROFILE; FAFSA; Noncustodial PROFILE. Priority filing deadline is 11/15. The Princeton Review suggests that all financial aid forms be submitted as soon as possible after October 1. *Need-based scholarships/grants offered*: College/university scholarship or grant aid from institutional funds; Federal Pell; Private scholarships; SEOG; State scholarships/grants. *Loan aid offered*: Direct PLUS loans; Direct Subsidized Stafford Loans; Direct Unsubsidized Stafford Loans. Applicants will be notified of awards on a rolling basis beginning 2/15. Federal Work-Study Program available. Institutional employment available.

BOTTOM LINE

Notre Dame, while certainly providing a wonderful academic environment and superb education, does reflect this in the cost of attending the college. Annual tuition is $55,046. With room, board, and required fees, students are looking at over $70,000 a year. Fortunately, over 75 percent of undergrads receive some form of financial aid.

FINANCIAL FACTS	
Financial Aid Rating	90
Annual tuition	$55,046
Room and board	$15,640
Required fees	$507
Books and supplies	$1,050
Average frosh need-based scholarship	$40,098
Average UG need-based scholarship	$40,175
% needy frosh rec. need-based scholarship or grant aid	96
% needy UG rec. need-based scholarship or grant aid	97
% needy frosh rec. non-need-based scholarship or grant aid	30
% needy UG rec. non-need-based scholarship or grant aid	28
% needy frosh rec. need-based self-help aid	86
% needy UG rec. need-based self-help aid	87
% frosh rec. any financial aid	63
% UG rec. any financial aid	75
% UG borrow to pay for school	42
Average cumulative indebtedness	$27,686
% frosh need fully met	100
% ugrads need fully met	100
Average % of frosh need met	100
Average % of ugrad need met	100

CAREER INFORMATION FROM PAYSCALE.COM	
ROI Rating	91
Bachelors and No Higher	
Median starting salary	$67,000
Median mid-career salary	$130,500
At Least Bachelors	
Median starting salary	$68,800
Median mid-career salary	$139,700
Alumni with high job meaning	49%
Degrees awarded in STEM subjects	28%

University of Notre Dame

University of Pennsylvania

1 College Hall, Philadelphia, PA 19104 • Admissions: 215-898-7507 • Fax: 215-898-9670

CAMPUS LIFE

Quality of Life Rating	88
Fire Safety Rating	84
Green Rating	95
Type of school	Private
Environment	Metropolis

STUDENTS

Total undergrad enrollment	10,183
% male/female	48/52
% from out of state	81
% frosh from public high school	60
% frosh live on campus	100
% ugrads live on campus	51
# of fraternities	
(% ugrad men join)	36 (30)
# of sororities	
(% ugrad women join)	13 (28)
% African American	7
% Asian	21
% Caucasian	41
% Hispanic	10
% Native American	<1
% Pacific Islander	<1
% Two or more races	5
% Race and/or ethnicity unknown	2
% international	13
# of countries represented	126

ABOUT THE SCHOOL

The University of Pennsylvania (commonly referred to as Penn), as one of the eight members of the Ivy League, gives you all of the advantages of an internationally recognized degree with none of the attitude. Founded by Benjamin Franklin, Penn is the fourth-oldest institution of higher learning in the United States. The university is composed of four undergraduate schools, including The Wharton School, home to Penn's well-known and intense undergraduate business program. This, along with other career-focused offerings, contributes to a preprofessional atmosphere on campus. That comes with an element of competition, especially when grades are on the line. Penn students love the opportunity to take classes with professors who are setting the bar for research in his or her field. Professors are praised for being "enthusiastic and incredibly well-versed in their subject," a group who is "passionate about teaching" and who will "go out of their way to help you understand the material." Penn students don't mind getting into intellectual conversations during dinner, but "partying is a much higher priority here than it is at other Ivy League schools." Students here can have intellectual conversations during dinner, and hit the frat houses later that night. Trips to New York City and Center City Philadelphia are common, and students have plenty of access to restaurants, shopping, concerts, and sports games around campus.

BANG FOR YOUR BUCK

Transparency is embedded in Penn's financial aid process. For 2017–2018, Penn committed more than $224 million of its resources for grant aid to undergraduate students. Over 82 percent of freshman who applied for aid

University of Pennsylvania

Financial Aid: 215-898-1988 • E-mail: info@admissions.upenn.edu • Website: www.upenn.edu

received an award, and Penn's financial aid packages meet 100 percent of students' demonstrated need through an all grant, all grant aid program. According to the school, the average financial aid package for incoming awarded first years in 2015 was $51,470. University Named Scholarships are provided through direct gifts to the university and privately endowed funds and enable Penn to continue to admit students solely on the basis of academic merit. The scholarship amount varies according to determined financial need. Staff at Penn provide strong support for applicants, with one student noting, "It was the only school to call me during the admissions process instead of just e-mailing me extra information."

STUDENT LIFE

This "determined" bunch "is either focused on one specific interest, or very well-rounded." Pretty much everyone "was an overachiever ('that kid') in high school," and some students "are off-the-charts brilliant," making everyone here "sort of fascinated by everyone else." Everyone has "a strong sense of personal style and his or her own credo," but no group deviates too far from the more mainstream stereotypes. There's a definite lack of "emos" and hippies. There's "the career-driven Wharton kid who will stab you in the back to get your interview slot" and "the nursing kid who's practically nonexistent," but on the whole, there's tremendous school diversity, with "people from all over the world of all kinds of experiences of all perspectives."

CAREER

Penn's Career Services is an amazing resource for students who wish to discover opportunities on- and off-campus. A bursting job board (with over 13,000 individual position postings), trips to New York City and Washington D.C. to learn about organizations and industries, as well as hundreds of

ACADEMICS

Academic Rating	84
% students returning for sophomore year	98
% students graduating within 4 years	85
% students graduating within 6 years	96
Calendar	Semester
Student/faculty ratio	6:1
Profs interesting rating	67
Profs accessible rating	68
Most classes have 10–19 students.	

MOST POPULAR MAJORS

Economics, General; Registered Nursing/ Registered Nurse; Finance, General

SELECTIVITY

Admissions Rating	99
# of applicants	44,491
% of applicants accepted	8
% of acceptees attending	67
# offered a place on the wait list	3,535
% accepting a place on wait list	72
% admitted from wait list	<1
# of early decision applicants	7,073
% accepted early decision	19

employer information sessions give students tons of chances to network and research fields. One neat perk: along with other offices like Civic House, Kelly Writers House, and Penn Global, Career Services provides funding to finance research and unpaid (or lowly paid) summer internships. Career days each year bring over 600 employers to campus (Amazon, IBM, and Bloomberg, to name a few), and PennApps, a weekend-long "hackathon" for student developers, draws prospective employers like Intel and Microsoft for sponsorship and presentations. Alumni mentoring is also available to help students find their path. Penn grads who visited PayScale.com report median starting salaries of $72,800.

GENERAL INFO

Activities: Campus Ministries; Choral groups; Concert band; Dance; Drama/theater; International Student Organization; Jazz band; Literary magazine; Marching band; Model UN; Music ensembles; Musical theater; Opera; Pep band; Radio station; Student government; Student newspaper; Student-run film society; Symphony orchestra; Television station; Yearbook. 350 registered organizations, 9 honor societies, 18 religious organizations, 36 fraternities, 13 sororities, on campus. **Athletics (Intercollegiate):** *Men:* baseball, basketball, crew/rowing, cross-country, diving, fencing, football, golf, lacrosse, light weight football, soccer, squash, swimming, tennis, track/field (outdoor), track/field (indoor), wrestling. *Women:* basketball, crew/rowing, cross-country, diving, fencing, field hockey, golf, gymnastics, lacrosse, soccer, softball, squash, swimming, tennis, track/field (outdoor), track/field (indoor), volleyball. **On-Campus Highlights:** University of Pennsylvania Museum, Institute of Contemporary Art, Walnut Street shops and restuarants, Annenberg Center, Franklin Field. **Environmental Initiatives:** Building optimization implementation, a program to optimize building systems in high-energy-use buildings to reduce their utility use and carbon footprint. This effort is enhanced by Penn's comprehensive building metering program.

University of Pennsylvania

FINANCIAL AID

Students should submit: Business/Farm Supplement; CSS/Financial Aid PROFILE; FAFSA; Institution's own financial aid form; Noncustodial PROFILE. Priority filing deadline is 2/15. The Princeton Review suggests that all financial aid forms be submitted as soon as possible after October 1. *Need-based scholarships/grants offered*: College/university scholarship or grant aid from institutional funds; Federal Pell; Private scholarships; SEOG; State scholarships/grants. *Loan aid offered*: Direct PLUS loans; Direct Subsidized Stafford Loans; Direct Unsubsidized Stafford Loans. Applicants will be notified of awards on or about 4/1. Federal Work-Study Program available. Institutional employment available.

BOTTOM LINE

A year's tuition is $51,156. You'll pay another $16,190 in room and board. Don't be alarmed: Penn offers loan-free packages to all dependent students who are eligible for financial aid, regardless of the family's income level. The average student debt, for the students who choose to borrow, is approximately $22,103. Students have noted the school's "generous aid program" as being "phenomenal."

FINANCIAL FACTS	
Financial Aid Rating	91
Annual tuition	$51,156
Room and board	$16,190
Required fees	$6,614
Average frosh need-based scholarship	$48,798
Average UG need-based scholarship	$48,787
% needy frosh rec. need-based scholarship or grant aid	99
% needy UG rec. need-based scholarship or grant aid	99
% needy frosh rec. non-need-based scholarship or grant aid	0
% needy UG rec. non-need-based scholarship or grant aid	0
% needy frosh rec. need-based self-help aid	100
% needy UG rec. need-based self-help aid	100
% frosh rec. any financial aid	45
% UG rec. any financial aid	46
% UG borrow to pay for school	24
Average cumulative indebtedness	$22,103
% frosh need fully met	100
% ugrads need fully met	100
Average % of frosh need met	100
Average % of ugrad need met	100

CAREER INFORMATION FROM PAYSCALE.COM	
ROI Rating	93
Bachelors and No Higher	
Median starting salary	$72,800
Median mid-career salary	$133,900
At Least Bachelors	
Median starting salary	$75,000
Median mid-career salary	$149,500
Alumni with high job meaning	47%
Degrees awarded in STEM subjects	21%

University of Pennsylvania

University of Richmond

410 Westhampton Way, University of Richmond, VA 23173 • Admissions: 804-289-8640

CAMPUS LIFE

Quality of Life Rating	97
Fire Safety Rating	94
Green Rating	95
Type of school	Private
Environment	City

STUDENTS

Total undergrad enrollment	3,147
% male/female	48/52
% from out of state	77
% frosh from public high school	58
% frosh live on campus	99
% ugrads live on campus	91
# of fraternities	
(% ugrad men join)	8 (22)
# of sororities	
(% ugrad women join)	8 (30)
% African American	8
% Asian	7
% Caucasian	58
% Hispanic	8
% Native American	<1
% Pacific Islander	<1
% Two or more races	4
% Race and/or ethnicity unknown	5
% international	9
# of countries represented	63

#62 BEST VALUE COLLEGE

ABOUT THE SCHOOL

At the University of Richmond, situated right in the West End of Virginia's capital, academic opportunities abound. No matter if they want to study abroad or conduct research, these 3,147 students have access to "unparalleled resources" and can easily broaden their horizons. Under The Richmond Guarantee, for example, every undergraduate student is eligible to receive a fellowship of $4,000 for a summer internship or a faculty-mentored research project. Of course, University of Richmond is quite strong in the sciences, as evidenced by their "good…admission rate to med school." And the university is also home to the "highly respected" Robins School of Business. Even better, all students benefit from "small" courses which allows for an "AMAZING" classroom experience. All courses are taught by members of the faculty (no teaching assistants), and most instructors endeavor to "make their classes difficult because they know we can rise to the challenge." They also make it quite evident that "they all really want their students to understand the material and succeed." Best of all, they are always "willing to meet outside of class to help."

BANG FOR YOUR BUCK

Undergrads proudly proclaim that "the financial aid programs [at Richmond] are amazing." Indeed, the university "gives great…aid to those who need it." The University of Richmond has a need-blind admission process and a guarantee to meet 100 percent of demonstrated need. For Virginia residents, whose parents earn $60,000 or less a year, University of Richmond will cover full tuition, room, and meal plan—with no loans. And all students, no matter their financial circumstances, are automatically considered for merit-based

University of Richmond

Fax: 804-287-6003 • E-mail: admission@richmond.edu • Website: www.richmond.edu

aid. This includes the Presidential Scholarship which covers one third of the cost of tuition, the Richmond Scholars Program which covers full tuition, room and board, and the Davis United World College Scholars which provides up to $10,000.

STUDENT LIFE

It's easy to have a good time at the University of Richmond. After all, "there are endless clubs and activities that you can get involved in." Indeed, students can participate in everything from "service organizations [and] religious groups [to] a cappella and dance troupes [to] academic [and] social fraternities." Additionally, "club sports teams and IM Sports (intramural) are pretty popular." Many undergrads assert that "Greek Life definitely dominates the social scene." We're told that a "high percentage of students are [involved]" and that "[frat] parties are the main attractions on weekend nights." Fortunately, these tend to be "open to all members of the student body" no matter your affiliation. And if fraternities and sororities aren't your scene, "there are always events being put on by the Center for Student Involvement and various student groups."

CAREER

Students at the University of Richmond triumphantly declare that the school's Career Services office is "incredibly helpful and thorough." It's "constantly reaching out to students" and manages to "foster great relationships" with several companies. Undergrads flock there to explore various majors and careers (the Career Advisors are even certified in analyzing the Myers-Brigg Type Indicator assessment) and to take advantage of fantastic programs like Spider Shadowing, which provides individuals with the opportunity to spend time with an alum or employer to learn more about a particular career. As if that wasn't enough, students can turn to the office for résumé reviews and interview prep. Industry-specific

ACADEMICS

Academic Rating	95
% students returning for sophomore year	94
% students graduating within 4 years	85
% students graduating within 6 years	87
Calendar	Semester
Student/faculty ratio	8:1
Profs interesting rating	95
Profs accessible rating	97

Most classes have 10–19 students. Most lab/discussion sessions have 10–19 students.

MOST POPULAR MAJORS

Biology/Biological Sciences, General; Business Administration and Management, General; Organizational Behavior Studies

SELECTIVITY

Admissions Rating	93
# of applicants	11,882
% of applicants accepted	30
% of acceptees attending	23
# offered a place on the wait list	3,653
% accepting a place on wait list	34
% admitted from wait list	2
# of early decision applicants	662
% accepted early decision	48

FRESHMAN PROFILE

Range SAT EBRW	640–710
Range SAT Math	650–750
Range ACT Composite	30–33
# submitting SAT scores	442
% submitting SAT scores	53
# submitting ACT scores	390
% submitting ACT scores	47
% graduated top 10% of class	56
% graduated top 25% of class	86
% graduated top 50% of class	96

DEADLINES

Early decision	
Deadline	11/1
Notification	12/15
Other ED Deadline	1/1
Other ED Notification	2/15
Early action	
Deadline	11/1
Notification	1/20
Regular	
Deadline	1/1
Notification	4/1
Nonfall registration?	No

preparedness programs like Q-camp, A&S NEXT, and the Jepson EDGE Institute ensure undergrads are able to translate their skills when it's time to job hunt.

GENERAL INFO

Activities: Campus Ministries; Choral groups; Concert band; Dance; Drama/theater; International Student Organization; Jazz band; Literary magazine; Model UN; Music ensembles; Musical theater; Pep band; Radio station; Student government; Student newspaper; Student-run film society; Symphony orchestra. 176 registered organizations, 7 honor societies, 14 religious organizations, 8 fraternities, 8 sororities, on campus. **Athletics (Intercollegiate):** *Men:* baseball, basketball, cross-country, football, golf, soccer, tennis, track/field (outdoor), track/field (indoor). *Women:* basketball, cross-country, diving, field hockey, golf, lacrosse, soccer, swimming, tennis, track/field (outdoor), track/field (indoor). **On-Campus Highlights:** Boatwright Memorial Library and 8:15 Coffee Shop, Weinstein Fitness Center, Tyler Haynes Commons, Carole Weinstein International Center, Heilman Dining Center ("D-Hall"). **Environmental Initiatives:** The University of Richmond has committed to being carbon neutral by 2050 with interim goals of 30% below 2008 levels by 2020 and 65% below 2008 levels by 2035. As of our last GHG accounting in 2017, we have reduced our greenhouse gas emissions 24% below 2008 levels. We accomplished this by installing a 205 kW rooftop solar array, transitioning from coal to natural gas for heating, completing dozens of energy efficiency upgrades, and setting a LEED Silver minimum requirement on all new construction.

University of Richmond

FINANCIAL AID

Students should submit: CSS/Financial Aid PROFILE; FAFSA; Noncustodial PROFILE. Priority filing deadline is 2/1. The Princeton Review suggests that all financial aid forms be submitted as soon as possible after October 1. *Need-based scholarships/grants offered*: College/university scholarship or grant aid from institutional funds; Federal Pell; Private scholarships; SEOG; State scholarships/grants. *Loan aid offered*: Direct PLUS loans; Direct Subsidized Stafford Loans; Direct Unsubsidized Stafford Loans. Applicants will be notified of awards on or about 4/1. Federal Work-Study Program available. Institutional employment available.

BOTTOM LINE

The University of Richmond charges $54,690 for tuition. Beyond that, students and their families pay $12,900 for room and board. UR estimates that books and supplies will cost undergrads an additional $1,100. And it's recommended that individuals set aside $1,000 to cover personal expenses. There are also $60 worth of direct loan fees. These figures add up to $69,750.

FINANCIAL FACTS	
Financial Aid Rating	**96**
Annual tuition	$54,690
Room and board	$12,900
Books and supplies	$1,100
Average frosh need-based scholarship	$45,282
Average UG need-based scholarship	$43,705
% needy frosh rec. need-based scholarship or grant aid	96
% needy UG rec. need-based scholarship or grant aid	97
% needy frosh rec. non-need-based scholarship or grant aid	19
% needy UG rec. non-need-based scholarship or grant aid	19
% needy frosh rec. need-based self-help aid	78
% needy UG rec. need-based self-help aid	79
% frosh rec. any financial aid	62
% UG rec. any financial aid	70
% UG borrow to pay for school	43
Average cumulative indebtedness	$27,406
% frosh need fully met	83
% ugrads need fully met	82
Average % of frosh need met	100
Average % of ugrad need met	100

CAREER INFORMATION FROM PAYSCALE.COM	
ROI Rating	91
Bachelors and No Higher	
Median starting salary	$59,800
Median mid-career salary	$107,500
At Least Bachelors	
Median starting salary	$60,700
Median mid-career salary	$117,500
Alumni with high job meaning	48%
Degrees awarded in STEM subjects	13%

University of Richmond

The University of Texas at Austin

PO Box 8058, Austin, TX 78713-8058 • Admissions: 512-475-7399 • Fax: 512-475-7478

#72 BEST VALUE COLLEGE

CAMPUS LIFE

Quality of Life Rating	89
Fire Safety Rating	84
Green Rating	90
Type of school	Public
Environment	Metropolis

STUDENTS

Total undergrad enrollment	40,329
% male/female	46/54
% from out of state	6
% frosh live on campus	63
% ugrads live on campus	18
# of fraternities	
(% ugrad men join)	46 (14)
# of sororities	
(% ugrad women join)	29 (20)
% African American	4
% Asian	22
% Caucasian	40
% Hispanic	23
% Native American	<1
% Pacific Islander	<1
% Two or more races	4
% Race and/or ethnicity unknown	1
% international	6
# of countries represented	96

ABOUT THE SCHOOL

Some students at the University of Texas at Austin (UT Austin) boldly make the claim that their school is considered the "Harvard of the South," and they would probably be able to make a strong case for it. Considered one of the best public schools in Texas, the massive UT Austin campus offers a world-class education through its wide array of programs in the sciences and humanities as well as state-of-the-art laboratories. Despite the large size of some of the classes, the students find their professors to be supportive. According to one student, "They are always willing to meet you outside of class, and they try their best to encourage students to speak up during class." Students flock to this research university not only for its robust academics but also for its famed athletic offerings. One student raves, "I think the greatest strengths are the level of education we receive and the athletics program. The classes here are very difficult and will prepare students very well for graduate schools or careers. The athletics program here is awesome." The football team (Go Longhorns!) certainly helps inspire the school's contagious school spirit. The school's 431-acre campus serves as home to a student body of over 51,000 (including graduate students) and offers boundless opportunities for students to get a rich and diverse social education. With over 1,100 student organizations, the campus is bustling with activities such as sports games, festivals, movie screenings, concerts, and cultural events. For those who need the rush of city life, the campus is just a few blocks away from downtown Austin, where students often frequent the numerous restaurants, bars, clubs, and live music venues, especially those on 6th Street, a major hot spot. Competitive academic programs, legendary athletics, a huge sprawling campus, the eclectic allure of Austin, a strong sense of Texas

The University of Texas at Austin

Financial Aid: 512-475-6203 • Website: www.utexas.edu

pride, and an unabashed love of a good party are the hallmarks of an education at the University of Texas at Austin.

BANG FOR YOUR BUCK

UT Austin works hard to make college affordable for the families of students who wish to attend. One effort, Texas Advance, provides scholarships to students with a family adjusted gross income up to $100,000. Many of these top-performing students will also be invited to participate in one of the university's selective academic-enrichment communities. 360 Connections set the tone once new students arrive on campus—these small groups help first-years make the most of all the opportunities for mentorship, research, internships and experiential learning that UT Austin has to offer. Meanwhile, the Office of Financial Aid offers money management information and programming needed to help all students and their families reduce the burden of unnecessary debt.

STUDENT LIFE

"Because of the huge Greek life at UT, a 'typical student' would be a sorority girl or fraternity boy," but—and it's a big but—such students "are hardly the majority, since UT is actually made of more 'atypical' people than most other schools. Everyone here has his own niche, and I could not think of any type of individual who would not be able to find one of his own." Indeed, "everyone at Texas is different! When you walk across campus, you see every type of ethnicity. There are a lot of minorities at Texas. Also, I see many disabled people, whom the school accommodates well. Everyone seems to get along. The different types of students just blend in together." Especially by Texas standards, "Austin is known for being 'weird.' If you see someone dressed in a way you've never seen before, you just shrug it off and say 'That's Austin!'"

ACADEMICS

Academic Rating	77
% students returning for sophomore year	95
% students graduating within 4 years	61
% students graduating within 6 years	83
Calendar	Semester
Student/faculty ratio	19:1
Profs interesting rating	71
Profs accessible rating	62

Most classes have 10–19 students. Most lab/discussion sessions have 10–19 students.

MOST POPULAR MAJORS

Computer and Information Sciences, General; Biology/Biological Sciences, General; Economics, General

SELECTIVITY

Admissions Rating	94
# of applicants	50,575
% of applicants accepted	38
% of acceptees attending	46
# offered a place on the wait list	0

CAREER

There is a huge career services presence at UT Austin, where each college has its own dedicated office. This way while all students have access to HireUTexas, the university's campus-wide job board, they also have resources tailored to their particular schools and interests. For instance, students in the College of Liberal Arts may take courses (for credit!) that complement and make the most of their internship experiences. And ScienceWorks is the online hub for College of Natural Sciences students looking for jobs, internships, mentors and professional development events. Job and Internship Fairs are usually organized by school as well with multiple chances to network and meet potential employers each year. UT Austin graduates who visited PayScale.com report a median starting salary of $60,700, and 50 percent derive a high level of meaning from their work.

GENERAL INFO

Activities: Campus Ministries; Choral groups; Concert band; Dance; Drama/theater; International Student Organization; Jazz band; Literary magazine; Marching band; Model UN; Music ensembles; Musical theater; Radio station; Student government; Student newspaper; Student-run film society; Symphony orchestra; Television station; Yearbook. 1,022 registered organizations, 5 honor societies, 89 religious organizations, 46 fraternities, 29 sororities, on campus. **Athletics (Intercollegiate):** *Men:* baseball, basketball, cross-country, diving, football, golf, swimming, tennis, track/field (outdoor). *Women:* basketball, crew/rowing, cross-country, diving, golf, soccer, softball, swimming, tennis, track/field (outdoor), volleyball. **On-Campus Highlights:** The Tower, Darrell K Royal-Texas Memorial Stadium, LBJ Presidential Library, Blanton Museum of Art, Student Activities Center. **Environmental Initiatives:** Incorporation of sustainability principles throughout the institution's approved Campus Master Plan (May 2013).

The University of Texas at Austin

FINANCIAL AID

Students should submit: FAFSA; Institution's own financial aid form. Priority filing deadline is 1/15. The Princeton Review suggests that all financial aid forms be submitted as soon as possible after October 1. *Need-based scholarships/grants offered*: College/university scholarship or grant aid from institutional funds; Federal Pell; Private scholarships; SEOG; State scholarships/grants. *Loan aid offered*: Direct PLUS loans; Direct Subsidized Stafford Loans; Direct Unsubsidized Stafford Loans. Applicants will be notified of awards on a rolling basis beginning 1/15. Federal Work-Study Program available. Institutional employment available.

BOTTOM LINE

For students who are Texas residents, the cost of tuition is $10,818, which makes the school very affordable for many. For any out-of-state students, the price tag jumps to $38,228 plus another $11,812 for room and board. Whether you're an in-state or out-of-state student, do not forget to factor in the additional cost of books and supplies, which add up to $700.

FINANCIAL FACTS	
Financial Aid Rating	77
Annual in-state tuition	$10,818
Annual out-of-state tuition	$38,228
Room and board	$11,812
Books and supplies	$700
Average frosh need-based scholarship	$10,222
Average UG need-based scholarship	$9,535
% needy frosh rec. need-based scholarship or grant aid	72
% needy UG rec. need-based scholarship or grant aid	77
% needy frosh rec. non-need-based scholarship or grant aid	53
% needy UG rec. non-need-based scholarship or grant aid	27
% needy frosh rec. need-based self-help aid	61
% needy UG rec. need-based self-help aid	65
% frosh rec. any financial aid	41
% UG rec. any financial aid	40
% UG borrow to pay for school	40
Average cumulative indebtedness	$24,244
% frosh need fully met	25
% ugrads need fully met	22
Average % of frosh need met	72
Average % of ugrad need met	70

CAREER INFORMATION FROM PAYSCALE.COM	
ROI Rating	91
Bachelors and No Higher	
Median starting salary	$60,700
Median mid-career salary	$112,800
At Least Bachelors	
Median starting salary	$62,100
Median mid-career salary	$118,000
Alumni with high job meaning	50%
Degrees awarded in STEM subjects	28%

The University of Texas at Austin

University of Virginia

Office of Admission, Charlottesville, VA 22906 • Admissions: 434-982-3200 • Fax: 434-924-3587

CAMPUS LIFE

Quality of Life Rating	87
Fire Safety Rating	90
Green Rating	96
Type of school	Public
Environment	City

STUDENTS

Total undergrad enrollment	16,290
% male/female	45/55
% from out of state	28
% frosh from public high school	72
% frosh live on campus	100
% ugrads live on campus	38
# of fraternities	
(% ugrad men join)	31 (31)
# of sororities	
(% ugrad women join)	16 (31)
% African American	7
% Asian	15
% Caucasian	57
% Hispanic	6
% Native American	<1
% Pacific Islander	<1
% Two or more races	5
% Race and/or ethnicity unknown	6
% international	4
# of countries represented	122

#12 BEST VALUE COLLEGE

ABOUT THE SCHOOL

The University of Virginia's offerings live up to Thomas Jefferson's presidential legacy. UVA seamlessly blends the academic advantages of the Ivy League with the social life and the price tag of a large state school. The wealth of academic and extracurricular activities available here is paralleled at just a handful of schools around the country, and the school "values academia while fostering an enjoyable atmosphere for students." While class sizes can be large, and getting into the courses you want can be difficult, students rave about their engaging and inspiring professors, "who care and keep students from being 'numbers.'" Graduation rates are among the highest in the country, and the university has one of the highest graduation rates for African-American students. UVA also takes its history and traditions very seriously. The student-administered honor code is a case in point; sanctions can be harsh, but only for those who disrespect it. "Students claim full responsibility for their grades and actions, while being engaged and challenged in all aspects of life," says a student.

BANG FOR YOUR BUCK

UVA has one of the largest per-capita endowments of any public school in the country and exerts a tremendous effort to ensure that its undergraduates have access to an affordable education regardless of economic circumstances. Around half of undergraduates receive some form of financial aid, and the university aims to meet 100 percent of every student's demonstrated need. There are loan-free financial aid packages for low-income students

University of Virginia

Financial Aid: 434-982-6000 • E-mail: undergradadmission@virginia.edu • Website: www.virginia.edu

and new Blue Ridge Scholarships for high achieving students with high financial need. There are caps on need-based loans for middle-income families. By limiting debt—or eliminating it altogether, in the case of students with the most need—UVA ensures that you can afford to attend the university as long as you can get admitted and maintain decent grades. Scholarships abound for Virginia residents, including the Virginia Commonwealth Award, which gives recipients up to $3,000 per academic year. There are plenty of other scholarships, too, available based upon need, academic achievement, and specific donor criteria. UVA's signature program, Jefferson Scholars, covers the tuition, fees, room and board of extraordinary students.

STUDENT LIFE

Students here "often get typecast as homogeneous and preppy." Overall "life at UVA is pretty chill, but when exams roll around life can be very hectic." Due to the top-notch academics, one student says, "during the week I typically spend most of my time studying." It's not all work and no play, however, as "people are committed to academics but play hard on the weekends. Parties off-grounds, going to bars, hanging out with friends, seeing shows and performances, going to dinner, etc." are all popular. "While the UVA party scene is definitely predominant, both the University and the city of Charlottesville provide plenty of alternative opportunities for entertainment." "It seems that almost every day of the week there is something university-sponsored to attend," says a student, and physical activity is big too: "[Students] like playing sports, going running, going hiking in the areas around Charlottesville, playing Frisbee on the lawn, etc. Everyone always seems to be outdoors during nice weather." The wealth of things to keep busy pays off for students. "Life at school is usually buzzing," says a student, and another raves that "I can't imagine being happier anywhere else."

ACADEMICS

Academic Rating	89
% students returning for sophomore year	97
% students graduating within 4 years	89
% students graduating within 6 years	94
Calendar	Semester
Student/faculty ratio	15:1
Profs interesting rating	81
Profs accessible rating	83

Most classes have 10–19 students. Most lab/discussion sessions have 20–29 students.

MOST POPULAR MAJORS

Biology/Biological Sciences, General; Economics, General; Business/Commerce, General

SELECTIVITY

Admissions Rating	97
# of applicants	37,182
% of applicants accepted	26
% of acceptees attending	39
# offered a place on the wait list	5,972
% accepting a place on wait list	60
% admitted from wait list	0

FRESHMAN PROFILE

Range SAT EBRW	660–730
Range SAT Math	670–770
Range ACT Composite	30–34
# submitting SAT scores	2,980
% submitting SAT scores	78
# submitting ACT scores	1,568
% submitting ACT scores	41
Average HS GPA	4.3
% graduated top 10% of class	90
% graduated top 25% of class	98
% graduated top 50% of class	100

DEADLINES

Early action	
Deadline	11/1
Notification	1/31
Regular	
Deadline	1/1
Notification	4/5
Nonfall registration?	No

CAREER

University Career Services offers all of the standard resources for undergrads, including advising and one-on-one career planning; job fairs and on-campus recruitment; internship and job search services; and professional development services like résumé building and interview coaching. It also offers specialized career events in a variety of fields, such as commerce, engineering, nursing, education, and government and non-profits. The new Internship Center is a hub for all things internship related, like the University Internship Program that provides field placement based on what students are learning in the classroom. One student raves that "UVA really excels in career training and placement." Career Exploration Workshops and other self-assessments ensure that undergrads are attuned to their personal styles and interests. "The students [at UVA] are very ambitious and career-focused," and out of alumni visiting PayScale.com, 48 percent report that they derive a high level of meaning from their jobs.

GENERAL INFO

Activities: Campus Ministries; Choral groups; Concert band; Dance; Drama/theater; International Student Organization; Jazz band; Literary magazine; Marching band; Model UN; Music ensembles; Musical theater; Opera; Pep band; Radio station; Student government; Student newspaper; Student-run film society; Symphony orchestra; Television station; Yearbook. 7 honor societies, 31 fraternity, 16 sororities, on campus. **Athletics (Intercollegiate):** *Men:* baseball, basketball, cross-country, diving, football, golf, lacrosse, soccer, swimming, tennis, track/field (outdoor), track/field (indoor), wrestling. *Women:* basketball, crew/rowing, cross-country, diving, field hockey, golf, lacrosse, soccer, softball, swimming, tennis, track/field (outdoor), track/field (indoor), volleyball. **On-Campus Highlights:** Rotunda/Academical Village (orig campus), Alderman and Clemons Libraries, John Paul Jones Arena, Football, Baseball, and Soccer Stadiums, Aquatic and Fitness Center. **Environmental Initiatives:** Academics: The University of Virginia offers 70+ courses in 8 different schools with significant focus on sustainability, including a global sustainability course, a new course model cross listed and taught jointly by faculty from Engineering, Architecture, and Commerce. In Spring 2011, the University created the interdisciplinary Global Sustainability minor.

University of Virginia

FINANCIAL AID

Students should submit: CSS/Financial Aid PROFILE; FAFSA. Priority filing deadline is 3/1. The Princeton Review suggests that all financial aid forms be submitted as soon as possible after October 1. *Need-based scholarships/grants offered*: College/university scholarship or grant aid from institutional funds; Federal Nursing Scholarships; Federal Pell; Private scholarships; SEOG; State scholarships/grants. *Loan aid offered*: Direct PLUS loans; Direct Subsidized Stafford Loans; Direct Unsubsidized Stafford Loans. Applicants will be notified of awards on or about 4/5. Federal Work-Study Program available. Institutional employment available.

BOTTOM LINE

There is a large disparity here between tuition and fees for in-state versus out-of-state students. That's not unusual, just something to note. It's also important to keep in mind that 100 percent of applicants with financial need have their needs met. The sticker price for tuition, fees, room and board, and personal expenses for Virginia residents is somewhere in the neighborhood of $30,294 per year. For residents of other states, it's more than twice as much at $61,785. The average undergraduate need-based scholarship totals $23,439.

FINANCIAL FACTS	
Financial Aid Rating	94
Annual in-state tuition	$14,509
Annual out-of-state tuition	$46,000
Room and board	$11,590
Required fees	$2,845
Books and supplies	$1,350
Average frosh need-based scholarship	$24,068
Average UG need-based scholarship	$23,439
% needy frosh rec. need-based scholarship or grant aid	88
% needy UG rec. need-based scholarship or grant aid	87
% needy frosh rec. non-need-based scholarship or grant aid	10
% needy UG rec. non-need-based scholarship or grant aid	7
% needy frosh rec. need-based self-help aid	59
% needy UG rec. need-based self-help aid	61
% frosh rec. any financial aid	57
% UG rec. any financial aid	52
% UG borrow to pay for school	34
Average cumulative indebtedness	$24,682
% frosh need fully met	100
% ugrads need fully met	100
Average % of frosh need met	100
Average % of ugrad need met	100

CAREER INFORMATION FROM PAYSCALE.COM	
ROI Rating	95
Bachelors and No Higher	
Median starting salary	$64,500
Median mid-career salary	$117,500
At Least Bachelors	
Median starting salary	$65,900
Median mid-career salary	$129,200
Alumni with high job meaning	49%
Degrees awarded in STEM subjects	23%

University of Virginia

University of Wisconsin—Madison

702 West Johnson Street, Suite 101, Madison, WI 53715-1007 • Admissions: 608-262-3961 • Fax: 608-262-7706

CAMPUS LIFE

Quality of Life Rating	95
Fire Safety Rating	83
Green Rating	60*
Type of school	Public
Environment	City

STUDENTS

Total undergrad enrollment	30,360
% male/female	49/51
% from out of state	35
% frosh live on campus	93
% ugrads live on campus	25
# of fraternities	
(% ugrad men join)	26 (8)
# of sororities	
(% ugrad women join)	11 (8)
% African American	2
% Asian	6
% Caucasian	71
% Hispanic	5
% Native American	<1
% Pacific Islander	<1
% Two or more races	3
% Race and/or ethnicity unknown	2
% international	10
# of countries represented	81

ABOUT THE SCHOOL

The University of Wisconsin-Madison is a distinguished research university that educates more than 30,000 undergraduates through over 9,000 courses and over 200 majors. In addition, the school operates under the principle that it should improve people's lives beyond the classroom: "the research UW-Madison conducts has made an incredible impact on the world." Accordingly, the school does its best to make sure that unique experiences like research are "an option for anyone." Unique experiences are somewhat of a theme for UW-Madison, which offers students a novel structure as well as variety of teaching techniques. First Year Interest Groups (FIGs) let students "take classes that complement each other and stay with the same group of students" for their first semester in college. Many teachers also incorporate "different types of real-world projects that combine class work with practical applications" as well as active learning, in which "students watch short lecture videos before class and work examples in class with the help of the professor and Teaching Assistants." Plus, students rarely have to worry about falling behind: "Tutoring happens around campus for almost every single class."

BANG FOR YOUR BUCK

UW-Madison offers a lot to in-state students, including a guaranteed period of free tuition to incoming freshmen and transfer students whose family's household adjusted gross income is $58,000 or less. A similar guarantee is also extended to first-generation Wisconsin residents who transfer from another UW school or select two-year programs. Additionally, the school maintains a listing of scholarship options on its Wisconsin Scholarship Hub.

University of Wisconsin—Madison

Financial Aid: 608-262-3060 • E-mail: onwisconsin@admissions.wisc.edu • Website: www.wisc.edu

Students do express the desire for the school to be "more affordable for out-of-state students," but others admit that once you're in the Madison fold, there are "lots of opportunities to enhance your education. There's always a speaker in your field to go listen to, there are always programs to join, and there is always research to conduct."

STUDENT LIFE

Madison's campus is "urban, but [the school] isn't in a big city," and the combination of the two offers the whole package: "Big Ten athletics, nightlife, lakefront views (and paths that go around them), and there's always a new restaurant to try." During the week, "people are extremely active in extracurriculars and research." The university has "speakers come in from all over the world to provide insight into breaking discoveries," and plenty of students are in attendance. On weekends, "more social things such as going ... out to dinner with friends" are popular, and the student unions "provide a host of recreational activities, events, [and] shows." But above all else, sports play a huge role here—"athletic games are sacred places for our Badger teams"—and they bring "lots of school spirit," which makes "the energy of the entire campus year-round ... amazing."

ACADEMICS

Academic Rating	85
% students returning for sophomore year	95
% students graduating within 4 years	62
% students graduating within 6 years	87
Calendar	Semester
Student/faculty ratio	17:1
Profs interesting rating	84
Profs accessible rating	82

Most classes have 10–19 students. Most lab/discussion sessions have 20–29 students.

MOST POPULAR MAJORS

Biology/Biological Sciences, General; Economics, General; Political Science and Government, General

SELECTIVITY

Admissions Rating	93
# of applicants	42,741
% of applicants accepted	52
% of acceptees attending	31

CAREER

Career Services are organized through the university's individual schools and colleges. However, the Career Exploration Center is available university-wide to help students focus their paths from the start through academic advising, workshops, and career assessment tools. This drilled-down approach to professional planning is a nice personalization in a large university. One student shares, "My career path was significantly influenced by a number of professors due to their ability to teach, care for students' success both in and

Range SAT EBRW	630–700
Range SAT Math	670–780
Range ACT Composite	27–32
# submitting SAT scores	1,584
% submitting SAT scores	23
# submitting ACT scores	5,736
% submitting ACT scores	84
Average HS GPA	3.9
% graduated top 10% of class	54
% graduated top 25% of class	90
% graduated top 50% of class	99

DEADLINES

Early action	
Deadline	11/1
Notification	12/31
Regular	
Deadline	2/1
Nonfall registration?	Yes

out of the classroom, and excitement for research." That last point is almost universally agreed upon as the biggest future-planning benefit to the school: With "an abundance of research opportunities in all fields," even first-years "can easily work in a lab, and if you're there long enough, there is potential for publication." Overall, the school offers an array of "great programs that make you an excellent candidate to potential employers."

GENERAL INFO

Activities: Choral groups; Concert band; Dance; Drama/theater; International Student Organization; Jazz band; Literary magazine; Marching band; Music ensembles; Musical theater; Opera; Pep band; Radio station; Student government; Student newspaper; Student-run film society; Symphony orchestra; Television station; Yearbook. 953 registered organizations, 27 honor societies, 26 fraternities, 11 sorority, on campus. **Athletics (Intercollegiate):** *Men:* basketball, cheerleading, crew/rowing, cross-country, football, golf, ice hockey, soccer, swimming, tennis, track/field (outdoor), wrestling. *Women:* basketball, cheerleading, crew/rowing, cross-country, golf, ice hockey, soccer, softball, swimming, tennis, track/field (outdoor), volleyball. **On-Campus Highlights:** Allen Centennial Gardens, Kohl Center, Memorial Union Terrace, Chazen Museum of Art, Babcock Hall Dairy Plant and Store. **Environmental Initiatives:** Our conservation efforts in the last four years have reduced campus energy consumption by over 1 trillion BTUs and water consumption by 178,000,000 gallons annually.

University of Wisconsin—Madison

FINANCIAL AID

Students should submit: FAFSA. Priority filing deadline is 12/1. The Princeton Review suggests that all financial aid forms be submitted as soon as possible after October 1. *Need-based scholarships/ grants offered*: College/university scholarship or grant aid from institutional funds; Federal Pell; Private scholarships; SEOG; State scholarships/grants. *Loan aid offered*: Direct PLUS loans; Direct Subsidized Stafford Loans; Direct Unsubsidized Stafford Loans. Applicants will be notified of awards on a rolling basis beginning 3/1. Federal Work-Study Program available. Institutional employment available.

BOTTOM LINE

Wisconsin residents pay a steal of $10,725 for tuition and fees while out-of-state residents must cough up $37,785. Minnesota residents get a break at $14,770. Room and board runs another $11,558 and new first-year students must pay an additional fee of $275. Aid is available to all students; the UW-Madison website offers a clean step-by-step process for obtaining financial assistance.

FINANCIAL FACTS	
Financial Aid Rating	97
Annual in-state tuition	$9,273
Annual out-of-state tuition	$36,333
Room and board	$11,558
Required fees	$1,452
Books and supplies	$1,200
Average frosh need-based scholarship	$13,556
Average UG need-based scholarship	$12,751
% needy frosh rec. need-based scholarship or grant aid	75
% needy UG rec. need-based scholarship or grant aid	77
% needy frosh rec. non-need-based scholarship or grant aid	8
% needy UG rec. non-need-based scholarship or grant aid	8
% needy frosh rec. need-based self-help aid	71
% needy UG rec. need-based self-help aid	73
% UG borrow to pay for school	46
Average cumulative indebtedness	$28,229
% frosh need fully met	38
% ugrads need fully met	34
Average % of frosh need met	76
Average % of ugrad need met	75

CAREER INFORMATION FROM PAYSCALE.COM	
ROI Rating	91
Bachelors and No Higher	
Median starting salary	$57,300
Median mid-career salary	$104,400
At Least Bachelors	
Median starting salary	$58,900
Median mid-career salary	$108,000
Alumni with high job meaning	50%
Degrees awarded in STEM subjects	33%

University of Wisconsin—Madison

Vanderbilt University

2305 West End Avenue, Nashville, TN 37203 • Admissions: 615-322-2561 • Fax: 615-343-7765

#13 BEST VALUE COLLEGE

ABOUT THE SCHOOL

Undergraduates are attracted to Nashville's Vanderbilt University, a mid-sized private research university, by its "diverse student body," "strong research" opportunities, and a "collaborative classroom culture." And while the education is "top-notch," Vanderbilt's nearly 6,900 undergrads here appreciate that there's a healthy "balance between academics, extracurriculars and social life." Students apply directly to one of Vandy's four undergraduate schools (College of Arts and Science, School of Engineering, Peabody College of Education and Human Development, or Blair School of Music). Across all four schools are opportunities for research, internships, and involvement in honors programs. Many students, especially individuals who are undeclared, really value the school's "good pre-major advising program." They're also quick to mention that they have access to "great tutoring services" as well. Even better, the clear majority of professors at Vanderbilt are "really invested in their students and go out of their way to see them succeed." Further, they know how to create a classroom environment that's "engaging." And they work hard to ensure that the course-work is both "challenging [and] rewarding." Best of all, professors here are "very accessible" and quite "willing [to offer both] their time and [their] resources."

BANG FOR YOUR BUCK

At first glance, it's easy to experience sticker shock when looking at the cost of a Vanderbilt education. In fact, every year the university distributes more than $41 million in aid to first-year students. Vanderbilt has pledged to meet

Vanderbilt University

Financial Aid: 800-288-0204 • E-mail: admissions@vanderbilt.edu • Website: www.vanderbilt.edu

100 percent of a family's demonstrated need solely with grants so students don't have to worry about paying back loans. Vanderbilt also sponsors several merit-based scholarships. Rather competitive, these scholarships are awarded to incoming students who demonstrate exceptional intellectual prowess. The three signature scholarships—The Ingram Scholars Program, The Cornelius Vanderbilt Scholarship, and The Chancellor's Scholarship—all cover full-tuition and offer a summer stipend for research, study abroad, a creative endeavor, or the required immersion Vanderbilt experience.

STUDENT LIFE

At Vanderbilt, life beyond the classroom is full of opportunity. As one student explains, "There are so many student-run and university-run events going on every single day. It's hard to choose which interesting and fun [ones] to go to!" For starters, there are numerous "cultural events [such as] Diwali, Cafe Con Leche, and the Asian New Year Festival." Many undergrads can also be found heading to the "student recreational center to either work out, play basketball, rock climb, play racquetball, or attend yoga, spinning, and other classes." Certainly, there are "tons of clubs and volunteer opportunities" with which to get involved as well. And, like many schools, students admit that "Thursday nights, Friday nights, and Saturday days are usually parties at frats, bars, or tailgates." Of course, when undergrads want a break from campus, they can "explore the food, music and culture" scene that Nashville has to offer.

CAREER

Vanderbilt's stellar Career Center does its utmost to help students meet their professional goals and dreams. Right from the beginning, undergrads can meet with a Career Coach assigned to work with their specific major. What's more, the Center makes meeting with said coach incredibly easy; you can get together

ACADEMICS

Academic Rating	94
% students returning for sophomore year	97
% students graduating within 4 years	89
% students graduating within 6 years	94
Calendar	Semester
Student/faculty ratio	7:1
Profs interesting rating	96
Profs accessible rating	96

Most classes have 10–19 students.
Most lab/discussion sessions have 10–19 students.

MOST POPULAR MAJORS
Economics; Human & Organizational Development; Medicine, Health, & Society

SELECTIVITY

Admissions Rating	99
# of applicants	34,313
% of applicants accepted	10
% of acceptees attending	49
# of early decision applicants	4,140
% accepted early decision	21

FRESHMAN PROFILE

Range SAT EBRW	700–760
Range SAT Math	750–800
Range ACT Composite	33–35
# submitting SAT scores	688
% submitting SAT scores	43
# submitting ACT scores	1,018
% submitting ACT scores	64
Average HS GPA	3.8
% graduated top 10% of class	89
% graduated top 25% of class	96
% graduated top 50% of class	99

DEADLINES

Early decision	
Deadline	11/1
Notification	Mid-December
Other ED Deadline	1/1
Other ED Notification	Mid-February
Regular	
Priority	1/1
Deadline	1/1
Notification	Late March
Nonfall registration?	No

in person, via Skype, or speak over the phone. Students can also tap into numerous online resources, taking career assessments, searching for internship listings, etc. Additionally, the Career Center sponsors a myriad of events throughout the academic year. For example, the office hosts industry specific "slams." These operate as fun, casual networking events wherein companies pitch themselves to students in rapid-fire rounds and then set up tables so interested individuals can further the conversation. Of course, students can rest assured that there are more traditional career fairs as well.

GENERAL INFO

Activities: Campus Ministries; Choral groups; Concert band; Dance; Drama/theater; International Student Organization; Jazz band; Literary magazine; Marching band; Vanderbilt International Relations Association; Music ensembles; Musical theater; Opera; Pep band; Radio station; Student government; Student newspaper; Student-run film society; Symphony orchestra; Television station; Yearbook. 423 registered organizations, 16 honor societies, 16 religious organizations, 15 fraternities, 14 sororities, on campus. **Athletics (Intercollegiate):** *Men:* baseball, basketball, cross-country, football, golf, tennis. *Women:* basketball, bowling, cross-country, golf, lacrosse, soccer, swimming tennis, track/field (indoor and outdoor). **On-Campus Highlights:** The Commons, The Wond'ry, Student Recreation Center, Student Life Center, Sarratt Student Center. **Environmental Initiatives:** Greenhouse gas emissions reduction-Overall greenhouse gas emissions from Vanderbilt's campus and medical center decreased by 12 percent from an all-time high reached in 2008—and by 7 percent from 2005 to 2011—even though Vanderbilt has seen significant growth in square footage, staff, students and research dollars over the last four years. GHG emissions per square foot have gone down 21 percent over the past seven years, which reflects a lot of hard work to improve the energy efficiency of existing buildings, some that are very old, as well as new construction and renovation projects that have incorporated excellent energy efficiency. GHG emissions per person, per student, per research dollar, per inpatient day and per ambulatory visit also have trended significantly in a positive direction since 2005. Most university greenhouse gas inventory reports

Vanderbilt University

do not include research and/or patient care activity, making Vanderbilt's report more comprehensive than most and also more comprehensive than what is now required by the Environmental Protection Agency.

FINANCIAL AID

Students should submit: CSS/Financial Aid PROFILE; FAFSA. Priority filing deadline is 2/3. The Princeton Review suggests that all financial aid forms be submitted as soon as possible after October 1. *Need-based scholarships/grants offered*: College/university scholarship or grant aid from institutional funds; Federal Pell; Private scholarships; SEOG; State scholarships/grants; United Negro College Fund. *Loan aid offered*: Direct PLUS loans; Direct Subsidized Stafford Loans; Direct Unsubsidized Stafford Loans. Applicants will be notified of awards on or about 4/1. Federal Work-Study Program available. Institutional employment available.

BOTTOM LINE

Vanderbilt students are currently charged $50,800 for tuition. Undergrads are required to live in university housing and pay $11,044 for housing and $5,866 for meals. All students also pay another $1,270 to cover student service fees. Books and supplies typically cost students an additional $1,294. And Vanderbilt ballparks personal expenses at around $2,874. These figures come to a total of $74,084.

FINANCIAL FACTS	
Financial Aid Rating	99
Annual tuition	$50,800
Room and board	$16,910
Required fees	$1,270
Books and supplies	$1,294
Average frosh need-based scholarship	$49,614
Average UG need-based scholarship	$49,076
% needy frosh rec. need-based scholarship or grant aid	99
% needy UG rec. need-based scholarship or grant aid	99
% needy frosh rec. non-need-based scholarship or grant aid	11
% needy UG rec. non-need-based scholarship or grant aid	7
% needy frosh rec. need-based self-help aid	49
% needy UG rec. need-based self-help aid	55
% frosh rec. any financial aid	66
% UG rec. any financial aid	65
% UG borrow to pay for school	21
Average cumulative indebtedness	$22,854
% frosh need fully met	100
% ugrads need fully met	100
Average % of frosh need met	100
Average % of ugrad need met	100

CAREER INFORMATION FROM PAYSCALE.COM	
ROI Rating	95
Bachelors and No Higher	
Median starting salary	$65,400
Median mid-career salary	$119,100
At Least Bachelors	
Median starting salary	$67,600
Median mid-career salary	$128,300
Alumni with high job meaning	52%
Degrees awarded in STEM subjects	23%

Vanderbilt University

Vassar College

124 Raymond Avenue, Poughkeepsie, NY 12604 • Admissions: 845-437-7300 • Fax: 845-437-7063

#50 BEST VALUE COLLEGE

CAMPUS LIFE	
Quality of Life Rating	88
Fire Safety Rating	89
Green Rating	90
Type of school	Private
Environment	Town

STUDENTS	
Total undergrad enrollment	2,436
% male/female	41/59
% from out of state	72
% frosh from public high school	64
% frosh live on campus	99
% ugrads live on campus	97
# of fraternities	0
# of sororities	0
% African American	4
% Asian	12
% Caucasian	56
% Hispanic	11
% Native American	<1
% Pacific Islander	0
% Two or more races	8
% Race and/or ethnicity unknown	<1
% international	9
# of countries represented	54

ABOUT THE SCHOOL

A coed institution since 1969, Vassar was founded in 1861 as the first of the Seven Sister colleges. Located in Poughkeepsie, New York, this private liberal arts school where there is very little in the way of a core curriculum allows students the freedom to design their own courses of study. This approach, students agree, "really encourages students to think creatively and pursue whatever they're passionate about, whether medieval tapestries, neuroscience, or unicycles. Not having a core curriculum is great because it gives students the opportunity to delve into many different interests."

Student life is campus-centered, in large part because hometown Poughkeepsie does not offer much in the way of entertainment. It's a very self-contained social scene; virtually everyone lives on Vassar's beautiful campus. A vibrant oasis, it's easy for students here to get caught in the "Vassar Bubble." There are clubs and organizations aplenty, and the school provides interesting lectures, theatre productions, and a wide array of activities pretty much every weeknight. Weekends, on the other hand, are more about small parties and gatherings. More adventurous students make the relatively easy trek to New York to shake up the routine.

The lack of core requirements is valued by students as "a great opportunity… to explore anything they want before settling into a major." The faculty is "super accessible" and "fully engaged in the total Vassar community." "My professors are…spectacular at illuminating difficult material," says a junior psychology major. Classes are small and "most are very discussion-based"; while academics are rigorous and challenging here, students

Vassar College

Financial Aid: 845-437-5230 • E-mail: admissions@vassar.edu • Website: www.vassar.edu

describe themselves as self-motivated rather than competitive, contributing to a relaxed and collaborative atmosphere.

BANG FOR YOUR BUCK

Vassar has a need-blind admissions policy and is able to meet 100 percent of the demonstrated need of everyone who is admitted for all four years. Vassar awards more than $69 million dollars in scholarships. Funds come from Vassar's endowment, money raised by Vassar clubs, and gifts from friends of the college and all are need-based. In addition to a close-knit community, beautiful campus, engaged professors, and rigorous academics, study abroad opportunities abound.

STUDENT LIFE

The students at Vassar are an eclectic group who "will do things in any way but the traditional way" and who revel in their individuality. Think "smart and passionate hipsters" out to prove they have something to offer the world. Students say "the vibe of the whole school is so chill," but does not hamper a "vibrant extracurricular scene." In fact, Vassar is "bursting at the seams" with over 170 student organizations. There are "a ton of intramural sports teams," several very popular a cappella groups, plenty of political organizations, a large performing arts contingent, and "basically anything else you can think of." New York City isn't far, but there are always a decent amount of weekend activities right on this close-knit campus such as "concerts, comedy shows, plays, dances, etc."

ACADEMICS

Academic Rating	94
% students returning for sophomore year	95
% students graduating within 4 years	88
% students graduating within 6 years	92
Calendar	Semester
Student/faculty ratio	8:1
Profs interesting rating	95
Profs accessible rating	90

Most classes have 10–19 students.
Most lab/discussion sessions have 10–19 students.

MOST POPULAR MAJORS

Psychology, General; Economics, General; Political Science and Government, General

SELECTIVITY

Admissions Rating	96
# of applicants	8,312
% of applicants accepted	25
% of acceptees attending	34
# offered a place on the wait list	1,138
% accepting a place on wait list	50
% admitted from wait list	8
# of early decision applicants	679
% accepted early decision	44

FRESHMAN PROFILE

Range SAT EBRW	680–740
Range SAT Math	690–770
Range ACT Composite	31–33
# submitting SAT scores	418
% submitting SAT scores	61
# submitting ACT scores	332
% submitting ACT scores	48
% graduated top 10% of class	61
% graduated top 25% of class	91
% graduated top 50% of class	98

DEADLINES

Early decision	
Deadline	11/15
Notification	12/15
Other ED Deadline	1/1
Other ED Notification	2/1
Regular	
Deadline	1/1
Nonfall registration?	No

CAREER

The Career Development Office at Vassar "helps students and almumnae/i envision and realize a meaningful life" after graduation. To that end, the CDO provides career and major exploration, sets up information interviews, and will even help students put together a four-year plan to maximize their college experience. Both Handshake and The Vassar Alumnfire network provide job and internship listings for summer and post-college. Typically, more than 90% of Vassar graduates report having employment, graduate school, or fellowships within six months of graduation. PayScale.com reports that the starting salary for recent grads is a median of $55,400 and that 52 percent of grads visiting their website believe their work makes the world a better place.

GENERAL INFO

Activities: Campus Ministries; Choral groups; Concert band; Dance; Drama/theater; International Student Organization; Jazz band; Literary magazine; Model UN; Music ensembles; Musical theater; Opera; Radio station; Student government; Student newspaper; Student-run film society; Symphony orchestra; Yearbook. 145 registered organizations, 5 honor societies, 12 religious organizations, 0 fraternities, 0 sororities, on campus. **Athletics (Intercollegiate):** *Men:* baseball, basketball, crew/rowing, cross-country, diving, fencing, lacrosse, soccer, squash, swimming, tennis, track/field (outdoor), volleyball. *Women:* basketball, crew/rowing, cross-country, diving, fencing, field hockey, golf, lacrosse, soccer, squash, swimming, tennis, track/field (outdoor), volleyball. **On-Campus Highlights:** Library, Bridge for Laboratory Sciences, Class of 1951 Observatory, Frances Lehman Loeb Art Center, Center for Drama and Film. **Environmental Initiatives:** Tree Campus USA & Landscaping choices—in 2012/13 CCS and B&G worked together to phase out the use of harmful pesticides on campus to more environmentally friendly products. Additionally, the switch to a salt water brine solution, has cut the campus's total usage of salt on campus by 50%.

Vassar College

FINANCIAL AID

Students should submit: CSS/Financial Aid PROFILE; FAFSA; Noncustodial PROFILE. Priority filing deadline is 3/30. The Princeton Review suggests that all financial aid forms be submitted as soon as possible after October 1. *Need-based scholarships/grants offered*: College/university scholarship or grant aid from institutional funds; Federal Pell; Private scholarships; SEOG; State scholarships/grants. *Loan aid offered*: Direct PLUS loans; Direct Subsidized Stafford Loans; Direct Unsubsidized Stafford Loans. Federal Work-Study Program available. Institutional employment available.

BOTTOM LINE

The sticker price at Vassar for tuition, fees, and room and board runs about $68,110 for a year. That said, Vassar has a need-blind admission policy, and financial aid is extremely generous. It's probably harder to get admitted here than it is to afford going here. Meeting financial standards is less important than exceeding high academic standards and intellectual pursuits that venture far outside the classroom.

FINANCIAL FACTS

Financial Aid Rating	**99**
Annual tuition	$54,410
Room and board	$12,900
Required fees	$800
Books and supplies	$900
Average frosh need-based scholarship	$51,903
Average UG need-based scholarship	$49,190
% needy frosh rec. need-based scholarship or grant aid	99
% needy UG rec. need-based scholarship or grant aid	99
% needy frosh rec. non-need-based scholarship or grant aid	0
% needy UG rec. non-need-based scholarship or grant aid	0
% needy frosh rec. need-based self-help aid	95
% needy UG rec. need-based self-help aid	97
% frosh rec. any financial aid	64
% UG rec. any financial aid	66
% UG borrow to pay for school	49
Average cumulative indebtedness	$21,473
% frosh need fully met	100
% ugrads need fully met	100
Average % of frosh need met	100
Average % of ugrad need met	100

CAREER INFORMATION FROM PAYSCALE.COM

ROI Rating	92
Bachelors and No Higher	
Median starting salary	$55,400
Median mid-career salary	$100,100
At Least Bachelors	
Median starting salary	$57,700
Median mid-career salary	$115,400
Alumni with high job meaning	52%
Degrees awarded in STEM subjects	24%

Vassar College

Wabash College

PO Box 352, 301 W. Wabash Av, Crawfordsville, IN 47933 • Admissions: 765-361-6225

CAMPUS LIFE

Quality of Life Rating	89
Fire Safety Rating	88
Green Rating	65
Type of school	Private
Environment	Village

STUDENTS

Total undergrad enrollment	881
% male/female	100/0
% from out of state	21
% frosh from public high school	87
% frosh live on campus	99
% ugrads live on campus	99
# of fraternities	
(% ugrad men join)	10 (64)
% African American	6
% Asian	1
% Caucasian	74
% Hispanic	9
% Native American	0
% Pacific Islander	0
% Two or more races	3
% Race and/or ethnicity unknown	2
% international	6
# of countries represented	17

#26 BEST VALUE COLLEGE

ABOUT THE SCHOOL

Indiana's Wabash College is one of only three remaining traditional, all-male liberal arts colleges in the United States. Offering its nearly 900 students the choice of 27 majors, about 70 clubs and organizations, and a rigorous academic curriculum, the school emphasizes critical thinking and clear communication while following the Gentleman's Rule, which states, "The student is expected to conduct himself at all times, both on and off campus, as a gentleman and a responsible citizen." The academics here are "difficult but superb [and allow students] to find solutions in any situation." And the school takes that seriously by administering "senior comprehensive exams [that] ensure students master the material and become true recipients of a liberal arts education." Faculty members also "encourage discussion and engagement in class to get students experience in communication and understanding complex topics." Professors are described as "dedicated to helping students hit the highest potential." Plus, their "office hours are frequent and [they are] never intimidating." Lastly, the "school spirit and tradition-oriented culture is second to none," as "everyone goes to games and activities that started over 150 years ago [and] still happen each year at Wabash."

BANG FOR YOUR BUCK

The school strives to make a liberal arts education affordable for everyone regardless of financial circumstances, and approximately 99 percent of enrolled students receive financial aid. Additionally, there are a number of merit-based scholarships available, such as Lilly Awards (tuition, standard fees, and room and board for exceptional and creative students), Snodell Scholarships (up

Wabash College

E-mail: admissions@wabash.edu • Fax: 765-361-6437 • Website: www.wabash.edu

to $15,000 each year for four years for residents of Chicago, northern Illinois, southern Wisconsin, and eastern Iowa), and Dean's and President's Scholarships (based on GPA and standardized test scores). For the most part, students "have equal opportunities to enjoy programs, such as immersion classes and career workshops" without paying additional fees, and funding for student research projects is available through a grants program and individual departments.

STUDENT LIFE

Wabash is "the last bastion of traditional masculine values and personal responsibility," so on weekdays "the vast majority of students are extremely committed to their studies and exceeding expectations in the classroom." Enrollees are also "encouraged to participate in activities outside of class, often for credit," and the school "fosters an environment of challenging each other and participating in important conversations about real issues." On weekends, students "are almost always at sports events, depending on the season." The area surrounding Wabash "is very rural, so life is centered around the campus"; luckily, "extracurriculars are easy to come by" and the college "does its best to host events of all kinds."

CAREER

The Schroeder Center for Career Development is a one-stop shop for students to hone their skills and choose their future paths while at Wabash, and students have access to career guides, online job and internship databases, job fairs, and networking events set up by the office. Wabash also organizes "events to connect with alumni and other business owners to give [students] as many opportunities to succeed as possible." One student boasts the utmost confidence in the career center: "If all else fails, Career Services will not."

ACADEMICS

Academic Rating	92
% students returning for sophomore year	86
% students graduating within 4 years	66
% students graduating within 6 years	71
Calendar	Semester
Student/faculty ratio	10:1
Profs interesting rating	99
Profs accessible rating	99

Most classes have 10–19 students. Most lab/discussion sessions have fewer than 10 students.

MOST POPULAR MAJORS

Economics, General; Political Science and Government, General; History, General

SELECTIVITY

Admissions Rating	85
# of applicants	1,336
% of applicants accepted	65
% of acceptees attending	32
# of early decision applicants	29
% accepted early decision	93

Around 25–30 percent of Wabash graduates enroll in professional or graduate school within five years of graduation, and the co-curricular WabashX programs in Global Health, Democracy and Public Discourse, the Center for Innovation, Business, & Entrepreneurship, and Digital Arts and Human Values help students specifically prepare for careers and post-graduate work through hands-on experience. This involvement is due in part to "the incredibly engaged and expansive alumni network" that will "help out any way [it] can" to "try to help guide a path for your career or just offer mentorship." It's "a testament to how special Wabash College truly is."

GENERAL INFO

Activities: Campus Ministries; Choral groups; Concert band; Dance; Drama/theater; International Student Organization; Jazz band; Literary magazine; Music ensembles; Musical theater; Pep band; Radio station; Student government; Student newspaper; Student-run film society; Symphony orchestra; Yearbook. 64 registered organizations, 9 honor societies, 4 religious organizations, 10 fraternities, 0 sororities, on campus. **Athletics (Intercollegiate):** *Men:* baseball, basketball, cross-country, diving, football, golf, soccer, swimming, tennis, track/field (outdoor), track/field (indoor), volleyball, wrestling. **On-Campus Highlights:** Allen Athletics and Recreation Center, Wabash Chapel, Fine Arts Center, Sparks Student Center, 1832 Brew Coffee Shop. **Environmental Initiatives:** Printing Quota that saved 240,000 sheets of paper in the first semester (among 900 students).

Wabash College

FINANCIAL AID

Students should submit: FAFSA. Priority filing deadline is 1/15. The Princeton Review suggests that all financial aid forms be submitted as soon as possible after October 1. *Need-based scholarships/ grants offered*: College/university scholarship or grant aid from institutional funds; Federal Pell; Private scholarships; SEOG; State scholarships/grants; United Negro College Fund. *Loan aid offered*: Direct PLUS loans; Direct Subsidized Stafford Loans; Direct Unsubsidized Stafford Loans. Applicants will be notified of awards on a rolling basis beginning 12/15. Federal Work-Study Program available. Institutional employment available.

BOTTOM LINE

Tuition runs $43,870, with room and board tacking on another $10,500, plus an additional $850 in Student Activity and Student Health fees. It may be a small school (around nine hundred students), but Wabash has one of the country's highest per-student endowments, and 99 percent of all students receive some form of financial aid.

FINANCIAL FACTS	
Financial Aid Rating	98
Annual tuition	$43,870
Room and board	$10,500
Required fees	$850
Books and supplies	$1,200
Average frosh need-based scholarship	$37,745
Average UG need-based scholarship	$32,979
% needy frosh rec. need-based scholarship or grant aid	98
% needy UG rec. need-based scholarship or grant aid	99
% needy frosh rec. non-need-based scholarship or grant aid	16
% needy UG rec. non-need-based scholarship or grant aid	14
% needy frosh rec. need-based self-help aid	84
% needy UG rec. need-based self-help aid	84
% frosh rec. any financial aid	100
% UG rec. any financial aid	100
% UG borrow to pay for school	91
Average cumulative indebtedness	$34,723
% frosh need fully met	85
% ugrads need fully met	80
Average % of frosh need met	97
Average % of ugrad need met	94

CAREER INFORMATION FROM PAYSCALE.COM	
ROI Rating	93
Bachelors and No Higher	
Median starting salary	$62,200
Median mid-career salary	$114,400
At Least Bachelors	
Median starting salary	$65,300
Median mid-career salary	$137,800
Alumni with high job meaning	54%
Degrees awarded in STEM subjects	34%

Wabash College

Washington University in St. Louis

Campus Box 1089, St. Louis, MO 63130-4899 • Admissions: 314-935-6000 • Fax: 314-935-4290

CAMPUS LIFE

Quality of Life Rating	96
Fire Safety Rating	97
Green Rating	95
Type of school	Private
Environment	City

STUDENTS

Total undergrad enrollment	7,356
% male/female	47/53
% from out of state	90
% frosh from public high school	57
% frosh live on campus	100
% ugrads live on campus	74
# of fraternities	
(% ugrad men join)	14 (26)
# of sororities	
(% ugrad women join)	10 (38)
% African American	9
% Asian	16
% Caucasian	51
% Hispanic	9
% Native American	<1
% Pacific Islander	<1
% Two or more races	5
% Race and/or ethnicity unknown	2
% international	7
# of countries represented	50

#48 BEST VALUE COLLEGE

ABOUT THE SCHOOL

The nearly 8,000 undergraduates at Washington University in St. Louis already enjoy a low 7:1 student-to-faculty ratio and 1,500 courses across 90 fields of study. But the pot is sweetened by the university's prestigious reputation in the research world: more than 3,000 projects take place each year, and it's "very easy to get involved in research and connect with world-renowned faculty." In addition to exploring through research, the school encourages students to expand their interests and combine multiple disciplines—80 percent of students double major or pursue minors, or take classes outside of their division. And that's easily accomplished thanks to WashU's "academic flexibility" and the fact that "there's always funding for student groups, student initiatives, university-run activities, [and] research." While "the academic environment is very advanced and can be challenging," the "professors are very knowledgeable and … provide as many resources [as possible] to do well in a class (review sessions, online notes, recorded lectures, etc.)." Furthermore, many classes at WashU incorporate non-traditional learning methods such as group focus on collaborative problem solving or experiential learning courses "where students are placed in teams and consult with local small businesses." They also don't waste any time getting there: even first-year seminars "sometimes include out-of-class components like research or travel."

BANG FOR YOUR BUCK

The university does not want money to stand in the way of students applying to WashU, and it meets 100 percent of demonstrated financial need for everyone admitted, including no-loan packages for families with an annual

Washington University in St. Louis

Financial Aid: 888-547-6670 • E-mail: admissions@wustl.edu • Website: wustl.edu

income of $75,000 or less. The school has numerous creative financing and payment plans available, and there are also merit-based scholarships available as well as the Signature Scholars program, which brings together students from across academic disciplines and cultural communities. Additionally, "the support systems in place for first-year students help ease the college transition immensely, and the administrators deeply care about the well-being of the students."

STUDENT LIFE

In short: "Campus life is exciting and lively," "the views of campus are breathtaking," and "the food ... is awesome." And it's busy too; "Very few people do nothing [or sleep] for more than two hours per day," shares an undergrad. Perhaps because "almost everyone's time is spent studying," it turns out that "most student groups at WashU have a social aspect to them" and "people usually turn to Greek life and/ or student run organizations for fun." So, though the "library is always filled," people are also "always playing Frisbee on the open fields" and "are excited to explore St. Louis."

ACADEMICS	
Academic Rating	92
% students returning for sophomore year	97
% students graduating within 4 years	88
% students graduating within 6 years	95
Calendar	Semester
Student/faculty ratio	7:1
Profs interesting rating	87
Profs accessible rating	85
Most classes have 10–19 students. Most lab/discussion sessions have 10–19 students.	

MOST POPULAR MAJORS
Engineering, General; Social Sciences, General; Business Administration and Management, General

SELECTIVITY	
Admissions Rating	98
# of applicants	31,320
% of applicants accepted	15
% of acceptees attending	38
# of early decision applicants	1,840
% accepted early decision	42

CAREER

The WashU Career Center hosts an Internship & Job Career Fair twice a year and even offers preparatory workshops leading up to it; it also maintains an online recruiting platform called CAREERlink where students can search for jobs, co-ops, and internships. There are a limited number of stipends available for students who wish to take unpaid internships over the summer, and academic credit is also available. Additionally, Career Interest Groups help aggregate all of the information about specific career paths, putting students, staff, faculty, and alumni in touch to create smaller communities and share guidance. "I have ... found the alumni network to be extremely strong and supportive through my recruitment processes," says a student. There are "great global opportunities" at WashU as well, and around 45 percent of students study abroad at some point.

GENERAL INFO

Activities: Campus Ministries; Choral groups; Concert band; Dance; Drama/theater; International Student Organization; Jazz band; Literary magazine; Model UN; Music ensembles; Musical theater; Opera; Pep band; Radio station; Student government; Student newspaper; Student-run film society; Symphony orchestra; Television station. 380 registered organizations, 19 honor societies, 18 religious organizations, 14 fraternities, 10 sororities, on campus. **Athletics (Intercollegiate):** *Men:* baseball, basketball, cross-country, diving, football, soccer, swimming, tennis, track/field (outdoor), track/field (indoor). *Women:* basketball, cross-country, diving, golf, soccer, softball, swimming, tennis, track/field (outdoor), track/field (indoor), volleyball. **On-Campus Highlights:** Kemper Art Museum, Whispers Cafe in Olin Library, Danforth University Center, Brookings Quadrangle, South 40 Residential Area.

FINANCIAL AID

Students should submit: CSS/Financial Aid PROFILE; FAFSA; Noncustodial PROFILE. Priority filing deadline is 2/1. The Princeton Review suggests that all financial aid forms be submitted as soon as possible after October 1. *Need-based scholarships/grants offered*: College/university scholarship or grant aid from institutional funds; Federal Pell; Private scholarships; SEOG; State scholarships/grants; United Negro College Fund. *Loan aid offered*: Direct PLUS loans; Direct Subsidized Stafford Loans; Direct Unsubsidized Stafford Loans. Applicants will be notified of awards on or about 4/1. Federal Work-Study Program available. Institutional employment available.

Washington University in St. Louis

BOTTOM LINE

Tuition is a hefty $54,250 and room and board is a solid $16,900, but fear not: the sticker price is just for show. The school is committed to cost not being a barrier, and it has eliminated need-based loans to students from families with incomes of $75,000 or less. First-year students who are Pell-eligible or from families with incomes of $75,000 or less will also receive $500 toward the purchase of a computer, $1,500 toward the cost of start-up supplies, and a $1,550 grant to replace the expectation that students work the summer before starting at Washington University.

CAREER INFORMATION FROM PAYSCALE.COM	
ROI Rating	92
Bachelors and No Higher	
Median starting salary	$64,800
Median mid-career salary	$114,900
At Least Bachelors	
Median starting salary	$67,300
Median mid-career salary	$123,500
Alumni with high job meaning	47%
Degrees awarded in STEM subjects	30%

FINANCIAL FACTS	
Financial Aid Rating	99
Annual tuition	$54,250
Room and board	$16,900
Required fees	$1,042
Books and supplies	$1,126
Average frosh need-based scholarship	$48,522
Average UG need-based scholarship	$47,335
% needy frosh rec. need-based scholarship or grant aid	96
% needy UG rec. need-based scholarship or grant aid	97
% needy frosh rec. non-need-based scholarship or grant aid	8
% needy UG rec. non-need-based scholarship or grant aid	5
% needy frosh rec. need-based self-help aid	71
% needy UG rec. need-based self-help aid	67
% frosh rec. any financial aid	49
% UG rec. any financial aid	48
% UG borrow to pay for school	27
Average cumulative indebtedness	$22,555
% frosh need fully met	98
% ugrads need fully met	99
Average % of frosh need met	100
Average % of ugrad need met	100

Washington University in
St. Louis

Wellesley College

Board of Admission, 106 Central Street, Wellesley, MA 02481-8203 • Phone: 781-283-2270 • Fax: 781-283-3678

CAMPUS LIFE	
Quality of Life Rating	88
Fire Safety Rating	98
Green Rating	93
Type of school	Private
Environment	Town

STUDENTS	
Total undergrad enrollment	2,375
% male/female	0/100
% from out of state	86
% frosh from public high school	62
% frosh live on campus	100
% ugrads live on campus	97
# of fraternities	0
# of sororities	0
% African American	7
% Asian	23
% Caucasian	38
% Hispanic	13
% Native American	<1
% Pacific Islander	0
% Two or more races	6
% Race and/or ethnicity unknown	<1
% international	14
# of countries represented	87

#44 BEST VALUE COLLEGE

ABOUT THE SCHOOL

Students spend a tremendous amount of time reading and writing papers at Wellesley. Spending part of junior year abroad is a staple of a Wellesley education. Wellesley Career Education offers grants and stipends, which allow students to pursue what would otherwise be unpaid research and internship opportunities. When they get their diplomas, Wellesley graduates are able to take advantage of a tenaciously loyal network of more than 35,000 alums who are ready to help students with everything from arranging an interview to finding a place to live. Wellesley's close-knit student population collectively spends large segments of its weekdays in stressed-out study mode. Students don't spend all of their weekdays this way, though, because there are a ton of extracurricular activities available on this beautiful, state-of-the-art campus. Wellesley is home to more than 160 student organizations. Lectures, performances, and cultural events are endless. Wellesley is twelve miles west of Boston, and access to cultural, academic, social, business, and medical institutions is a powerful draw. On the weekends, many students head to Boston to hit the bars or to parties on nearby campuses. While enrolling nearly 2,400 undergraduates, Wellesley offers a remarkable array of more than 1,000 courses and fifty-four major programs; plus, "you can cross-register at MIT (and to a limited extent at Brandeis, Babson, and Olin.)" From research to internships to overseas studies, Wellesley "provides great resources and opportunities to all its students."

Wellesley College

Financial Aid Phone: 781-283-2360 • E-mail: admission@wellesley.edu • Website: www.wellesley.edu

BANG FOR YOUR BUCK

With an endowment worth more than $1.5 billion, Wellesley is well-equipped to serve its students. Admission is completely need-blind for U.S. citizens and permanent residents. If you get admitted (no easy task), Wellesley will meet 100 percent of your calculated financial need. Most financial aid comes in the form of a grant; it's free money, and you'll never have to pay it back. Packaged student loan amounts are correlated to family income. No student will graduate with more than $15,200 in packaged student loans. Students from families with a calculated income between $60,000-$100,000 will graduate with no more than $10,100 in packaged student loans. And students from families with the greatest need, with a calculated income of $60,000 or less, will graduate with $0 in packaged student loans.

STUDENT LIFE

Because Wellesley is an academically rigorous school full of driven women, "most of the weekday is spent in class or studying." But when students want to take a break from the books, "there are always seminars and panel discussions and cultural events to attend. The diverse community and the multitudes of campus groups means there's always something to do." Once the weekend hits, "there's a large split. There are girls that don't party, or hardly party. And then there are girls who party every weekend." "On campus parties are hard to find and are normally broken up because of a noise complaint from a studying neighbor." As such, "the girls who are interested in men frequently spend their weekends venturing off campus to MIT or Harvard for parties," or head into Boston for "a girl's night out—go to a movie, maybe see a play, go karaoke, or just have dinner in the city." But no matter how you want to spend your free time, Wellesley has you covered: "It's nice to know that whatever you feel like doing on a

ACADEMICS

Academic Rating	95
% students returning for sophomore year	96
% students graduating within 4 years	78
% students graduating within 6 years	90
Calendar	Semester
Student/faculty ratio	8:1
Profs interesting rating	95
Profs accessible rating	90

Most classes have 10–19 students. Most lab/discussion sessions have 10–19 students.

MOST POPULAR MAJORS

Computer Science; Psychology, General; Economics, General

SELECTIVITY

Admissions Rating	97
# of applicants	6,631
% of applicants accepted	20
% of acceptees attending	47
# offered a place on the wait list	1,909
% accepting a place on wait list	65
% admitted from wait list	3
# of early decision applicants	802
% accepted early decision	31

Friday night, you'll always have company—whether you want to stay in and watch a movie or go into Boston to party."

CAREER

The typical Wellesley woman is often described as "career oriented" by her peers, and fortunately "Wellesley has an amazing alumni network and a career service center that helps students gain access to all sorts of job, internship, and community service opportunities." Wellesley Career Education offers ample resources, including career advising, help with finding jobs and internships, and tools for students seeking to continue their education in graduate school. True to its name, the center also offers guidance for women looking for service opportunities within existing organizations on and off-campus, and even offers funding for students looking to start their own initiatives. The support doesn't end after students graduate: "Wellesley's alumnae network is one of the strongest I found in my college research, and Wellesley's career placement services will assist alumnae no matter how much time has passed since they graduated."

GENERAL INFO

Activities: Campus Ministries; Choral groups; Concert band; Dance; Drama/theater; International Student Organization; Jazz band; Literary magazine; Model UN; Music ensembles; Radio station; Student government; Student newspaper; Student-run film society; Symphony orchestra; Television station; Yearbook. 160 registered organizations, 7 honor societies, 30 religious organizations, 0 fraternities, 0 sororities, on campus. **Athletics (Intercollegiate):** *Women:* basketball, crew/rowing, cross-country, diving, fencing, field hockey, golf, lacrosse, soccer, softball, squash, swimming, tennis, track/field (outdoor), track/field (indoor), volleyball. **On-Campus Highlights:** Wang Campus Center, Davis Museum and Cultural Center, Clapp Library and Knapp Media Center, Science Center, Lake Waban.

Wellesley College

FINANCIAL AID

Students should submit: CSS/Financial Aid PROFILE; FAFSA; Noncustodial PROFILE. Priority filing deadline is 2/15. The Princeton Review suggests that all financial aid forms be submitted as soon as possible after October 1. *Need-based scholarships/grants offered*: College/university scholarship or grant aid from institutional funds; Federal Pell; Private scholarships; SEOG; State scholarships/grants; United Negro College Fund. *Loan aid offered*: Direct PLUS loans; Direct Subsidized Stafford Loans; Direct Unsubsidized Stafford Loans. Applicants will be notified of awards on or about 4/1. Federal Work-Study Program available. Institutional employment available.

BOTTOM LINE

The total cost for a year of tuition, fees, and room and board at Wellesley is over $70,000. However, this school has the financial resources to provide a tremendous amount of financial aid. Your aid package is likely to be quite extensive, and students leave with just $16,122 in loan debt on average. That's chump change for an education worth more than $250,000.

FINANCIAL FACTS	
Financial Aid Rating	97
Annual tuition	$53,408
Room and board	$16,468
Required fees	$324
Books and supplies	$2,050
Average frosh need-based scholarship	$52,881
Average UG need-based scholarship	$50,752
% needy frosh rec. need-based scholarship or grant aid	97
% needy UG rec. need-based scholarship or grant aid	95
% needy frosh rec. non-need-based scholarship or grant aid	8
% needy UG rec. non-need-based scholarship or grant aid	7
% needy frosh rec. need-based self-help aid	93
% needy UG rec. need-based self-help aid	94
% frosh rec. any financial aid	60
% UG rec. any financial aid	56
% UG borrow to pay for school	51
Average cumulative indebtedness	$16,122
% frosh need fully met	100
% ugrads need fully met	100
Average % of frosh need met	100
Average % of ugrad need met	100

CAREER INFORMATION FROM PAYSCALE.COM	
ROI Rating	92
Bachelors and No Higher	
Median starting salary	$58,900
Median mid-career salary	$106,200
At Least Bachelors	
Median starting salary	$60,500
Median mid-career salary	$115,100
Alumni with high job meaning	55%
Degrees awarded in STEM subjects	34%

Wellesley College

Wesleyan University

70 Wyllys Avenue, Middletown, CT 06459-0265 • Admissions: 860-685-3000 • Fax: 860-685-3001

CAMPUS LIFE

Quality of Life Rating	87
Fire Safety Rating	93
Green Rating	96
Type of school	Private
Environment	Town

STUDENTS

Total undergrad enrollment	2,922
% male/female	45/55
% from out of state	93
% frosh from public high school	52
% frosh live on campus	100
% ugrads live on campus	99
# of fraternities	
(% ugrad men join)	4 (4)
# of sororities	
(% ugrad women join)	1 (1)
% African American	6
% Asian	7
% Caucasian	54
% Hispanic	12
% Native American	<1
% Pacific Islander	<1
% Two or more races	6
% Race and/or ethnicity unknown	3
% international	12
# of countries represented	54

ABOUT THE SCHOOL

Connecticut's Wesleyan University emphasizes a "practical idealism" in its open curriculum, in which students propose an academic plan to their faculty advisors and readjust each semester as interests and strengths develop. The school offers forty-five majors, seventeen minors, and twelve certificates, with over one thousand classes available to just 3,000 students, not to mention countless study abroad opportunities and First-Year Seminars (all of which are writing-focused). The school is "very good about making sure you can study a range of things and still get the credits you need in your major(s)," and "the course offerings are diverse and great." Professors are "experts in their field and make learning challenging, yet rewarding," and class sizes are small so that "student-professor relationships are more easily facilitated." In addition, "student-student relationships are easier to maintain." In fact, students themselves are often core of the curriculum, as "everyone contributes wonderfully idiosyncratic thoughts built from past experiences within their own niches through the same mode of communication: education."

BANG FOR YOUR BUCK

Resources abound at Wesleyan, and there are more than 800 individual tutorials and private music lessons available to students, as well as numerous opportunities to get involved in graduate-level research. The school participates in the Twelve-College Exchange Program, where students can apply to study at one of eleven New England colleges for a semester or the full year, like a domestic study abroad. Most students also complete a senior thesis or capstone

Wesleyan University

Financial Aid: 860-685-2800 • E-mail: admissions@wesleyan.edu • Website: www.wesleyan.edu

project (such as independent research) in an area that interests them most, which is an excellent showcase for results. There is no time lost to mindlessness here; the fluid general education requirements set up by Wesleyan University "really allow students to explore a broad spectrum of subjects while also figuring out what they like or dislike," so they can figure out if they like something else while still fulfilling their major requirements with a "lower risk factor."

STUDENT LIFE

Wesleyan students are "Hip, passionate, socially conscious," as well as "really dedicated and artsy," but there is a surprisingly strong athletic culture to be found, and games of all sport teams are in high attendance. Students take full advantage of the liberal arts experience and curiosity runs far and wide (a "very strange brilliance"), and "many are passionate about their niche interest." People "don't generally take themselves too seriously, even as they're doing incredible things academically," and overall, students are "hard-working and know how to relax with friends, too." The school is "big enough not to feel suffocating, small enough to feel comfortable," and even has its own movie theater that plays new releases. There is a highly diverse international student population (the school offers a full tuition scholarship to one student from each of eleven Asian countries each year), and all are "reflective snapshots of the various cultures around the world"; "everyone has something unique or weird (in a good way) about them."

CAREER

The Gordon Career Center has "many helpful resources for applying to summer internships and jobs after graduation," and works individually with students to design career paths based on the overlap of interests, rather than straight

ACADEMICS

Academic Rating	92
% students returning for sophomore year	96
% students graduating within 4 years	85
% students graduating within 6 years	89
Calendar	Semester
Student/faculty ratio	8:1
Profs interesting rating	93
Profs accessible rating	89

Most classes have 10–19 students. Most lab/discussion sessions have 10–19 students.

MOST POPULAR MAJORS

Psychology, General; Economics, General

SELECTIVITY

Admissions Rating	96
# of applicants	12,706
% of applicants accepted	17
% of acceptees attending	36
# offered a place on the wait list	1,965
% accepting a place on wait list	56
% admitted from wait list	0
# of early decision applicants	1,080
% accepted early decision	38

trajectories from a major. Due to the interdisciplinary nature of the school, students have multiple and wildly varying interests (for instance, a double major in physics and theatre), and "no one can be placed in a traditional box." Students are truly free to make their own schedules and pursue the career they desire here, all with the support of the faculty. "Not once have I been discouraged from pursuing my interests, and the encouragement to follow these passions has caused a spark in me to bring them together," says a theater and science in society double major.

GENERAL INFO

Activities: Campus Ministries; Choral groups; Concert band; Dance; Drama/theater; International Student Organization; Jazz band; Literary magazine; Model UN; Music ensembles; Musical theater; Pep band; Radio station; Student government; Student newspaper; Student-run film society; Symphony orchestra; Yearbook. 263 registered organizations, 2 honor societies, 10 religious organizations, 4 fraternities, 1 sorority, on campus. **Athletics (Intercollegiate):** *Men:* baseball, basketball, crew/rowing, cross-country, diving, football, golf, ice hockey, lacrosse, soccer, squash, swimming, tennis, track/field (outdoor), track/field (indoor), wrestling. *Women:* basketball, crew/rowing, cross-country, diving, field hockey, golf, ice hockey, lacrosse, soccer, softball, squash, swimming, tennis, track/field (outdoor), track/field (indoor), volleyball. **On-Campus Highlights:** Center for the Arts, Freeman Athletic Center, Center for Film Studies, Olin Memorial Library, Van Vleck Observatory. **Environmental Initiatives:** Energy conservation activities resulting in a 28% reduction of energy consumption campus wide and the construction of 3 PV solar system with a combined output of 215 kW.

Wesleyan University

FINANCIAL AID

Students should submit: CSS/Financial Aid PROFILE; FAFSA; Noncustodial PROFILE. Priority filing deadline is 2/15. The Princeton Review suggests that all financial aid forms be submitted as soon as possible after October 1. *Need-based scholarships/ grants offered*: College/university scholarship or grant aid from institutional funds; Federal Pell; Private scholarships; SEOG; State scholarships/grants. *Loan aid offered*: Direct PLUS loans; Direct Subsidized Stafford Loans; Direct Unsubsidized Stafford Loans. Applicants will be notified of awards on or about 4/1. Federal Work-Study Program available. Institutional employment available.

BOTTOM LINE

Tuition, room and board, books (estimated), and fees run $73,928 for first-year and sophomores, but the university is committed to price not being a barrier to those who want to attend and meets all financial need. Almost $64 million of solely need-based financial aid is distributed to 42 percent of Wesleyan students, with the average award coming in at $50,051.

FINANCIAL FACTS	
Financial Aid Rating	97
Annual tuition	$56,704
Room and board	$15,724
Required fees	$300
Books and supplies	$1,200
Average frosh need-based scholarship	$50,083
Average UG need-based scholarship	$50,051
% needy frosh rec. need-based scholarship or grant aid	98
% needy UG rec. need-based scholarship or grant aid	99
% needy frosh rec. non-need-based scholarship or grant aid	4
% needy UG rec. non-need-based scholarship or grant aid	3
% needy frosh rec. need-based self-help aid	99
% needy UG rec. need-based self-help aid	99
% frosh rec. any financial aid	47
% UG rec. any financial aid	47
% UG borrow to pay for school	36
Average cumulative indebtedness	$23,454
% frosh need fully met	100
% ugrads need fully met	100
Average % of frosh need met	100
Average % of ugrad need met	100

CAREER INFORMATION FROM PAYSCALE.COM	
ROI Rating	91
Bachelors and No Higher	
Median starting salary	$61,600
Median mid-career salary	$117,000
At Least Bachelors	
Median starting salary	$63,000
Median mid-career salary	$135,000
Alumni with high job meaning	56%
Degrees awarded in STEM subjects	21%

Wesleyan University

Williams College

PO Box 487, Williamstown, MA 01267 • Admissions: 413-597-2211 • Fax: 413-597-4052

CAMPUS LIFE

Quality of Life Rating	90
Fire Safety Rating	60*
Green Rating	87
Type of school	Private
Environment	Village

STUDENTS

Total undergrad enrollment	2,020
% male/female	52/48
% from out of state	86
% frosh from public high school	54
% frosh live on campus	100
% ugrads live on campus	93
# of fraternities	0
# of sororities	0
% African American	8
% Asian	13
% Caucasian	50
% Hispanic	13
% Native American	<1
% Pacific Islander	0
% Two or more races	5
% Race and/or ethnicity unknown	3
% international	8
# of countries represented	56

#7 BEST VALUE COLLEGE

ABOUT THE SCHOOL

Founded in 1793, Williams College emphasizes the learning that takes place in the creation of a functioning community: life in the residence halls, expression through the arts, debates on political issues, leadership in campus governance, exploration of personal identity, pursuit of spiritual and religious impulses, the challenge of athletics, and direct engagement with human needs. The school is an "amalgamation of the most thoughtful, quirky, and smart people that you will ever meet as an undergraduate." The rigorous academic experience "is truly excellent," and a typical student says, "I feel like I am learning thoroughly." Professors are accessible and dedicated. Distinctive academic programs include Oxford-style tutorials between two students and a faculty member that call for intense research and weekly debates. These tutorial programs offer students an opportunity to take a heightened form of responsibility for their own intellectual development. In January, a four-week Winter Study term allows students to take unique, hands-on pass/fail classes.

BANG FOR YOUR BUCK

The endowment at Williams totals over $2.5 billion. This colossal stash bountifully subsidizes costs for all students, including the cost of books and course materials for any student receiving financial aid and the costs to study all over the world. The fact that Williams is simply awash in money also enables the school to maintain a need-blind admission program for domestic students—including those who are undocumented or have DACA status—

Williams College

Financial Aid: 413-597-4181 • E-mail: admission@williams.edu • Website: www.williams.edu

and meets 100 percent of the demonstrated need of all students. More than half of the college's international students—59 percent to be exact—receive financial aid and their average grant exceeds $65,000 annually. Merit-based scholarships are a historical artifact here. All financial aid is based purely on need. Convincing this school that you belong here is the difficult part. If you can just get admitted, Williams guarantees that it will meet 100 percent of your financial need for four years. You will walk away with a degree from one of the best schools in the country with little to no debt.

STUDENT LIFE

The typical Williams student is "quirky, passionate, zany, and fun." As one junior reports, "Williams is a place where normal social labels tend not to apply...So that football player in your theater class has amazing insight on Chekhov and that outspoken environmental activist also specializes in improv comedy." Nestled in the picturesque Berkshires of Massachusetts, campus is "stunning" and secluded, which means there is a real sense of community and caring here. Entertainment options include "lots of" performances, art exhibits, plays, and lectures. Some students have a healthy "obsession" with a cappella groups, and intramurals are popular, especially Ultimate Frisbee and broomball ("a sacred tradition involving a hockey rink, sneakers, a rubber ball, and paddles"). On Mountain Day, a unique fall tradition, bells ring announcing the cancellation of classes for the day, and students hike Stony Ledge to celebrate with donuts, cider, and, of course, a cappella performances. Opportunities for outdoor activities abound.

ACADEMICS

Academic Rating	99
% students returning for sophomore year	99
% students graduating within 4 years	90
% students graduating within 6 years	95
Calendar	4-1-4
Student/faculty ratio	7:1
Profs interesting rating	98
Profs accessible rating	99

Most classes have fewer than 10 students. Most lab/discussion sessions have 10–19 students.

MOST POPULAR MAJORS
Economics; Math; Biology

SELECTIVITY

Admissions Rating	98
# of applicants	9,560
% of applicants accepted	13
% of acceptees attending	43
# offered a place on the wait list	1,772
% accepting a place on wait list	37
% admitted from wait list	12
# of early decision applicants	748
% accepted early decision	34

FRESHMAN PROFILE

Range SAT EBRW	710–760
Range SAT Math	700–790
Range ACT Composite	32–35
# submitting SAT scores	305
% submitting SAT scores	57
# submitting ACT scores	312
% submitting ACT scores	59
% graduated top 10% of class	89
% graduated top 25% of class	97
% graduated top 50% of class	100

DEADLINES

Early decision	
Deadline	11/15
Notification	12/15
Regular	
Deadline	1/1
Notification	4/1
Nonfall registration?	No

CAREER

The '68 Center for Career Exploration at Williams empowers students to forge their own career path and gives them all the tools they need to get started. Each semester's calendar is packed with informational sessions, and cover letter writing or job fair success workshops. The aptly named "Who Am I & Where Am I Going" workshops helps students explore potential fields, and many students complete "real world" internships or work experience before graduation. The Williams Network connects students with opportunities and the "extensive alumni network" helps graduates get plum jobs all over the world. Graduates who visited PayScale.com report an average starting salary of $67,500 and 51 percent find a great deal of meaning in their work.

GENERAL INFO

Activities: Campus Ministries; Choral groups; Concert band; Dance; Drama/theater; International Student Organization; Jazz band; Literary magazine; Marching band; Music ensembles; Musical theater; Opera; Pep band; Radio station; Student government; Student newspaper; Student-run film society; Symphony orchestra; Yearbook. 150 registered organizations, 2 honor societies, 0 fraternities, 0 sororities, on campus. **Athletics (Intercollegiate):** *Men:* baseball, basketball, crew/rowing, cross-country, diving, football, golf, ice hockey, lacrosse, skiing (downhill/alpine), skiing (nordic/cross-country), soccer, squash, swimming, tennis, track/field (outdoor), track/field (indoor), wrestling. *Women:* basketball, crew/rowing, cross-country, diving, field hockey, golf, ice hockey, lacrosse, skiing (downhill/alpine), skiing (nordic/cross-country), soccer, softball, squash, swimming, tennis, track/field (outdoor), track/field (indoor), volleyball. **On-Campus Highlights:** Paresky Center, Sawyer Library, Science Center, Williams College Museum of Art, '62 Center for Theatre and Dance, Williams Bookstore.

FINANCIAL AID

Students should submit: CSS/Financial Aid PROFILE; FAFSA; Noncustodial PROFILE. Filing deadline is 1/15. The Princeton Review suggests that all financial aid forms be submitted as soon as possible after October 1. *Need-based scholarships/grants offered*: College/university scholarship or grant aid from institutional funds; Federal Pell; SEOG; State scholarships/grants. *Loan aid offered*: Direct PLUS loans; Direct Subsidized Stafford Loans; Direct Unsubsidized Stafford Loans; Institutional student loans for international students. Applicants will be notified of awards on or about 4/1. Federal Work-Study Program available. Institutional employment available.

BOTTOM LINE

Williams College is very similar to an Ivy League school. It has boundless, state-of-the-art resources in everything; a diploma with the Williams brand name on it will kick down doors for the rest of your life; and it's absurdly expensive. The total retail price here for tuition, room and board, and fees comes to about $72,270 per year. Financial aid here is beyond generous, though, and you'd be insane to choose a lesser school instead because of the sticker price.

FINANCIAL FACTS	
Financial Aid Rating	99
Annual tuition	$56,970
Room and board	$14,990
Required fees	$310
Books and supplies	$800
Average frosh need-based scholarship	$56,933
Average UG need-based scholarship	$55,621
% needy frosh rec. need-based scholarship or grant aid	100
% needy UG rec. need-based scholarship or grant aid	100
% needy frosh rec. non-need-based scholarship or grant aid	0
% needy UG rec. non-need-based scholarship or grant aid	0
% needy frosh rec. need-based self-help aid	83
% needy UG rec. need-based self-help aid	87
% frosh rec. any financial aid	50
% UG rec. any financial aid	52
% UG borrow to pay for school	41
Average cumulative indebtedness	$15,496
% frosh need fully met	100
% ugrads need fully met	100
Average % of frosh need met	100
Average % of ugrad need met	100

CAREER INFORMATION FROM PAYSCALE.COM	
ROI Rating	96
Bachelors and No Higher	
Median starting salary	$67,500
Median mid-career salary	$127,500
At Least Bachelors	
Median starting salary	$68,500
Median mid-career salary	$142,200
Alumni with high job meaning	51%
Degrees awarded in STEM subjects	32%

Williams College

Worcester Polytechnic Institute

Admissions Office, Bartlett Center, Worcester, MA 01609 • Admissions: 508-831-5286 • Fax: 508-831-5875

#32 BEST VALUE COLLEGE

CAMPUS LIFE

Quality of Life Rating	92
Fire Safety Rating	77
Green Rating	92
Type of school	Private
Environment	City

STUDENTS

Total undergrad enrollment	4,571
% male/female	62/38
% from out of state	55
% frosh live on campus	97
% ugrads live on campus	49
# of fraternities	
(% ugrad men join)	13 (33)
# of sororities	
(% ugrad women join)	6 (36)
% African American	3
% Asian	5
% Caucasian	63
% Hispanic	9
% Native American	<1
% Pacific Islander	<1
% Two or more races	2
% Race and/or ethnicity unknown	8
% international	9
# of countries represented	69

ABOUT THE SCHOOL

Worcester Polytechnic Institute is a medium-size university in Massachusetts with a primary focus on technology and the applied sciences. Undergraduates can choose from more than fifty majors and minors across fourteen academic departments, and though the school is world-renowned for engineering WPI prides itself on offering an extremely flexible curriculum that emphasizes the importance of a well-rounded education. In addition to abundant research opportunities, the school offers several options to complete projects in the sciences and humanities. These include an Interactive Qualifying Project that challenges students to apply technology to solve a societal problem, often by working and studying abroad. Students say that these programs "give [them] a chance to learn real world skills and work together rather than against each other." "I love the fact that WPI develops technical professionals' soft skills and doesn't only focus on the numbers," students say, and while there are some unpopular professors most "genuinely want all of their students to not just succeed academically but to understand the material." Furthermore, the majority are "interested in helping students, and don't prioritize their own research above being a good professor."

BANG FOR YOUR BUCK

WPI offers several financial aid options in the form of scholarships and grants, loans, and work-study. Need-based aid comes from a variety of State and Federal programs, such as the Pell Grant, as well as institutional scholarships. The school also offers an extremely high number of merit-based scholarships for which students are automatically considered upon application, with

Worcester Polytechnic Institute

Financial Aid: 508-831-5469 • E-mail: admissions@wpi.edu • Website: www.wpi.edu

several awards that average $12,500 to $25,000. There are special merit scholarships available to students of color, and to students studying in specific disciplines such as chemistry or pre-med. Each incoming first-year student receives a global scholarship of up to $5,000 to remove any barriers to study abroad. Ninety-seven percent of students are receiving merit- and/or need-based aid, and many students cite financial assistance as a determining factor in their decision to attend WPI.

STUDENT LIFE

Though "the work in classes requires you to spend significant time studying," WPI is "a place for more than just rigorous academics." Thirty to 40 percent of students are involved in Greek life and there are abundant clubs and activities on campus. "Students are very involved in campus organizations" and in addition to structured groups there are dances, a winter carnival, Saturday gaming nights, a comedy festival, a play festival, and weekend movie nights, among many other offerings. Off campus in Worcester, "there are constantly shows and concerts, there is an ice rink, a climbing gym, and movie theaters." Many students also travel to Boston on weekends. "At WPI you are always on the go with work, academics, and extra curricular activities, but we are the best time managers I know."

CAREER

Due to WPI's emphasis on real-world experience and applied science and technology, it's not surprising that the students are a career-focused bunch. All students participate in three projects, some with external sponsors, before graduation. The Career Development Center is generally well regarded, offering career fairs and company presentations, services like résumé building and interview prep, and advice for students on how to use networking and social media to their advantage. A WPI education is "about preparing

ACADEMICS

Academic Rating	93
% students returning for sophomore year	96
% students graduating within 4 years	82
% students graduating within 6 years	87
Calendar	Semester
Student/faculty ratio	13:1
Profs interesting rating	87
Profs accessible rating	91

Most classes have fewer than 10 students. Most lab/discussion sessions have 20–29 students.

MOST POPULAR MAJORS
Mechanical Engineering; Computer Science; Biomedical Engineering

SELECTIVITY

Admissions Rating	95
# of applicants	10,584
% of applicants accepted	42
% of acceptees attending	29
# offered a place on the wait list	3,202
% accepting a place on wait list	34
% admitted from wait list	14

FRESHMAN PROFILE

Range SAT EBRW	630–710
Range SAT Math	670–750
Range ACT Composite	29–33
# submitting SAT scores	897
% submitting SAT scores	70
# submitting ACT scores	317
% submitting ACT scores	25
Average HS GPA	3.9
% graduated top 10% of class	64
% graduated top 25% of class	93
% graduated top 50% of class	100

DEADLINES

Early action	
Deadline	11/1
Notification	12/20
Regular	
Deadline	2/1
Notification	4/1
Nonfall registration?	No

students for successful careers in their respective fields upon graduation through practical applications of the knowledge and skills that are taught," and "a large percentage of the student body will leave WPI with a fairly good job when they graduate." Evidence seems to bear out that observation, as WPI has been frequently cited for graduating their students into high-paying careers. Beyond the finances, 52 percent WPI alumni visiting PayScale.com report feeling as though their job has a high level of meaning.

GENERAL INFO

Activities: Campus Ministries; Choral groups; Concert band; Dance; Drama/theater; International Student Organization; Jazz band; Literary magazine; Model UN; Music ensembles; Musical theater; Pep band; Radio station; Student government; Student newspaper; Symphony orchestra; Yearbook. 227 registered organizations, 19 honor societies, 8 religious organizations, 13 fraternities, 6 sororities, on campus. **Athletics (Intercollegiate):** *Men:* baseball, basketball, crew/rowing, cross-country, diving, football, soccer, swimming, track/field (outdoor), track/field (indoor), wrestling. *Women:* basketball, crew/rowing, cross-country, diving, field hockey, soccer, softball, swimming, track/field (outdoor), track/field (indoor), volleyball. **On-Campus Highlights:** Quadrangle, Campus Center, The Goat's Head Restaurant, Gordon Library, Sports & Recreation Center.

FINANCIAL AID

Students should submit: CSS/Financial Aid PROFILE; FAFSA; Noncustodial PROFILE. Priority filing deadline is 2/1. The Princeton Review suggests that all financial aid forms be submitted as soon as possible after October 1. *Need-based scholarships/grants offered*: College/university scholarship or grant aid from institutional funds; Federal Pell; Private scholarships; SEOG; State scholarships/grants. *Loan aid offered*: Direct PLUS loans; Direct Subsidized Stafford Loans; Direct Unsubsidized Stafford Loans. Applicants will be notified of awards on a rolling basis beginning 12/21. Federal Work-Study Program available. Institutional employment available.

BOTTOM LINE

Tuition and fees for a year at WPI are listed as $51,604, with room and board totaling an additional $15,302. In addition to many merit-based scholarships WPI offers a numerous need-based programs, with 98 percent of first year students receiving some form of financial aid. Between robust aid packages and lucrative career prospects for graduating students, Worcester Polytechnic Institute could be a great investment for those interested in the science, technology, and engineering fields.

CAREER INFORMATION FROM PAYSCALE.COM

ROI Rating	93
Bachelors and No Higher	
Median starting salary	$73,600
Median mid-career salary	$135,500
At Least Bachelors	
Median starting salary	$75,200
Median mid-career salary	$142,100
Alumni with high job meaning	52%
Degrees awarded in STEM subjects	86%

FINANCIAL FACTS

Financial Aid Rating	89
Annual tuition	$51,604
Room and board	$15,302
Required fees	$716
Books and supplies	$1,000
Average frosh need-based scholarship	$24,500
Average UG need-based scholarship	$23,502
% needy frosh rec. need-based scholarship or grant aid	100
% needy UG rec. need-based scholarship or grant aid	97
% needy frosh rec. non-need-based scholarship or grant aid	29
% needy UG rec. non-need-based scholarship or grant aid	25
% needy frosh rec. need-based self-help aid	46
% needy UG rec. need-based self-help aid	48
% frosh rec. any financial aid	99
% UG rec. any financial aid	91
% frosh need fully met	61
% ugrads need fully met	45
Average % of frosh need met	82
Average % of ugrad need met	78

Yale University

PO Box 208234, New Haven, CT 06520-8234 • Admissions: 203-432-9300 • Fax: 203-432-9392

#6 BEST VALUE COLLEGE

CAMPUS LIFE

Quality of Life Rating	92
Fire Safety Rating	62
Green Rating	95
Type of school	Private
Environment	City

STUDENTS

Total undergrad enrollment	5,938
% male/female	50/50
% from out of state	92
% frosh from public high school	57
% frosh live on campus	100
% ugrads live on campus	84
% African American	8
% Asian	19
% Caucasian	42
% Hispanic	13
% Native American	<1
% Pacific Islander	<1
% Two or more races	6
% Race and/or ethnicity unknown	<1
% international	11
# of countries represented	118

ABOUT THE SCHOOL

As one of the triple towers of the Ivy League, when you say you attend "Yale, you don't really have to say much else—those four letters say it all." Beyond the gothic spires ("It reminds me of Hogwarts," says a student) and ivy-clad residence halls, Yale University truly lives up to its reputation as one of the preeminent undergraduate schools in the nation. At this world-class research institution, 5,000-plus undergraduates (who are "are passionate about everything") benefit not only from "amazing academics and extensive resources" that provide "phenomenal in- and out-of-class education," but also from participation in "a student body that is committed to learning and to each other." Cutting-edge research is commonplace and great teaching the norm, and three quarters of courses enroll fewer than twenty students. A popular test-the-waters registration system allows students to sample classes for up to two weeks before they commit to their schedule, and the school "encourages its students to take a range of courses." "The wealth of opportunities in and out of the classroom made the choice very clear to me," says a student. The education they're getting prepares them for leadership on a massive scale. Case in point: Yale alumni were represented on the Democratic or Republican ticket in every U.S. presidential election between 1972 and 2004. Still, no matter the end result, it's clear that "the people at Yale are genuinely interested in learning for learning's sake, not so that they can get a job on Wall Street."

Yale University

Financial Aid: 203-432-2700 • E-mail: student.questions@yale.edu • Website: www.yale.edu

BANG FOR YOUR BUCK

Here's a shocker: you don't have to be wealthy to have access to a Yale education. Thanks to a multibillion-dollar endowment, Yale operates a need-blind admissions policy and guarantees to meet 100 percent of each applicant's demonstrated need. In fact, Yale's annual expected financial aid budget is larger than many schools' endowments. Yale spends more than $140 million dollars on student financial aid annually. The average scholarship award is around $50,000, and it's entirely need-based—no athletic or merit scholarships are available. Seven hundred and fifty Yale undergraduates will have a $0 expected parent contribution next year—that's more than 10 percent of its student body. Yale even provides undergraduates on financial aid with grant support for summer study and unpaid internships abroad.

STUDENT LIFE

A typical Yalie is "tough to define because so much of what makes Yale special is the unique convergence of different students to form one cohesive entity. Nonetheless, the one common characteristic of Yale students is passion—each Yalie is driven and dedicated to what he or she loves most" which "creates a palpable atmosphere of enthusiasm on campus." Yale is, of course, extremely challenging academically, but work doesn't keep undergrads from participating in a "a huge variety of activities for fun." "Instead of figuring out what to do with my free time, I have to figure out what not do during my free time," says a student. There are more than 300 student groups on campus including the Yale Daily News, the oldest collegiate daily newspaper still in existence, as well as "singing, dancing, juggling fire, theater . . . the list goes on." Many students are politically active and "either volunteer or try to get involved in some sort of organization to make a difference in the world."

ACADEMICS

Academic Rating	**91**
% students returning for sophomore year	99
% students graduating within 4 years	88
% students graduating within 6 years	97
Calendar	Semester
Student/faculty ratio	6:1
Profs interesting rating	**82**
Profs accessible rating	**79**

Most classes have 10–19 students.

MOST POPULAR MAJORS

Economics, General; Political Science and Government, General; History, General

SELECTIVITY

Admissions Rating	**99**
# of applicants	35,307
% of applicants accepted	6
% of acceptees attending	70

CAREER

As its name would suggest, the Yale Office of Career Strategy (OCS) offers a host of resources to students before they even embark on the job hunt. A comprehensive collection of online career profiles helps students gain an overview of potential fields, and walk-in appointments with career advisers ensure that all of their questions get answered. OCS sponsors numerous internship programs, often drawing upon Yale's extensive alumni network for leads on opportunities. The Yale Career Network is another great way to network with keen alumni. Yalies report median starting salaries of about $70,300, and 60 percent of those grads who visited PayScale.com say they find a high level of meaning in their work.

GENERAL INFO

Activities: Choral groups; Concert band; Dance; Drama/theater; Jazz band; Literary magazine; Marching band; Music ensembles; Musical theater; Opera; Pep band; Radio station; Student government; Student newspaper; Student-run film society; Symphony orchestra; Television station; Yearbook. 350 registered organizations, on campus. **Athletics (Intercollegiate):** *Men:* baseball, basketball, crew/rowing, cross-country, diving, fencing, football, golf, ice hockey, lacrosse, sailing, soccer, squash, swimming, tennis, track/field (outdoor), track/field (indoor). *Women:* basketball, crew/rowing, cross-country, diving, fencing, field hockey, golf, gymnastics, ice hockey, lacrosse, sailing, soccer, softball, squash, swimming, tennis, track/field (outdoor), track/field (indoor), volleyball. **On-Campus Highlights:** Old Campus, Sterling Memorial Library, Yale Art Gallery, Beinecke Rare Book and Manuscript Library, Payne-Whitney Gymnasium. **Environmental Initiatives:** The university pledged to a greenhouse gas commitment of 43% below 2005 levels by 2020.

Yale University

FINANCIAL AID

Students should submit: CSS/Financial Aid PROFILE; FAFSA; Noncustodial PROFILE. Recommended filing deadline is 3/1. The Princeton Review suggests that all financial aid forms be submitted as soon as possible after October 1. *Need-based scholarships/grants offered*: College/university scholarship or grant aid from institutional funds; Federal Pell; Private scholarships; SEOG; State scholarships/grants; United Negro College Fund. *Loan aid offered*: Direct PLUS loans; Direct Subsidized Stafford Loans; Direct Unsubsidized Stafford Loans. Applicants will be notified of awards on or about 4/1. Institutional employment available.

BOTTOM LINE

Annual tuition to Yale is $55,500. Room and board in one of Yale's residential colleges is $16,600 per year, bringing the total cost to about $72,100 annually, not to mention costs of books, supplies, health insurance, and personal expenses. Yale guarantees to meet 100 percent of all students' demonstrated financial need; as a result, the cost of Yale education is often considerably lower than the sticker price.

FINANCIAL FACTS

Financial Aid Rating	99
Annual tuition	$55,500
Room and board	$16,600
Books and supplies	$3,670
Average frosh need-based scholarship	$57,954
Average UG need-based scholarship	$56,602
% needy frosh rec. need-based scholarship or grant aid	100
% needy UG rec. need-based scholarship or grant aid	100
% needy frosh rec. non-need-based scholarship or grant aid	0
% needy UG rec. non-need-based scholarship or grant aid	0
% needy frosh rec. need-based self-help aid	75
% needy UG rec. need-based self-help aid	85
% frosh rec. any financial aid	51
% UG rec. any financial aid	52
% UG borrow to pay for school	16
Average cumulative indebtedness	$14,575
% frosh need fully met	100
% ugrads need fully met	100
Average % of frosh need met	100
Average % of ugrad need met	100

CAREER INFORMATION FROM PAYSCALE.COM

ROI Rating	97
Bachelors and No Higher	
Median starting salary	$70,300
Median mid-career salary	$138,300
At Least Bachelors	
Median starting salary	$73,900
Median mid-career salary	$151,500
Alumni with high job meaning	60%
Degrees awarded in STEM subjects	22%

Yale University

NOTES

NOTES

NOTES

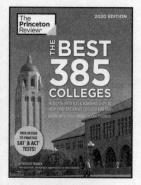

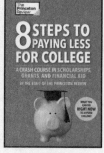